Mind Design and Minimal Syntax

Mind Design and Minimal Syntax

WOLFRAM HINZEN

OXFORD
UNIVERSITY PRESS

Great Clarendon Street, Oxford, OX2 6DP,
United Kingdom

Oxford University Press is a department of the University of Oxford.
It furthers the University's objective of excellence in research, scholarship,
and education by publishing worldwide. Oxford is a registered trade mark of
Oxford University Press in the UK and in certain other countries

© Wolfram Hinzen 2006

The moral rights of the authors have been asserted

First published 2006

All rights reserved. No part of this publication may be reproduced, stored in
a retrieval system, or transmitted, in any form or by any means, without the
prior permission in writing of Oxford University Press, or as expressly permitted
by law, by licence or under terms agreed with the appropriate reprographics
rights organization. Enquiries concerning reproduction outside the scope of the
above should be sent to the Rights Department, Oxford University Press, at the
address above

You must not circulate this work in any other form
and you must impose this same condition on any acquirer

Published in the United States of America by Oxford University Press
198 Madison Avenue, New York, NY 10016, United States of America

British Library Cataloguing in Publication Data
Data available

Library of Congress Cataloging in Publication Data
Data available

ISBN 978-0-19-927441-3

For my lovely children,
Konstantinos and Ariadne

Contents

Preface .... *ix*
Acknowledgements .... *xv*

Part I: Naturally Human

1 Introduction 3
   1.1 Humans as natural objects 3
   1.2 The study of human nature 11
   1.3 Human design 24
   1.4 The fate of human nature in the twentieth century ... 32

2 Against metaphysical naturalism 55
   2.1 From methodological to metaphysical naturalism 55
   2.2 Rationalist method from Galileo to Chomsky 66
   2.3 Double standards 79

3 Biological internalism 89
   3.1 Biology before unification 89
   3.2 Mind as function: A critique 95
   3.3 God or natural selection or…? 105
   3.4 Epilogue on explanation and necessity 110

Part II: Deducing Variation

4 Prior to function 117
   4.1 Language growth 117
   4.2 Language and communication 128
   4.3 Language as a social construct 139

5 Beyond the autonomy of syntax 150
   5.1 What is syntax? 150
   5.2 Explanation in linguistic theory 161
   5.3 Human phrase structure 170
   5.4 Transforming the phrase 194
   5.5 Why is there movement? 208
   5.6 The proper interpretation of LF/SEM 220

Part III: Rational Mind

  6 Good Design! 239
     6.1 Phases and cascades: Beyond LF 239
     6.2 Epistemology for mental organs 250
Conclusions 272
References 278
Index 295

Preface

As we move from one line to the next in the following sequence of expressions, the fog gradually clears:

> y;jdf[39r"#a-9875JKVxsclsjdli7@@
> sruo fo dlrow siht ni gninaem si ereht
> ours of world this in meaning is there
> there is meaning in this world of ours

Without quite knowing why, or what happens to us, words arrange themselves in a way that they seem meaningful to us. We cannot see or hear meanings (we haven't got sense organs for them), in the way we can see words or hear sounds. Even after many decades of 'naturalizing philosophy' unclarity prevails over what exactly a thought is that we express by a meaningful sentence, and how it arises from or relates to physical processes such as the electrical activity of the brain. We can describe many aspects of the transition from acoustical patterns to meaningful expressions, but only if we presuppose what is to be explained, the human faculty of language. Yet, whatever meanings are, nothing could be more evident than that some linguistic expressions carry determinate meanings, while others do not, and that we can have very specific and intricate intuitions on what these meanings are.

Whatever mind and meaning are, then, this book adopts a fundamentally 'realist' attitude towards them as phenomena of the natural world. There are linguistic expressions, some of which are meaningful; and we can describe their meanings, experiment with them and study them, while bracketing, for the moment, the ontological problem they pose. Meaning arises in organisms with an appropriate internal complexity and evolutionary history that we can form hypotheses about; and it has empirically attestable properties that we can study naturalistically. This book seeks to describe the structural principles on which our human apprehension of meaning depends. More than any other introductions to linguistic theory it emphasizes philosophical assumptions on the nature of mind and meaning on which linguistic theory rests and that it has crucial implications for.

From the present perspective, studying the 'mental' is no different methodologically from studying the 'natural': this book centrally opposes a *methodological dualism*. Moreover, just as the study of our 'bodily' organization has a fundamentally *internalist* aspect—what organs mature in ontogeny is a function of genetic factors and laws of development—it assumes that the study of our 'mental organization' should have this aspect too. In particular, it will claim, contrary to prevailing externalist orthodoxy, and to the extent that meaning patterns with linguistic form, that what meanings human linguistic expressions carry has little to do with how these expressions relate to the world. Neither need it relate to what beliefs we hold. On the contrary, how we relate to the world generally depends on our grasp of meaning, our possession of certain concepts and of structural principles that organize them.

In short, meaning is a structural and internalist phenomenon, relating to the emergence of order and of complex organization in the human language faculty, and other cognitive systems inside the mind interfacing with it. Linguistic form (syntax) moreover, I argue, does not merely act as a negative constraint on what expressions can mean, or which expressions are 'well-formed'; it positively explains why certain expressions mean what they do, what human meaning is like, and why it is like that. I will describe this internalist position as essentially parallel to one found in theoretical biology, where a position that its nineteenth century defenders called 'formalism' or 'rational morphology' allowed for the autonomous study of animal form, disregarding the external *conditions of existence* that drive such organic forms in or out of existence on the evolutionary scene.

Other than the functionalist, who will unfailingly ask the question 'What is it *for* ?', the formalist will emphasize principles for the emergence of structural complexity inside the organism. Often, he will claim explanatory priority for the latter, diminishing the explanatory role that functions and adaptation play. The study of mind, in the present perspective, is the study of structural organization in no other sense than the biological formalist's study of organic complexity, while addressing a level of reality more abstract than that usually addressed in the life sciences. It is formalism applied to the structure in nature that the mind is. As my bracketing of the ontological issue indicates, this naturalism will be a purely methodological stance in which no ontological questions of 'materialism' or 'physicalism' are prejudged. The closest predecessor for the notion of form used here may be W. v. Humboldt's notion of the 'Form of human language', on which Chomsky (1966: 19, fn. 39) remarks that it amounts to much the same thing as the modern notion of the 'generative grammar' of a language. Interestingly, and in contradistinction to the notion of form used in formal logic, it included both syntactic and semantic structure.

Formalism and functionalism, S. J. Gould has suggested,

represent poles of a timeless dichotomy, each expressing a valid way of representing reality. Both poles can only be regarded as deeply right, and each needs the other because the full axis of the dichotomy operates as a lance thrown through, and then anchoring, the empirical world. If one pole 'wins' for contingent reasons of a transient historical moment, then the advantage can only be temporary and intellectually limited. (Gould 2002: 312).

This would give both formalism and functionalism equal rights to existence, as complementary rather than contradictory perspectives on the same explanandum. Though I am sympathetic to this view, this book makes the stronger claim that in some cases a formalist perspective may be more useful and allow a deeper explanatory depth. I further claim, following Chomsky, that human language is a good example. Gould's balanced dichotomy should alert us to the current predominance of functionalist and externalist thinking about the mind, even in research that falls outside the theory of mind that traditionally labels itself 'functionalist'. My primary overall aim in this book is to give formalism in the sense above a place in the current landscape of the philosophy of mind, and introduce the kind of study of the human language faculty—namely, generative grammar—that gives rise to my claims.

Apart from a methodological naturalism and internalism, this book wishes to articulate a *rationalist* position. In this tradition, the mind is credited with rational structures intrinsic to it as a natural object, structures it uses to interpret the world and its experience. This crucially empirical claim about the structure of mind is, from the present point of view, the essence of rationalism as a philosophical tradition, which continues to this day. Rationalism is then a claim about the intrinsic rational contents of the human mind—its *analytic* content—and a commitment on its factual internal *design*. As in the case of an animal's organ, or the universe at large, our mind's structural organization is a matter of empirical fact. We want to know what this design is like, what its nature and organizing principles are, hence what our nature is. Design can be good or elegant, and it can be bad, inefficient and convoluted, design that no rational designer would ever have contrived. Looking at our human mind, we would like to know which of these attributes describes it best.

Can we, in particular, give substance to the idea that the design of the language faculty is a form of 'elegant' or 'perfect' design? Its design might be deemed perfect if, say, it provided a maximally efficient solution to some task it is required to fulfil, but also if it was 'necessary', in the sense that it had all and only the elements it *needed* to have to be usable at all, hence was a form of 'minimal' design. Perfect design is not what we expect in evolution in general, where natural selection, in Jacob's phrase, is a form of 'tinkering' with given organismic designs: in general, evolution cannot engineer new designs from scratch to meet the demand of some new task. It has no foresight into a future in which certain designs will be needed. 'Blind' and mindless, it drags on and makes do with whatever organismic structure does a job *well enough*. Hence we expect nature to contain flawed and makeshift designs, one famous example of which may be human eye design, which a rational engineer, in Dawkins' words, would 'laugh at': photocells point away from the light source rather than towards it (Dawkins 1986: 93).

Human language may well seem badly designed too, as indeed it has seemed to many philosophers in the Fregean tradition, if we look at it under a certain perspective. As a communication device, for example, it is probably flawed in crucial respects, containing lots of structure that seems sub-optimal, redundant, or worse. But the mistake may lie with our perspective. Perhaps language is perfectly designed in the way of pairing sounds with meanings, using a minimum of resources to accomplish this mapping, without these sound-meaning pairs necessarily being 'ready to use'. The question of mind design is not an *a priori* one, and even if a hypothesis of perfect design were to fail, the apparent imperfections in our object of study, which only an actual exploration of this hypothesis could reveal, will be of interest. Where we find an aspect of the design not as we would rationally expect it, we will have something interesting to explain.

Our foray into the field of generative grammar will thus lead us to explore the 'minimalist thesis' that even minimal design specifications for features that the faculty of language *needs* to have to play its role in the functional organization of the mind—together with general, non-language-specific, properties of computational systems in nature—actually *suffice* to rationalize the structure which this faculty is empirically found to have. There is no structure apart from the one it needs to have. Any extent to which we could vindicate such a thesis would be surprising, and it would clearly open up an entirely new perspective not only on language, but also on human nature, on empirical grounds.

My aim to advertise a position may perhaps seem modest—especially from a theoretical linguistic perspective—were it not for the fact that the formalism and rationalism I will develop has been in eclipse for much of twentieth century philosophy, with a concomitant loss of a former prime topic of the rationalist tradition, human nature. Much current philosophy still rests on three pillars, externalism, metaphysical naturalism, and functionalism, which are precisely the pillars that centrally characterized Skinnerian behaviorism (Chomsky 1959). The meanings of these terms have changed, but it is worth asking how much. There are various philosophical tendencies today that are said to be 'rationalist', be it because of their emphasis on the objectivity of reason (Nagel 1997), their commitment to some substantive notion of innate knowledge (Fodor 1981, 1998), or their defence of some version of *a priori* knowledge (Peacocke 2002). Yet, human nature, as a theoretical concept, figures in none of them in any central way. Aspects of all these rationalisms will figure in the present one, but the rationalism developed here is a unique brand, as it combines with an internalism and methodological naturalism in what I think is an unfamiliar way in philosophy today.

So, on the one hand this book is addressed to philosophers, whom I invite to join me in a journey through the world of theoretical linguistics, a field still disconnected from much research and education in the analytic philosophy of language. On a most general level, my message is that language is of an *intrinsic*, not merely an instrumental, interest to us as philosophers: language is *more* than a deficient tool for the expression of our thoughts, a code for propositional contents, an idiom to be 'regimented' by the means of modern logic, or an instrumental device for representing reality or for communication. The point of language in its ordinary use, to put it somewhat drastically, is not to relate us to the external world, but actually to *free* our mind from the control of the external stimulus, from having to talk about the world as it actually is, as opposed to how it might be, was or will be. The hallmark of human language use is its creativity, or the *lack* of a connection to the immediate physical context and the adaptive challenges it poses. As a consequence of that, humans alone may have a history: lacking language, all non-humans animals are stuck in the here and now.

On the other hand, this book is directed to students and researchers of all persuasions who work in the language and cognitive sciences. I hope to convince them that all research on the human language faculty, no matter how data-driven it may seem, always rests on philosophical ideas and ideals. Indeed it must be, given the prevailing unclarity on such matters as mind and meaning. Generative grammar not other than cognitive or functionalist linguistics are also, and at heart, philosophical projects. Realizing this, and patiently addressing the philosophical issues involved, might help us to gain a deeper understanding of intellectual divides that keep disuniting the field in unproductive ways.

It is particularly clear that the Chomskyan version of generative grammar and the Minimalist Program (MP) as its most recent incarnation, are also and inherently philosophical projects, at least if we understand philosophy in the traditional sense of seventeenth and eighteenth century 'natural philosophy'. Moreover, Chomsky is the philosophical thinker in which I see the above trias of methodological naturalism, internalism, and rationalism come together, and although this book does not claim to be a correct analysis of his views, or even attempts one, virtually all that follows is inspired by what I take to be these views. The degree of perfection of the design of our mind, in the sense above, is the MP's main question. Crucially, the MP is a piece of (formalist) computational *biology* for me: it is neither an expression, nor even supportive of functionalism, be it in the broad sense above, or in the specific sense of the metaphysical doctrine in the philosophy of mind that runs under this label, including the Fodorian 'Representational Theory of Mind'.

By and large, I regard contemporary work in the study of human language as vindicating the denial by seventeenth and eighteenth century thinkers of a 'representational theory of mind'. According to that theory, the mind derives its content from the way it 'mirrors' an environment, and mental representations are relationally defined as inner signs or stand-ins for outer objects. I shall dispute that this particular idea is prominent in any way in the 'natural philosophies' of either Galileo, Descartes, Locke, Hume, or Leibniz. It is because I find these historical connections not only fascinating but positively helpful in understanding our current philosophical predicament that this book devotes so much of its space to early modern thought.

As a consequence of these aims, one half of this book (Chapters 1–3), will speak more to philosophers, while the other half (Chapters 4–6) will speak more to linguists. But since my interdisciplinary effort is genuine, my hope is precisely to have linguists read the former half, and philosophers the latter, even though they might find just these parts occasionally more hardgoing.

Taking Minimalism as an inspiration, my first aim, in Part I, will be to resuscitate a formalist framework for thinking about human nature, considered as a central topic for philosophical inquiry, and as a basis for the philosophies of mind and language. The study of the human mind, for me, *is* the study of (human) nature, mentality being one of the latter's crucial aspects.

In Chapters 4–6, I turn directly to human language and give an introduction to the generative framework with an eye on philosophical and epistemological implications, and the explanatory vision that motivates the generative enterprise. Chapter 5 contains what I hope to be a self-contained introduction to current generative grammar. Chapter 6 pulls the various strands of the book together in a synthesis that is centred on the question of human mind design.

Acknowledgements

Chomsky's *The Minimalist Program* fell into my hands accidentally in the spring of 1999. As sometimes happens with books that fall into one's hands, I thought 'tremendously interesting', but also wondered, 'would anyone take this *really* seriously'? The idea in question was the idea of *Minimal Mind Design*—the idea of rationalizing the human language faculty as a perfect solution to a problem of satisfying minimal design specifications. Inquiring a little further, I found that its author certainly was serious about what he was saying, *very* serious. Not long afterwards, the quiet and peaceful surroundings of the medieval city of Regensburg, embedded in lower Bavaria, turned out to be a perfect place to pursue increasingly arcane ideas. I wish to express my heartfelt thanks to many people for simply looking with *sympathy* at what I was doing, but also for supporting it in any way they could, and for providing me with a wonderful environment to work in: especially Hans Rott, Carsten Reinhardt, Christoph Meinel, Wolfgang Gebhardt, Holmer Steinfath, the history of science group at large, and Andreas Eidenschink and Maria Kronfeldner.

As I explored the paths that led to this book I benefited in various ways from the help of, and conversations with David Adger, Umberto Ansaldo, Cedric Boeckx, Andrew Carstairs-McCarthy, Noam Chomsky, John Collins, Kit Fine, Jerry Fodor, Norbert Hornstein, Hans Kamp, Ruth Kempson, Michiel van Lambalgen, Giuseppe Longobardi, Paul Pietroski, Tanya Reinhardt, Martin Stokhof, Georges Rey, Benjamin Shaer, Neil Smith, and Helmut Weiss. I would like to express my gratitude to Massimo Piattelli-Palmarini and James McGilvray, as well as two anonymous referees for Oxford University Press for reading the manuscript and commenting generously. John Davey, my editor from Oxford, has from the start been a pleasure to deal with, and I thank him warmly for his almost immediate interest in this project. Jess Smith has done a formidable job in likening the language of this book more to English. Whatever the reader may think of my English, without her everything would be much worse. My greatest thanks, however, go to Juan Uriagereka, whose interest and help, at a stage when I hardly knew what I was talking about, was one of the happiest incidents of my career. My indebtedness will be obvious throughout, while any mistakes will of course remain my own.

Two postdoctoral fellowships at Columbia University and New York University, both generously funded by the Swiss National Foundation of Science, were particularly inspiring. Equally important were two other research stays in the US, one at the Departments of Linguistics and Philosophy in Maryland, another at MIT, both made possible by personal research grants from the German Research Council (DFG).

This book started out as an old-style 'deutsche Habilitation', which was 'typically German' not just because of that, but also because of its voluminous dimensions: by and large, my referees were unanimous that I had written two books rather than one. I am grateful to my editor, John Davey, for proposing an elegant way of achieving weight loss—publish two slim(mer) volumes instead. The second volume (Hinzen 2006a), also to be published by Oxford University Press, will be more technical in nature and will buttress the present framework through an internalist treatment of exactly those dimensions of language where the externalist view is putatively strongest, namely names (reference) and truth.

Part I
Naturally Human

1

Introduction

1.1 Humans as Natural Objects

In this chapter I develop the idea of a 'science' of human nature, conceived in much the same way as the Enlightenment and Cartesian naturalists understood it. The Enlightenment project of a 'Science of Man'

> was, very broadly speaking, expected to provide a description of the nature and extent of human cognitive capacities, of the way the mind works, as well as afford an understanding of the processes by which human beings come to be the way they are, the manner by which they acquire their character and individuality, their tastes, desires and ends (Tomaselli 1995: 229).

This enterprise evolved against the presupposed background of the new Galilean ('anti-Aristotelian') science, taking over its intrinsic assumptions and limitations, rather than as a separate 'philosophical' undertaking that is methodologically distinct from it. Far from being centrally an 'epistemological' project in the modern sense of an attempt to secure or justify our knowledge of the external world, the science of man is 'foundational' in a rather different sense: the knowledge of human nature was to be in the service of an *advancement* of science and culture. The aim is not to prove the *legitimacy* of given claims to knowledge (in the sense of an 'accurate representation' of the external world), or to offer a special 'philosophical' *adjudication* between various such claims, but, quite simply, to bring about a deepening and furthering of human knowledge. David Hume, who most strikingly gave content to the project, argued in his *Treatise of Human Nature* (1739–40/1978) that epistemology, ethics, aesthetics, and politics were all anchored in the study of human nature and depended on an understanding of it.[1] Also '*Mathematics, Natural Philosophy,* and *Natural Religion,* are in some measure dependent on the science of Man; since they lie under the

---

[1] The connection with ethics seems particularly important. For Rousseau, in his *De l'inégalité parmi les hommes* (1755), it seemed that the principles of ethics and 'natural jurisprudence' could only be deduced from insight into the nature and constitution of man. Without a proper idea of human nature, he argued, there was bound to be uncertainty and obscurity in the definition of natural right. The idea seems natural and has repercussions in contemporary ethics. In Singer (1999), for example, human nature—which Singer thinks of in Neo-Darwinian adaptationist terms—comes out as a negative constraint for the feasibility of any moralist's vision of reforming society. I take up this point at the very end of this book.

cognizance of men, and are judged of by their powers and faculties' (Hume 1739–40/1978: xv). Hence we must grasp 'the nature of the ideas we employ, and of the operations we perform in our reasonings'.[2]

The scientific revolution that set the stage for Hume's idea introduced the new science of mechanics and revived the ancient atomic theory of matter that figured in various forms in the works of Galileo Galilei, Joachim Jungius, Pierre Gassendi, the 'British Platonists' (Ralph Cudworth, Herbert of Cherbury, Henry More), and, in particular, Robert Boyle's 'New corpuscular philosophy' (1666). The new atomism raised fundamental epistemological issues concerning the knowability of matter that figure centrally in the work of Berkeley, Hume, and Locke (Rogers 1996). Their predecessor Galileo had regarded perception not as a representational participation in the true structure of the real, but as a subjective interpretation imposed on the structure of atoms as acting on our sense organs (Shea 1998: 804). According to Locke, the inner constitution and nature of material things remains unknown to creatures like us. By the very constitution of our minds, we are bound to be agnostic about the atomic microstructure of matter (Brandt 1988: 663–5).

A scepticism of this sort is not a scepticism about the 'reality of the external world'—this being whatever the sciences investigate—it is a statement of the fact that intuition, sense experience, and ordinary common sense are no guides to the real, give us no access to its corpuscular structure. As Galileo had assumed, ordinary things have a complexity that escapes mathematization. To understand anything, one has to look away from the world of the senses and employ *idealizations* that *distort* nature as known to us. Science works only in highly simplified domains, and its language is not ordinary language, but the language of mathematics.[3] On the other hand, Galileo argued that it is ludicrous to deny any reality to ideal geometrical forms figuring in physical explanations and call them 'imaginary', given that they alone let us understand anything in nature in 'non-magical', that is mechanical, terms (Fischer 1994: 178).

In this vision of nature, we lose the idea of a purpose. For the Aristotelians, the world existed for the sake of man. Science was not only earth-centred but human-centred: it had to make sense in relation to man, and various theories of the world had to combine into a vision of a coherent, rational, and aesthetically appealing whole (Shea 1998: 810–1). For Galileo, by contrast, blind mechanisms act in this world of ours. We do not recognize our ordinary conceptions in

---

[2] The idea, plausible in itself, has a certain resemblance to what is discussed today under the name of an 'anthropology of science' (Atran 1990).

[3] Thus, in the *Dialogo* (1632), 355, Galileo applauds those who, by the mere power of their intellect, distrusted the testimony of their senses ('did violence to their senses'), and who made their reason (*ragion*) the master over their belief (*credulità*). See Shea (1998: 808) for comments. In modern times, the same Galilean stance is famously formulated by Weinberg (1976), who spoke about 'abstract mathematical models of the universe to which at least the physicists give a higher degree of reality than they accord the ordinary world of sensation'.

the ideas of the new science, such as the discovery that a feather and a cannon ball fall with the same acceleration (if dropped in a vacuum). It stands to reason that this is 'absurd', just as Galileo's speculation about 'a highly spiritual substance (...) that is flooding through the universe, goes through all things without a resistance (...)' seems absurd from a common-sense point of view (Galileo 1615, quoted in Fischer 1994: 179). The world as seen through the lenses of the new science becomes a strangely unfamiliar place.

Picking up on the Galilean intuition of geometrical forms as inherent in physical matter, Descartes developed a stunning scientific *oeuvre*, a 'natural philosophy' comprising optics, physics, geometry, chemistry, astronomy, anatomy, navigation, physiology, and other sciences. Carrying Galileo's methodological commitment to mechanical explanations much further and developing it into a metaphysical world view, he stipulated that

'occult qualities' cannot be accepted as having any explanatory value, that contact action is the only means by which change can be effected, and that matter and motion are the ultimate ingredients in nature (Gaukroger 1993: 174; cf. Toulmin and Goodfield 1962: 156–69).

The final causes of the scholastics, Descartes tells us, do not exist (*Discours* Part V, Section 2, *Principia* Part 1, Section 28). Renaissance naturalism, which saw the cosmos as a living organism, a holistic system containing non-mechanical forces of 'attraction' and 'repulsion' that act at a distance, was unintelligible. Mechanical models set a new standard for intelligibility (Machamer 1998), the reduction of a natural phenomenon (the tides, celestial motion, etc.) to something that one could comprehend as working like a complex machine, a system of connected parts setting one another in motion. In this vein, Galileo ridiculed Kepler for his assumption of a magical 'attracting force' acting between the moon and earthly water, and offered a (wrong) mechanical model instead (Fischer 1994). Galileo's criterion of true understanding of some natural phenomenon was that we could in principle 'duplicate [it] for ourselves by means of appropriate artificial devices' (Machamer 1998: 69). Both the scope and the limits of mechanical models in science (including the science of the mind) will occupy us throughout this book.

Galilean-Cartesian science equally renounced a certain kind of 'why'-question, Galileo's message in the *Saggiatore* (1623) being that science was to bring nature into a mathematical form, rather than to dig deeper into the 'true natures' of things and their ultimate rationales (post-Newtonian science would later further denounce certain 'how'-questions as well). Galileo ventured no guesses as to the 'true nature' of water, air, fire, and earth, or of the sun or the moon, idealizing natural objects to whatever extent necessary to see them instantiating mathematical laws. Leaving 'secondary' properties of matter, which essentially depended on our contingent ways to apprehend nature (taste, colour, sound, and smell), out of account was a price to pay for the new science, a conclusion that Hume would later extend to 'primary' properties such as extension and solidity as well (Hume

1748/1975, section XII, part II, §123: 155). For the purposes of science, at least, Galileo contended, nature was to be looked at as a more or less organized structure of moving and interacting atoms, which to some extent was mathematically describable.

When Hume envisaged applying this new science to the study of human nature, Aristotelian essentialism as understood in the scientific revolution was long gone. Idealizations employed in the new science were not essences. Figuring out the nature of light or atoms in physics was not a matter of understanding the 'essence' of light, or the indivisible, in something like the ordinary senses of these notions. Science attributed physical properties to things, and the description of the real entailed abandoning our common-sense conceptions.

Descartes was particularly concerned with mechanical models in physiology. Just as the universe was a big clock, the animal was an automaton, two prominent metaphors described by Descartes in sections 7 and 9 of part V of his *Discours* (1637/1984). These could serve as leading metaphors for modern science as such, for which the world is not an indivisible whole, an integral organism, but something that can be broken down into independent parts and non-purposive mechanisms that can be studied in isolation. Modern science, as Lewontin puts it, 'sees the world, both living and dead, as a large and complicated system of gears and levers' (Lewontin 1993: 12). It is plainly absurd to explain why watches indicate the time by appealing to 'hidden qualities' or 'time-indicating powers'. They work mechanically, by means of cogs and wheels, and there are no mysteries in how this happens: nothing is hidden, there is no occult. Even so, Descartes believed the human soul harboured the 'creative principle', with its distinctive form of 'mental causality', since human behaviour did not appear to be mechanically triggered, in the way animal motion might be (a point to which I return at greater length below). Some natural philosophers and physiologists in the early eighteenth century (such as Julien de la Mettrie), as well as some in the early seventeenth (such as John Hobbes), regarded this as a half-hearted stopgap position on the way to a truly mechanistic world view. Revived in the second half of the twentieth century as the doctrine of 'machine functionalism' (though with differences, to which I return), the idea of *homme machine* has inspired our thinking ever since.

As Chomsky has pointed out frequently (Chomsky 2000, 2002), it is one of the remarkable puzzles of the scientific age that the Galilean-Cartesian dream of a world free of the 'occult' came to be seen as unrealistic, and quite possibly unachievable. The dream was shattered when by the end of the very century in which the 'mechanical philosophy' was born, Newton *re-introduced* 'occult forces' into nature by means of his force of gravitation, crucially acting at a distance. On the continent, Huygens would protest that Newton's 'Principle of attraction' was 'absurd'. Leibniz agreed, calling gravity 'an occult quality' of the very same type that the mechanical philosophy had denounced, a quality 'so very occult, that it is impossible that it should ever become clear' (quoted in Torretti

1999: 76–7). Newton in essence agreed, too, with Huygens's verdict, deeming the idea that gravity should be an inherent property of matter 'so great an absurdity that I believe no man who has in philosophical matters a competent faculty of thinking can ever fall into it' (letter to Bentley, 1693, quoted in Torretti 1999: 78). Although he lacked a cause for these properties of gravity, Newton concluded in the *Principia* that 'it is enough that gravity really exists'. Unlike Leibniz (cf. Leibniz 1704/1996, preface: 23), Newton did *not* encourage the assumption of a missing, though unknown, mechanical cause, as the cause in question seemed of a radically different kind, and the mechanical philosophy seemed to positively preclude finding it.

As Chomsky also emphasized, this remarkable development saddled physics with a *new* and *lower* standard of intelligibility than Galileo had hoped for: the goal becomes 'intelligibility of theories, not of the world', which we may have to acknowledge as unintelligible to us (Chomsky 2002: 68, 2003: 263). Immaterial agents were back on the physical scene, and the machine, the mechanical universe, was shattered (Rogers 1996: 50–4), leaving behind the 'ghost' that was thought to inhabit it, or, for Hume, a nature whose secrets are hidden in utter obscurity. The acquiescence expressed in Newton's 'it is enough' suggests a radical departure from the ideal of a science based on certain and self-evident first principles such as Descartes had propounded.

For Locke, while the mechanical philosophy was wrong, it was nonetheless clear, insofar as our understanding goes, that 'bodies can act on one another only through contact, since it is impossible for us to comprehend that a body can act on what it does not touch; for this would mean that it could cause an effect where it is not'; Newton's 'gravitation from matter to matter', though working in a way 'incomprehensible' to us, proved that God could do something that could neither be derived from our conception of body nor explained through our knowledge of matter. As he crisply put it in his correspondence with the Bishop of Worcester, 'our comprehension is no measure for the power of God' (quoted in Leibniz 1704/1996: 18, 23). This fundamental epistemic problem is why Locke also suggested that there could be no principled conceptual argument against the possibility that matter can think. Until some new way of formulating the mind–body problem could be found, there was the possibility that we could be pieces of 'thinking matter', since there was nothing to prevent God from 'superadd[ing] to matter a faculty of thinking' (Locke 1690/1975, IV, chapter 3, section 6: 541). If gravitation proved mysterious to the human mind, but had a naturalistic explanation by means of laws all the same, why couldn't the same state of affairs exist in the case of thinking as well? Matter had ceased to be wholly 'material', and though one could continue to defend the Cartesian dualism of two substances, it had become pointless, as Leibniz notes (Leibniz 1704/1996: 20), to insist on the *immateriality* of the second substance of mind.

While Newton had still thought of forces as 'agents of divine action' in the material world, these soon became subject to secularization (Golinski 1995: 321).

According to the eighteenth century materialists, matter was 'self-acting', or, as we would say today, self-organizing. Citing the growth of crystals, Diderot and LaMettrie argued, against the 'vitalists', that this was true even of the inorganic world (ibid.: 323). LaMettrie, pushing Albrecht von Haller's physiological work to a radical conclusion, contended that matter was neither alive nor dead, neither with nor without sensation. Such distinctions had nothing to do with the nature of the bodies involved, but solely with their mode of *organization*, a 'functionalist' idea in essence. Thinking was a property of organized matter, as much as electricity, capacity for movement, solidity, or extension (Toulmin and Goodfield 1962, part III, esp. 317–8).

Ghostlike as the shattered machine became, one would expect subsequent scientific thinkers to have tried to restore it, but the machine remains shattered today. The world does not appear to work mechanically or to uphold our intuitive notion of 'cause', reckoned by Joseph Fourier, Auguste Comte, and later Bertrand Russell, to be a relic of a pre-scientific 'metaphysical' age. Modern physics can make little sense of our common-sense notion of a 'solid body'. When Maxwell introduced the field concept, a body came to be thought of as a 'disturbance' of the field: it is like the wave caused by throwing a stone in a pond. The field itself is 'structured through matter', as Metzner (2000: 47) puts it. Schrödinger gave up on the notion of the particle altogether, and quantum theory introduced further mysteries, from non-locality to the conclusion that given the role of the observer and his conscious decisions, the 'material' world is not wholly 'material' at all (see further Davies and Gribbin 1991 on what they call the 'matter myth', and Stapp 2004 on the lack of support from within contemporary physics for materialism as an intuitive metaphysical theory and as defended in the philosophy of mind).[4]

Science thus has not reinvested the notion of matter—contrary to what current disputes on 'materialism' and 'physicalism' (Gillett and Loewer 2001) would suggest—with the coherence it attained in Descartes and then lost at the end of the seventeenth century (Chomsky 2000: 84–5, 2003: 258–65). From then on, it seems, 'matter' became an indefinite catch-all term for whatever science would concoct. Scientific insight increased in the meantime, but not apparently in the sense of lending any metaphysical coherence to the distinction between the 'mental' and the 'natural' or 'physical'.

Given that the new science induced a widespread belief in the 'unknowability' of nature, and a deep scepticism with regard to 'ultimate truth' as claimed by metaphysicians, it is no surprise to find that Hume's 'science of man' shared this

---

[4] Contemporary studies in the history of physics, specifically of Lorentz's work, interestingly reveal how well into the twentieth century the lack of mechanical explainability of physical action in the field prevented progress and prolonged the acceptance of the aether, as a putative material 'carrier' for the waves propagating across the field. In Lorentz's case, sticking to intuitive mechanistic intuitions was a real hindrance for progress towards Einsteinian general relativity, which Lorentz apparently completely misunderstood in its revolutionary consequences (Brouwer 1980).

strictly non-metaphysical spirit.⁵ As the only 'solid foundation' for the other sciences, Hume wrote, the science of man must itself be based on a firm foundation of careful 'experience and observation'. Its objective to further knowledge was no more ambitious than that of 'natural philosophy', philosophy as an integral part of the sciences of the day (Hume 1739–40/1978: xvii). The science of man did not aim at essences, its inability to 'explain ultimate principles' being a defect it shared with 'all the sciences'. The 'anti-foundationalism' of this enterprise, in contemporary epistemological terms, is important and striking. Human nature, whatever that is, is not a matter for 'philosophizing', in the sense of the 'Aristotelians' and scholastics.

The spirit of 'rationalism' in Hume's enterprise may seem to diverge from Humean verdicts that we call 'empiricist' today, but Hume's 'empiricism' is not entirely clear-cut. It is not only rooted in Cartesian naturalism, but has explicit rationalist elements,⁶ which would seem to be implied in adopting a notion of human nature in the first place. Locke's label as an empiricist must count as similarly doubtful (even though his *method* was empirical—like that of any other 'natural philosopher' of the time).⁷ Quite possibly, *any* inquiry into human

---

⁵ In the *Enquiry Concerning Human Understanding*, Hume asserts that 'the powers and forces, by which [the course of nature] is governed, be wholly unknown to us'. We 'are ignorant (...) of the manner in which bodies operate on each other: Their force or energy is entirely incomprehensible' (Hume 1748/1975, section V, part II, §44, 54. We are equally 'ignorant of the manner or force by which a mind, even the supreme mind, operates either on itself or on the body' (ibid., section VII, part I, §57, 72).

⁶ Hume accepted that parts of knowledge do not derive from observation, but from the 'original hand of nature' (cf. Hume 1748/1975, section IX, §85: 108). Striking is his suggestion that certain (associative) operations of the mind 'are a species of natural instincts, which no reasoning or process of the thought and understanding is able either to produce or to prevent' (Hume 1748/1975, section 15 part I, § 38: 46–7), a notion with a noteworthy relation to the 'learning instincts' described later in this introduction, in the sense of the ethological literature (Marler 1991). Intuitively speaking, language acquisition by a normal child, if not prevented by brute force, is a process which indeed 'no reasoning or process of the thought and understanding is able to either produce or to prevent'. In a similar vein, Hume 1748/1975, section V, part II, §45: 55, speaks about nature having 'implanted in us an instinct', and in the first mentioned passage Hume elaborates that an instinct is a 'mechanical power, that acts in us unknown to ourselves; and in his chief operations is not directed by any such relations or comparisons of ideas', hence not on the standard tools on which empiricist learning theories are based. Later in the same work he effectively suggests, strikingly emough, that externalist and empiricist doctrines, in the sense of both a belief in mind-independent external objects of which we then form representations, and a faith in sense experience, is nothing but the expression of a 'powerful instinct of nature', 'infallible and irresistible', 'a universal and primary opinion of all men'. In other words, an empiricism and externalism of this sort is innate. Philosophy has to *correct* this basic instinct, which wrongly suggests to us the existence of external objects causing our representations of them (Hume 1748/1975, section XII, part I, §118–9: 151–3). A version of the 'natural instinct theory' of innate ideas is also defended by Leibniz, who speaks of innate ideas as inborn 'inclinations, dispositions, capacities or natural powers' (Leibniz 1704/1996: 9).

⁷ The question what a Lockean 'idea' is has vexed commentators. In particular, it is not clear at all that these are 'images' that 'stand for' or 'mirror' external things, and when Locke in book IV of the *Essay* considers what '*Knowledge* the Understanding has by those *Ideas*', it seems one might class him as a rationalist with equal justification: ideas internal to the mind ground our knowledge. They are the

nature should be classified as 'rationalist': an empiricist view would then hold that there is no such thing as a human nature to study, because human beings are the product of their contingent experiences, and a matter for historical narrative. I return to the methodological content of rationalism, and the many ways in which empiricism, though crucially not the Cartesian naturalism that Fodor (2003) ascribes to Hume, tends to be linked to a methodological dualism in the study of 'mind' and 'body'.

Despite the interest in the study of human nature that prevailed during the Enlightenment, much discussion centred on whether mankind might in the end turn out to be 'the plaything of time and historical circumstances' (Tomaselli 1995: 232). M. le Roi, in his *Encyclopédie* entry for 'Homme (morale)' (1765), despaired that man defied definition, and that human motivations were too diverse to fall into a pattern that would allow theoretical study. We find similar sentiments in Rousseau and Diderot. The important point here is that overwhelming human diversity was regarded as an essentially *frustrating* fact, which rendered a certain theoretical project fruitless, though not invalid. It did not point to *another* theory, based on some kind of new and historical conception of human nature, but to a theoretical defeat.

In sum, the early modern notion of human nature was that it was a matter for naturalistic inquiry. There was no great concern to draw a boundary between natural and 'non-natural' aspects of human nature, or argue for a principled difference in experimental method. Rather than starting from metaphysical distinctions and divides, including that of mind and body, it positively denounced such aprioristic distinctions. More relevant distinctions are those made between the mechanical and the non-mechanical, between explanations by causes and explanations by laws, and between the mathematical and the brutely empirical. Epistemologically, the understanding of human nature was meant to go as far as that of other sciences (which, according to most authors, was not very far), and there were no aspirations in the 'science of man' for some 'essence of man', or human uniqueness.[8] In particular, there was no claim to the effect that humans are of their essence 'natural', whatever this metaphysical

---

material on which it builds, the element in which our understanding lives (see Tipton 1996 for a careful assessment of Lockean 'empiricism').

[8] Since naturalistic inquiry of its nature does not provide essences, it is not surprising that a study of human nature so conceived won't tell us much about what we common-sensically mean when using the word *human being* or *man*. We do not know whether to call a fertilized egg at certain early stages a *human being*, for example, but science does not answer these questions, which is why they are a matter of public debate. The science of human nature will also not be intrinsically concerned to capture human uniqueness (the latter, with respect to some or other human trait, would be an empirical result). If there are homologs of features of human nature in creatures on Mars or in the animal kingdom elsewhere, this says nothing against them not being features of human nature. This stance on my topic may seem disappointing, but it is also liberating, as it implies that human nature is not a matter of public debate and conceptual analysis, but empirical research, which leaves other conceptualizations of man—in poetics, common sense and culture—simply untouched.

notion, which does not arise in naturalistic inquiry, might mean. 'Being natural' is not a human property but rather the characterization of a mode of *inquiry*. In other words, a methodologically naturalist research program such as Hume's gets as far as it gets, depending on whether there are any aspects of humans that do not vary arbitrarily with circumstances. An overwhelming diversity would show the program to be theoretically fruitless, or simply too difficult, but not illegitimate on conceptual or metaphysical grounds.

1.2 The Study of Human Nature

With so much history in place, let us now ignore three centuries that intervene between the Cartesian naturalists and us. Let us simply mimic the early modern philosophers and look at humans in the same way as one might study physical organs, ants, volcanoes, galaxies, or brains, but not politics, prime ministers, or art exhibitions, which are not conducive to explanation from a naturalistic perspective. We will assume that humans, like other natural objects, such as stars, apples, and brains, have a *history*. But there is a higher level of abstraction where we can, as elsewhere in the sciences, ignore history and describe humans as falling under laws.[9] As elsewhere in nature, these laws act and manifest themselves in historical circumstances, and depend on antecedent conditions which are historically given, but they are not a matter of historical circumstance themselves. But are there laws of human nature? The methodological naturalist will regard this as an empirical question: as le Roi's worry quoted above suggests, variation *might* be arbitrary and not fall into a coherent pattern. But then again, it might not, given a suitable level of abstraction. Where surface variation ends or reveals itself as surface variation only, human nature begins. We cannot tell *a priori* where this happens, or if it does.

We may then, not only propose to study human nature, but ask, what is its design like?[10] What kind of design do we exhibit? And why are we the way we are? This is to go beyond a merely empirical and descriptive enterprise, since we wish to know why what we find is the way it is. We are trying to make sense of us.

In this regard, consider a useful, threefold distinction made by Williams (1992: 6), between the organism-as-document, the organism-as-artefact, and the organism-as-crystal. The first perspective is adopted by evolutionary biologists primarily interested in unique evolutionary histories, organisms as outcomes of unrepeatable contingencies, which get documented in features of the organisms themselves. Here we may recall Gould's famous statement that if we were to 'rewind the tape of evolution', it is unlikely that there would be a human species

---

[9] Hume puts it very well: '[M]an is a being, whom we know by experience, (...) and whose projects and inclinations have a certain connexion and coherence, according to the laws which nature has established for the government of such a creature.' (Hume 1748/1975, section XI : 144)

[10] Note that here we are proposing human nature as a choice of subject for study which one may be interested in or not. We are no more making a metaphysical claim for its existence than Hume did.

again (see Gould 1989). Evolution is not a 'path to (adaptive) perfection', predictable from the kind of conditions under which humans had to survive; it is like history itself: unpredictable, unlawful. This first perspective remains vital even in the light of requirements made by the developmental process, or the organism's individual morphogenesis, where 'a moderate [genetic] disturbance is countered by a control mechanism that prevents the disturbance from redirecting the process' (Williams 1992: 6). Chance will be less of an explanatory force, that is, as development forces stability of regulatory genes, allowing changes only where not too many traits are disturbed at once (Schank and Wimsatt 2001).

The second perspective views organisms as *machines*: they have a design that *suits a particular purpose*. Just as in the case of any artificial machine that you encounter, the complex design you see will only become understandable once you know what it was made for. In other words, the function rationalizes the design.

The third perspective, finally, views the design of the organism as the outcome of a structure-building process which involves laws of form and natural constraints that induce restrictions in the space of logically possible designs and force nature to generate only a tiny amount of a much larger spectrum of forms. Here it is the crystal that serves as a useful analogy, not, e.g., the heart. The design of a snowflake exhibits an inherent geometry, a sixfold symmetry. In explaining it, extraneous factors like temperature, humidity, or air pressure will play a role. However, to say that these external factors *explain* the internal structure would be as strange as saying that the water we give to a plant causes it to develop in the way it does. Just as the plant's development will be a matter of what species of plant it is, and of internally directed principles of growth for which external factors are merely necessary conditions, the crystal is primarily explained internalistically, by laws of form.[11]

All three perspectives are equally legitimate when looking at a natural object, such as a human being. Humans are a mixture of history, artefactuality, and law. But whichever perspective leads to the most fruitful results in some particular case will depend on the object being studied, and the particular trait under consideration. It is the third perspective that this book emphasizes, for the case of human language. Although studying the nature of humans under this perspective will necessarily entail studying *functions* they carry out, it will not involve viewing, as a matter of methodological principle, organic design as intrinsically *functional*, or as serving a purpose. This matters, as we shall see, because surviving conceptualizations of human nature (say, in evolutionary psychology) by and large depict it as intrinsically functionally designed. The human linguistic mind, in particular, is thought to be the result of the external shaping of selective forces,

---

[11] Crystallization has been a leading metaphor in the history of science, playing a vital role in how the ancient Platonic idea of Form became naturalized in early modern science (Emerton 1984). It seems an apt example of how brute matter, just by itself, reaches a state of ordered and symmetrical form; in many ways, it seems like the inorganic analogue to the kind of self-organization found at the level of living systems (Kauffman 1993).

acting on the communicative functions and other effects of subcomponents of the language system as a whole, eventually composing it, piece by piece, in a gradualistic fashion (see Jackendoff 2002; Pinker and Jackendoff 2005).

While I come to that later, I note here that the intuitive notion of human nature as such does not invite a functionalist perspective in the sense of the second perspective above, despite the predominance of the latter in current revitalizations of the notion of human nature (e.g., Pinker 2002). The point is that, intuitively, the *nature* of a thing is what it *is*, irrespective of what *happens* to it, or how it is *used*. This is not to say that our ordinary notion of human nature is *inconsistent* with humans fulfilling certain functions or serving certain purposes. But if they do fulfil such functions, we want this to *follow* from their nature. It is seriously offensive (and certainly not *true*, we think) to say, of a person doing the house cleaning, that it is in the nature of this person to do the house cleaning. This would be in the sense in which some philosophers in Ancient times held that it was in the *nature* of a slave to be a slave, a doctrine that Plato's *Meno* subversively opposed by saying it was in the nature of a slave to know geometry (and to do so without education). It appears to be a general feature of our inquiry when determining the *nature* of something that we idealize from contingent functions.

Our intuitive notion of our nature conflicts in a similar way with the view of us as intrinsically *historical*. The example just given suggests that our *grasp* of the concept of the human differs at different historical periods, while there is a sense in which the *concept* itself is relevantly the same. At an earlier point in Western history, our grasp of it was consistent with some humans being slaves: in the perception of the time, it was in the nature and order of things. In our perception, it is not. Nobody is born a slave, or to do the housecleaning, we hold. But we do not say, today, that our grasp of the concept of human nature is just *ours*, and that the earlier periods were *right* in allowing slavery, because they had a *different concept*, justifying their practices relative to *it*. Our tolerance of the views of others stops at a point. We are not saying that slavery is out because *our own practice of legislation* happens to forbid it, and we would not regard *that* as the reason for not allowing it. On reflection we will concede that our own legislation is simply a contingent historical phenomenon which as such provides no justification for *anything*. We would rather, if we had to, try justifying our legislation in terms of the *content of some concept*, conceived ahistorically, however imperfectly we may be able to perceive it. Because of what it is to be human, we might say, even an Ancient slave was not, of its nature, a slave.

I am claiming, then, rightly or wrongly, that in ethical judgement-making we feel ourselves bound by transhistorical and universal principles. The obvious objection to this is: 'But hey, even if you are right, this universality is only what we *think*—it's not necessarily for real!', to which the obvious reply is, 'If this is what we *do* think, why should we distrust our thinking?' In science generally speaking we do not know whether what we think is right. We just try to convince ourselves by all means available, think it, test it, and hope for the best!

Despite an overwhelmingly functionalist perspective that biology has had in the nineteenth and twentieth centuries, there is a simple sense in which evolutionary biology suggests no close connection between the nature and the contingent use or function of a thing either. There is no such thing as the function that the jawbone, say, as a particular organic form, as such has. At some point in evolution we see it in reptiles, at others we encounter it being used (in well-suited ways) as a noise amplifier in mammals. The Panda's thumb seems like a piece of functional design fitted for holding bamboo shoots, but it really is a modified wrist bone. Our lowered larynx allows us our particular mode of vocalization, but it is used for size exaggeration in deer as well. The vertebrate forelimb has bones in a particular homologous arrangement that is relevantly the same in whales and cats, and horses and humans, hence being used for very different purposes. In any of these cases and others like it, contingent *function* will tell us little about intrinsic *form*. Re-use of old materials and forms is a trick that evolution plays routinely, and humans are good at it, too, as when applying an artefact created for one purpose to another purpose.

The deeper rationale for this dissociation of form and function within evolutionary biology is that there is a 'tremendous "inertia" of form in evolution' (Lewontin 1998: 117), implying a conservation of given morphological forms 'despite dramatic changes in function' (Maynard Smith and Szathmáry 1995: 243). Evolution does not invent structures to suit new purposes. A form even at one single point in evolutionary time may have *several* functions, all maybe contributing to reproductive success. No form or structure has the power to *determine its use*, hence none of these uses allows direct conclusions as regards the form so used. The actual function of a thing is a historically contingent matter, often a happy accident. Organic and non-organic devices can be *employed* (by evolution, or the scientist) to serve certain functions, as in the case of the jawbone, or the case of a molecule, which is created in the laboratory and used to destroy a particular bacterium. But it is not in the *nature* of these things to be used for those purposes, even if they happen to be perfectly fitted to suit these roles.

It may well be true, on the other hand, that such things as the jawbone or a particular chemical molecule would not *exist* without them serving particular functions. There is as much a dissociation of nature and function, as there is a dissociation of nature and conditions of existence. The above molecule might have been created by nature, rather than in the lab, for some reason, in which case its conditions of existence would have been different, without this implying any change in its nature. The molecule may also have *never come about*: no scientist may have thought of creating it. While it would not have *existed* then, its internal structure and architecture, being as such something abstract, would have been what it is. If it had been created, it would have had *that* structure.

It is in this sense, not only that the actual conditions of existence of a thing do not determine its nature, but, also, that to have a certain nature, a thing need not exist. The fact that the tides *exist* is irrelevant to *understanding* them. They could be a thought-up phenomenon not existing on this planet for some historically accidental reason, and we could still understand their mechanism completely, in the way we could understand the mechanism of an imaginary machine. Physicists think of our universe as having a certain nature and certain design features, say as consisting of certain very simple fundamental laws. But they might think up another possible universe obeying different laws, maybe less simple ones. This other universe would not exist, but that would be a contingent fact, and the universe would still have a certain nature. Today's physicists may turn out to be wrong, and that different sort of universe might *be*, for all we can tell, the actual one. Will it change its nature, just because we now realize it happens to exist? What changed is merely which possible world is (or which we have reasons to judge) actual.

Existence makes a difference, then, but not necessarily one that concerns the nature of a thing, a consideration reminiscent of Kant's, that there is no difference in the nature of potential 5 *Thaler* and actual 5 *Thaler* that I have in my pocket, although there is a contingent and historical difference in existence, a higher-order predicate according to Kant. A version of the same idea surfaces in Sartre's famous existentialist argument that there is no such thing as human nature, for from mere *existence* (Heidegger's *Geworfenheit*), no human *nature* could be extracted. The existentialist's point is that the conditions under which a thing exists do not only leave its nature *underspecified*; as such they do not determine it *at all*. The idea that neither the uses nor histories of entities determine their nature is equally a premise in some biologists' arguments, discussed later on, that there is no point to the notion of a human nature. For their reasoning, schematically, is this: the human, as genetically given, is essentially historical and varied, its variance being a matter of how it adapts to an environment in which it finds itself and which exerts selective pressures on it. Therefore, there is no human nature (Hull 1978).

All in all, then, there are some initial reasons to believe that the question of human nature actually does not have much to do with the question of conditions of existence, functionality, or 'design for a use'. But this won't prevent us from investigating functions human organisms happen to carry out, things like metabolism, immunization, breathing, or language. We notice in particular that all complex organisms are highly structured internally, or *modular*: any organism has a number of relatively independent sub-systems—organs—which are dedicated to certain tasks: the immune system, the breathing system, the circulatory system, the digestive system, and so on.[12] They are holistically dependent sub-systems whose function supports a more complex whole, which we aim to

---

[12] Modularity of subsystems—from molecules to organs and body segments—may more generally be a fundamental design principle in the biological world, as something that constrains the way external selection can modify or re-organize an organism in evolution (see Schlosser and Wagner 2004 and Raff 1996, esp. chapter 10, for discussion).

understand by sorting out systems that have relatively distinctive characteristics interacting in systematic ways.

It is in this informal sense of 'organ' that we may suspect 'organs of the mind' as well. We may in particular isolate one cognitive competence, say our faculty of language, and aim to characterize its distinctive principles, if there are any, viewing it as a component of the mind/brain, described abstractly. The brain itself, indeed, is internally differentiated, and 'is no more plausibly a blank slate with unlimited plasticity in response to its environment than is a mind' (Cherniak 2005).[13]

Given empirical support for modular organization in the mind/brain and the pervasiveness of modularity in the biological world more generally, the heatedness of debates on 'modularity' and Chomsky's 'hypothesis of the language organ' seems misplaced. The 'modularity of mind' is not assumed in the Chomskyan approach as a matter of methodological principle. It simply so happens, as Chomsky puts it, that a human infant, but not her pet kitten, reflexively categorizes parts of the confusion around her as 'linguistic', and that richly structured capacities enter her peculiar modes of human thought and action during development. But in other ways, both the infant and kitten 'develop along a rather similar path in acquiring capacities to deal with many other aspects of the world' (Chomsky MI, version of 2000: 89). Fromkin (1997) summarizes several decades of empirical research following up the suggestion of characterizing language as an 'organ' of the mind, autonomous and independent of other cognitive abilities yet interacting with them in use:

> The more we look, whether at studies of neonates or development or lesions or blood flow studies of cognitive processes or ERP and fMRI studies, the more we find that knowledge and processing of language is separate from the ability to acquire and process other kinds of knowledge, that the asymmetry between general knowledge and linguistic knowledge shows language to be independent of general intellectual ability, and that language itself, as well as other cognitive systems are distinct both anatomically and functionally (Fromkin 1997: 23).[14]

A modular perspective in the sense above does not exclude principles structuring other 'organs' from being applicable to the linguistic domain; the Minimalist Program, we shall see, explores this very idea centrally, e.g., by turning domain-general principles of computational efficiency into explanatory tools in the domain of language. Clearly, a more general theory of mental function that would maintain the standards of empirical and explanatory adequacy of given

---

[13] Paul Broca began defending the modularity of the brain on the basis of anatomical and aphasiological studies the 1860s. Since then, the question has continued to be a matter for debate. For a review of recent confirmations of Broca's original suggestions on the modularity of language see Grodzinky (2004); see also Stowe, Haverthort, and Zwarts (2005).

[14] See Smith and Tsimpli (1995) for a particularly striking case study of the dissociation of language from general cognition and communicative ability; see also Curtiss (1977), Yamada (1990), and Damasio (1999).

theories of linguistic function is intrinsically desirable, even if it were to prove much of the traditional descriptive apparatus of linguistic theory an artefact. Nor is there any assumption that mechanisms that form a part of the human faculty of language will all be language-specific in the sense of being uniquely adapted to language (Hauser, Chomsky and Fitch 2002). A claim about the functional dedication of a system as a whole (that is, viewed as a dedicated organ) implies nothing about the functional specialization of the mechanisms entering it, which may not be 'for language' at all (see Chomsky MI, version of 2000, fns. 4, 6).

Talk of 'organs' neither commits us to a kind of developmental 'fixity', nor to other aspects of the modularity notion introduced specifically by Fodor (1983) and criticized by Karmiloff-Smith (1992). While it seems plainly true that the difference noted between the child and her kitten relates to their differences in genetic endowment, this is not to say in any way that cognition develops deterministically as prespecified by the genes. Indeed it is a classical assumption of Chomskyan biolinguistics that the human language faculty, viewed as a distinctive subsystem of the human mind, undergoes *state changes* during human development in the light of experiential data. This is an important respect in which 'modularity', in the present sense, does *not* contrast with either 'learning' or 'development'. An appropriate formulation seems to be that human language develops along its internally determined course, whatever the internal determinants, developmental as well as genetic, are.

There is, finally, no presumption that language is an 'input system' in Fodor's sense, a system with proprietary inputs which pass on information from the external environment through a system of sensory transducers that output data in a format suitable for some 'central', domain-general processing system (dealing with the fixation of belief, rational planning, building up encyclopedic knowledge, etc.). In this book, indeed, the language faculty will be viewed as reaching more deeply into the caverns of the mind. In particular, I will take it to account for kinds of *judgements* that we make and their meanings, while not regarding judgement-making intrinsically as an instance of the formation of *belief* in the Fodorian sense.

Pursuing the path of a methodological naturalism, then, we will try to determine the structure of putative 'mental' organs in much the way that we do so in the case of 'physical' ones. We will try to determine, on some suitable level of abstraction, the mechanisms by means of which they achieve the distinctive functions they achieve, assuming (basically, out of ignorance and the absence of viable alternatives) that these mechanisms are located and *internally represented* in the brain. For all we can tell, syntactic structures are not located in the foot, the air, or the mind of God.[15] Since languages do not only exist as external systems of

---

[15] Syntactic structures could also be abstract structures, like those of arithmetic, and as such be located nowhere (see Langendoen and Postal 1984; Katz and Postal 1991). I won't be able to discuss this alternative here, which I think is not as far removed from the perspective of this book as it may at first seem.

communication, but are *known*, and since any human language is a system with *infinite* generative power (there being no apparent finite limit to the expressions you can at this moment generate or comprehend), but we are finite, it seems that the language we know *must* be *finitely represented* in our heads. It cannot be a finite set of objects outside our heads (air pressure wave changes, movements of molecules, etc.), given that *it* is not finite; in any case, if it existed outside of us, we would have to assume that internal mechanisms enter into the process of using and knowing it.

Although talk of systems of knowledge being internally represented in the brain has been an issue embarrassingly difficult and controversial to discuss, the point just made may, I hope, be seen as a very simple one. It so happens that for little Freddy to know a language, he has to know many things: a system of phonological rules, a lexical system, and a syntactic system, among others. There is a fact about him, presumably related to his brain, which makes him know these things. Part of what has proved problematic here are the common-sense connotations of the words 'knowledge' and 'representation', which will lead us to ask the question: what are the systems that we are claiming to be 'internally represented' representations *of*? Need there not be something external for internal linguistic representations to apply to? But the question is puzzling, for a language is what it is *by virtue of* the internal representations that neonate children begin to spontaneously form: there isn't as much as a *sentence* out there, to be represented by us, without them.

Human mental activity, we are assuming, splits into a number of subcomponents with distinctive functions, in the way of organs of the body. In both cases, external functioning will depend on internal structures enabling it. The properties of these structures are an empirical matter of fact, including the question of whether they are relational in the sense that the common-sense notion of representation suggests. If the answer to that question is *yes*, then the internal structures *are* not the systems of knowledge whose cognitive representation we wish to describe; rather these systems will be something other than the internal structures, which will themselves merely externally *relate* to these systems, perhaps by way of some mechanism of 'intentionality'. If the answer is *no*, the systems of knowledge simply *are* structures in the mind, invoked to explain what we think we cannot otherwise explain. It is clear that the second, negative answer is more parsimonious, invoking, by dropping one relatum, fewer empirical commitments than the positive answer, and hence should be preferred everything else being equal.

Qua 'mental' organs, then, we assume these mind modules are internally represented in the brain somehow. We may view them as specialized circuits which are segregated into functionally specialized subsystems themselves. Chomsky made the classic case for the existence of a 'language organ' which has the specialized purpose of acquiring knowledge of human linguistic sound and meaning. Another important putative module is TOM ('theory of mind'), dedicated to the computation of intentional states of agents and the origin of 'folk psychology' (Baron-Cohen 1995; Leslie 1994). Neurotypical children acquire that latter skill at roughly the same age and after reaching the same developmental milestones, which has led many psychologists to conclude that our notions of belief and intentional action are part of human nature, separate from general-purpose intelligence rather than learned on the basis of it.[16] Other prominent modules that have been argued for are numerical competence (Wynn 1998; Hauser & Spelke, in press), the classification of plants and animals (folk biology), intuitive ('folk') physics, face recognition, moral reasoning, and social relations, to name but a few (Hirschfeld and Gelman 1994 provides an overview).

The specialized neural circuits in question may also be called innate 'instincts to learn' in Marler's (1991) sense, instincts that have provided a classical case against the behaviourist variant of empiricism. If brain organization consists of one or more of such task-specific learning devices, there is no such thing as learning in the ordinary and the empiricist's sense, namely a unitary process that is relevantly the same across different domains. There would be, in particular, no general-purpose 'associative learning' mechanism as posited in empiricist learning theories ever since Hume: an idea that will, Gallistel suggests, turn out to be the 'phlogiston of psychology' (see Gazzaniga 1997: chapter 5; and see Gallistel and Gibbon 2001).[17] Domain-specific learning systems of this kind provide animals with a predisposition to deal with stimuli in specific ways, which these stimuli do not by themselves suggest. They may be called 'knowledge-acquisition systems', on the ground that learning, intuitively, is the acquisition of knowledge, and also because, intuitively, a human who speaks a language knows a great deal about its properties. It is knowledge whose development we can empirically study and experiment with as the human infant develops. In the light of frequent philosophical criticisms that such knowledge does not deserve to be called 'knowledge', it must be emphasized that the word 'knowledge' is simply used in its ordinary sense here: it is perfectly intuitive, for ears uncontaminated by philosophical theories of knowledge, to say that children know these things, this being the *explanation* of *why* they act in the way they do. As a word of ordinary language, the notion of knowledge and its various translations will have too many shades of meaning for them all to be consistent with the usage just introduced, but this would seem quite expected. There are also more technical

---

[16] Leslie's (2000) interesting discussion of approaches claiming to explain how such notions might be induced from experiential evidence suggests that no such approach has in any sense been successful so far.

[17] If it does, the term 'learning' will share the fate of the Ancients' terms 'air', 'earth', or 'fire', which were likewise meant to be natural kind terms, but turned out to be human descriptive artefacts that science could make no use of. The same is possible for our terms 'belief' and 'thought'. In their use in epistemology, rationality theory, philosophy of mind, and common sense, these terms *are* paradigmatically domain-general, as we can have beliefs or thoughts just about anything, and a belief is partially defined by the general notion of a truth-conditional content.

reasons for speaking of systems of knowledge in the case of human linguistic competence: one reason being, in particular, that such knowledge has an algebraic and richly deductive structure, and that experience cannot 'falsify' or 'rectify' it, being *conditioned* by this very system of knowledge.

A learning system in the present sense is thus a mechanism for converting experience into knowledge—experience that is radically underspecified with respect to that knowledge. Insects in particular learn to know their position, by computing how fast they have been moving, in what direction, and for how long; birds use their knowledge of the celestial pole of the night sky to hold their southward course during the night-time portions of their first migratory flights (Gallistel 1990). The search for a mechanism that gives ants, birds, or bees a knowledge of their position is methodologically essentially the same as the search for a mechanism in the human brain that allows children to acquire knowledge of language. No methodological or ontological dichotomies arise between studying innate predispositions in birds who recognize the syllables characteristic of the song of their species, or in human babies, who appear to be equipped with 'innate expectations' as well, and go through similar stages as birds do in the process of acquiring speech (Eimas 1985; Mehler and Dupoux 1994; Boysson-Bardies 1999).

In the generative tradition, we assume that linguistic competence involves a system that stores information in long-term memory, the *cognitive system*, which contains structures that get *used* or *accessed* on occasions, through systems of *performance*. Performance systems seem to enjoy some partial independence from the cognitive system, in that they can be replaced (as when switching from spoken to a sign language). But a competence-performance distinction also makes sense on the basis of other empirical and methodological reflections. Clearly, we cannot simply assume that the grammatical rules that are internally represented in the brain of a human are, at the same time, processing or parsing rules, or are intrinsically related to the use to which the cognitive system of language is factually put. While there is an obvious and non-controversial sense in which a theory of parsing English will incorporate a theory of a person's knowledge of English rather than, say, her knowledge of Chinese, an intrinsic connection between a theory of that knowledge and a psycholinguistic theory of parsing would be a further empirical result. It is an expression of methodological caution, then, in order not to prejudge this further question, to firstly characterize *what* we actually know—our system of linguistic knowledge—in the most *neutral* possible terms, and view this as the *basis* for the actual use to which that system is put in communication (rather than as providing a direct theory of that use: see Chomsky 1965: 9). Language use is clearly richer as a domain of inquiry, as many other interacting neurological and psychological mechanisms help to determine the actual physical output of language that is produced and comprehended.

Viewed in this way, the competence-performance distinction reflects the methodological decision to start with less rather than more, and to build up complexity as one goes along. It is an instance of the distinction between structure and function that we find in the life sciences more generally and in neurobiology in particular, where the causal relationship between these two things is a central question. Thus the nineteenth-century physiologist Claude Bernard contrasted 'anatomy (the stable morphological organizations or "structures") with physiology (the dynamic processes by which an organism acts on the outside world or on itself)' (Changeux and Dehaene 1996: 128). A distinction between a mental grammar as a part of our neuroanatomy (competence) and neuromuscular behaviour involved in speech production and comprehension (performance) is parallel to Bernard's. At a still more basic level, the competence-performance distinction is present in physics, where all sorts of factors may distort the result of an experiment predicted on theoretical grounds, yet this need not shake our conviction that there is one outcome that the experiment *should* yield if these factors are controlled for.

It is also a fundamental tenet in the rationalist tradition, beginning with Plato's *Meno* (85c-d), that there is nothing incoherent, generally speaking, in the idea that a given cognitive system is latently there, but for some contingent reason never used, or not fully used. Thus, had it not been for his accidental encounter with Socrates, the slave boy interrogated in the *Meno* might never have exploited his capacity for geometry. Even so, to conclude that he would not have had this capacity seems quite absurd. There are populations in this world, Eskimos among them, who have a rudimentary indigenous mathematics that does not exploit the human faculty of number in the way we do. It would seem strange to posit that Eskimo children lack numerical capacity when the lack of a number system is more plausibly a matter of cultural difference, and what *use* they make of it.[18]

Our cognitive system of language, too, may be *there* (internally represented somehow), even if not used, for some contingent reason. Communicative skills may break down while grammatical competence remains intact; and due to temporary brain lesions, say, it may be that the cognitive system underlying language use cannot be accessed for some period. Then, as Chomsky has pointed out, the effects of the lesion may cease and the knowledge come back. Pending miracles, one supposes it has been there somehow during this period, even though it wasn't used, and unusable. Chomsky (2000: 27) even envisages the fantasy of some crazy scientist who has discovered the neural basis of how our brains store information about linguistic structures and rewires our brains so that the cognitive system of language outputs not to the performance systems to

---

[18] Non-human primates have surprising abilities in numerical computation (Carey 1998: Wynn 1998). Sulkowski and Hauser (2001) report on experiments demonstrating the capacity of rhesus monkeys to spontaneously compute (in single trials, without training) the outcome of subtraction events. Since it would be very surprising if such abilities were entirely absent in humans, and for many other reasons cited in these works, we should question whether the capacity to represent numerals is a 'cultural construction'.

which it factually outputs now, but to others, which use human linguistic structures for a different purpose, such as locomotion. The moral of the story, I suppose, is that if our human language system might in principle be used quite differently than we use it now, then it does not, as a system of knowledge described purely formally, intrinsically relate to its factual use. As a system of knowledge, it cannot look into and has no power over the performance systems that use it, which are independently constituted, and may change or fail without the cognitive system changing or failing. It is a matter of empirical fact (but no more) that the cognitive system of language is used to communicate, manipulate, refer, deceive, or joke. It relates to these behaviours in the sense that it *enters* into them in historical circumstances, but it does not *consist* in them, still less *cause* them (let alone *be caused* by them).

To claim that simply because the system is used for some purpose, it can be understood in *terms* of its being so used, is an instance of the fallacy of deriving structure from function that I mentioned above. How form *should* derive from function or performance in the specific case of language is quite a mystery. When coming to a foreign country whose language we cannot understand we are able to make sense of the circumstances we are in by means of our own thoughts, and would also be able to make sense of the thoughts of the people we meet, were it not for the different sound structure of the language they use, which for us gives no indication of what their thoughts are. The two structures, sound and meaning, are completely different, having different constituents and relations on them. Hence meaning is not a matter of sound, and the language system itself, being a way of *relating* sound and meaning, does not reduce to *either*, being more abstract and 'central' to the mind than either of them.

Note that a mechanism abstractly characterizing how sounds and meanings *are* related according to the system of knowledge of language says nothing in itself about how they will *actually* come to be related in performance. Thus people misspeak or get confused, use expressions that are generated by the mechanism but too complex for anyone to parse, or use expressions with meanings that they do not happen to have according to the mechanism. A nice example of the last point is the expression *No head injury is too trivial to ignore*, which in performance is almost unfailingly taken to express the meaning, *No matter how trivial a head injury is, it should not be ignored*. But the expression does not have that meaning. It means *No matter how trivial a head injury is, it should be ignored*.[19] Mismatches such as these, which may arise in performance, allow no direct conclusions about the function or mechanism relating sound and meaning itself. What an expression would be 'sensibly', 'rationally', or 'usually' interpreted as saying need not be what it means. The system has its own mind, so to speak, working by its own idiosyncratic principles, apparently not 'rational' ones (in something like the sense of rational decision theory). There is similarly no rational ground, but

[19] I owe this example to John Collins.

only a purely syntactic one, for why in the expression *When did he note that she had deceived him* we may be inquiring both about the time of the noticing and the time of the deception (one answer could be: *on Sunday, but I only noticed it on Monday*), whereas in *When did he note how she had deceived him*, it can only be the time of the noticing.

Note that claims about human linguistic competence have no intrinsic relation to possible claims about the language 'organ' being an expression of the human *genome*, or the issue of whether or not it evolved in some important sense through a gradual process of adaptation by Neo-Darwinian principles. These questions are secondary ones. That we are interested in systems of knowledge as such, in partial abstraction from (adaptive) behaviour, history, and use, is a crucial difference to claims about human nature made in sociobiology (Wilson 1978; Dawkins 1976/1989) and evolutionary psychology (Pinker 1997, 2002; Pinker and Jackendoff 2005; Plotkin 1997; Cosmides and Tooby 1997).

An immediate anthropological consequence of the present approach to human nature that surfaces in this section is an expectation that there are *limits* to human systems of knowledge. A rat is naturally endowed with the ability to make sense of certain things in its environment, while other things remain inscrutable to it. There appears to be little reason to believe that we should be an extraordinary exception in nature in this respect, by having an ability to acquire in principle knowledge of anything we like (Chomsky 2000: 83; see also McGinn 1994: chapter 1, who draws on this Chomskyan point). Only on the opposite view, that our brains house a 'generalized learning device' rather than a number of specialized learning modules, would we expect there to be no natural limitations to what we could in principle learn. Given a long enough life, sufficient energy, and funding, we might learn just about anything. But if the intrinsic structure of our cognition imposes factual limits on which domains and problems we can, with some success, apply our cognitive apparatus to, an important implication for human nature arises: that there are likely to be principled limitations to human knowledge in certain domains. In particular, there appears no reason to suspect that our minds must be 'well designed' for particular uses such as doing philosophy. Somehow, it seems as if we do not get very far in resolving philosophical questions, such as the question of free will, despite no lack of effort on our part.

That evolution should have designed our minds functionally so as to be able to come up, in principle, with a solution to any question we can make intelligible to ourselves, appears to be a widespread misunderstanding of the rationalist position I will be introducing (see, e.g., Rorty 1990: 280, to whom I return). If rationalism is based on the biology of our minds, exactly the opposite is to be expected. The same presumption may also be the reason why we tend to wrongly assume that how we arrive at and apply concepts must be somehow *transparent* to our minds (that we know what and how we think and speak, or why we apply concepts when we do so).

1.3 Human Design

The human mind as such and its 'organs' *have* a particular design, on the nature of which given theories will take their respective commitments. I talk here about 'design features' in a completely general way, implying nothing about design intentions, which we do not assume in the natural realm. Human linguistic expressions in particular have certain construction principles, whose rationale we would like to understand, say the universal distinction between sentences like *John said that* and Noun Phrases (NPs) like *John*. Once we have noted such design features, we can ask meta-theoretical questions, such as whether the design is essentially functional or adaptive. Clearly, not all design is functional. We admire the perfect design of the bee's honeycomb pattern, e.g., but searching for a functional explanation in cases such as this would be a blind alley, as the explanation of this design pattern apparently has nothing to do with adaptive function. We also seem to have a general grasp of a distinction between design-for-a-use as envisaged on an occasion, and design irrespective of such a contingent use. Thus the human eye has a particular intricate design, whose structural optimality is a subject of debate. But to say that it is bad design because we cannot see well in the dark, or because our eyesight declines as we get older, is a piece of evaluative discourse that is irrelevant to the study of the natural world.

Design, as I am using the word, is of its essence something that we *study* rather than *do*. This contrasts sharply with the use of 'design' in software engineering, say, or in the design of an *artificial mind* that can carry out certain tasks. Advances in artificial intelligence need not tell us anything about human mind design. Suppose we constructed some artificial device with a 'mind' so nifty that it fooled people into believing they were conversing with a human being when they talked to it. If that were the case, the device would pass what is called 'Turing's Test' (Turing 1950). On one understanding of what that would mean, it would show the correctness of a metaphysical theory of the mental, which says that mental processes are of their essence computational. That understanding immediately raises the problem what we do with phenomena that are informally characterized as 'mental', but that cannot be modelled computationally—mathematical thinking, for example, if Penrose (1994) is right, or vast areas of everyday reasoning, if Fodor (2000) is right. Clearly, a metaphysical theory should not prejudge *whether* Penrose or Fodor are right, an entirely empirical issue.

On another and related understanding, the test suggests a criterion for the appropriateness of our use of mental vocabulary; hence, for when we could or should say that a computer 'thinks'. In this case, the test will consist, apart from a brute engineering task, in a suggestion for a convention regarding the use of a *word*: it specifies a concrete condition on when it is appropriate to use the term 'mental'.

On either understanding, the device's success in passing the test would allow no conclusions about the structure of the mind considered as a natural object, for in a study of this type it is irrelevant how we *call* things, and what metaphysical views we hold on what the essence of the 'mental' is. Indeed, it would not follow that our mind *is* a computer, even though it could be true that certain aspects of its performance can be described computationally. In a similar way, designing an artificial language allows no empirical conclusions on human language design. Its design will depend on the designer's purposes, or what he wants to use his language for. The design of human natural language is simply what it is. The artificial language may be specifically designed to enable communication, but this would not necessarily tell us anything about natural language design. A prosthetic leg, equally, may (one day) work (relative to certain task specifications) in just the way that a natural one does. It may even serve to deepen our understanding of natural legs (suggesting say, that they do, indeed, work in a mechanical fashion, rather than being moved by the soul's spirits). Mind–computer comparisons may be interesting in similar ways, and recall the comparisons made between the universe and a clock in the seventeenth and eighteenth centuries. No ontological issues—metaphysical issues concerning 'what something is', or a universal 'leg-type', capturing the 'essence of legs'—arise from such comparisons. It is unclear why insight into the design of mind should wait for the definition of some 'essence of the mental', or a number of general 'mental state types', that would be independent of our specifically human biology, an idea as unreasonable as insisting on the need for an unbiological universal 'leg-type' (see comments in Chomsky 2003: 261 and see further Section 1.4 below).

Whether such metaphysical moves take place or not, the empirical-experimental task of studying the actual design of legs, universes, or human minds remains. For the purposes of the latter task, the study of self-organizing neural nets or morphogenetic processes in chemical matter (Turing 1952)—if it also leads to a kind of 'thinking' that passes the Turing Test—is as worthwhile as software engineering in the symbolic paradigm. That is, there is no intrinsic relation between some device's passing the Test and its being a serial computer or symbol-processor, and hence between the Turing Test and the functionalist view of the mind and its metaphysics. In particular, the mind's 'matter' may *matter*, as Leiber (1995) puts it, contrary to what the functionalist holds. In short, there is no argumentative route from the fact that something passes the Turing Test to the correctness of the 'physical symbol hypothesis', the hypothesis that our minds perform computations over mental symbolic representations.

The best understanding of Turing's (1950) suggestion to develop machines passing the Turing Test may thus be that it is, quite simply, a piece of standard science, on a par with mechanical models in physiology or astronomy, rather than being an attempt at a definition of 'what intelligence is', an attempt to 'develop a functionalist theory of mind', or 'a criterion of the mental'. It does not contribute to a philosophical, or conceptual-metaphysical problem, but rather does *exactly the opposite*: by suggesting how to *avoid* such questions, which Turing calls 'absurd' in the very first lines of his paper. Like Turing, I doubt that there is an essence or a mark of the mental. Whether and in what sense human mental processes are 'intentional', in particular, is an empirical issue, not a conceptual one. Organisms exhibit empirically distinct features that we loosely classify as 'chemical', 'electromagnetic', 'mental'. We use these terms to indicate domains of inquiry, but not because we know what the mental or the chemical of its nature is. We do not use mental vocabulary to describe what we do because we know what mental properties *are*, and find them instantiated in some organism. That would be like saying that we do not call chairs 'mental' because we know they do not have a mind, whereas we know we do. But there is no 'essence of the mental' enshrined in ordinary language that prevents us from assigning a mind to the chair. If chairs began moving in strange ways, their mentality would become an established fact. It is just that so far, no rich internal structures have had to be posited to explain how they behave.

In short, mind design is an instance of organic design, an empirical given for which we try to find a rationale, and the abstract computational modelling of the mind does not imply a commitment to the truth of functionalism as a metaphysical or philosophical position. Furthermore, the question of the rationale of the design we find should not be prejudged, by stipulating that human mind design must be functionally understood, in the sense that the function rationalizes the structure. Functional equivalence, as between an artificial mind and the human one, does not address our question.

A more interesting idea for our purposes is that nature sets a *standard for design perfection*. To understand this idea, suppose that we have come up with a theory of some natural object that makes it appear somewhat weird: it has no *appeal* to us, makes no good *sense*, or *bewilders* us. We look and say: this is not the design that we, in the light of given constraints that we know of, would have chosen. In fact we might then suspect: this cannot be what nature is really like, the mistake is in our description. Maybe this *is* how nature is, but this can only be a conclusion of last resort. The assumption we see at work here is that nature sets a *standard* of perfection: if its design comes out as imperfect, the fault is ours. If this is *nature*, it *is* perfect.

This is clearly no functional notion of perfection, as nature serves no purposes. It is much more of an aesthetic notion, but none the worse for that. To seek perfection in nature has been a vital heuristic in the history of science, 'a very profitable objective', as Dirac (1968) puts it. The heuristic is to derive testable predictions from the assumption that nature realizes 'perfect' solutions. Given some intuition of what perfect design would be, say planets moving in perfect spheres, the heuristic is to try *vindicating* this idea of design. The prediction we make is perfectly refutable, as when we find that the planets move in ellipses. But such 'imperfection' will call for a special explanation. Further inquiry will be called for, contrary to when design is as we expect it to be, in which case there is no incentive to ask any further *why* things are as we find them to be. Questions arise when we find things not to be as we think they should be.

There is thus more than a methodological or 'aesthetic' dimension to assumptions about design optimality, as these address potential features of *reality*, quite irrespective of our *theories*. It is precisely our *theories* that, even if they are best theories for some domain, we may call into question if they do not make reality fall out in the way we expected.[20] In a certain way, assumptions about design optimality in nature may even seem *epistemologically unavoidable*, being preconditions to scientific inquiry as such.[21] It seems impossible to even imagine our course of inquiry if we were to assume that nature tends to be always *more* complex than we think, that it tends to work with design principles that seem maximally convoluted or unexpected for minds like ours. Nature as we find and describe it is in this sense *bound* to make sense to us.

While the perfect design assumption is apparently real in physics, it is more surprising to make it in psychology or biology. Yet, the question of whether the design of our minds realizes a perfect solution will centrally occupy us here. This is the question of *minimal mind design*. If psychology was a 'special science' with explanatory principles and methodologies radically different from those of physics, the transfer of the idea of perfection to the mind would be surprising. If we view the mind as a natural object that is in principle a part of physics, the idea may still remain surprising, but it should by no means be rated bizarre. In the domain of language, the question would be whether that particular organ is designed so as to be a perfect solution to the task of relating sound and meaning.

We return here to our earlier question whether the mind is more like a machine or a crystal. Kepler (1611/1959), using thought experiments, first wondered whether the snowflake's symmetry properties could be traced to some hypothetical microscopic regularity in their atomic structure. If matter was composed from tiny, identical particles, he reasoned, certain macroscopic ('emergent') properties would primarily depend on the forces causing the organization of the microscopic particles, not their material composition or even their shapes.[22] In particular, particles of some given shape naturally pack together in certain ways rather than others. If you put one coin on the table, and ask how many you

---

[20] Even principles like Occam's razor reflected an 'ontological' trend in late medieval Aristotelianism, rather than a merely methodological one. Aristotle's assertions in *Phys.* I. 4. (188a19) (on the advantage of Empedocles' assumption of a parsimony of explanatory principles), and in *Phys.* I. 6. (189a: 11–12), have a methodological flavour, too, but when referring to these very passages (and to Occam's razor) in his *Praelectiones Physicae* (1630), Jungius tells us 'Naturam autem sapientissima, idioque nec deficiens in principijs suis nec superflua' (Jungius 1630 (1982): 96), which makes just the kind of assumption of design perfection in nature that I have described here.

[21] I owe this point to conversations with Christoph Meinel.

[22] See Stewart (1998: 31–6) for an exposition of this view from a more modern viewpoint, an account on which I rely.

can pack naturally around it, the answer is—as a consequence of the laws of geometry—six, and these fit perfectly. You can then continue building structure, obtaining a tight honeycomb pattern. (In fact there is, provably, no better—denser, no more *optimal*—way of packing coins than this.) The optimality follows from mathematical laws for fitting a given shape into a given region: again the functionality of this patterning, as in the honeycomb pattern, is a consequence, not a cause.[23]

By and large, modern science has changed the details but not the spirit of Kepler's proposal: there are atoms in matter, and they pack efficiently, so as to minimize energy. In short, the snowflake seems indeed 'intelligently designed' to achieve a regular geometry, but what matters is the sheer necessity for the form (a sixfold symmetry) to arise. The complex structural design of snowflakes is a side-effect of natural principles of efficiency and optimality, while the emergent structure itself arises from interactions between the constituents of the system on a local level. In essence, I will read the Minimalist Program as entailing the real possibility that human *meaning* might be a side-effect of structural growth in some analogous sense—arising, too, as an emergent pattern from local interactions between words in the course of a syntactic derivation (see Section 6.1).

Any vindication of design perfection, be it in the case of nature or mind (if we wish to make a difference here), will have a tremendous epistemological benefit. Wherever we find what we think is 'perfect design', there is a sense in which there is nothing more to explain, in which the enterprise of knowledge comes to an end (although this is not meant to suggest that our intuitions as to what perfection is are settled once and for all, and cannot be shaped gradually in the light of inquiry and insight itself; or that we won't still have to learn how the brain works so as to *implement* such perfect design). The point is that if design is perfect, we have vindicated the basic 'Galilean' intuition of the 'perfection of nature' (Chomsky 2002, chapter 2), and there is no such question as *why* nature is perfect. The only thing we need in this case is a *generative principle* that *gives* us that perfect design, an explanation that will then be complete and pose no further questions regarding external conditions, historical origins, evolutionary pathways, the structure of the brain, etc. There would be, to be sure, a *history of growth* for the crystal, but studying this history, or development, if it was just a way of implementing our generative principle, would be close to irrelevant: it would show the historical realization of a process governed by ahistorical laws.

Beyond epistemological consequences, there would be anthropological ones. As noted, structural perfection is what we primarily expect in the physical universe only, not the living one, in which another scientific aesthetic has reigned. If the

---

[23] Kepler himself explores the honeycomb pattern as an organic analogue to snowflake crystallization, it being equally, Kepler suggests, an instance of a maximally efficient way of building a pattern. Without being capable of pursuing this pattern intentionally (or on 'reflection', as Kepler says), the bee just builds it by a 'natural instinct'.

Neo-Darwinian evolutionary biologist is right, man is a historical fabric, cobbled together in a process that is largely one of historical accidents on which the forces of natural selection then act in ways that no law can predict.[24] There are no laws for how species become extinct or thrive. Natural selection itself is no law, but a blind, purposeless and basically 'stupid' mechanism that sorts among morphological forms appearing on the evolutionary scene, and may well assemble hopeless designs of the kind a watchmaker would, were he blindfolded (or drunk, in addition). Very concretely, Gopnik (1990) diagnoses the human language faculty as a Rube Goldberg machine *par excellence*; Jackendoff (2002: 161), summarizing its design, concedes: 'It is not elegant'; and Pinker and Jackendoff (2005: 27) find the faculty 'useful but imperfect, just like other biological systems'.

In the case of the human cognitive apparatus at large, people have found that it is 'a kludge, a collection of *ad hoc* systems that somehow get the job done' (Gazzaniga 1997: 114). The living world is full of oddities and strange solutions that, in Jacob's phrase, a 'reasonable God would never have used' (Jacob 1982: 34). Darwin himself emphasized the structural and functional imperfections of life (e.g., in his work on orchids), as opposed to his theological contemporaries who defended the idea of organized beings pre-ordained by an omniscient creator. Evolution employs principles of 'least effort' (say, in using old materials to new purposes), but not in the sense of conservation laws in physical systems, say, or minimal distance or locality principles of movement as we will encounter them in the organization of the human linguistic system. With the exception of pop-versions of Darwinism deriving from the work of Spencer and others, there is crucially *no* meaning of evolution driving organisms to an ever higher perfection in some linear fashion.

While, for Spencer, evolution could only end in the establishment of the greatest perfection and the most complete happiness, for Darwin there is no point to the assertion that it refers to a *necessary* process of increasing perfection, complexity, and specialization (see further Hinzen 2005a). There is no factual question whether one Rube-Goldberg machine concocted by evolution's tinkering is 'better' or 'more perfect' than any other. It just so happened that in its local context, it had adaptive advantages with respect to competitors that at this point occupied the same evolutionary scene. Evolution's products, such as the eye, *work*, and they are adaptive, but there is no functional sense in which the eye 'works well'. Clearly, if our eyes allowed us to see in the dark, they would be better, and although man's supreme intelligence is 'good for' many things, we might as well come to think that it has been a gross maladaptation, should it prove to be what eventually drives us to extinction.

---

[24] Nature is a 'tinkerer' (Pierre Jacob's famous word was *bricoleur*), 'an opportunistic maker of gadgets, a "satisficer" who is always ready to settle for mediocrity if it is cheap enough' (Dennett 1995: 225). You may expect organisms cobbled together by the accidents of their respective histories if nature is a tinkerer, but not elegance in organismic design.

Searching for design perfection in some functionalist and adaptationist sense may be in vain, then, but this isn't, again, the notion of design that we are after. While the vertebrate eye is not good for seeing in the dark, it isn't well-designed in one respect that is independent of such contingent functions: as Dawkins (1986: 93) notes, each photocell is 'wired in backwards, with its wire sticking out on the side nearest the light'. The photocells are how we expect them—pointing towards the light—only in invertebrates, like octopus and squids. The vertebrate eye has additional complexity, in short, that we would not rationally expect. Here then there is an empirical question, similar to questions we will meet in the language case, about whether or not (and if not, why) a given natural object fulfils rational design expectations, given the basic function it is dedicated to. This is a question untouched by our verdict that evaluative or 'Spencerian' notions of 'good design' have no factual content.

It may be encouraging, on the other hand, that structural perfection in the biological world, though unexpected under conditions of genetic tinkering, is ultimately less in a principled conflict with known evolutionary mechanisms than popular perception suggests. If we look at the cardiovascular system of vertebrates as a fractal space filled by a network of branching tubes, and assume a form of 'minimal design'—energy dissipated by this flow system is minimized—we derive stunning empirical predictions that seem by and large correct, throughout the realm of life (West et al. 1997). An equally spectacular example is Cherniak's 'best of all possible brains' hypothesis, departing from the principle 'save wire' (Cherniak 1995). It is a central function of the brain to connect, and given computer models of how such wiring might be perfected, the finding is that refinement we actually find in the brain is discernible down to a 'best-in-a-billion' level. This is structural organization, Cherniak argues, which, despite being formidably functional, has no functional rationale in its use, but rather comes '"for free, directly from physics", i.e., [is] generated via simply exploiting basic physical processes, without intervention of genes'. A final example for an unexpected form of perfection in the living world may be the near-universal chemical basis of life itself, where, equally, the apparent fact that we may have the 'best of all possible genomes' has baffled scientists (see Conway Morris 2003: chapter 2, for an overview and references).

Given such examples, the question of the perfection of the human language faculty cannot be prejudged, and Gopnik's or Jackendoff's claims, cited above, will have to be judged on their empirical merits. Any approximation to perfection we *were* to find in the domain of the human language faculty would make human language rather more similar to objects in the physical world, leading to a rather interesting and entirely unexpected kind of (non-metaphysical) 'physicalism' as regards human language and mind. It need not be true, in short, that in some crucial sense the human linguistic mind, and maybe the mind more generally, is a Neo-Darwinian adaptation that evolved in response to particular socio-ecological problems, and has design features causally related to the probability of reproductive success (Pinker and Bloom 1990). The empirical study of mind design should *tell* us whether that is true. The following claim (in this generality) is not a fact, but something we would like to *know*:

constraints on cognitive design derive from a world of hungry predators and unwilling prey (...). Consciousness and cognition are not made in Plato's heaven, but in the competitive Darwinian world where small improvements in sensorimotor control give an organism a predatory and reproductive edge (Churchland 1996: 284).

No such claim about human nature *needs* to be true, and none should depend on *a priori* stipulations that it 'must' come out right. This is the methodological importance of the question of mind design. The point of asking 'how perfect' the human mind is, is not to show it perfect, but to give empirical substance to the claim that it is not, if indeed it is not.

In the same way, intuition may suggest as strongly as it wants that the mind's capability of 'representing the external environment' (a contingent function) *must* be the cause of its internal structure and form—that the mind is of its *essence* a 'medium of representation', an instrumental device, a great 'mirror of nature' (Rorty 1980), a bearer and conveyer of 'truth-conditional contents'. If only one could bring the functionalist to concede that this question is *empirical*. Language and words may well *be* tools or instruments in some sense, as Wittgenstein suggested, crucially making no *additional* suggestion that they exist and have the structure that they have *because they are used* for what they are used for.[25] Even intuitively it is not clear that the peculiarities of the human conceptual system has any rationale in functional utility.[26] Nor is there any evidence that language, though used in certain ways in specific circumstances rather than others, *describes* these circumstances, in the sense that the circumstances are independent from their mode of description. What we *see*—a *person*, rather than a *body*, say—will itself *depend* on the concepts we are built to employ.

Consider finally implications of the question of design perfection for internalism. The more perfect mind design was the more, internalism would win the day. As in the case of the crystal, the role of environmental factors will be a matter of setting external conditions within which an internally directed process of structural growth takes place. In the perfect case, external conditions would not even have to be mentioned. In the imperfect case, the environment would enter as a source of contingency interacting with natural law. Ice crystals after all allow for very different shapes, given their sensitivity to a variety of external conditions,

---

[25] Wittgenstein explicitly contrasts *speaking* with *cooking*, saying that the latter is defined through its purpose, the former not. This is part of what it means for grammar to be 'autonomous'. See Wittgenstein, *Zettel* (1992: 347). Right here, Rorty (1995) goes beyond Wittgenstein, suggesting that what language games we play depends on their utility.

[26] Why, indeed, would it be less useful not to have the concept of a *person*, say, but to have a different concept in its place, say that of a human-like but computer-directed zombie?

including temperature, air currents, and humidity.[27] These will ultimately defeat any ambitions to predict the actual shape of particular snowflakes in the real world environment, which sets a determinate limit to internalist inquiry (in the same way that history as such does). There is an excessive variance, that is, deriving from embedding internalist laws into an external environment. Any such conclusion is fully consistent with the other one, however, that each and every snowflake is built by the same internal principles of growth. The point is general: even an excessive variance from individual to individual in the case of humans is *as such* no obstacle to claims about laws of human nature.

I have now outlined human nature as a topic for theoretical inquiry, and given my reasons for thinking that vindicating design perfection in human nature is something interesting to try. But so far I have ignored virtually all the complications that surround this topic. Human nature is a battleground. It may even be a kind of consensus in the humanities today that the very idea of human nature is a historical relic from the eighteenth-century Enlightenment, of which the nineteenth century quite rightfully deprived us, and which the twentieth century rightly took care not to re-establish, was it not for the sociobiologist's unfortunate revival of it. I address some of the reasons for this contention in the following final section of this chapter. It is also a fact that twentieth-century analytic philosophy has been consistently pursuing a path that is in many ways opposed to the broadly rationalist and internalist assumptions about human language and mind that have been flowing into my exposition above, and which I will elaborate throughout this book. This is not even to mention historians of philosophy whose reading of the seventeenth-and eighteenth-century traditions widely diverges from my own reading here. Chapter 2 will be devoted to these philosophical issues; in Chapter 3, I more fully discuss denials of human nature within biology itself.

1.4 The Fate of Human Nature in the Twentieth Century

To start with the Continental tradition, it seems that for Heidegger, for example, there was no 'nature' in my naturalistic sense to the human at all. Interestingly, Heidegger not only reacted fiercely against any idea of making man's *animality* a part of his humanity, but against *any* stipulation of a human 'essence', in the sense of the metaphysical tradition. Man was not to be the metaphysicians' 'rational animal', a composite of an animalic body and a disembodied 'rational soul' or 'true self'. Sartre's classical verdict 'Il n'y a pas de nature humaine' builds on Heidegger's: man has no definition, no essence that, as in the case of artefacts, could precede his existence and rationalize it.

---

[27] Thus an ice crystal needs atmospheric conditions of $-15°C$ to grow. As the temperature falls, the ice crystal tips (the branch-like protrusions growing out of the hexagon) get sharper. At warmer temperatures, the ice crystals grow slower and smoother, resulting in less intricate shapes.

Heidegger's anti-humanism was widely accepted and developed in France, where Foucault and Derrida, building additionally on Nietzsche, joined forces in discussing *Les fins de l'homme*.[28] At the same time Heidegger involved a new form of *Dasein* that was meant to replace the old metaphysical idea of rational man. *Dasein* was to inaugurate an entirely new and 'post-metaphysical' way of thinking about ourselves. But Heidegger's practice took the form of a *historical reconstruction* (or rather deconstruction) of our metaphysical history, a history of (mis-)understanding the nature of Being and ourselves, according to him. There is no scope here for a non-historical notion of human nature.

Heidegger's project to overcome the 'rational animal' remains intriguing. To this day philosophy is centred on man's rationality: his beliefs, desires, and intentions, in terms of which human actions are rationalized. The prime preoccupations of philosophy are the *normatively evaluable* features of the mind: things like when it is correct to assert something, what makes something true, or when a belief is justified. These features are at the same time the main obstacles to viewing the mind as a part of the natural world. The puzzle is how to reconcile the intrinsic normativity of mind, meaning, and morality with the world as described by modern science, in which rationality appears to have no place (McDowell 1996 is a paradigmatic expression of this kind of concern). There is a 'realm of law' and a 'realm of reason', and they do not fit, giving rise to reductionism, anomalous monism, and other such attempts to close what appears to be a deep divide.

Heidegger's philosophy addresses these efforts, but his cure is radical: to abandon the conceptual scheme of the *animal rationale* altogether, and to dissolve the human into the history of the self-eventuation of Being (the *Ereignis*, the *Seinsgeschick*). His critique of modern philosophy has much to contribute to my approach here, but his vision takes us in the opposite direction: to put it bluntly, while Heidegger turns man into something like a purely spiritual being that has no animal 'part' at all, I view him, including aspects of his 'reason' such as his ability to use his faculty of language, as a part of nature. Because of this, and because Heidegger's critique seems essentially directed against an essentialist picture of man as the rational animal (which I do not support), the broadly Heideggerian tradition, as much as I respect it, will play no role in what follows.

Twentieth-century *analytic philosophy* at large might be viewed as gradually moving from a strictly positivist empiricism to a more liberal pragmatism, a trend that begins with Quine's *Two Dogmas*, continues with Davidson (who brings down further dogmas of the old doctrine), and finally leads up to different kinds of pragmatism and 'relativism' as defended by Putnam and Rorty today. While Quine's pragmatism is retained by the latter two authors, along with his refusal to recognize 'analytic truths' which appears to have been near-universally adopted, his staunch defence of *scientism*—the priority of the physical

---

[28] Cf. Derrida (1972). For an extensive review of these currents, see Ferry and Renaut (1985).

description of reality over any other—is now finally rejected. There are many languages, the language of science being only one among them, but none of them 'describes or represents reality', or has more rights to the truth than any other. This leaves us with a version of philosophy that makes no claims to produce *necessary* truths, be it in the sense of traditional metaphysics or 'truths of reason', or in the sense of 'truths of meaning' as opposed to 'truths of facts'. But it is a philosophy that also does not produce *contingent* empirical truths, on a par with the sciences.

Having been eradicated in the early empiricism and positivism on grounds of its association with rationalism, human nature remains absent in this new philosophy, as human beings for Rorty *are* the 'plaything of historical circumstances', a product of accidental external forces or history, be it cultural or evolutionary. This contention has an affinity with what a radical empiricism would predict, for here as well the mind of an individual at a moment in time is formed by what has happened to it in its experience. When this idea is pushed to an extreme, the mind becomes the proverbial blank sheet of paper: as experience, culture and history unfolds and the paper fills, the mind 'gets written'. Before that, there is no script according to which it performs. As such, the mind has no relevant internal structure by means of which we could define its nature (an innate general learning mechanism, which even the empiricist must allow, won't do in this regard). *Education* is what gives an empty mind a form and a content from without, or perhaps gives an individual a mind in the first place.[29] We should be wary about any claim made for an essential human nature, as it will have to be a stipulation, reflecting religious or metaphysical dogma, cultural bias, politics, or power.[30]

While Rorty would call himself a pragmatist rather than an empiricist, the affinity of his position with the empiricist one seems in this way perspicuous enough: the mind is 'possessed' by the culture it happens to be embedded in. The point is further manifest in Rorty's use of Freud in arguing for the purely historical, contingent, and experiential growth of human conscience, considered as a basis and origin of moral judgement (Rorty 1986). Your morals are the outcome of your history and the contingencies of how you happen to have invented and re-invented yourself. While, on anyone's view, it will have to be allowed that the human 'body' is appropriate for biological study, Rorty's view

---

[29] We would thus not predict, e.g., that there is a fundamental unity between the mind of the !Kung, a 'primitive' hunter-gatherer population scattered in small groups across Botswana, Angola, and Namibia, and our minds. There will be no basis for such a unity, which there clearly is, looking at the structure of the language they speak, the thoughts they think, or the kinds of emotions they can have. See Gazzaniga (1992: 98–90) for some comments and references on the !Kung.

[30] To many, indeed, the positing of a human nature has manifested no more than an inclination towards a political conservatism. Saying that particular institutionalized behavioural patterns in human societies derive from human nature is, on this view, to make an apology for not aiming to change the status quo.

assumes that the human 'mind' is in principle 'malleable' and determined from without, hence no topic for biology, if there is such a thing as the human mind at all. We note the influence of a strange psychology–biology divide here, a 'methodological dualism', that will concern us again later on (Section 2.3). At the same time, note that this position has a certain intuitive and common-sensical feel to it: for intuitively, while our body exhibits a clear structure and morphology, our minds do not. If we let our native empiricist inclinations guide our judgements, we might feel inclined to suggest that this alleged mind-thing simply does not exist. After all, it is invisible. But let us be fair to this fascinating piece of intellectual history and look at Rorty's own articulation of this sort of view in some detail:

> Contemporary intellectuals have given up the Enlightenment assumption that religion, myth and tradition can be opposed to something ahistorical, something common to all human beings qua human. Anthropologists and historians of science have blurred the distinction between innate rationality and the products of acculturation. Philosophers such as Heidegger and Gadamer have given us ways of seeing human beings as historical all the way through. Other philosophers, such as Quine and Davidson, have blurred the distinction between permanent truths of reason and temporary truths of fact. Psychoanalysis has blurred the distinction between conscience and the emotions of love, hate and fear, and thus the distinction between morality and prudence. The result is to erase the picture of the self common to Greek metaphysics, Christian theology and Enlightenment rationalism: the picture of an ahistorical nature centre, the locus of human dignity, surrounded by an adventitious and inessential periphery (Rorty 1990: 280).

What then are philosophers doing, other than preaching scepticism (it very much seems that the sceptic has finally won in the battle over what Rorty calls the 'epistemological problematic')? This is a question that Rorty, quite consequentially given his premises, answers by appeal to the 'priority of democracy over philosophy': there is no grounding that the latter could offer for the former, which itself has no grounding at all. If 'philosophy' means 'disputes about the nature of human beings and even about whether there is such a thing as "human nature"' (ibid.: 285), the claims it makes on behalf of such an ahistorical human nature cannot lend any deeper authority to social policy in liberal democracies. The latter is not a matter of ahistorical truth but simply of how various sorts of reflective equilibria are induced locally and historically within given communities. If a philosophy made claims to the truth that conflicted with liberal policy and tolerance of the views of others, then democracy should take precedence over philosophy, and philosophy has to become a private matter, in much the way that religion is (in Western societies). Characterizing approvingly the position of John Rawls, Rorty writes:

> Truth, viewed in the Platonic way, as the grasp of what Rawls calls 'an order antecedent to and given to us', is simply not relevant to democratic politics. So philosophy, as the explanation of the relation between such an order and human nature, is not relevant either (ibid.: 291).

In other words, we are losing the very idea of truth on a world-view such as this as well, where humans are said, not to aim at the truth, but increased prosperity. In the naturalism I develop here, having that idea is a crucial and possibly humanly unique feature of our cognition that needs to be explained rather than explained away (see Hinzen 2003a, 2005b, 2006b). One might agree with Rorty (or Rawls) in the above quote, if the notion of human nature really had to be the philosophical and essentialist concept that Rorty takes it to be. But this is not the notion I side with here (nor is it the notion we find in Hume or Locke, according to my reading in Section 1.1). As Rorty characterizes the concept, it is embodied in what he calls the Enlightenment idea of reason, for which 'there is a relation between the ahistorical essence of the human soul and moral truth that ensures that free and open discussion will produce "one right answer" to moral as well as to scientific questions' (ibid.: 280). But why could the notion of human nature not simply be an empirical one? Why could we not want to find out, naively, about the workings of the human mind, much as we attempt to find out about the principles of the immune system or planetary systems? Rorty's doubts about 'whether there *is* such a thing as "human nature"', it seems, can only arise if a methodological dualism as regards 'mental' and 'physical' aspects of human nature is adopted from the start, a dualism I will centrally reject here.

Human nature will thus in the present work not necessarily be a source of norms, let alone of ultimate truths such as Rorty's '"one right answer" to moral as well as to scientific questions'. But Hume would not have thought of offering any such thing, his aim being to increase the intelligibility of an object of nature. Still, it may well be that the structure of our minds includes a moral faculty that has the power to resolve particular moral issues, in the sense that we arrive at a reasoned verdict concerning them, and that any problem that we can identify as moral would also be a subject of moral assessment for us. But then again, our moral faculty, like the language faculty, interacts with others that unavoidably influence our judgements; as a consequence, the verdicts that our moral faculty yields need not be accessible to us, just as in the case of language not every grammatical expression is so accessible (say, because of memory limitations). In any case, our understanding of our own nature is much too limited to literally deduce policy decisions from it. It is a mind *without* a definite nature, a nature that would confine it to certain domains and limit its powers, which might be turned into what Rorty calls the Enlightenment rationalism's faulty vision: a universal and in principle unlimited problem-solving capacity, designed to get things right about a mind-independent world that it is designed to represent.

In essence, then, my assessment of Rorty's verdict against human nature comes down to the view that its explicit and implicit claims about the mind do not seem to be based on empirical evidence but on a selective intellectual tradition, and a strange, perhaps empiricism-based, methodological dualism that denies that the 'mind' is accessible by naturalistic inquiry in the way the 'body' is.

While pragmatism is clearly not hospitable to a notion of human nature, it is maybe more astonishing that the contemporary *philosophy of biology* returns an essentially negative answer to the question of human nature, too. '[M]odern biology sees itself as a deeply historical science', biologist Stuart Kauffman says, with regret (Kauffman 1995: 22). Organisms in Darwinian biology are viewed as 'largely *ad hoc* solutions to design problems cobbled together by selection' (Kauffman 1993: 26), a theme we have encountered before. There is no deeper explanation or rationale for our existence than history affords, according to this view. Ernst Mayr has lifted this contention to a matter of methodological principle for biology, arguing that laws and experiments have no significant place in biology. Its method is *historical reconstruction*, the testing of 'competing historical narratives', a method that Mayr contrasts with that of physics on principled grounds.[31] Evolutionary psychologists, transferring the historical method of explanation in Neo-Darwinian biology to psychology, equally consider 'introducing the time factor'—i.e., history—as crucial to the study of human mental traits (Plotkin 1997).

An essential background for these pervasive conclusions is *population thinking* in biology, which identifies species by their history. Species, that is, are mere varieties: they are not 'Aristotelian' natural kinds, written into the fabric of nature, but temporally extended collections of interbreeding individuals that will be quite different among themselves, genetically and behaviourally. As reproductively isolated populations become geographically separated, different environmental pressures act upon them, and will eventually lead to a change in gene frequencies in a way that reduces the fertility of inter-population crosses: new species with more or less distinctive traits arise.

Ultimately, on this view, all members of a species are unique; conceived collectively, a species can only be described in statistical and historical terms. If organisms are essentially determined by their DNA, and there is no reason to think that all human beings share the same genes, 'human being' denotes no more than a statistical average. It will be unlikely, in fact, that all and only humans exhibit a particular trait. If deprived of human universals in this sense we might as well be claiming that there is no human nature, unless we assume what is called the 'monomorphic' mind, or that something is true for the mind that is not true for traits like blood type, eye colour, or hearts: a uniform underlying genetic constitution. Hull summarizes the situation as follows:

If species are interpreted as historical entities, then particular organisms belong in a particular species because they are part of that genealogical nexus, not because they possess any essential traits. No species has an essence in this sense. Hence there is no such thing as human nature. There may be characteristics which all and only extant human beings

---

[31] 'Evolutionary biology, in contrast with physics and chemistry, is a historical science (...). Laws and experiments are inappropriate techniques for the explication of such events and processes. Instead one constructs a historical narrative, consisting of a tentative reconstruction of the particular scenario that led to the events one is trying to explain' (Mayr 2000: 80).

possess, but this state of affairs is contingent, depending on the current evolutionary state of *Homo sapiens*. Just as not all crows are black (not even potentially), it may well be the case that not all people are rational (even potentially) (Hull 1978: 358).

Some biologists, such as Mayr, give these ideas a political dimension. Population thinking is said to contrast with *typology*, according to which, Mayr says, nature consists of a limited number of natural kinds, essences, or 'types'. Species are judged according to whether they are closer to, or more removed from, some ideal, one way in which they are 'supposed to be'. Since variation cannot be accommodated, this 'mode of thinking leads to racism' (Mayr 2000: 82). But while it may be true that there is no meaningful notion of design perfection in some evaluative sense—some notion of an ideal type to which all species aspire— it would still not follow that variants can 'depart indefinitely', to use Darwin's and Wallace's phrase, from their original form. There might be structural types that constrain such departures, cross-cutting species differences, hence depriving Mayr's political consequences of any force. As for Hull, it is a strange bias to assume that the only basis for a notion of human nature would be the universal distribution of a certain trait. Nothing like that has been assumed in the previous sections, where, quite simply, *systems of human knowledge* were at stake, without any assumption that these are necessarily or wholly genetically based, exhibit no variance, or are (in all their subcomponents) unique to all and only humans. Hull provides no argument that, if we actually cared to look at the mind and what structures it exhibits, some of these might turn out not to be accidents of genetic history. I return to Mayr's and Hull's verdict in Chapter 3.

As much as one can use Neo-Darwinian biology to argue against human nature, however, one can use it to argue for it. Indeed, writers making claims in favour of a human nature today, such as Dawkins (1976/1989, 1998), Wilson (1998), Dennett (1995), Plotkin (1997), or Pinker (1997, 2002), do it largely on the basis on which writers such as Hull reject it: the 'Neo-Darwinian Synthesis' (NDS). For this tradition, there *is* a human nature, hence there *are* internal constraints and conditions on which human behaviour, mentality, and morality depends. These internal determinants are the *genes*, of which the organism as a whole is a *creation*, an ephemeral *vehicle* through which the genes interact with an environment. In Dawkins' terms, it is a 'survival machine' (Dawkins 1976/1989: 21), designed by its genes to carry them into the next generation and enhance their share of the gene pool. The genome is itself a product of natural history, of the slow and gradual action of natural selection on accidental mutations that may turn in any directions at any times. There is no hidden rationale to our nature and existence, and no sense to the notion of a 'possible animal' or a 'possible organ'. Everything is possible in history, in principle, as long as natural selection allows it. Man is *chance*, and man is *selected*.

The NDS which began in the 1920s and 1930s, and 'hardened' (Gould 2002: 518– 84) in the 1940s and 1950s, combined Darwin's by then widely accepted theory of evolution, on the one hand, with Mendelian and molecular genetics, on the other. Given these two main strands of the NDS, we may expect to find two aspects of any notion of human nature coming from within it: its historicity, and at least a tendency to neglect the role of *organismic development*. Relevant to the latter neglect was Weismann's (1885) distinction between the *soma* (somatoplasm) and the *Keimbahn* (germ plasm) in organisms such as us: while the somatic cells are destined to perish after a lifetime, only the genetic material in the sex cells gets transmitted to future generations, and is potentially immortal. If this is so, our bodies cannot be the beneficiaries of natural selection: *they* don't survive or reproduce themselves. What benefits from their actions are the gene lineages that produce them; the genes alone have the power to copy themselves and project a lineage into the future.

Although Weismann did not know about Mendel's experiments, he identified the chromosomes within the germ cell nuclei as the physical carriers of hereditary determinants. Evolutionary change occurs via modifications of this hereditary material, not the organism: the relation between the germ cells and the soma is one-way, in that, while the former direct growth in development and are thus the origin of natural form, there is no information flowing back from the organism to the germ cells ('Weismann's barrier'). Lamarckian inheritance of acquired characteristics through the germ cells is impossible. Contrary to Lamarck's opinion (and Darwin's too, to some extent), the external environment does not directly act on the organism. It merely *selects* among traits produced by *internal* determinants. Weismann's barrier provided a perfect basis for the rise of molecular genetics after the rediscovery of Mendel's work. It allowed the calculation of heredity in terms of well-defined rules, crucially without a need to understand just *how* the genes act during organismic organismic development.[32]

According to Dawkins (1976/1989), if genes were to build an organism that would not tend to behave selfishly, they would probably not be replicated much, hence not be found in future generations. In short, organisms will tend to inherit genes with a propensity to make an organism that is 'successful', meaning that they turn it into a 'well-designed machine—a body that actively works as if it is striving to become an ancestor' (Dawkins 1995: 2). Note the 'as if': literally bodies do not 'do' anything on this picture. As a machine, we act blind to our own deeper motives, while our contingent environments give us opportunities to reproduce or not. We are simply the latest triumph of the genes' efforts to increase their number in organisms built by them. Without our ancestor's selfishness we would not exist.

---

[32] 'All that was necessary was to see the effect of genes on the characters of the adult organism, so that their presence or absence could be registered: tall plants signified the presence of particular genes affecting height, red flowers signified the presence of particular genes making red pigment, and so on. *How* genes acted to produce their effects could be put aside while the rules of their segregation and transmission were worked out' (Goodwin 1994: 27).

The implications of this idea extend well into the domains of ethics, meaning, human nature, and the purpose of life. Thus 'good' is not the 'good for society', as there is no such thing as group selection. Group welfare, if accidentally arising from a basically selfish behaviour of organisms in that group, is a 'fortuitous consequence' (Dawkins 1995: 142). The meaning of life? It has none, being a meaningless dance to the music of DNA:

> In a universe of blind physical forces and genetic replication, some people are going to get hurt, other people are going to get lucky, and you won't find any rhyme or reason in it, nor any justice. The universe we observe has precisely the properties we should expect if there is, at bottom, no design, no purpose, no evil and no good, nothing but blind, pitiless indifference (ibid.: 155).

Current thinking in biology, then, seems to offer two seemingly contradictory perspectives on the notion of human nature: while the one group emphasizes population thinking and rejects the existence of an Aristotelian idea of human nature, the other argues for a new and rather bleak vision of human nature, backed up scientifically by Neo-Darwinian biology. The former group holds that the notion of human nature that the other group propagates is based on empirical assumptions that are too strong, and hence suggests that the notion should be abolished altogether.

While pragmatism and the philosophy of biology in the respective senses above are technically parts of analytic philosophy, let us now turn to the latter's core domains, the *philosophies of language and mind*. By and large, it seems as if the philosophy of language is even less sympathetic to the notion of human nature than the philosophy of biology. We see much of it devoted to arguing that a naturalistic inquiry into human language viewed as a natural object is simply not possible, be it because of an assumed 'normativity' of language, or because a naturalistic study of this kind suggests a 'mentalism' that is regarded as inconsistent with 'Wittgensteinian' verdicts against a 'private language' (on which more in Chapter 4). Part and parcel of Frege's philosophy, still lying at the heart of analytic philosophy, is a commitment to the objectivity and normativity of thought, a guiding theme in analytic philosophy and logic ever since. Given a basic anti-psychologistic commitment that philosophers in the Fregean tradition share, these philosophers have largely focused on *mind-external* entities (thoughts, propositions, referents), while the human mind as an empirical domain for naturalistic inquiry has received little attention.

If the mind enters this scene of philosophical reflection, it often does in an instrumental role: it is a device for *representing* the old Fregean mind-external thoughts, propositions, or 'semantic contents'. This gives us a version of the Computational-Representational Theory of Mind (CRTM). Just as, for Russell, expressions of a natural language are defined functionally as external 'signs' depicting more or less suitably the structure of mind-external propositions, the CRTM's 'expressions' of the internal 'language of thought' (LOT) are functionally defined 'symbols' in much the same sense: their rationale is their representational role. Trivial and arbitrary as expressions are on this picture, there must be *propositions* distinct from them, which *really* carry the burden of semantic content. A 'science of expressions' of the sort that I will describe in Chapters 4 and 5 would then be quite beside the point: the *thoughts* matter, on this view, not their representations. Why concern oneself with the representations themselves, as a philosopher? It will thus be important to see that there can be a *non-functional* perspective on expressions (namely, as sound–meaning pairs), which has no need for a notion of mind-external propositions at all.

The Russellian notion of a proposition effectively replaced the more traditional Kantian notion of a *judgement*, which will be vital in this book, and is introduced in Section 5.3. We may note here that a judgement as conceived by Kant is *not* a notion of empirical psychology (it differs in that it carries a normative force, which no psychological structure as such does), but then neither is it a mind-external object like a proposition. Prior to its expulsion from philosophy and logic, it thus occupied an interesting middle ground.

Russell's project of a 'philosophical logic' was concerned with extracting the 'knowledge [of logical forms involved in all understanding of discourse] from its concrete integuments, and [...] rendering it explicit and pure' (Russell 1914: 53). As Lepore and Ludwig (2002) put a version of the same idea, philosophical logic attempts to find a way of 'getting clear about the nature of reality through getting clear about the forms of our thoughts or talk about it' (Lepore and Ludwig 2002: 55). This project—being one of 'purification'—suggests a sense in which the philosophy of language, if based on it, is not a naturalistic project, or a part of natural science. Human languages rather become part of a 'translation project', the project of converting their 'natural deficiencies' into the logical idiom, where the structure of the 'thoughts' that they convey only imperfectly is made fully transparent. Again, languages themselves provide no more than 'external signs'. What is to be made transparent are the structures of the *thoughts* or inferential *commitments* supposedly expressed in human linguistic expressions, not the structures of actual natural language *meanings*. The approach has little use for such a notion of *linguistic meaning* as something that plays an independent theoretical and explanatory role, and cannot be collapsed into the notion of a *thought expressed* by a sentence, or a *belief conveyed* by it.

What, however, does it mean to 'get clear about the nature of reality'? People study proteins, ecologies, galaxies, brains—but what is it to study *reality*? If we look at how people actually try to determine the nature of proteins, ecologies, etc., we find that their way of approaching reality does not require the invoking of clarified forms of our thought and talk *about reality*, in particular not those embedded in natural languages. Scientists use experiments and inquiry, but do not contemplate the forms and contents of their thoughts, nor that of their 'talk about reality'. Hume's science of human nature, equally, uses experiments and inquiry, since no insight need flow from clarifying ways in which we ordinarily *think* and *talk* about human beings and the world. Studying how we talk and think about things *is* a vital topic, but it is a chapter in the science of human nature that we may call, with Chomsky (2000), 'ethnoscience'. It is a chapter of anthropology, describing how humans behave. The quote from Lepore and Ludwig is again paradigmatic in manifesting a functionalist perspective on human thoughts, which views these not as natural objects among others that we could study as such, but as *means* employed in the service of representing reality (whatever that notion amounts to). As noted, Chomsky's study of the mind as I will depict it is crucially not concerned with mental *representation*—as a relation between mind and world, and a function that the mind carries out—but with mental *representations*, considered as specific natural objects that enter into language use and are invoked to explain it.

So far, then, the Russellian project of a philosophical logic appears as a normative and non-naturalistic one. All in all it seems fair to say that the philosophy of language has rarely been particularly concerned with human language as such, a task it has left to linguistics. Central disputes such as realism versus anti-realism that have characterized it are *metaphysical* at heart. Discussions of names often have an *epistemological* flavour, and are tied to foundational theories of knowledge, such as theories of 'knowledge by acquaintance' as opposed to 'knowledge by description'. The 'direct reference' theory of names is not so much a theory of language than a theory about the mind's *access* to the world, the question being whether it is *mediated* (through internal representations, Fregean *Sinne*, etc.) or not. If reference is 'direct', language alone, merely by virtue of what its words mean (that is, on this view, what *reference* they have) provides us with the immediate and robust world connection that the Cartesian tradition is thought to dispute (a crucial misreading of this tradition, according to Section 1.1).[33] By contrast, the more *indirect* and mind-mediated this connection becomes, the more the shadow of the 'Cartesian ghost in the machine', the 'worldless self', or the 'inner realm of consciousness' in which internal representations figure, rears its head, a supposed 'characteristic anxiety' of modern philosophy (McDowell 1996). An enormous literature on 'empty names' such as *Pegasus* or *Hamlet* appears as an expression of the same epistemological worry, too.[34] If the meaningfulness of a word does not, factually speaking, depend on any mind–world connection (since there is no referent), how on earth do we tie meaning and mind to the world at all? The mind seems to work without the world!

---

[33] On the other hand, no linguistic mechanisms have ever been proposed that actually explains why reference *is* direct (such a mechanism is discussed in Hinzen 2006a).

[34] '[T]hought without a relation to things in the world is empty', Putnam avers (1992: 383). Empty names, or thoughts about heaven and hell, suggest this conclusion to be radically wrong. At this point often the suggestion is made that thoughts about Pegasus are really about pictures of Pegasus. But this can hardly be, as humans strictly distinguish between animals and pictures. I return to this when discussing reference at the end of this volume, in Section 6.2.

The epistemological task of refuting scepticism and relativism also motivates the widely shared concern for solving the Kripkean 'rule-following problematic', a sceptical problem of formidable dimensions, often supposed to rule out the idea that rules can be followed 'in private'. The most frequent solution to this problem has an *externalist* drive and points in a *non-naturalistic* direction, by virtue of its invocation of the intrinsically *social* and *normative* aspect of meaning. It is in this problem where the almost exclusive emphasis on the *public* and *norm-governed* aspects of language in philosophy, as opposed to its internal and biological ones, has one of its deepest motivations.

While philosophies of language have *postulated* that language 'must' be public, however, rather than being an intrinsic property of the human mind, this is not yet to give an empirical account of what a 'public norm-governed language' *is*. As we shall see, it is difficult to give an empirical content to this notion (and if we give it an empirical content, it need not lend credibility to the *normativity* of language; see below and Section 4.3). In actual empirical studies of structural aspects of language, no such thing as public languages, consisting of mind-external symbols and public rules for how to manipulate them, are invoked.[35] Field research on the ecology of language, on language contact and language change through migrations, population drift, and societal reorganizations, has no use for the concept either (see, e.g., Mufwene 2001).[36] Nor do naturalistic studies of communication systems in the animal kingdom (Hauser 1996) demand it.

It may seem obvious that whenever a French speaker comes to learn Bantu, he thereby hits upon a 'public and norm-governed' entity, which exists 'outside' or independently of speakers, and is then somehow transferred to him by his Bantu-speaking teachers. But no such entity needs to be invoked. The French speaker unavoidably comes equipped with his native knowledge of one human language, one aspect of which is a cognitive state encoding information about the sound and meaning structures of its expressions, as built by certain structural principles. The Bantu teacher is in a certain cognitive state, too, encoding partially overlapping information, to the extent that the structure of Bantu and French are subject to the same structural principles. When sound waves of Bantu utterances reach the French speaker's ears, he tries to construct their sound and meaning on the basis of what he knows, hears, and sees. That is a matter of internal computational processes, triggered but not determined by external (visual, acoustic, etc.) stimuli. Eventually, the two speakers will communicate. As the new Bantu speaker moves to new regions of the country and stimuli change, his newly acquired language changes too: speakers tend to accommodate their idiolects to local

---

[35] One of the very few attempts in print to actually defend some such notion on empirical grounds is Millikan (2003).

[36] Mufwene's (2001) approach to these matters, in particular, is fully compatible with the notion of a language as a mentally represented internal structure, determined by universal principles and parameters.

circumstances. It may even be that when our speaker finally settles in a remote region, his language and that of his first teacher have become so dissimilar that they can't communicate any more (just as speakers from the north of Germany may find it hard to communicate with those from the south). In this case we have a phenomenon similar to biological speciation in the population-genetic sense.

There is indeed this concrete and plausible sense in which languages are rather like species as viewed by a population geneticist. A 'language' like Bantu or German, on this conception, is a temporary arrangement of communicating agents speaking more or less alike, shifting historically as people migrate, institutions change, wars break out, and idiolects blend into one another. The notion is of dubious use if we wish to find out about the structure of the human language faculty, but it makes empirical sense.[37] This is still not the notion of 'public and norm-governed language', however, that the philosophical tradition has been invoking. For on the present population-theoretic view, language is still a matter of the individual, even though these individuals gather in populations.

I come back to these points in Chapters 2 and 4. It is enough here to have identified some sources of why human nature has not been a topic of study in the philosophy of language, and could not naturally be one, given its assumptions and aims. To be sure, it is very interesting to tie the analysis of language and meaning to metaphysical and epistemological concerns, and I do so here myself, but the nature of the enterprise becomes obscure if entities are being invoked that play no role in the empirical and naturalistic study of language. This affects notions like 'public norm-governed languages' as much as the notion of 'reference' (see Chomsky 2000, and Section 6.2 below). Again, the epistemological motivation for the latter notion is clear, but what is needed is an empirical argument that there really is this 'reference-relation' that has the desirable epistemological conclusions that I mentioned above. In short, although we have touched only upon a few central philosophical issues and concerns in the philosophy of language, we know enough to say that the characterization of human language as an aspect of human nature, subject to naturalistic study in the present sense, is a vision orthogonal to that field of inquiry, and often in contradiction with it.

In the *philosophy of mind*, an adherent of *eliminative materialism*, when asked about human nature, might reply that there is no such thing as meaning and mind (Churchland 1981). The 'official eliminativist thesis', in Lycan's formulation, is that 'no mental ascription has ever been true' (Lycan 2003: 20). In other words, saying that Freddy knows English, e.g., or that he understands it, but does not know French, are false. For there is no such thing as understanding, which we could truly talk about. Now, that claim could simply mean that in a naturalistic inquiry into some domain, ordinary language terms such as 'understanding' or

---

[37] However, determined as languages on the population level are by all imaginable forces of human history, they hardly lend themselves to naturalistic theorizing.

'knowledge' play no role, or get discarded. That is to be expected, when we recall how physics has discarded ordinary notions of movement, causation, or solidity, when talking about the natural world. Tables and chairs, too, do not figure in physical theories, and no physical theory can account for what it is for something to be a table, in our understanding. That the situation in a natural science of the mind could be different is hardly to be expected. So there is one sense here, in which the 'official thesis' in question is uncontentious.

This is not so for *functionalists* in the philosophy of mind, whose substantive disagreement with the eliminative materialists centres on this issue. What allows there to be a substantive issue in the first place is the shared agreement that the common-sense vocabulary that we use to talk about the mind are *theoretical terms* of a folk or common-sense *theory*, in the same way in which *proton* is such a theoretical term in physical theory (Lycan 2003: 19). The disagreement then is that the functionalists say this theory is largely true, while the eliminative materialists say it is false. On the face of it, assuming this basis for the dispute is like assuming that our notion of a table is a part of a 'table theory', and that just as a scientific psychology will vindicate or falsify our folk psychology, physics vindicates or falsifies our folk physics. This point of view is rather surprising, given that common sense and science, serving such radically different purposes, do not compete for truth. No sense of contradiction arises when we say that the sun sets. The case in question seems to be a simple case of the irrelevance of one vocabulary to another.

There is another sense, however, in which the 'official thesis' seems implausible at best, namely the literal and perfectly ordinary sense of the assertions that Freddy understands English, feels pain, wants his Mom, etc. Plainly, these claims may be true, and they become controversial *only* the moment we saddle ourselves beforehand with a *metaphysically loaded* notion of 'mentality' according to which something is 'mental' only under certain criteria (intentionality, perhaps). If we then have metaphysical doubts about mental states so conceived, we could discard statements to the effect that Freddy is in one of those as false. Thus, here we discover a metaphysical bias in eliminative materialism, which flies in the face of the assumed 'naturalism' of the approach, and cannot itself be grounded naturalistically. Clearly, however, our ordinary talk about persons knowing languages, understanding French, believing in God, etc., is *not* metaphysically loaded in this fashion. As we noted before, 'mental' may be used as a term with no metaphysical import, as an indication for a domain of inquiry, empirically but not metaphysically distinct from the domains we indicate under labels such as 'chemical', 'optical', or 'physiological'.

Eliminative materialism may also be the *methodological* claim that the mind should be studied at the neurological level rather than on the level of rule-based computations over abstract mental representations, a proposal that reflects a clear methodological dualism, given that naturalistic inquiry will naturally seek *whatever* levels of abstraction yield interesting theories. There cannot be *a priori* verdicts on which such levels are or are not suitable for naturalistic inquiry.

No matter whether understood as a metaphysical or a methodological claim, the framework does not invite the question of human nature in the present sense. As for the metaphysical claim above, without a human mind there is presumably no human nature; as for the second, a connectionist neural net of the sort employed by eliminative materialists to model human cognitive processes has no nature in itself, as its structure and content derives from whatever it is that it 'learns', or is trained to 'know'. This in turn is a contingent matter of how the connectivity of its nodes is set up and then modified in the course of its exposure to inputs, starting from random connection strengths. But we clearly wouldn't say that a knowledge or skill we acquire through extensive training (or accidentally, through history) tells us something about human nature. It is surely not in the nature of humans, for example, to know how to write—uncontroversially, as many humans lack that skill. We might well say, on the other hand, that the mind's nature and therefore human nature, is, on this picture, its malleability. Empty within, it acquires its content from without. It has a nature, and this is a *capacity to learn*.

The eliminativist picture is often recommended on the grounds that an enterprise like Universal Grammar, which sets out to study the innate structures of the human language faculty, is thought to be 'non-biological' in nature, and not backed up somehow by studies of the brain at a lower level of abstraction.[38] But a unification problem of the kind we are facing when choosing higher 'psychological' levels of abstraction is a standard problem in the history of science, not a disaster that should lead us to metaphysical conclusions about the non-existence of the mind as described in such psychological models. By a similar logic as the one of eliminative materialism, Chomsky notes,

one could have argued not long ago that there is a terrible crisis for the study of matter and organisms in terms of colors, valence, the solid state, and a multitude of other properties;

---

[38] In a critical section titled 'Mind Without Biology' Edelman (1992) criticizes the cognitivist/functionalist approach to the mind—one of which he thinks is generative grammar: 'One of its most curious deficiencies is that it makes only marginal reference to the biological foundations that underlie the mechanisms it purports to explain. The result is a scientific deviation as great as that of the behaviourism it has attempted to supplant. The critical errors underlying this deviation are as unperceived by most cognitive scientists as relativity was before Einstein and heliocentrism was before Copernicus' (Edelman 1992: 14). But if little can be learned about syntactic computations, which we have reason to believe must be there, by looking at neurons, it is hard to understand why generative grammar should be given up for neuroscience. (For a recent advance in isolating the functional correlates of morphological and syntactic processing in the brain see Moro *et al.* 2000, and for a general discussion of the meaningfulness of relating syntax to the brain, Grodzinsky and Amunts 2006.) As Edelman's discussion of Chomsky makes clear, he completely misunderstands Chomskyan linguistics as a form of functionalism wedded to some sort of 'objectivist' model-theoretic semantics. To say, with Edelman (1992), that generative grammar is 'unbiological' is like saying, with an equal lack of motivation, that Kauffman's (1993) biology is 'unbiological', or that Gregor Mendel's biology was 'unbiological', since it simply consisted of abstract laws of inheritance, with a then unknown molecular basis.

and earlier, for the investigation of electricity and magnetism, planetary and celestial motion, etc. Virtually the whole of science was in crisis because of the huge gap between what had been learned about these topics and the principles of the mechanical philosophy (or even much more recent physics) (Chomsky 2000: 104).

That is, theories offering some insight and explanatory schemes had been offered at certain times for things like valence, which could not be made sense of in the physics of the time. The theories developed and prospered, while people ignored the unification problem. As science progresses, a unification problem may come to pass—something that may happen and has happened in many and unexpected sorts of ways, and usually not by means of plain reduction (probably not in the case of Mendelian and molecular genetics, and certainly not in the case of nineteenth-century chemistry). The linguistic theory of Universal Grammar for now imposes *demands* on such a unification, or on what the sciences operating at a lower level of abstraction will have to account for: it will have to yield the structures that modern syntax has unearthed, as long as we consider these structures right, which does not seem to be disputed by eliminativists, who focus on a metaphysical or methodological claim instead. This is in the same sense in which the body of doctrine developed in chemistry around the turn of the last century imposed demands on physics for what a unification of matter would have to achieve (Chomsky 2002: 69). In contrast to chemistry in the nineteenth century, on the other hand, even the beginnings of a body of doctrine are missing in the case of the phenomena that most intrigued the Cartesians, the creative and apparently uncaused ordinary use of language: 'lacking that, questions of unification cannot be seriously raised' (ibid.: 55).

That we may have to wait for a substantive revolution in physics for the mental to be understood in terms of it (or at least an expansion of it through the addition of new fundamental entities and laws), is, we might note at this point, what many metaphysical dualists have held. Chomsky's assertion that the terms of ordinary common-sense understanding (no matter whether we are talking about *table* and *chair* or about *thinking* and *feeling*) and those involved in scientific understanding 'belong to different intellectual universes' (Chomsky 2000: 138), and that unification will depend on an 'expansion' of physics rather than on reduction, *is* a dualistic statement of sorts. We might ask what *makes* the two kinds of vocabularies so radically different, and whether their seeming radical difference does not indicate a deeper metaphysical divide of the kinds metaphysical dualists have been claiming. Knowledge of physics teaches us nothing about how ordinary human concepts figure in our understanding, a fact about human concepts at large, not only those used in talking about our mental life. Plainly, no amount of physical description of some object (in terms of quarks, strings, electromagnetism, and so on) would ever reveal what is most obvious to *us*, as we look at it: say, that it is a *table*.

I think that even prior to a unification on the basis of some revolution in (or expansion of) physics, it is possible that we will discover or become convinced of a principled difference of 'mental' reality and neurophysiological reality (see further Section 2.1). In the absence of that, lack of unification may be a sheer lack of luck or cognitive resources. Whatever the reason, there is no merit in trashing explanatory theories of the human language faculty that we have, if neurological theories yield no deeper insight than linguistics and Universal Grammar do. No one would trash embryology for superstring theory, computer science for electrical engineering, or economics for quantum mechanics, as Rey puts it (Rey 2003: 153); although engaging in these reductions, as Chomsky points out, would seem rather more plausible than jettisoning generative grammar for neuroscience, where unification is lacking in a more severe way still (Chomsky 2000: 114).

What *empirical* reasons are there to believe that we can understand the structure in the human mind (more or less wholly) in terms of what happens to it? Note that the following review of problems will affect 'eliminativist connectionism' only, not the encompassing one that Smolensky (2000) reasonably defends. Smolensky (2000: 590–1) emphasizes *'the indeterminism of the basic connectionist commitments toward most central issues of cognitive theory'*, including the nature of mental representation, modularity, and nativism. In turn, he correctly notes that generative grammar is not wedded to discrete (ungraded) representations, modularity, or some particular version of nativism, all working assumptions that have merely 'enabled substantial progress' in addressing the basic explananda of linguistic theory. On the grammar-based strategy for connectionism that Smolensky proposes, there is no longer a principled clash between the two frameworks, as I think there need not ever have been, once connectionism is seen as a theory addressing issues of common concern, namely how our knowledge of language and computations on which it depends are realized in a neural substrate. In the absence of an explanatory alternative to a duality of structured mental representations and algebraic rules in our cognition, on the one hand, and elements of statistical learning, on the other, it is hard to see the possibility of a principled dichotomy of frameworks (Pinker and Ullman 2004; Yang 2004).

Smith (2002: 113) notes (and see Smith and Tsimpli 1995) that human language-learning subjects are unable to learn structure-independent rules, or form structure-independent generalizations (see Section 5.3 for an explanation of these terms), while a connectionist net can do that with ease. On the other hand, connectionist networks have intrinsic difficulties in learning things that children learn spontaneously. Thus, in particular, because the knowledge they acquire will of necessity be experience or training-based, there will be a natural problem in getting networks to generalize from finite data received in training to a rule that applies to an infinite domain (Marcus 2001: 47). Networks must rely on local regularities in a given range of data presented to them. Having no rules at their disposal, the networks can only learn from changes in the 'connection between one unit and another on the basis of information that is locally available to the connection' (McClelland and Rumelhart 1986: 214).

Marcus (2001: 38–9) illustrates that primate cognition is not 'local' and experience-dependent in this sense with the apparent primate capacity to freely (without explicit instruction) abstract algebraic (rather than statistical) rules. A relevant task is the grasp of the grammatical pattern ABA, of which *ga ti ga* or *li ti li* would be instances, and to judge new and unfamiliar patterns such as *wo fe wo* as instances of the same grammar (as opposed to *le we we*, say) (Hauser, Weiss, and Marcus 2002). To take an example from human language, children find it natural to continue the series 'a rose is a rose, a lily is a lily, a tulip is a tulip, a blicket is a...' with '...blicket', no matter what a blicket may be. Standard connectionist nets don't (Marcus 2001: 50). To understand the rule for continuing, the point is, experience (or familiarity with a new input and its phonetic properties, or its potential similarities with items in the training set and statistical co-occurrence patterns therein) is irrelevant. In learning, *ignoring* experience is as vital as building on it. What is needed and manifest is a grasp of an *abstract relationship* between *typed variables*, of the form 'any X is an X', taken to hold universally for infinitely many things that can be values of the variable X.

In the case of learning the regular past tense, this means that children must instantiate the abstract variable 'verb stem' by a value, say *walk*, and attach the morpheme -*ed* to it. McClelland and Rumelhart's network, trained to generalize verbs to their past-tensed forms, correctly predicted *malked* and *splang* for the novel inputs *malk* and *spling*. But it transformed the novel and unsimilar input *ploanth* to *bro*, and *frilg* to *freezled*, something humans would never do. As Pinker remarks when discussing this issue, a network that tells us something about humans needs to tell us why human children inflect weird verbs they will likely not have heard, such as *to out-Gorbachev someone*, in the right way; why they form the past tense of the homophonous *wring* and *ring* systematically in *different* ways; and why they build the past tenses of *derived* verbs such as *ring* in *ringed the city* in a *regular* way, even though they are homophonous to *irregular* verbs such as *ring* in *she rang up*. Pinker suggests that verbs based on noun roots cannot have past tenses listed together with their roots in memory, which is why they always turn out to be regular, even if their sound pattern points in a different direction. These seem to be genuine quirks that characterize the specifically human mind. As Pinker (see Gazzaniga 1997: 117–9, 122) points out in his discussion of past-tense learning models, we *can* go and wire up a neural net, train it with the relevant inputs, and declare victory if it yields those quirks on the basis of those inputs. But the victory would be spurious, as it seems strange to suggest, either that we are specifically wired for these quirks to come about (these features of language seem rather to follow from more general and fundamental principles not specific to the examples), or that we are specifically taught to inflect in those ways rather than others (see further Pinker and Ullman 2004).

For an illustration from logic, consider the exclusive-*or* function, something achieved by children at the earliest stage at which they can be tested (see Crain and Pietroski 2001, for discussion). This function yields the answer 'true' to an odd number of '1's in the input, so that 10, e.g., comes out true, while 11 comes out false. Marcus (1998) trained Elman's network on 15 of the 16 possible numbers of inputs in a four-bit version of the problem. Tested on the sixteenth input, the model generalized in the wrong way in most instances. If, e.g., the novel input was '1111', the network would falsely assign 'true', apparently because the most similar inputs in its training set had had that response, e.g., '1110', '1101', '0111', '1011'. In short, experience-dependent judgements by similarity yield wrong generalizations of a kind we don't find in humans. If humans naturally do what connectionist nets have great difficulties in doing, and connectionist nets naturally do what humans do not, then connectionist nets look like a bad model of human nature.

As Marcus (1998) notes, we know that, if we are told that all gronks are bleems, and all bleems are blickets, all gronks are blickets. Our mind is endlessly productive in this fashion, a power that is conditioned, not on co-occurrence patterns, but abstract relationships between expressions semantically related to one another in systematic ways. In particular, for the above inference to go through, the sentences in question must have *discrete constituents* which reoccur *identically* (with the same meaning) in other syntactic positions in other sentences. This *systematicity* of human (and perhaps primate) thought, first prominently noted by Fodor and Pylyshyn (1988), has posed a challenge to connectionist learning models that has not been met to date (Hadley 2004).

Summarizing, the problem with eliminative materialism is that it competes philosophically or metaphysically, where it should either address questions of *implementation*, or else compete *empirically*, on the lines of Smolensky (2000), for explanatory power as a theory of particular phenomena related to the human language faculty. On its empirical merits as an alternative linguistic theory I have thrown some doubt. As a metaphysical theory, it seems that in part it is an obvious and trivial claim, pointing to a disparity between ordinary and scientific vocabulary. But while there is a disparity, there is no competition; belonging to different 'intellectual universes' also means not describing the same universe. Methodologically, ontological qualms should most certainly *not* induce the misguided intuition that something has to be 'eliminated'. A positive difference in vocabulary has to be recognized, but no issue of elimination arises, despite an issue of irrelevance, given certain scientific aims. Given current standards of scientific understanding, an inquiry into the mind will try to avoid describing the mind using mental vocabulary; and it will seek levels of abstraction of whatever kind seem useful to address, leaving the resolution of the issue of metaphysical dualism to the future, and bracketing ontology for now.

Opposing *functionalist* philosophers of mind do not quite 'eliminate' the mind, but, weirdly enough, are committed to endorsing a similar consequence:

for if functionalists are right, there is a sense in which the mind is still not subject to theoretical and naturalistic study. Functionalism, as noted, suggests the 'computer model' of mind, taking inspiration from Turing's (1950) proposal about programming a computer that would react appropriately to anything somebody would say in its presence. As I argued in Section 1.2 when discussing the significance of the Turing Test, the proposal that psychology should devote itself to software engineering (describing abstract and substrate algorithms for particular tasks) is of unclear interest to the project of finding the intrinsic structures of the human mind, as much as is the attempt to define a metaphysical theory of 'mental state types' that are independent of their biological underpinnings, and hence may be found in robots, Martians, and octopuses as well. Functionalism, crucially, *is* this kind of metaphysical speculation on what the essence of the mental is, arriving at the conclusion that

mental states and events are functional states and events in either a computational or a teleological systems-theoretic sense of 'functional' (Lycan 2003: 24).

This functionalist proposal on what mental states, ontologically speaking, are, seems similar to the odd suggestion that we specify what tables and chairs of their essence are, rather than abstract from tables and chairs and our common-sense understanding of them, when turning to the nature of matter as Galilean physics has proposed to study it. As a metaphysical thesis on the nature of mental states, however, functionalism takes the ontological/metaphysical status and relevance of our common-sense talk of mental states for granted, and proceeds from there to propose a solution to the mind–body problem.

The solution is not merely that certain limited aspects of our mental life can be studied computationally, but that we *are* serial computers: there are physical symbols encoded in the brain that get manipulated according to computational rules so as to mediate between certain inputs and outputs. This conclusion is not proposed on empirical and behavioural grounds, as it is by researchers on animal cognition (see Gallistel 1998, and Section 1.2), but on the grounds of a general 'theory of mind' which aims to fit the 'mental' into the physical world. Computers are no offence to a 'naturalistic' worldview, with which mentalistic talk has been thought to conflict, ever since Skinner attempted to put psychology on a 'scientific' basis.

While being 'naturalistic', then, the idea is neither *eliminativist*, nor an *identity theory* in the sense that the mind is the brain. The programs that the computer stores in long-term memory are not pieces of matter, but they are not immaterial either: rather, they correspond to a certain *arrangement* or *organization* of matter, which is why the matter itself can vary, and the computational processes running in it still be the same. Functionalism thus does not require us to eliminate mental states from our worldview, for we have now found a method to ontologically *reduce* them. Talk of beliefs and desires is now neither irrelevant to a scientific psychology (in the way that talk of tables and chairs is in physics), nor plain false (as in eliminative materialism); they cannot be either irrelevant or false, because of their specific stipulated nature or essence: they are functional states, and as such they are as 'real' as the internal states of any computational machine that mediate its behaviour.

Functionalism gives some metaphysical comfort to the modern 'materialist' or 'physicalist', and it is clearly motivated by some such 'naturalism'. Yet there is an anti-naturalistic dimension to it. The study of mind in functionalism is indifferent to the biological matter in which the various functions of mind are carried out, *functional equivalence* being what counts. Functionalism lifts the independence from biology to the level of a methodological principle, backed up by the metaphysical claim that mental state types, while indeed being 'natural kinds', are not 'human-biological kinds' (Lycan 2003: 18). An alternative and more plausible view would be that the description of the mind at the level of 'mental' mechanisms, more abstract than 'biological' mechanisms, simply reflects a lack of understanding—and unification—that we hope to overcome. As Randy Gallistel observes:

> We clearly do not understand how the nervous system computes. We do not know what are the foundations for its ability to compute. We do not understand how it carries out the small set of arithmetic and logical operations that are fundamental to any computation, the operations that are part of the basic instruction set in any computer ever developed, including massively parallel computers and neural net computers. We do not, for example, understand how neurons multiply, add, and compare the values of variables. (...) [C]omputational descriptions of psychological processes will prove to be a necessary intermediary in the process of linking psychological processes to their neural realization (Gazzaniga 1997: 77–8).

In other words, we cannot unify our computational description of the brain in terms of algorithms with a description on the level of cells, no matter whether we posit operations in neural nets or in algebraic and rule-based accounts.[39] But again, the unification problem here does not mean that the independence of the algorithms from the brain is a principled one, or lies in the *nature* of mind (as it would if our minds simply were computer programs); or that advances of understanding on the level of human cells would be necessarily irrelevant.

Contrast this view with Lycan's, quoted above, or with Block's (1995) assertion that functionalism's 'computer model of mind is profoundly *unbiological*' (ibid.: 390, his emphasis). For cognitive science, Block says, 'it does not matter' whether one chooses an implementation in 'gray matter, switches, or cats and mice'. Biology or physics is irrelevant to psychology, and physical mechanisms will not enter into characterizations of cognitive processes and psychological

---

[39] Note that connectionist approaches are not quite concerned with the biology of the mind ('organically based intelligence': cl. Elman *et al.* 1996: 104) either, despite their claim to be closer to the neural level (a questionable claim, given the current level of understanding, as Marcus (2001: 30) points out).

explanations. If we constructed automata that, in accordance with some imposed criterion, mimic our cognitive achievements, 'we will naturally feel that the most compelling theory of the mind is one that is general enough to apply to both them and us', Block argues, as opposed to 'a biological theory of the *human* mind [which] will not apply to these machines' (Block 1995: 391).

But this generality is bought at the expense of subject matter: the question of human nature (of 'human-biological' kinds) is simply by-passed, if the 'most compelling' theory were so general as not to say anything specific about humans or the kind of structures and mental representations specifically found in humans. An alternative theory, supported with evidence from human biology or from biological constraints on possible organic functioning on this planet, could surely be more compelling. Why should we have to say that any suggestions about abstract principles for the computation of expressions are compelling only if they apply to devices with a different underlying biology and/or physics—Martians, say?

On a more basic level, I see no reason to deny, and reason to affirm, that explanations of human linguistic competence may exploit *hardware* properties of the kind of matter brains are made of. In particular, it is unclear whether a universe that, unlike ours, was purely Newtonian, would support syntactic computation that the human linguistic mind arguably performs (particularly the kinds of long-distance causal relationship between elements of a syntactic tree that we will encounter in Chapter 5). Not just any computation will work in any physical universe (see further Penrose 1994; Stapp 2004). Functionalism might thus perhaps better be viewed as a 'theory of rationality in general', or of 'rational processes in general', rather than as an empirical and explanatory theory of the human mind, a different task.

All that said, one fundamental insight of functionalism remains, although we have quoted it to be an insight of the eighteenth century, and although I consider it to be a claim about the computational *modelling* of mental processes more than a claim about what they of their essence or ontologically are: mind is not matter, but form, or the *organization* of matter. Mind is a *formal* concept, not a material one. Interestingly, it is precisely the functionalist idea thus understood, or the idea of prioritizing form over matter, that has given rise to a new paradigm in the theory of *life*. Artificial life research undertaken with a view to determining principles for a 'general biology' (Langton 1988; Kauffman 1995b, 2000) claims that life does not consist in matter, but originates from the structural organization of matter. Life is multiply realizable, too, in just this sense: it need not, according to this view, be carbon-based, for example, and is not tied to such accidents of history.

In *this* sense, the functionalist paradigm has entered into biology itself, and there can be no claim about 'independence from biology' here. Life is a biological phenomenon that is now studied on the basis of abstract and general principles, for the sake of understanding earth-bound life better in the light of *other* conceivable life forms falling under the same general principles. But no non-biological 'type of life' is posited, and no metaphysical theory of life, which would depend on our ordinary concept of 'life', is endorsed here. In a similar way we may expect insight into human knowledge of language to flow from a comparative study of communication systems in other animals (Hauser 1996). But here again we do not thereby expect any insights about what 'the mental in general' or 'as such' is, a task that could only depend on our conceptual intuitions of what 'mental' means, which may be simply irrelevant for the empirical study of the actual minds that we wish to understand.

Functionalism as a philosophical doctrine clearly does not proceed, even programmatically, from the basis of the positive insight just formulated, to the task of *finding* the organizational principles that give rise, say, to linguistic forms in the hardware of the human brain. Usually functionalism is coupled to a form of externalism, whereas the fundamental insight of functionalism, that mind resides in structural organization (or form) rather than matter is an *internalist* and *formalist* one: mind or life are not explained by the contingent functions that a complex organism takes up to an environment, but by internal and autonomous principles for the organization of form. From this point of view, the truth of functionalism is a form of formalism, which is what I defend here.

In the next chapter I will develop a version of naturalism that seems incompatible with any of the currents in the philosophies of mind and language I have reviewed in this chapter, and to which I will return at various points in what follows.

2

Against Metaphysical Naturalism

2.1 From Methodological to Metaphysical Naturalism

Post-Newtonian standards of intelligibility allow for mysterious 'immaterial' forces rather than merely mechanical causal interactions among colliding particles. If 'nature' is what the natural sciences unravel, it is intelligible to whatever extent the sciences afford intelligibility, which means mostly leaving aside, with Galileo, ontological qualms about what things 'really are'. Saying that the mind is a part of nature is to indicate that anything is a potential object of naturalistic inquiry of this kind. This broad methodological naturalism does not address such questions as what the essence of the 'natural' or the 'mental' is; it offers a 'theory of mind' no more than a 'theory of matter', although it does engage in a study of various mental *phenomena*.

In essence, then, methodological naturalism as I here describe it is just 'natural philosophy' in the original sense of Galileo, Locke, Hume, or Descartes. What Locke was asking was:

'How can we escape the appeals to authority, the confusion of words for things?' Locke's answer to this question (...) was clear, it is repeated many times in the *Essay*: make careful observations, compile histories of phenomena, do not be misled by language, study things not words (Yolton 1990: 70).

Today we credit philosophers such as Locke with inaugurating enterprises such as 'empiricism' and 'epistemology'—enterprises that we regard as narrowly 'philosophical' and distinguish from standard natural science. Rorty (1980) in particular sees what he calls the 'epistemological problematic' arising in this period, triggered by what he terms an 'indirect representative' theory of perception. No doubt, if the notion of an 'idea' is that of an inner representative of outer objects, something like an 'object' located in the 'inner arena' of the mind in which the external world gets 'mirrored', epistemological scepticism is a problem that is likely to arise; it will also eventually be hard to resist. If there are such representatives standing proxy for external ones, they will all too easily seem like the 'veil' preventing the sort of 'direct access' to the external world which it has been a prime preoccupation of modern philosophy to secure. Questions of realism and anti-realism will also be an unavoidable consequence of the representational theory of ideas, given that wherever there are relationally understood representations, there will be a question of whether they really 'reach out' to the external world, or not.

It seems to be precisely this picture of inner sensations or representations of outer things that Wittgenstein opposes in his 'Private Language Argument'. But 'mental representations' as used here are crucially *not* relational in the sense above. They are posited for behavioural reasons, given a lack of other explanatory constructs that would serve for the same explananda. Contrary to the ideas that Wittgenstein criticized, however, it is not mental entities that are referred to by the expressions we use. The use partially explains the meaning of these expressions, in the sense that the meaning is a matter of how it is processed in the mind by several of its interacting components or systems. On the other hand, these mental representations partially explain the use, in that the latter will depend on certain competence systems being there in the first place, and a certain cognitive endowment at large (a human nature). All of this seems consistent with Wittgenstein's central verdict that one should not construe the meaning of terms of 'inner sensations', 'ideas', etc., 'nach dem Muster von "Gegenstand und Bezeichnung"' ('according to the model of "object and sign"', PU, §293). Words do not refer to their meanings, in particular, but express them; and even when they are words used to talk about ordinary material objects, they are not understandable as mere signifying devices whose meaning derives from the objects they signify: we cannot tell *which* objects they signify before we know the words' meaning and how they are used (see further Chapter 6, and Hinzen 2005a).

While the representational model attacked by Wittgenstein is often ascribed to seventeenth-and eighteenth-century thinkers, though—else one wonders who ever defended the views that Wittgenstein spent his life criticizing—Yolton argues persuasively that it is questionable to impose such modern conceptions on them. To be 'in' the mind, Arnauld explains, is 'to be conceived', not to be a picture that represents something (Yolton 1990: 65). The core of the theory of 'ideas' from Descartes to Reid, Yolton asserts, takes them not to be 'inner objects' but 'ways of knowing'. They are not 'signs of the corpuscular structure' of the universe, but signs in terms of which we know of or are acquainted with experience, so that the 'world as known *is* the world of ideas' (Yolton 1984: 213).[1] There is a fundamental difference between physical and cognitive reality: knowing is not

reading off properties of the world from our sensations or ideas. The representative function of ideas is not a sign function: ideas are not signs of things, they are the interpretations of, or cognitive responses to, physical motion (Yolton 1990: 62).

The *causal* relation between physical objects and our bodies is inadequate for cognition; ideas in particular do not *resemble* their causes at all. Locke argues that there is no '*necessary* connection between "the bulk, figure, and motion of several

---

[1] Which is again crucially not to say that we stand in some mysterious 'relation' to these ideas, or 'perceive' them somehow.

Bodies about us" and the sensations or ideas they produce in us', a paradigmatically non-empiricist contention, it would seem (Yolton 1990: 66). For Hume, not only are secondary qualities of objects, such as 'hard, soft, hot, cold, white, black' not in the objects themselves, hence not representations of properties or things out there, but also neither are 'supposed primary qualities of extension and solidity'. Hume takes this insight to argue against 'the evidence of the sense or the opinion of external existence', again a paradigmatically empiricist and externalist opinion (Hume 1748/1975, section XII, part II, §123: 155).[2]

As for Descartes, he taught that all universals are modes of thinking or ways of knowing (*Principia*, part I, §§58–9); that most properties we attribute to external things do not capture what they really are (ibid., part II, §4); and that our sensations of sensory qualities like light, tone, colour, warmth, etc. may be exactly the same, no matter whether an external object actually causes it. The actual structures of the external objects which affect our nerve endings are utterly different from our conceptions of them, hence cannot cause or explain them (ibid., part IV, section 198).[3] As for Leibniz, he contends it is nothing but prejudice that the natures of things are outside to start with, and then enter into the mind somehow (Leibniz 1686/1996, §§26–8).

It is not clear how any of these doctrines invite the relational and externalist conception that there are 'inner ideas', which derive their 'content' from being 'representations' *of* mind-external 'properties' or 'objects'. Consequently it seems doubtful, by and large, that seventeenth-and eighteenth-century philosophers supported a relational understanding of mind. Rorty, by contrast, reads Descartes's 'epistemological' project as that of overcoming 'scepticism', hence as a *foundationalist* one. The method in the quest for absolute certainty is alleged to be the inspection of 'ideas' in Rorty's sense, found in the 'inner arena' of the *cogito*. The result is a tendency to diminish the role of experiential–experimental methods over *a priori* ones in Descartes's conception of method.

This coheres well with a standard picture of Descartes's work, as well as with the *Meditation*'s stress on certainty. The Ego's reflections on his cogitations, however, may rather have been conceived of as an attempt to *systematize* human knowledge, to show all particularized truths to be intrinsically connected and to follow from one another in a single chain of reasons (Schulthess 1998: 73–7). It seems doubtful whether the common caricature of Descartes's philosophy as 'certifying to oneself' the contents of one's 'inner representations' and

---

[2] Fascinatingly, Hume adds that the empiricist and representationalist stance is not so much a false philosophical doctrine as a 'natural instinct' of all men, which, when held against reason, 'carries no rational evidence for it' (ibid.).

[3] One verification of the last idea is the actual disparity between the acoustic level of linguistic analysis, and the phonetic/phonological one, the former of which addresses an outer physical reality, the latter an inner one, and where indeed the properties of the inner representations cannot be attributed to the outer ones (see Anderson and Lightfoot 2002, ch. 6, and Kenstowicz 1994 for discussion).

introspections could be applied to a systematization of human knowledge of this kind.

Yolton (1990: 68) stresses that the method of ascertaining the *cogito* is not found or applicable in the other scientific domains that Descartes was mainly concerned with, where what counted was observation and experiment. We should be careful to extrapolate, from Descartes's few narrowly philosophical essays, on what he thought about the enterprise of knowledge at large (Clark 1982). Similar observations hold for Locke, who

> was writing with scientists in mind (...) These medical men did not look to their own inner states in order to diagnose illness: they watched carefully the symptons and signs as they developed. (...) The 'philosophy' Locke knew was 'natural philosophy', that is science. What his account of the origin, extent and limits of knowledge did was urge us to be careful observers, make detailed natural histories of symptoms and phenomena, so that we might discover better the workings of nature. Only an experimental knowledge of nature was possible, never, he insisted, a demonstrative science, a science of certainty or incorrigibility (Yolton 1990: 68–9).

Yolton rejects the modern label 'Lockean empiricism', since all that can mean is that Locke was undertaking a standard observational science of nature, including human nature. On similar grounds, doubts arise with respect to the modern label 'epistemology', as Locke's studies in the workings of the mind were psychology for him, closely related to physiology. If so, there is little point for Rorty to criticize Locke's efforts at discovering the principles of mind as

> confusedly thinking that an analogue of Newton's particle mechanics for 'inner space' would somehow be of 'great advantage in directing our Thoughts in the search of other Things', and would somehow let us 'see, what Objects our Understandings were, or were not fitted to deal with' (Rorty 1980: 137).

Michael Friedman confirms the essential *absence* of Rorty's 'epistemological problematic' in the early modern philosophers. While fundamentally sceptical about the reach of scientific understanding, they do not seem to have had any problem with the 'reality of the external world':

> the philosophers of the modern tradition [from Descartes] are not best understood as attempting to stand outside the new science so as to show, from some mysterious point outside of science itself, that our scientific knowledge somehow 'mirrors' an independently existing reality. Rather [they] start from the *fact* of modern scientific knowledge as a fixed point, as it were. Their problem is not so much to justify this knowledge from some 'higher' standpoint as to articulate the new *philosophical* conceptions that are forced upon us by the new science (Friedman 1993: 48).

While philosophers understood themselves as scientists, it was natural for scientists to address questions of 'philosophy', and to call themselves 'natural philosophers', starting with Newton's *Mathematical Principles of Natural Philosophy* (1687). Robert Greene's *Principles of the Philosophy of Expansive and Contractive*

Forces appeared in 1727, John Rowning's *Compendious System of Natural Philosophy* in 1735–43, James Hutton's *Dissertation on Different Subjects in Natural Philosophy* in 1792. Naturalists called themselves 'philosophers' well into the 1800s. John Dalton published his *New System of Chemical Philosophy* in 1808/1810, Humphry Davy his *Researches, Chemical and Philosophical* in 1800. The groundbreaking hypothesis of William Prout on the structure of chemical matter was published in two papers in the *Annals of Philosophy* (1815/1816). A science like chemistry included considerations called 'metaphysical' because they were held to be speculative, such as assumptions about atoms, which were 'theoretical, metaphysical entities, which could not be seen, touched, or tasted', and for which Dalton, it was thought, despite his assignment of atomic weights to them, could not provide a 'proof of physical existence' (Brock 1992: 165). 'Metaphysics' was not apparently something other than science, but just an expression for its more theoretical and experimentally unconfirmed upper reaches.

The integration of philosophy with science persisted up to Kant, who still had a 'Ph.D.' student, Jeremias Richter (1762–1807), who would later become famous for the development of Stoichiometry, which allowed the calculation of supposed weights of phlogiston in substances. Under the supervision of Kant, Richter wrote a thesis on the use of mathematics in chemistry (Brock 1992: 130). Only later, in the decades after Kant did philosophy become autonomously institutionalized as an academic discipline. Before then, philosophy was science, and science included 'philosophical' issues. 'Naturalism' in philosophy was no issue; philosophy as such was methodologically naturalistic, and no argument for any such naturalism was asked for.

Predictably, it is at this juncture that the perennial dispute about the scientific status of philosophy would arise, which still plagues philosophers today. German hermeneutics developed the sense in which the humanities had their own kind of *Verstehen*, thought independent of the scientists' *Erklären* (explanation). Two attempts to resolve this instability emerged: either to reduce philosophy to science (or the philosophy of science), the stance taken by Carnap and later Quine, whose dictum 'philosophy of science is philosophy enough'[4] speaks for itself; or to discard science (and logic) as irrelevant to philosophy, and to engage in *Fundamentalontologie* instead, which was Heidegger's decision. There is little doubt that Wittgenstein, temperamentally, followed Heidegger at this juncture more than Carnap, trying to finish off in the *Tractatus* what he regarded as the 'science part' of philosophy, this being what was most trivial about it. In this booklet he also stated clearly that 'philosophy is none of the sciences', thereby stating what presumably had become a plain sociological fact by that time (*Tractatus*, 4.111). Contemporary pragmatists such as Rorty have a closer affinity with Quine's reduction of philosophy than with Heidegger's foundationalist

---

[4] Quoted without reference in Rorty (2001).

reinstitution of it: Rorty's 'priority of democracy over philosophy' is a way of exorcizing philosophy as well.

With the Carnap–Heidegger dichotomy in the early twentieth century we are facing nothing less than 'the parting of the ways' (Friedman 2000) between continental and analytic philosophy that effectively took place in the 1930s,[5] itself an expression of the uncertain status of philosophy as an academic discipline after it ceased to be 'natural philosophy'. Why has today's 'naturalism' become a controversial philosophical doctrine in *metaphysics*? I do not think that there is any way to reach a deeper understanding of contemporary naturalism without acknowledging the *sociological* developments in the nineteenth century that made such a doctrine *possible* in the first place.

Today, naturalism has come to mean a materialist version of *monism*. It is an 'ontological' position, the claim that 'everything is physically constituted' (Papineau 2001: 3). Its agenda is to overcome a supposed metaphysical divide: a divide between two realms, 'mind' and 'body', the 'mental' and the 'physical', 'norms' and 'laws', with 'mental causation' being an apparent bridge between them. It is a *metaphysical* monism of this sort that, we shall see, can ground a *methodological* dualism according to which a naturalistic inquiry into language and human nature is misguided because the 'mental' and the 'physical' are in principle to be studied by different methods. There is no necessary conflict, on the other hand, as I see it, between the present *methodological* naturalism and a *metaphysical* dualism, a point I have hinted at, and to which I return shortly.

Is there any rational ground from switching a purely methodological for a metaphysical naturalism? What has changed since the post-Newtonians concluded that the universe did not work as Descartes or Galileo had suggested? Descartes's matter—a 'Plenist' conception of some substance filled with small, hard corpuscles in constant motion—was intuitively as different from 'mind' and spiritual ingredients as one could imagine. Newton, by contrast, accepted the vacuum. Much of the universe was empty space, including what appeared to be solid bodies. What prevented their penetration and disintegration were the forces acting between and integrating their components. An important later concept of Newton's was the aether, thought to be composed of small mutually repulsive particles. This concept developed into a theory according to which attractive

---

[5] One can locate the split rather precisely, or at least symbolically, in the 'International University Course' in Davos, Switzerland (17 March–6 April 1929), which marked the replacement of the older generation by the younger generation within German philosophy. As has not been widely noticed, Carnap attended this meeting as well, where Cassirer and Heidegger were the prime figures, and agreed with Heidegger on the demise of metaphysics, even though drawing opposite conclusions from it. While Heidegger broke with the epistemological tradition of Neo-Kantianism completely, and denied the centrality of logic to philosophy, Friedman (2000) argues that Carnap may be regarded as having tried reducing Kant's theoretical philosophy to its logical-methodological component, transforming Kantian epistemology into modern logic and philosophy of science.

and repulsive forces interacted in an antagonistic way so as to sustain activity in nature. Newton's forces rose to epistemological importance in Locke, who identified them with 'powers' of matter, which would also be powers to affect the human senses. This inspired the matter theory of the leading scientist Joseph Priestley (1733–1804), who *reduced* matter to 'powers', concluding that 'solid matter' was an illusion and there was no 'substration' of matter independent of its 'powers'. The distinction between matter and spirit had collapsed. (Yolton 1983)

This conclusion suggests that we must have a different notion of matter today that now enables us to draw distinctions such as 'body' versus 'mind' (or 'physical' vs 'mental') again, giving rise to a 'mind–body problem' that many post-Newtonians thought incoherent. But if anything, physics has furthered this effective erosion of the common-sense conception of 'solid bodies' that began in Newton, and it seems as if 'materialism' in something like Priestley's curious sense is what we are left with today. This was crucially *not* a reductive view, but rather the insight 'that the kind of matter on which the [Cartesian] two-substance view is based does not exist'. As Yolton puts it:

with the altered concept of matter, the more traditional ways of posing the question of the nature of thought and of its relations to the brain do not fit. We have to think of a complex organized biological system with properties the traditional doctrine would have called mental *and* physical (Yolton 1983: 114; and see Chomsky 2000: 113 for discussion).

Why is it that contemporary 'physicalists' and 'eliminative materialists' revise this conclusion in *one crucial respect*, by saying matter is *only physical*? This is in *exclusion* of the mental being part of the physical, quite unlike what the eighteenth-century philosophers thought, hence equally unlike the naturalism about the mind that Priestley, Locke, Hume, LaMettrie, and others practised. It is through this crucial difference that a doctrine hailed as a truism by Priestley, given that the old pre-Newtonian notion of matter was gone, becomes a controversial metaphysical and philosophical thesis. If eighteenth-century materialism is encompassing, why is today's materialism either 'eliminative' or reductive?

Strangely, it is often suggested that the very metaphysical dichotomies that figure in current thinking are a *product* of early modern natural philosophy, and Cartesian dualism in particular, averred to be a paradigmatically non-naturalistic stance. True, Descartes calls the mind a separate 'substance', an individual that is a bearer of properties: but this does not mean the mind is a kind of 'thing' or 'object', the reason for the previous conclusion being merely that '*nothing* does not have any states or properties', as the mind does, hence there must be a *substance* that has these states and properties (*Principia*, part I, section 11). That moreover cannot be the *physical* substance, since while we cannot think of ourselves as *not thinking* (whatever we doubt we are or do), it does not seem in the same way essential to a physical substance that it thinks.[6] Few would like to defend a dualism of substances today, but it is an empirical question, then and now, whether it is a truth about the world that there are two such substances in it that are distinct and cannot be reduced to one another: that is, a bearer of physical and a bearer of mental or psychological properties.

As noted, Chomsky (2002: 56) argues that with the downfall of the Cartesian notion of body a possible basis for such a principled distinction fell away, and materialism collapsed. Still, it would seem a mistake to conclude from this the impossibility of a rational inquiry into the reducibility or 'supervenience' of meanings, morality, or the Self. Contemporary arguments for dualism do not depend for their coherence on a pre-Newtonian physics or contact mechanics. For example, substance dualism, as defended by Lowe (2004), appeals to distinct identity conditions for persons and bodies (as well as any parts of those bodies); while property dualism as defended by Chalmers (1996), does not involve a dualism of substances, and exploits the intuition that however the mental may arise from the physical (understood as whatever post-Newtonian physical theory told us about it), we can think of the latter as being deprived of the former, which is to say that the former cannot be essential to the latter, however lawfully it may be *connected* to it. Dualism as defended by Penrose (1994) appeals to the non-computability of mental processing, while dualism as defended by Stapp (2004), appeals to the conceptual structure of modern physics itself. All four dualist proposals are clearly framed within an overall project of naturalistic inquiry (see specifically Chalmers 1996: 127–9, 170–1), and it would be way too quick to exclude even a dualism of substances merely on the grounds that post-Newtonian physics deprived us of a basis for a distinction that Descartes's physics still provided.

Neither will doing away with this physics eradicate an empirical difference that Descartes spotted between humans and machines. Unlike a computer, which acts as it is programmed to do (or acts randomly), a human action on an occasion seems neither programmed nor random, while being appropriate all the same. Though often predictable, specific human behaviours, for all we can make out, are, if non-pathological, never compelled, in the sense that, whatever one does, one could have acted differently.

Descartes's criterion for distinguishing a human from a machine concretely demands that, first, the machine must use *language* in the normal way that we do (that is, language use should be incited but not determined by input or circumstances), and second, it should be *universally adaptable*. The latter test

---

[6] In modern terms, such as those of Chalmers (1996), while a subject incapable of thinking is inconceivable, it *is* conceivable that despite all the evidence you may have that your neighbour has conscious mental states like you, he really is only a 'body', a zombie who has no 'inner life' at all, while behaving as if he did.

criterion is particularly interesting: each machine works only by being specialized or programmed in some way or other, which implies it will break down when facing most other tasks. But human reason is a *universal* instrument, Descartes points out, hence not specialized or *specifically adapted* to circumstances it is programmed to react to in some way. It is unlikely, Descartes remarks, that any machine could achieve this universality by having sufficiently many interacting 'organs' or computational modules (specialized programs) as parts.

There is, to be sure, one instance of mechanical causation of human behaviour, the case of phobias, where the subjects cannot help but to react in a manner that seems clearly controlled by and predictable from the stimulus (such as a snake). But this one case where stimulus freedom fails is a pathological one,[7] and not even human emotional reactions are stimulus-controlled. The more we move in the direction of language use, the more abstract and indirect become the relations between the internal mechanism that is triggered and the causal trigger itself.[8] We may equally check what happens if a human is prompted by an *internal* stimulus, such as a pain. There again seems to be no behavioural trait causally-mechanically determined by this. Even if, statistically, feeling pain engenders crying out in pain, there *is* nothing in particular I *must* do when sensing a pain, no matter how strong it is, as we know anecdotally from torture.

The reason that Descartes's empirical test criterion seems still so compelling is that the model of mechanical causation is firmly enshrined in our common-sense understanding. As Locke said, it is not in any way 'comprehensible' to us that causation should work in a different way, or that body A could be moved by body B *without* being in mechanical contact with it. Looking at my computer screen, I cannot print characters without actually *hitting keys*. And I cannot hit keys by just *looking at them* either. But then, consider how you evoke an idea or a thought in my mind, say that a behaviour of mine is shameful. *Looking at me* need not invoke it. *Telling me* about it need not invoke it. A behavioural pattern of which the thought is *true* need not invoke it. On the other hand, *if* you succeed in invoking it, then it is *not* because you triggered a necessary and mechanical reaction on my part: actions do not evoke shame in the way that onions make you weep. To begin with, you must be able to make sense of that notion of shame and be naturally capable of feeling it (else nothing will invoke it). Given that capability, you will then have to actually invoke the feeling in your mind. Even assuming that I am naturally capable of the relevant reaction, no amount of physical interaction between you and me involving acts of mechanical causation in the sense above

---

[7] Fodor (1990) defines a *reflex* as a 'mechanism of environment-behaviour correlation which connects the tokening of a specific sort of condition in the world with the tokening of a specific sort of behavioural response to that condition'. He argues very plausibly (against Dretske's account) that 'mental events don't have specific effects *or* specific causes'. The illusion to the contrary is produced 'by taking as a paradigm the sort of mental state that mediates a behavioural *reflex*' (p. 33).

[8] Apparently, Descartes did not talk of 'mental causation', reserving the separate notion of 'occasioning' for what moves the mind when it comes up with an idea (Yolton 1990: 59–60).

seems like a sufficient condition for a particular mental reaction such as this to occur in me (in the sense in which it *is* a sufficient condition, under normal conditions, for a particular character to appear on my screen when a relevant key is hit). *Given* a common-sense notion of mechanical causation, there *is* no mechanical induction of a human behaviour by a stimulus.

We should therefore be *puzzled* by statements such as: 'Causal relations involving mental events are among the familiar facts of everyday experience' (Kim 1996: 125).[9] In fact, they are not! Leaving aside the fact that most of our thoughts don't concern the situation in our immediate surroundings, we see that even in a case where we stand right in front of a tree under epistemically ideal conditions, and we don't circularly characterize this situation as being one in which we are looking at *a tree*, there is no reason to say that we are *compelled* to either say or think that we see *a tree*. Kim is not thinking about phobias, surely, where our reaction *is* so compelled? He may not run causation and determination together, but then, if we don't do that, the notion of causation is not that of mechanical causation, and the question is what notion it is (nor would a statistical notion do in instances such as this: there is also no statistical norm on what we utter next given that we are standing in front of a tree).

When discussing mental-to-physical causation, Kim intends there to be a relation between Jones's decision (a 'mental event') to reach for a spoon, say, and his actually reaching for it. But *which* mental event is supposed to mechanically cause me to reach for a spoon? I know of none. Likely we should not answer: your *decision* to take the spoon. Our criterion for something (such as a neural event) being a 'decision to reach for a spoon' is that this very act occurs and is perceived and described in intentional terms. If I were to constantly make 'decisions to take spoons' (given normal physical conditions), and nothing ever happened, it would seem unlikely that I ever decided to take the spoon. The 'mental event' of deciding is not an act that it seems we can separate off from the taking of the spoon, so as to make it a sufficient condition for it.[10]

Explaining acts by mechanical causes, even if they did exist, moreover seems *inconsistent* with our common-sense notion of an *act* (else criminal punishment would make little sense, and robots might commit murders). Ordinary understanding does not forbid that Jones's *brain*, while he undergoes what we describe as 'decision-making', is subject to a description appealing to mechanisms. But this is a far cry from saying that the brain or cognitive sciences providing such

---

[9] It might be remarked at this juncture that we say thinks like 'He made me do it', invoking some notion of causation. But when reflecting on a causal sense that this might have, I notice myself either thinking about cases where another person induced behaviour on my part without me wanting it, or else about cases where a superior orders an inferior to do something, a situation in which, when questioned, the latter might reply with this kind of assertion. In the first case, it is not *me* who did anything; in the second, I could have acted differently (strictly speaking, my answer is inadequate).

[10] This is a Wittgensteinian line of thought. For his notion of a 'criterion' see *Das Blaue Buch*: 48f–9.

mechanistic descriptions analyse human decisions and actions. They analyse mechanisms which *enter* decision-making and action once decision-making and acting, as common-sensically understood, take place. There is no scientific explanation as to why Jones decides to reach for a spoon. *We* of course 'explain it' by saying 'he decided to do so (wanted it, etc.)', but we do not mean, when we say that, that certain mechanical causes induce Jones's behaviour. As I am using the English word (action), he would *not* in fact have *acted* in this case at all. 'Mental causation' (whatever that is) is quite different from mechanical causation; we don't know how they relate.[11]

It should thus also surprise us that it is precisely the notion of mechanical or machine-like causation that figures in the explanation of behaviour and mental causation in functionalism. The latter assumes that there are correlations between causal interactions among symbolic structures represented in our brains, on the one hand, and rational relations among the (relational) meanings of these symbolic structures, on the other. Suppose, e.g., that there is a physical symbolic object in my brain, call it A, in one of Block's (1995) examples, denoting, on the semantic side, a shark-thought and a physical object, B, denoting a danger-thought. Then the functionalist holds there is a causal relation between A and B (a process of 'thinking') that is like a transition from one of a machine's states into another. But while it may be true that a shark-thought may incline me towards a danger-thought, and in fact a decision not to swim, it appears to be an empirical falsehood to say that I am *compelled* to think such a thought, or think it by default, even if the shark-thought came first. *No* thought, it seems, has another thought as a known (or anyway empirically attested) causal consequence, in the sense of causation we are discussing. Importantly, then, in what follows, mental mechanisms that I will talk about and that generative grammar has appealed to will *never* be mechanisms employed in the service of inducing and explaining human actions. They are mechanisms involved in computations within a cognitive system, which run when this system is enacted (and then in the absence of intentions and decisions).

It may seem like an unpalatable conclusion that mental 'causation', whatever the sense of this word, is both real and cannot be modelled computationally, but it is not clear what would empirically warrant another conclusion. We need not be ashamed to concede that the study of human nature today need not involve a solution to the problem of the causation of behaviour, or indeed have that as its major concern. There *need* not be a theory offering a solution to this problem at all, just as there need not be a theory in physics of how a body mechanically causes another body's movement without being in contact with it. In this latter case, we are content with having a law that allows us predictions and explanations

---

[11] As Chomsky (2002: 59) remarks, even lower-level phenomena such as how we direct our attention on different objects in a visual scene at will, escape serious scientific treatment, if we attend to the aspect characterized by 'at will'.

even without knowing mechanical causes. This suggests that if we *had* laws for human behaviour, the remaining problem of how behaviour is *caused* would have the same status as the problem of how bodily behaviour is caused by other bodies. On this view, while mental causation *appears* more mysterious than physical causation, this is because laws of behaviour are lacking, *not* because there is a metaphysical problem here that is inherently more mysterious than the body–body problem that Newton faced and left unresolved. But then again, given the nature of human behaviour, what would 'laws of behaviour' be? And why should we believe that there is any such thing?

In conclusion, although I reject metaphysical naturalism in the contemporary sense, rationalism as I here develop it is open to a dualistic metaphysics, and one might even point out that it is the explosion of the Cartesian 'machine', supposedly housing the 'ghost' of our minds, that should make us *unprejudiced*, within our project of a naturalistic inquiry into this exploded world, as to what kinds of properties and substances it may or may not contain: there simply *is* no conceptual connection between 'naturalism' (in the present methodological sense) and 'materialism'.

2.2 Rationalist Method from Galileo to Chomsky

Galileo is often said to have been an experimental scientist, an artisan, and engineer, but this is not in contradiction with another interpretation, going back to Koyré (1939/1966), which emphasizes the primacy of the intellect over experience in Galileo's science, and the primacy of mathematical models over an empirically given reality. This would be to read his physics as a form of Platonism set against the then prevalent Aristotelianism, though hardly a metaphysical version of Platonism, even less a form of Pythagorean mysticism according to which mathematics could provide evidence for physical truth (see further Shea 1998: 799–802). Mathematics (geometry) is a language, rather, in which Galileo assumes nature is written, there being no other way to understand the world. Platonic ideas are here simplified models or explanatory principles, from which the general features of reality, though not single objects in all their complexity and (in part subject-dependent) details, can be grasped.

A new conception of experiment was an inherent aspect of the scientific revolution that Galileo helped to instigate. Most crucially, experiment came to be seen not as a recording of data or fact-collecting, on the basis of which theories were formed, but rather a way of actually constructing a machine that one could understand to mechanically produce effects that a given mathematical model predicted (Machamer 1998). Experiments were a way of *interfering* with the natural order of things, not of representing it, which is in direct opposition to the Aristotelian view. An object shows its true nature not by exploring its natural and holistic connections with other things, but by putting it in an artificial circumstance where it establishes accidental and 'unnatural' connections with other objects. This is the way in which, as Shea puts it, Galileo could free the Aristotelian tradition from an empiricism that 'was its main weakness' (ibid.: 800). Science is not fact-recording or world representation. To gain knowledge, we must *discard* an enormous amount of evidence and facts in the face of a simple mechanical model that proves predictive and explanatory, while being inconsistent with other phenomena—as those did who believed *without* and *prior* to the telescope that the earth moves.

Galilean method then consists, first, of *engaging in idealizations*—in particular, viewing objects as geometrical forms, and employing a non-Aristotelian notion of abstraction—and, second, of *designing experiments*, in which a phenomenon under investigations is artificially simplified in a way that allows one to direct questions at it that are answerable unambiguously. In what follows I regard these two aspects of Galilean method as a common core in a rationalist approach to science, no matter what the phenomenon in question may be, mental or physical. Building a generative grammar of any one human language is nothing other than building an abstract machine that, if it was internally represented in the brain, would produce the infinite output of that language.

Experiment retains its crucial role in Descartes. The more he advanced theoretically, Descartes tells us, the more he found that *observations* became necessary, and at the end of section 3 of part 6 of the *Discours* (which reads like an author's plea for external funding), he laments over the costs incurred in making the relevant experiments ('expériences'). But, as we shall see in a moment, Descartes adds an element largely absent in Galileo, and he introduces a slightly different conception of the relation between theory and experiment, while retaining the Galilean conception of idealization.

The novel element transpires when Descartes complains, in a letter to his patron Mersenne, that Galileo had never *deduced*—with the required certainty—the properties of real objects from higher principles (see Shea 1998: 802). This deductive method in scientific inquiry contrasts with both the Newtonian method of induction (to which Hume would some decades later draw his critical attention), and the Baconian method of fact-collecting, where theoretical generalizations are only to be made tentatively after the gathering of empirical data. Cartesian method proceeds the other way around, from some new theoretical conception or model to experiments and observations that will show its worth or worthlessness. A good theory or model is one that brings a variety of natural occurrences into a wider and coherent scheme of thought—without necessarily having done extensive fact-collecting for every step while forming it.[12]

---

[12] 'If people look at all the many properties (...) and the fabric of the entire world, which I have deduced in this book from just a few principles, then, even if they think that my assumption of these principles was arbitrary and groundless, they will still perhaps acknowledge that it would hardly have been possible for so many items to fit into a coherent pattern if the original principles had been false' (Descartes 1644/1983, part IV: 205; see also 1637/1984, part VI, section 10: 123–4).

Theoretical discovery on this view obeys no 'method'. It does not quite matter how ideas spring from our minds creatively, or where they come from.[13] Whatever hypothesis makes good sense of a larger number of varied examples wins (though, we should note, mere 'coverage of data' is also not *as such* what counts, an attitude corresponding to an instrumentalist attitude to science that Descartes surely rejected). It seems perfectly adequate for these reasons to call this way of proceeding *anti-foundationalist*, and to contrast it with a *foundationalist* empiricism, where every theoretical step and non-observable theoretical conception has to be derived from experience. Instead of the latter strategy, Descartes speaks of 'seeds of the truth' that we happen to find in us (*Discours*, part 6, section 3; cf. *Principia*, part 1, section 13).

The same conclusion seems appropriate for Galileo, given his essentially *practical* method of justification and abstinence from essentialist inquiry. Anti-foundationalism in the present sense was also an essential aspect of the doctrines of Plato, the originator of 'innate ideas' or 'seeds of the truth'. Plato strikingly described the process of understanding as 'the dawning of ideas we find occurring in us, like in a dream' (*Menon*, 85c), hence as a non-methodical and indeed *irrational* process: the ideas are just there somehow, they swim to the surface. We do not know where they come from, and simply use them, even though we cannot justify them (see also Popper 1959).

This understanding of rationalist or Cartesian method is not, on the other hand, quite the one that famous foundationalist passages like the following in the *Principles* (1644/1983) suggest:

> I frankly admit that I know of no material substance other than that which is divisible, has shape, and can move in every possible way, and this the geometers call quantity and take as the object of their demonstrations. Moreover, our concern is exclusively with the division, shape and motions of this substance, and nothing concerning these can be accepted as true unless it be deduced from indubitably true common notions with such certainty that it can be regarded as a mathematical demonstration (Descartes, *Principia*, part II, article 64).

But the role of a deductivist method in Descartes's methodology is very easily overstated, and Descartes himself was well aware of its pitfalls. No truths about the physical world—the distance of planets from the sun, the motion of comets, the colours of the rainbow, the nature of quicksilver, etc.—follow from metaphysical first principles or 'truths of reason' such as the *cogito* or the existence of a good God (Gaukroger 1993). Descartes is unambiguous that deduction cannot *justify* anything, and is no method of discovery. Rather it is a *mode of presenting* things one already knows, which themselves have been reached analytically by means of problem-solving.[14] Gaukroger thus suggests the relevance even for

---

[13] 'It is their eventual performance that counts—and that is judged by deducing their implications, and matching these conclusions against Nature' (Toulmin and Goodfield 1962: 163).

[14] Descartes explicitly rejects the mode used by ancient geometers proceeding deductively like Euclid, such as Pappus and Diophantus, as inadequately depicting (in fact as 'hiding' or 'covering up')

Descartes of a difference that we make today between a systematizing kind of 'textbook science', in which everything is so *presented* as to 'follow from the axioms', and a 'laboratory science', in which these truths are actually *found* (for contemporary views of this distinction see Hacking 1983, 1992). Descartes's *Principia* on this account is a piece of textbook science, by contrast, say, to the earlier *Optics* or *Meteors*. It deduces scientific results, leaving their justification as a matter of observation and experiment, which are part of a scientific *practice*, with very possibly no particular 'method of discovery' at all.

On the other hand, it is not clear why this seemingly anti-deductivist stance on scientific method needs to be *inconsistent* with deduction from 'first principles' in the sense of the previous quote. As pointed out above, in a rationalist deductive method it does not particularly matter where our hypotheses come from (what experiment we derive them from). Taking them as *given*, we make deductions from them. These deductions then acquire an empirical content through a testing of predictions they yield. Specifically, Descartes's views about experiment suggest that experiments demonstrate *which* of a number of theoretical models of a particular phenomenon construed on *a priori* and principled grounds is real in our factual, physical world. This would be importantly *consistent* with Gaukroger's insistence that deduction as understood by Descartes is no method of discovery. For discovery is of what *exists*, and this is what only observation and experiment can show. But the reasoning remains a deductive one from causes to effects, not an inductive one from effects to possible causes suggested by them:

My own procedure has been the following: I tried to discover the general principles or first causes of all that exists or could exist in the world, without taking any causes into consideration but God as creator, and without using anything save certain seeds of the truth which we find in our own minds. After that I examined what were the first and commonest *effects which could be deduced from these causes*; and it seems to me that by this procedure I discovered skies, stars, and earth, and even, on the earth, water, air, fire, minerals, and several other things which are commonest of all and the most simple, and in consequence the easiest to understand. Then, when I wanted to descend to particulars, it seemed to me that there were so many different kinds that I believed it impossible for the human mind to distinguish the forms or species of objects found on earth from an infinity of others which might have been there if God had so willed. Nor, as a consequence, could we make use of things unless we discover *causes by their effects*, and make use of many experiments (Descartes, *Discours*, 1637/1984, part 6, section 3; in the translation I follow Garber 1992: 293–4; italics mine).

As for 'particulars', '[c]ertainly he intended animals and human beings', Garber (1992: 296) writes, 'magnets (...) and other reasonably complex terrestrial phenomena'; descending to these particulars is to give 'an account of what

how they actually discovered their truths (see further Gaukroger 1993: 170–1, 183). See also Descartes (1637/1984) *Discours*, part II, section 6, where Descartes finds the ancient geometric 'analysis' and the modern 'algebra' too abstract to have any use at all ('d'aucun usage') in the application to natural phenomena.

these particulars are, i.e., and account of their natures, their internal structures'. 'What God wills', is, in my terms, which possible world becomes real (or which nature comes to exist): this will be just a historical fact, and there is no more to say about it. The role of experiments in the above quote is puzzling at first, given that we seem to find a straightforward reversal of the rationalistic ethos of 'deduction of effects from first principles' described in the beginning of the passage. It may seem as if Descartes admits the need for experiment over and above *a priori* and deductive thinking, in the sense of a necessary deduction of *causes from effects*, rather than vice versa. Should one conclude that the method of science in Cartesian rationalism is, after all, no different from what we call today the *hypothetico-deductive method*: reasoning from effects to causes by gathering experimental results and framing a hypothesis that explains these data? The hypothesis is then supported if it explains the experiment, coverage of data being the hypothesis's right to existence.

This latter conception of method would be consistent with a purely instrumentalist notion of theory, however, and with explanatory principles being 'mere' hypotheses that have no status except for their utility in deriving a given effect. We surely have reason to believe such conceptions absent in Descartes. Moreover, by the early seventeenth century, a traditional instrumentalist attitude towards astronomical theories had long been given up, in favour of a more realistic attitude among their best practitioners, including Copernicus, Brahe, Kepler, and Galileo, who opposed the Aristotelians in this respect as well (Shea 1998: 810). It does not seem an attractive conclusion that Descartes upheld his ideal of rationalist science, but, when facing actual explanatory practice, renounced that ideal and resorted to experimental reasoning from effect to cause.

Indeed we need not draw that conclusion. One function of experiment in Descartes is to search for facts that are *not* apparent, facts which, once found, have then to be explicated by deduction, conforming to the same standards of certainty and deduction that Descartes usually emphasizes. In the following passage, which follows the above, a *second* function of experiment reveals itself:

After this, reviewing in my mind all the objects which had ever been presented in my senses, I believe I can say that I have never noticed anything which I could not *explain easily enough by the principles I had found*. But I must also admit that the powers of nature are so ample and vast, and that these principles are so simple and so general, that I hardly ever observed a particular effect without immediately recognizing several ways in which it could be deduced. My greatest difficulty usually is to find which of these ways (of deducing the effect) is correct, and to do this I know no other way than to seek several experiments such that their outcomes would be different according to the choice of one or another way of deducing the effect (ibid.).

In short, once a particular fact is found, it can be explicated in a great many (too many) different ways: it is compatible with too many explanations, deductions, and principles. It is with respect to this difficulty that the *second* role for experiments comes in: they are *crucial experiments* (Garber 1992: 133), allowing us to discern, among various possible explications of a phenomenon, which deduction is the real one. Harvey's explication of the movement of the heart, Descartes thought, was perfectly *possible*, although his own was *real*, on the grounds of experiments described in the *Discours*, part V (and in the *Description du Corps Humain*, cf. Garber 1992: 133). Put differently, experiments tell us about a historical fact, an aspect of God's will: they distinguish 'objects found on earth from the infinity of others which might have been there'. Crucially, then, the experiment, rather than *determining* the theories, *selects among them*. Theory formation and model-building, as one might put it, if somewhat bluntly, proceed independently of the world and experience; the actual theory or model one ends up with is an expression of the creative activity of the mind, modulated by what experience suggests.

If we had an exhaustive list of causes that are conceivable for our minds, then crucial experiments eliminating all but *one* of these causes *would* make us know with the desired absolute certainty that the remaining cause is the true one. Descartes's rationalist account of scientific method is then *not* the hypothetico-deductive one: the aim *is* true explanation by appeal to reasons that our minds can conceive, not merely explanation by appeal to a hypothesis obtained by induction that happens to agree with all observations and experiments: 'Experiment is required, not as in Bacon or in more modern theories of experimental method to *start* possible lines of *induction*, but to *close off* possible lines of *deduction*' (Garber 1992: 136; my emphasis). We are still reasoning here from previously known causes to possible effects. It is merely that from experiments we learn about *actual* effects. This is sensible also because our ability to *explain*, as such, is no guide to *truth* (or that the explanation is correct). As Hacking (1982: 84) points out: explanation as such is *too easy*. In my terms, it does not guarantee *existence*. Quite similarly, the problem with explanatory models in early versions of generative syntax, we shall see, was not that they did not cover the data (generate the relevant languages), but that the derivations/explanations employed lent no credibility to their reality or existence. The generative principles were *too powerful*, and they had to be matched against constraints arising from the study of human language acquisition (see Section 5.2).

The scientific practice of the Minimalist Program shows some interesting historical affinities with Cartesian-rationalist method as now sketched. In particular, we will re-encounter the method of deduction from first principles (though, again, mere deductive coverage of data will not be what counts for explanatory benefit). Thus, viewing language as an optimal solution to a design problem—meeting conditions on usability for a language organ newly introduced into the brain—is a way of construing the language faculty *on principled* grounds. These will then guide the construction of particular generative rule systems, and there will be an entirely empirical question about whether one such perfect solution—as there may be several—is real. Again there is an emphasis on the development of a coherent system of human grammar as the latter *might* look like, and only subsequent to that a question how to fit actual human languages into this system. Factual utterances and public language uses are no more than effects here, to be deduced from a highly abstract account of linguistic structure, built up from a small number of explanatory principles and conceptual necessities.

By way of contrast, consider the foundationalist idea of wishing to *ground* our theoretical abstractions, and to trace their *origins*. Early in the history of generative grammar, philosophers such as Quine suggested that phrase boundaries were descriptive artefacts whose actual 'psychological reality' was to be doubted. 'Psychological experiments' were proposed, in which the perceptual displacement of 'clicks' was studied as potential 'psychological evidence' for the 'psychological reality' of perceptually invisible phrase boundaries as postulated (see Bever, Fodor, and Garrett 1974; and Chomsky 2002: chapter 4, 126–7, for comments on the history). The click experiment was such that a tape was played with some text. A noise was put somewhere, and the experimental subjects hearing the text were asked where they heard the noise. Interestingly, experimental subjects do not hear it where it is, but displace it somewhere else. This raises natural questions. Why is it displaced? Is it because the subjects unconsciously perceived some cohesive unit that they did not want to be interrupted? Could phrases be discovered by appeal to the preservation of such 'Gestalt' properties?

These experiments were to Quine's liking, the idea being that linguistic evidence needs checking against psychological evidence, though that was thought not to be true the other way around, a rather strange asymmetry: why should psychologists exclusively be in the role of *testing* linguistic theories, rather than contribute directly to them? (And why might there not be linguistic evidence for a psychological theory?) Indeed, putting the experiment to test is what naturally happens *first* when trying to put an experiment to theoretical use, rather than testing the linguistic theory. Thus, simple linguistic tests suggest that in *you spilled this*, there is no phrasal constituent [$_{?P}$ you spilled], although there is a (verb) phrase [$_{VP}$ spilled this]. Thus, you cannot ask a question that would return *you spilled* as an answer; on the other hand, you can ask questions that have the syntactic constituents as answers: 'What did you spill?' Answer: [$_{NP}$ this]. 'What did you do?' Answer: [$_{VP}$ spill this]. 'Who spilled this?' Answer: [$_{NP}$ you]. Hence one concludes that *you spilled* is not a constituent. On the assumption, moreover, that only a syntactic constituent can be elided, but not a non-constituent, we now predict that *you spilled* should not be deletable in ellipsis: and indeed, while in *you spilled this, and so did Manfred* (*spill this*), or in *Spill this is what you did*, the VP is deleted, there is no similar way to delete *you spilled*. Given such conclusions, and our reasonable concidence in them, we want, the psychological experiment to confirm them: the *experiment* is tested, not the theory, and may be rejected if it does not yield the right result.

This interpretive and evaluative process is not mechanical: it is a matter of judgement. There is no algorithm, Chomsky points out in the discussion cited, for interpreting the significance of an experiment with respect to a theory, and if the experiment yields wrong results in clear cases, the experiment may be rejected, not the theory. If the finding of the click experiments had been that the click got invariably displaced into the middle of the phrase (or a word), one presumably would have concluded that the Gestalt property was such that the click is placed right in the middle of the phrase (rather than that every phrase has two halves). Phrase structure theory is not what is revised, but the interpretation of the experiment. An indeterminacy lies in what the *experiment* tells us, not in theory-formation. While Quine (somewhat strikingly) argued that there was no 'fact of the matter' regarding phrase boundaries qua 'psychological' posits (see Quine 1960: 303), there rather appears to be no 'fact of the matter' regarding how to interpret the experiment (see Chomsky 2000: 58).

The moral of the story is that one should tend to take the ontological commitments of a theory seriously: if a novel theory says, on the basis of evidence, that phrase boundaries exist, the acceptance of that (and the assumption that there *is* a 'fact of the matter', even if the theory turns out false) should not depend on the extraneous standards of another, supposedly more fundamental science and its assumed experimental method.

Designing experiments is not a *recording* of phenomena—listening to how people use language, what they happen to say when, etc.—but a *creation* of them: phenomena that might have never been recorded in nature otherwise, or that we would never have attended to. On the basis of a linguistic theory, an experiment may be designed that tests a speaker's intuitions on something she would almost never say, potentially leading to interesting judgements that may turn out to have a more systematic significance. We cannot go and listen to utterances, and wait for an explanatory theory to arise from that. On the contrary, the theory *tells* us which data to record, and there are no mechanical *techniques* for finding data that might be relevant to discover answers to theory-determined questions about language structure. When Edward Sapir first found phonetic illusions—phonemes that native speakers have intuitions about but which objectively are not there in their phonetic output—it is obvious that merely recording output would not have served him well. As Hacking puts the general point:

One chief role of experiment is the creation of phenomena. Experimenters bring into being phenomena that do not naturally exist in a pure state. These phenomena are the touchstones of physics, the keys to nature, and the source of much modern technology. (...) Most of the phenomena, effects, and events created by the experimenter are like plutonium: they do not exist in nature except possibly on vanishingly rare occasions (Hacking 1982: 71–2).

Instead of saying that experiments *bring something into being*, we could equally appeal to the dissociation between nature and existence that I mentioned before.

The role of experiment is to *demonstrate existence* for a *nature* that one has determined. It creates an *effect*, for a known *cause*, in much the Cartesian sense. It is not that the cause *becomes known* to us through the experiment: this would be like saying that by seeing a concept that figures in our understanding to be instantiated, we thereby know the concept. On the contrary, we have to know the concept in order to see *it* instantiated. Kant's Thaler do not change in their features when I realize that I have them in my pocket.

This leads us, for the first of what will be many times in this book, to doubt the point of saying that a theory or concept 'represents the world', or stands in some inherent connection with phenomena out there. For Galileo, the point may have seemed obvious, for he frankly concedes that for it to be true that ideal geometric forms are inherent in nature, you have to abstract from an enormous amount of 'noise' (or empirical details). You have to distort the phenomena somewhat, and it is just expected that given the complexity of the real world, the laws you state won't be true in it. They will be attestable only in highly idealized conditions, conditions that have to be constructed artificially. The idea of science as representation seems misplaced here. For Descartes, if we succeed in providing experimental evidence that shows a theory or concept to be real, that does not show that there was a 'representation relation' between our concept and the world in the first place. It shows a historical fact: that a certain concept is instantiated. But that concept, Descartes tells us, is almost unavoidably only one among many, all of which are perfectly good causes of my observation of the relevant instance or phenomenon. Only one of them is an *actual* cause in our world, we may assume, but it is not clear how or why a concept becomes intrinsically 'related' to its instance, by being so instanced. There are concepts in our minds, and some of them happen to be instanced, as experiments show, but again, why do we need *representational relations* between the concept that is instanced and the world for this to be so? What we need are *concepts*, on the one hand, and *experiments* showing which of them have *instances* in our world, on the other. The representational theorist needs concepts and instances of them, too, but over and above these he has representational relations, which I see no use for.

The *natures* of things, also, I have argued, are as such independent of whether the things having them exist. Determining such natures does not derive from what exists, but depends essentially on our theoretical imagination and theory-internal criteria of success. We never know whether the concepts we are currently entertaining, be it *phlogiston, aether, aquatic animal, LF,* or *electron*, actually exist, in the sense of having an instance in this world. Whatever theory of some such theoretical conception, X, we entertain, the addendum 'if X exists' changes nothing in our theory. As we shall see in Chapter 5, in generative grammar we can use phrases such as 'LF as a level of representation in the human linguistic brain, if it exists, has such and such properties', leaving the question of actual existence aside, as a matter that only the future will tell. In this sense, talk about theoretical entities, whatever they are, is predicated on the presupposition of existence. Theoretical progress will eventually have more to say about existence, but for our theory to develop we need not speculate on existence. The relation of 'representation' or 'reference' seems in this way to be at odds with a rationalist conception of knowledge and scientific inquiry. As John Yolton, quoted above, says, 'the world as known *is* the world of ideas' (or what I have just been calling 'concepts'), and existence does not add to the *content* of our ideas, even though it does to the relevance of using these ideas in the description of our world.

It is in this context that doubts expressed by Chomsky about the usefulness of a notion of 'reference' have their place. Here is how Chomsky responds to the philosophical charge that to understand the semantics of science and make scientific discourse intelligible to us, we have to posit referential relations between scientific concepts and entities in the world:

Pre-Avogadro, chemists were using 'atom' and 'molecule' interchangeably. To render what they were saying intelligible, do we have to assume that they were referring to what are now called 'atoms' and 'molecules' (or what they *really* are, which no one today may know)? After the Bohr model of the atom was available, it was proposed that acids and bases be understood as potential acceptors or donors of electrons, which made boron and aluminium chlorides acids alongside of sulphuric acid (...). Were earlier scientists *really* referring to boron as an acid? Must we assume that in order to render their views intelligible? To take a simpler example, closer to home, must we assume that structural phonologists, 40 years ago, were referring to what generative phonologists call phonological units, though they hotly denied it—and rightly so? Structuralist phonology is surely intelligible; without assuming that there are entities of the kind it postulated (...).

What is required in all such cases is some degree of shared structure. In none of them is there any principled way to determine how much must be shared, or what 'similarity of belief' is required. Sometimes it is useful to note resemblances and reformulate ideas, sometimes not. (...) Nothing more definite is required to maintain the integrity of the scientific enterprise or a respectable notion of progress towards theoretical understanding (Chomsky 2000: 152).

That is, 'talking about' or 'referring to the same thing' is a variable notion about which nothing of great generality can be said. To explicate it, or the intelligibility of scientific progress, we do not need the notion of reference. We *need* to bring out a difference between doing science and science fiction, but *here* the notion of reference is of no help. What distinguishes Bohr's *electrons*, Galen's *Four Humours*, Democritus' *atoms*, Descartes's *tubes with animal spirits*, or our notions of *phoneme* or *IP* from the categories of astrology is not that the former have reference, the latter not. It is rather that the former categories prove theoretically fruitful in ways that the latter do not. As a *consequence* of that fact—a fact about the course of our understanding and scientific progress—rather than a presupposition for it, we may say that the former categories capture an aspect of the real world and in this sense conclude that they have reference. But we could not distinguish a good theory from a piece of science fiction by figuring out whether the terms of the one have 'real reference', while those of the other have not. Indeed it is part of the essence of the externalist notion of reference itself that how we *identify* referents by means of our concepts and understanding is *not* what decides over what our terms 'actually refer' to. In this way, 'actual reference' is an irrelevant notion for deciding which theory is better than another. Making decisions that something 'really exists', in Newton's words, is a matter of whether *we* accord reference to one term or not. This is not a matter of 'figuring out reference', but of interpreting experiments, comparing theories, and judging their fruits.

Given ideas that are or arise in our minds, science is an attempt to fit experimental data with our ideas and conceptions rather than vice versa. Brock's *History of Chemistry* offers striking examples of the way this happens, and leads to further doubts about the notion of *discovery*, over and above those about the notion of reference. Literally understood, the notion of discovery suggests the opposite of Galilean idealizations and experimental interference with nature. Discovery, intuitively speaking, is of what already exists, and it is, when given an empiricist connotation, like the mind's hitting upon something, which then induces in the mind an explanatory concept *of* that thing. Neither the rationalist's idea of idealizing entities in nature fits this notion of discovery, nor his way of matching data with a given theoretical model.

Consider Dalton, who, building on Lavoisier, invented chemical atomism in the late eighteenth century. Abolishing the previous theory of the identity of matter and all material substances, he land the ground for atomism by fixing a determinable empirical property of the supposed 'atoms', namely relative atomic weight. He assumed that compounds were formed by 'chemical synthesis', a process essentially depending on laws of composition for which Dalton assumed certain rules of simplicity (for example, having a binary composition, rather than a ternary one), none of which were in any way evident or suggested by data. Brock (1992: 138) calls them 'arbitrary', and apparently this difficulty plagued chemists for another fifty years.

Humphry Davy found Dalton's theory not simple enough. Dalton's atomism, married as it was to Lavoisier's elements, required an unattractively large number of atoms (nearly 50 kinds) which corresponded to that number of elements. Could the universe's design be so ugly? Davy 'found it impossible to believe that God would have wished to design a world from some fifty different building blocks' (Brock 1992: 160). His concern to preserve the intuition of nature's perfection stimulated William Prout (1785–1850), who was intrigued by the much simpler Aristotelian doctrine that all substances were *modifications* of a primary matter. He famously noted that the atomic weights of the elements were identical to integral multiples of the atomic weight of hydrogen. Maybe one should not say that he 'noted' this, for he rounded up his findings so as to get the whole numbers which alone would make his theory elegant and attractive. Nature *approximates* perfect solutions, but maybe does not realize them quite so often. Prout thus wondered whether hydrogen could be the basis of all matter, so that elements arose by clumping together such and such volumes of hydrogen. This, through a term coined by Berzelius, became known as 'Prout's hypothesis', a tantalizing speculation, so 'pretty' that experimentalists became tremendously intrigued by it, attempting to make it come out right. 'A continuous source of inspiration to chemists and physicists' well until the early twentieth century, 'the work done in support or refutation proved incredibly fruitful' (Brock 1992: 162).

With the advent of isotopes in the 1920s it was finally seen why Prout's hypothesis was essentially correct. With an advance in theoretical understanding of atomic theory, the data collected over the decades finally formed a coherent and rational pattern: they made sense. Importantly, much of the inquiry before was not driven by 'ontological concerns'; indeed, these were largely brushed aside ('Atoms are round bits of wood invented by Mr Dalton', H. E. Roscoe said, in 1887: see Brock 1992: 128), but this did not prevent progress. Instead of asking what these atoms 'really' *were*, inquiry was driven by the intuition that a simple and pretty law should come out right and a reason for an emerging pattern should be found. In the same sense, as we shall see, the Minimalist Program in linguistic theory is driven by an elegant and tantalizing speculation: that the laws of natural language reduce to the barest essentials, those minimally needed for the language 'organ' to interface with non-linguistic systems in the mind/brain, as well as entirely general laws applying to computational systems in nature. Data may prove too recalcitrant to make some such hypothesis come out right empirically. But it is too intriguing to simply dismiss.

Did Prout *discover* the unification of matter? His was rather a theoretical proposal, a visionary hunch, involving posited entities, versions of which, in the course of history, came eventually to seem more trustworthy than other candidates, as experiments suggested their existence. Did *Dalton* discover the atom? Does it make sense to even ask whether what atoms in something like today's sense were 'really there' for Dalton to be able to hit upon them? Or was it not rather that Dalton's mind creatively came up with an intriguing *concept*, which some given data did not seem to rule out, and which then proved fruitful in the creation of further data, so that it became eventually established or selected?

However these questions might be finally answered, there are reasons for doubt about the strategy of insisting that science is intrinsically a 'representation' of the world or 'about' it, rather than a way of experimenting with *concepts*, reflecting the course of our theoretical understanding, in the light of which we then attempt to arrange messy and recalcitrant data (parts of which we create) into a pattern that makes some coherent sense to a mind structured like ours. Engaging in experiments will never mean that we can compare our concepts with the things that we conceptualize in terms of them. In the case of language, anyhow, there simply does not seem to be any phenomenon in nature to compare our human concept of an Inflectional Phrase (IP) with, e.g., again, it is not clear why over and above such theoretical concepts, on the one hand, and their possible experimentally established *existence* (in the present sense) on the other, we need the metaphysical notion of *reference* too, and the related notion of 'representation of the world'. We can clarify and improve our concepts, and test experimentally whether the empirical phenomena we face allow them to be useful. If they are, we suggest our concepts have existence: they are not 'empty', in Kant's sense. But there are no metaphysical conclusions to be drawn from this as regards the 'real' or 'ultimate' structure of the world.

None of this is to point in any sense in the direction of a 'coherence theory' of knowledge, if this entails that we cannot interpret our scientific theories realistically, or attribute reality to them. That we need not draw metaphysical conclusions does not mean that the theories that we creatively devise do not either fit or not fit the world. Chomsky, indeed, plausibly suggests that we should 'attribute "reality" to whatever is postulated in the best theory we can devise' (Chomsky 2000: 95), be it animal spirits, rational spirits, the aether, or gravitational waves. The progress of science alone will resolve disputes over the actual existence of things whose bearing on reality we assume. There was no sense, really, for H. E. Roscoe, cited above, to tell Dalton that his atoms 'had no reality', or were a mere figment of his imagination. Whatever body of theory chemistry had before the 1920s, this theory had whatever 'reality': it had. Our concepts cannot by their nature fall short of 'reality', it may just happen that some concepts make better sense of the phenomena than others. Pegasus fails badly in this respect, and the aether has ceased to fare much better, though it once did. There are concepts we use, and there is the world, and there are fashions as well as progress, in which various concepts become selected for their use in making sense of the world. But the world does not determine the concepts (or experiment the theory), nor do concepts seem to tell us something ultimate about the real nature of the world.

From this we can also derive the recommendation not to *prioritize* the kind of sense that scientific concepts make of this universe over the sense that concepts like *sunset* make of it in the language of lovers. Only if concepts *were* intrinsically relational or representational would there be a temptation to say that *scientific* concepts have a monopoly on capturing the represented world. If concepts are not intrinsically representational, as I argue here, and scientific research is experimentation with conceptual structures we find occurring in our minds, then there is no reason to suggest that scientific concepts 'represent better' or more accurately the world than any other vocabulary that is the outgrowth of human mental creativity. There is much to recommend an idea we seem to find in Descartes, that natures of things as we determine them in thought relate contingently to the world, their instantiation being a historical matter, or that the scientist experiments with mental structures, so as to make some use of them.

Overall, then, rationalism in the philosophy of science is not quite understood here as a distinctive philosophical doctrine, as some of its basic commitments, such as the role of experiment and idealization, its anti-foundationalism as well as its explanatory direction from causes to effects, may be more deeply inherent in modern Galilean science as such. Rationalism thus understood has ontology flow from theory, rather than theory constrained by ontology; and it does not have a clear *methodological* content in the sense of suggesting some specifically 'rational method' of discovery, or a method for inferring possible causes from given effects. More appropriately, experiments are designed to create effects from known causes.

I will return to the idea that the Minimalist Program's practice is Galilean science applied to the mind. For now let us turn to *empiricist* constraints on inquiry, many of which I will argue reflect a methodological dualism rather than naturalism and underlie the implicit or explicit oppositions in various philosophies to a rationalist account of human nature. Having argued against such empiricist constraints on inquiry, we will be in a position to readdress biological objections to the notion of human nature in Chapter 3.

2.3 Double Standards

Being a methodological dualist, in Chomsky's (2000: e.g., 112) terms, means to judge science by a 'double standard'. On the one hand, physics, chemistry, or biology are reckoned to be basically self-justifying, or to set standards of rationality and justification. Their results are not held to be subject to the critical assessment of philosophers. On the other hand, the sciences of man, such as the cognitive sciences or linguistics, are not. Independent criteria are brought to sit in judgement over the evaluation of scientific success or the entities postulated by a theory; e.g., special evidence—'psychological evidence'—is demanded if linguistic theories are to be interpreted realistically. Such criteria effectively prevent these new sciences from being received, in the way I suggest they should be, as studies of human nature and have frequently led to the rejection or reinterpretation of the generative framework that I am assuming here.

A particularly prominent instance of this scepticism towards generative grammar, mentioned in the previous section, is the view that the abstract underlying structures posited in it have no 'psychological reality'. On this view (see, e.g., Devitt and Sterelny 1987; Devitt 2003), the generative theory of syntax is not about the mind. It is about something else, called 'linguistic reality', distinct from 'psychological reality'. Generative grammar, on the other hand, at least as I will present it in Chapters 4 and 5, *makes* no claims about 'psychological reality', only to reality, in the sense of the previous section (the sense in which we should 'attribute "reality" to whatever is postulated in the best theory we can devise' (Chomsky 2000: 95)). The notion of 'psychological reality' does not enter in its formulation,[15] nor does 'linguistic reality'. The notions are as irrelevant as those

---

[15] In all fairness, it has to be noted that the notion did enter, historically. I consider this a strategic mistake.

of 'chemical reality' would have been when levelled against chemistry prior to the twentieth century, when it was still disunified with physics.

All the same it *is* assumed in generative grammar that the abstract grammatical structures posited are represented in the mind/brain. Surely, the relevant structures are not visible in the external acoustic output of actual utterances. They can also not be regarded as statistical patterns in human speech behaviour. Theories of actual mental grammars in human heads claim to be *true* of these structures of mental representation, no matter how ignorant we are about their underlying nature at the neuronal level.

Davidson famously argues that these assumptions are unsound, or rather superfluous. It

> does not add anything to this thesis [a descriptive model of the speaker's linguistic competence] to say that if the theory does correctly describe the competence of an interpreter, some mechanisms in the interpreter must correspond to the theory (Davidson 1986: 438).

But standard accounts of animal communication systems such as bee dance *do* take the form of a search for actual mechanisms that implement processes described at the computational level, aiming for a unification of cognitive psychology and neurobiology (Hauser 1996; Gallistel 1990). It would seem that according to Davidson, naturalistic inquiry of this kind must be abandoned for an entirely different one, at least in the case of the *human* communication system. Substantive arguments are needed for such a methodological dualism. It clearly seems that facts about brain structure, evolutionary and ontogenetic pathways, etc., might well constrain possible theories of the recursive procedure underlying the generation of human linguistic expressions, hence subjecting it to empirical tests. We shall also see that in the Minimalist Program much of the design of human grammars is held to have to do with how syntactic computations meet interface representations between language and thought (the semantic interface, SEM), on the one hand, and language and sound (the articulatory-perceptual or 'sensorimotor' interface, PHON), on the other. That is, much of language design is constrained by how a cognitive system is embedded in the rich context of the modular architecture of the mind/brain.

For a concrete example, sentential syntax might have derived evolutionarily from the structure of the human syllable, itself deriving from the reconfiguration of the vocal tract due to consistent bipedalism (Carstairs-McCarthy 1999). If so, a deeper understanding of a central design feature of human language *will* crucially depend on the internal anatomy of the human organism. While these internal aspects do not act as constraints when setting up logical formalisms supplied with a model-theoretic semantics, it seems essentially bizarre to suggest on *a priori* grounds that they do not matter for a description of human knowledge of language.

Other constraints have been proposed for what *evidence* a theory claiming 'psychological reality' rather than merely 'linguistic reality' is allowed to build on.

For the linguist, Quine stipulates, though not for the biologist, 'the behaviorist approach is mandatory', the reason being that in acquiring language:

we depend strictly on overt behavior in observable situations (...). There is nothing in linguistic meaning (...) beyond what is to be gleaned from overt behavior in observable circumstances (Quine 1987: 5).

For Davidson, equally, what counts as relevant evidence is 'what is open to observation', namely 'the use of sentences in context' (Davidson 1990: 300). And according to Devitt and Sterelny, for 'linguistic evidence' to qualify as 'psychological' it must be of the 'behavioral sort needed to throw light on what is going on in the head' (Devitt and Sterelny 1987: 143).

Factually speaking, none of these strictures is observed by linguists, and much of the body of theory that has been collected over the last decades would simply not be there if the constraint *had* been obeyed. Linguists have posited categories that are phonetically null, and these cannot obviously be witnessed in 'overt behavior in circumstances', but are posited to explain semantic phenomena that otherwise have no better explanation. Phonemes, too, which build up phonetic representations underlying speech, cannot be 'gleaned' from the acoustics or physics of speech; nor could word meanings be acquired by a creature lacking the necessary concepts to grasp them, by having that creature look at what people do and say. Linguists also regularly appeal to structures in Japanese to make hypotheses about the underlying structures of German, which seems natural, as the same kind of mental organization underlies and enables the learning of both (as we notice when the German child is transferred to Japan). Electrical brain activity, too, is a subject of study relevant to the understanding of linguistic structures. Evidence, in short, comes from wherever it comes, and there is no need or motive to restrict it beforehand.

There is then a question of whether we should *revise* current linguistic theorizing so as to make it accordant with these strictures. Some writers, endorsing Davidson's claims, such as Stokhof (1999, 2002) appear to recommend just this. Like Quine, Stokhof argues that the stipulated paucity of permitted evidence is a requirement, following directly from what the epistemic situation of the language-acquiring child and the person engaged in communicative interactions is like. This is because the investigating scientist, the child, and people generally have only emitted noises to go on, which they may register. Over and above that, they may pick some features of the situation, test assent and dissent when prompting the person to be interpreted with a question like 'Is this an X?', and apply domain-general methods of logical induction.

But human organisms when acquiring language are, non-controversially, in certain internal biological states. Behaviourism applied to the structure of physical organs is out of the question, non-controversially, as no one proposes to reduce the structure of such organs (brain, immune system, visual system, etc.) to what can be 'gleaned' from the external environment (light, nutritional inputs, parental love, etc.). To say the same *is* controversial in the case of the human mind is, again, a kind of methodological dualism that requires excessive justification in the light of a scientific practice that routinely proceeds otherwise. It is often as if philosophers draw a red line: the mental is different, somehow, for them, and different and special constraints apply before a theory pretending to be about the mind may be realistically interpreted; *its* evidence, but not evidence in biology elsewhere, is tightly constrained.

The behaviourist-empiricist will have to agree that a child acquiring language, too, is in a certain internal biological state that bears on its task, and can at least distinguish linguistic utterances from noises, in a way a cat cannot, no matter what input and reinforcements we give it. What he may sensibly doubt is what *role* this biological state plays in the acquisition of linguistic competence, and how *rich* its internal structure is. On the view that Quine and Davidson consider 'mandatory', it would seem that the internal structure would simply be very poor. Maybe it is reduced to the most primitive basis for general learning, such as having notions of identity and difference, or the ability to generalize from similarity. Call this the 'empty organism theory', which nothing *a priori* rules out, even though it would be ridiculed with respect to vision, metabolism, the liver, the growth of the embryo, etc. Note that, surely, the language system *does* exhibit features of organs whose growth is internally directed in this fashion, such as having critical periods of growth and only a loose dependence on external factors, which always play a necessary role only, never a sufficient one (see Chapter 4).

The empty organism hypothesis is as such a perfectly acceptable empirical research program, and maybe should be regarded in this way and then judged on its merits, rather than as a philosophical position or arbitrary stricture that dictates some methodology is 'mandatory'. The problem for any such research program will be that there are certain known linguistic and developmental facts to be explained, things that *any* theory of language would have to account for. Generative grammar has unearthed structural facts about human languages, and most prominent *philosophical* critics of the Chomskyan program in linguistics, such as Rey (2003a), Searle (2002), Nagel (1995), Devitt and Sterelny (1987), or Devitt (2003) do not question any of *these*. Hence the empty organism theorist has to derive *these structures* from the kind of evidence he permits, noises and air pressure waves scattered across contexts in a statistical distribution, *without* appealing to internal structures in the organism, except for structure of the most primitive and domain-general sort. That is, by collecting data about assent and dissent, or 'the uses of sentences in context' (although this is somewhat misleading, for we are dealing with noises, but in no way with *sentences*, on the behaviourist view), the empiricist will eventually have to arrive at phrases, projections, principles of covert movement, the subjacency principle, and so on, none of which is anywhere near visible in 'observable behaviour' characterized as such, i.e., non-linguistically.

The mandatoriness of the restriction was said to derive from the fact that the child, the interpreter, and the theorist face the same sort of impoverished data. But it seems clear that they do not face them in the same way. If they aren't empty organisms, we should expect them to be rather *differently* organized internally. The linguist comes along with his attained linguistic competence and world knowledge, but also his scientific competence and explicit knowledge of linguistic structures as underlying expressions in other languages. The interpreter also has attained linguistic competence, and world knowledge. The child by contrast is deprived of world knowledge and has a language faculty set in an initial state at the beginning of language acquisition, destined to develop in certain ways during the critical age associated with that particular system of knowledge. It would seem that the brains of these three people are different in the light of what they know, hence that they come with different preconditions when facing the data. No conclusions for methodology, it would seem, can be derived from the alleged similarity of their epistemological situation.

Suppose we posited grammatical mechanisms explaining certain patterns, and assumed these entered into language use, guiding linguistic behaviour. Quine (1972) forbids this. We are to speak of 'guiding' only when the rules are 'consciously applied' to 'cause' behaviour. When this is not the case, we just speak of a physical body obeying certain laws, such as a planet (see similarly Rey 2003). In the latter case of mere obeyance, we do not assign 'psychological reality' to some theoretical conception of the organism obeying the rules. That is, in the case of falling bodies, planets, etc., we may go ahead and postulate 'physical reality' to a particular conception of the nature of the object involved, but without a 'conscious application' of rules there is no analogous 'psychological reality' in the case of humans.

Why this stricture? What makes for the difference between the laws of language and the laws of gravity? The difference, Chomsky argues (2000: 95), is one of complexity. We obviously cannot account for the properties of the state that the language faculty of the child has attained and for the way it enters into language use, on the assumption that the brain has mass and obeys gravity. We have to assume *more* internal structure. Hence, to begin with, we say there is a language faculty in the child, but not in the planet, or the cat. This faculty has an initial state, say at birth, and a final state, in which the child recognizes certain distinctions and makes certain judgements. Then we try to account for the difference between the former and the latter state, and for how it is bridged in development, by appeal to certain principles. These, we say, organize the child's cognitive activity so as to rule out the forming of certain structures and to rule in others, making language acquisition possible in the way it happens.

Methodologically, our way of proceeding in the case of the planet and the child appears alike, and the surplus of structure is similar to the surplus of structure we need to account for insect navigation or bird song. The child is not studied differently from the planet, or the bee, or the bird. In all these cases, again we 'attribute "reality" to whatever is postulated in the best theory we can devise' (Chomsky 2000: 95). Organisms are just vastly more intricate than planets. But no, Quine insists we are not describing the mind of the child (the 'psychological reality' problem again). We may not speak of our guiding principles being 'mentally represented' in the child, though not in the planet. This Quinean stance clashes with a naturalism as understood in the present volume, and the naturalism that Quine made famous now proves to be of a very different sort.

Rey's recent papers (Rey 2003a, 2003b) raise other questions. According to Rey, a defender of functionalism and the Representational Theory of Mind (RTM), the linguist positing linguistic structures in the organism (or its brain) should not say that the structures he is positing are *there* in the brain. He should say instead that there are structures in the brain that *represent* the first sort of structures, this representational nature of mental states being intrinsic to them. The notion of representation here is the standard philosophical one: a relational notion, representations being representations *of* something that is external to the representations themselves. In short, we should not talk about verb phrases in the mind/brain, as we will. Rather, we should talk about certain structures in the brain *representing* those verb phrases. But what is the point of introducing this 'representation' relation? Why, instead of simply and straightforwardly making a theory about the contents of the mind, make a theory about structures *representing* the contents of the mind?

In personal communication, Rey suggests that if one postulates something like movement processes—dislocations of phrases in a phrase marker, see Section 5.4—one would not want to take the theory of Movement *literally*, in the sense that these movements really go on somewhere inside the brain. This problem would be avoided, Rey argues, if one were to say that there are merely internal representations in there that *represent* the movement processes. But the problem need not be avoided in this fashion, and standardly isn't. The abstract characterizations that generative grammar provides are meant to be true of the mind/brain, but do not commit us to describing the reality thus characterized in the very same terms as used in the abstract theory. At the level of cells, very likely, much of our descriptive apparatus will prove inadequate. In the meantime, nothing prevents us from taking our characterizations to be true of structures represented in the mind, rather than representations of these structures.

Devitt, similarly, recognizes Chomsky's point that 'knowing a language involves internal representation of a generative procedure' (quoted in Devitt 2003: 108), and, with what appears to be a jump of his imagination, interprets this to mean that speakers 'stand in a *propositional attitude to representations of* [*the rules of language*]', hence in terms of a *relational* characterization of the knowledge in question. But there is no talk of propositional attitudes in the quote taken from Chomsky (at least in the technical philosophical sense, where these things are indeed relational), and no assumption of a representational theory in the sense that the internal mental structures in question (which the child undoubtedly needs) are representations of something else. Devitt makes a concrete suggestion for what this something else is, namely the linguist's *theory* of the child's language faculty, so that the child comes out as a theorist: 'That theory, hard-won by the linguist, is precisely what the speaker tacitly knows' (p. 109). But this is hard to believe. I see no more reason for a plant to have a theory of how its organs grow than for the child to have a theory of what the structures of its language are (see further Leslie 2000 and Chomsky 2003: 316ff. for discussion of the 'theory theory').

In Rey's case, as in that of the other philosophers above, it is as if there is something deep and mysterious about the mind. Something else is suggested as a topic of inquiry, be it *behaviour* (Quine), *representations* with certain mental 'contents' (Rey, Fodor, Devitt), or *neural nets* implementing the relevant structures, as in eliminative materialism. Rey's proposal, in particular, because it focuses on the *content represented* by structures in the mind—whatever these representational structures are—reverses the logic of formalism as understood here. What matters in formalism are the internal structures, not the 'intentional contents' they may come to be related to in the course of being accessed by performance systems. The structures are indeed assumed to contribute to our being able to ascribe certain contents to organisms, and to explain their functioning, but I see no good reason why we should move up to a level of abstraction where we pick out the structural-physical forms in the organism by reference to the contents and functions that they contingently come to relate to when used.

Devitt and Sterelny (1987: 142–6) offer different grounds for requiring a stronger form of evidence for theories of the mind. They cite the problem that theorie of the computational system of language on offer (in 1987) have too many alternatives. We cannot feel sure enough about our theories of grammar to attribute them to the mind. They are just arbitrary algorithms, and if there is one such algorithm, there are many (pp. 142, 145). But while in formal languages, indeed, an algorithm is defined by its purpose, and there will unavoidably be many algorithms fulfilling the same purpose, human grammar design is a matter of fact (our mind is structured in whatever way it is structured), even if we never figure it out. For this reason each proposal for an algorithm is a proposal for *what the algorithm is*. As such it will be *true or false*, and it seems wrong to suggest that a theory of some domain cannot be realistically interpreted as long as it has no competitors. When scientific theories are underdetermined by evidence there is only one sensible response: to improve these theories as best as one can. We should not doubt their 'reality', because the existence of alternatives doesn't prevent a theory from having empirical content. As this is true of all *standard* scientific domains in the core natural sciences, and uncontroversial there, why should it be controversial in the case of the human language faculty? Why does a standard and familiar fact suddenly become fatal? It is not clear what grounds there are for assuming this dualistic stance.

In this connection it is interesting to note that moving towards an elimination of possible theoretical variants may require movement *up* the scale of abstraction, rather than down (cf. Chomsky 2002: 94). Suppose one assumes the existence of such a thing as a 'passive construction', as in *John was seen*. The theorist is then forced to decide whether *John is expected to be smart* is a passive construction too. But one might also classify the latter as another 'construction', namely the 'raising construction', on the grounds that *John* moves up ('raises') to the beginning in *John is expected to be smart*, while being interpreted in a different position in that structure (as in *It is expected that John is smart* or *It is expected for John to be smart*, where *it* has replaced the position of *John* in the raised cases). At one point in generative grammar, this apparently was a genuine case of indeterminacy, with no basis for deciding the question. The question arose whether the indeterminancy was principled and fatal. Interestingly, progress essentially eliminated the very question, as it abandoned the notion of a 'construction' as such, be it 'passive' or 'raising'. In its stead came the general principle of dislocating ('moving') something elsewhere in the clause under certain conditions, yielding the earlier supposed 'constructions' as mere emergent effects.

This example illustrates how indeterminacies in theory formation can be overcome in generative grammar, not by probing deeper into some 'psychological reality', but by *increasing* the level of abstraction, in a way that seems in fact standard in the sciences: if you find new principles that encompass previous ones, without inducing further complexity, adopt them. This result is in a marked contrast with the one that Quine continued to urge in Quine (1986), namely to achieve 'psychological adequacy' for the rule systems of generative grammar by moving *down* the scale of abstraction, and undertaking 'psychological experiments' and the study of speech development, the 'temporally successive increments in the native's actual learning of the language', a 'system of habits he successively acquires' (p. 186).

Searle (1992), not unlike Quine, finds that the state of the human language faculty at a given time—a set of rules to compute the properties of sound and meaning of an infinite number of expressions—is not a 'psychological' state, because 'it is incapable of giving rise to subjective conscious thought whose content consists of those rules themselves' (Nagel 1995: 109). Only if there is 'conscious access *in principle*' (a 'potential for consciousness'), can psychological reality be granted. In an interesting response to this, Chomsky (2000: 95–6) asks us to consider a standard account of linguistic variance in terms of left–right orientation. English is 'left-headed': the *left* edge of the phrase [*loves the kid*] determines the nature of the *whole* phrase, so that it comes out as a *verb* phrase. Japanese is *right*-headed, by contrast, a mirror image of English. Hence, we may suggest, English children set a 'head parameter' in one way, Japanese ones set it in another. None of them is aware of this parameter, or 'has conscious thought' of it; nor have their parents or schoolteachers. Hence, Nagel and Searle would tell us, the theory postulating the existence of the head-parameter is not about the mind. It does not 'cross the body–mind divide', as Chomsky puts it. The question is why. Why reserve the notion of 'mind' for only those mechanisms that we have a conscious apprehension of?

To make good their claim that psychological reality is to be denied to generative rules, Nagel and Searle must suppose that conscious access in the case of language is impossible in principle. That is, there couldn't in principle be a species, S', which was just like our species, S, and used the same grammatical mechanisms as we do, but was different in having conscious awareness of them. For, in that case, we would still be capable in principle of the conscious awareness that was said to be needed for psychological reality, and psychological reality has been denied. But then, why should we agree on the impossibility of a species S', which in fact seems perfectly possible? And what should prevent us from positing something like a left–right parameter as guiding our linguistic judgements and as part of our linguistic knowledge?

Chomsky (2000: 95–6) points out there *is* in fact, in the case of humans, the actual biological possibility of what we just supposed: two species behaving alike but differing only in awareness, the case of blindsight. A blindsighted person distinguishes reliably between certain perceptual stimuli, but unlike normally sighted persons has no awareness of her discriminatory power, and judges the stimuli to be identical. Blindsight arises from brain injury, but if it were propagated by a genetic mutation, it is possible that a species wholly comprised of blind sighted individuals could arise, which would differ from our own species in lacking awareness of and being unable to report perceptual mechanisms which remain operative. Viewed in this way, the Searle-Nagel point seems an arbitrary restriction on what is possible in the case of language. Just as the blindsighted species seems biologically possible, S' seems biologically possible. But then, by Searle and Nagel's own lights, we should have to conclude that the grammatical mechanisms in question do after all have the psychological reality that they were denied. It is a contingent fact about human nature that some of our mental aspects happen not to be conscious.

Looking at this line of argument, the only thing that should surprise us is why we engaged in it in the first place: the whole question of whether or not there could be a species S' is entirely irrelevant with respect to the question of whether or not we should posit a left–right parameter as an explanation for order phenomena in English and Japanese. The consciousness issue simply seems to be irrelevant to this explanatory concern.

In this section I have discussed a representative sample of twentieth-century philosophical misgivings regarding a form of research that claims to be no more than a methodological naturalism applied to the mind and mental structure, and hence human nature. Special constraints have been proposed for the study of mind that are factually unobserved in linguistic practice; others have been based on arguments concerning how 'psychological' and 'linguistic' reality, or psychology and biology differ, but none seems clear or motivated enough to warrant strictures on naturalistic inquiry, which proceeds on its own course, stipulating structure when and where it is needed for explanations. Let us thus, in the next chapter, return to the challenge from the philosophy of biology that I left hanging in Section 1.4, and the vision of human nature that it implies.

3

Biological Internalism

3.1 Biology before Unification

Let us begin by returning to the verdict that the standard population-biological species concept, in conjunction with the standard measure of genetic variability we find in the human population, disallows any talk of a common 'human nature'. To start with, this point will lose force if our claim about aspects of such a universal human nature will not intrinsically depend on any claim about genetic (in)variability, as ours does not. We may claim, for example, that all human languages that children unfailingly develop (except in cases of serious pathology) are structurally alike and acquired alike, and detail this empirical claim by a theory of Universal Grammar (UG). By doing this, we have not claimed that the genetic basis of UG is the same in all humans; moreover, if UG fell from heaven rather then being encoded in our genes, nothing in our theory of UG or the claim that it characterizes an aspect of human nature would change, nor its degree of correctness. We independently know that the same morphology may develop in the organism despite significant differences in the genes that code for it. Nonetheless, the assumption of genetic identity has proved to be and remains a useful idealization of the facts. Genetically based language impairments like Williams Syndrome and Special Language Impairment clearly arise only now and then as rare deviations, and do not disturb the general uniformity or lead to genuine variety in some meaningful sense (cf. Jackendoff 2002: 98). Generally speaking, positing a universal type around which human speech behaviour patterns neither excludes variance in these behaviours, nor evolution.

Language development may not only be evolutionarily too recent to allow for much genetic variation, but the physical, external constraints within which language develops may also be too *weak* in this particular case (Chomsky 2002: 147, crediting the point to Jerry Fodor). Constraints to be met for an evolving cognitive system would be *strong* only if the environment exhibited specific structures that the organism *has* to meet in order for its genes to survive. If, e.g., children had an innate cognitive system of object recognition, a 'folk-physics' that pre-structured their experience so as to predict that solids offer no resistance to other solids falling through them, we would expect with some justification that such a system would be directly affected by the physical structure in the environment: the mismatch between environmental conditions and their internal cognitive construction would be vast, and the system would be unlikely to prevail. It is not clear, on the other hand, why *language* should be 'attuned' to the environment in some such way.

There do not seem to be specific conditions that language has to meet to prevail, except for being usable (communication, moreover, is possible in the absence of the specific structures we find in human language—all species communicate). True, we use language to talk about the world, but there do not seem to be constraints on doing so as specific as those we expect in a system detecting object permanence. There is no selective advantage in changing language to cope with *particular* conditions, an observation leading to doubts with respect to the project of assigning language an adaptive function and explaining it in those terms. In short, not only might there not have been enough time to tinker with the language faculty, there might also have been no evolutionary *point* in changing it. This gives two different rationales for genetic stability. The weaker the connection of language is to the outside world, the more stable we expect language to be across changes in environmental conditions.

As for Mayr's verdicts on the 'political incorrectness' of the 'typological' tradition, these arguments seem to have no basis. Lewontin (1993: 36–7) asserts that 'about 85 per cent of all identified human genetic variation is between any two individuals from the same ethnic group', and only 7 per cent lies between major human races in Africa, Europe, Asia, and Oceania. The typologist as I understand him here has obviously no reason to dispute such facts. He posits types where a given variation falls into a pattern, not where it doesn't. Traditionally, empirical arguments for human universals across surface racial differences have in fact been direct arguments *against* racial discrimination and *for* a universal rights movement. In the opening paragraph of the *Discours*, Descartes makes the classical remark that what he calls *bon sens*, the basic capacity for sound judgement or for telling truth and falsehood apart (essentially, *common sense*), is the 'most widely distributed good of the world', by its nature the same in all humans, who all possess that capacity as a whole, though using it differently. We may take this as an empirical assertion of the existence of one universal type, relative to which racial differences are simply irrelevant.

Whatever type we posit (and whatever nature of humans) will depend on observation and inquiry, and on whether positing some universal type has an explanatory significance with respect to the variation it is meant to encompass. The significance cannot be predicted, as it will depend on the actual development and explanatory scope of the relevant theory. Regarding human language, it is a basic empirical observation that all healthy humans have it, acquire it in relevantly similar ways, and can learn in principle any variety of it in an effortless fashion (at the relevant age). Still, virtually nobody in the early twentieth century would have predicted that there would eventually be grounds to detail an account of how precisely it is that all human languages pattern in essentially the same way, despite quite radical differences on their respective surfaces. Clearly, human linguistic competence might have turned out infinitely variable, a theoretically intractable domain not lending itself to any deeper explanation. Who would have thought that English, on the one hand, and Mohawk or Jemez, languages spoken by a few thousand speakers under quite different cultural conditions, would reduce to some rather trivial differences (Baker 2001)? In short, it could have turned out that there are no 'types' underlying all human languages, or even groups of them.

If, in the case of language or other cognitive competences we find (or posit, I should say, in the light of my doubts about discovery) universal types, this will not mean that empirically found variation among human languages was 'non-essential and accidental' (Mayr 2000: 81).[1] On the contrary, variation provides crucial data, as the *differences* between human languages must now be grasped as possible *variants* of the same underlying type (namely, UG), the number and kind of such possibilities being restricted by the nature of this type itself (whose existence commits us to such a thing as an *impossible language*). The point is that a given nature or underlying abstract 'plan' allows effective realizations within a *range of possibilities* that it demarcates. Variance is extremely 'relevant' and 'non-trivial', because each variance is a *prima facie challenge* to the typologist's hypothesis of essential unity. When the typologist posits a fundamental 'plan' underlying Tetrapod limb structure, say—'the pentadactyl limb'—he does not exclude some Tetrapods actually possessing fewer than five digits on any limb, some possessing more, and some possessing different numbers of them on the fore and hind limbs. The point of positing a type is that it allows for a certain variance, while limiting it in other respects. Assuming a Unity of Type in this and other instances will further invite interesting questions when facing a Tetrapod with a four-digit hand: 'Which is the missing finger? Why is it missing?' (cf. Webster and Goodwin 1996: 140–2). A type, in short, is not an 'essence' in some pre-modern metaphysical sense, but an *explanatory principle*, posited for and justified in terms of its explanatory power (see Section 3.3).

Concerning claims in the Neo-Darwinian Synthesis (NDS) that biology is a 'deeply historical' science (Mayr 2000, 2002), it is important to note that the unification of biology at the time was *incomplete*, as it did not include biological subdisciplines such as developmental biology (in particular embryology). Embryology uncoupled from evolutionary biology around 1900, staying separate from it until about 1980 (Arthur 2002). Developmental biology was not concerned with 'ultimate causes' in the sense of nineteenth-century biology—that is, the choice between 'God or natural selection'—asking instead for 'proximate' causes or mechanisms for the unfolding of the embryo. Functional explanations

---

[1] I will in particular not, in talking about certain abstract types characterizing human nature, be making a claim about the correctness of some neo-Aristotelian species concept, or a claim about something that all and only humans share (human uniqueness, on which see further below).

are irrelevant here, as the structure that the embryo or any other bodily organ gradually develops in ontogeny has no causal explanation in how useful or functional the end result of this ontogenetic process will eventually be. In this context, observations about the function of X set a problem rather than answering it: what a solution demands is a set of mechanisms. The developmental biologist's notion of an explanation was thus rather like that of standard experimental science: it was a search for *laws*, early examples being the generic developmental laws of von Baer and Haeckel in the early and middle nineteenth century. Contrary to the Neo-Darwinian's focus on adaptation as the main fact for biologists to explain, the developmental biologist's primary and crucially distinct explanandum was and is the *origin of form* (Amundson 1994; Kauffman 1993).

The NDS *remains* incomplete to this day. Biology is not unified, and there seems to be little basis at present for claiming what biology 'of its essence' is. There is the pending task of *truly* unifying biology through an integration of development and evolution ('evo-devo'), an idea that can accommodate quite different ideas about biology as a science. One of the most frequently quoted assertions within the NDS and today's evolutionary psychology has been Theodosius Dobzhansky's dictum 'in biology, nothing makes sense except in the light of evolution'. A recent article asserts that research has turned this dictum on its ear: 'Evolution, it turns out, makes no sense except in the light of biology—developmental biology, to be precise' (Pennisi 2002).

A particular emphasis in the emerging field of evo-devo is on 'generic' physical mechanisms that operate in morphogenesis and pattern formation quite independent of genetic tinkering (see Newman and Comper 1990; Newman and Müller 1999; and Arthur 2002, for recent reviews). These are mechanisms broadly applicable to both living and non-living systems, evoking the explanatory role of physical determinants of animal morphology, such as adhesion, surface tension, gravitational effects, viscosity, phase separation, and reaction-diffusion coupling. Many morphogenetic and patterning effects are the inevitable outcome of physical properties of living tissue on which generic mechanisms act. These have a prime explanatory role, shaping given 'morphological templates' at early stages of evolution. Subsequent evolution of genetic mechanisms can stabilize, refine, and conserve these, while not providing a basis for evolutionary novelty, in the sense of qualitative morphological changes with a discontinuous deviation from the ancestral state, by contrast to the much more frequent gradual changes realized through modifications in size, proportion, and shape.

Generic mechanisms are said to be responsible also for the continued generation of morphological novelty, and to be ultimately involved in the establishment of the individualized and heritable construction units of morphological evolution. While genetic control of developmental systems is undisputed, 'even in highly controlled forms of development the realization of morphology, particularly at the level of organogenesis, continues to depend on non-programmatic, epigenetic, mechanisms' (Newman and Müller 1999: 3). Relevant to these mechanisms are 'physicochemical, topological and biomechanical factors, as well as generic, stochastic and self-organizational properties of developing tissues, and the complex dynamics of interactions between these tissues'. The cause for the majority of novelties is said to be epigenetic in origin, hence not to lie with the genome. This internal causal factor would provide an explanation for the 'punctuated' character of the emergence of novelty in evolution: while the relative constancy of gene change predicts an equally constant rate of morphological change within an evolutionary lineage, the fossil record documents rapid jumps in form and structure, calling for an epigenetic causal factor between genome and form (Newman and Müller 1999: 4). Given an apparent lack of close correlation between genetic and morphological changes, developmentalist research of this variety explores the 'side-effect hypothesis', according to which genomic changes are ultimately peripheral to the problem of the origin of novelty or morphogenesis (Müller 1990). As Müller points out (ibid.: 120–1), if population genetics is not predictive of organic structures, the question of the origin of form becomes a genuinely internalist research program, replacing the methodological externalism that defines the gene-centred adaptationist program, a point to which I return.

It seems by now an established fact that mathematical patterns in plant geometry (such as the Fibonacci pattern), while possibly being adaptive, have no adaptationist significance or rationale; they are not random 'frozen accidents' of genetic evolution, reinforced by natural selection. Plants grow such patterns by mathematical rules of the physical world, working hand in hand with the plant's genes of course, but sparing them much of the work in the generation of natural order, and actually restricting their power: apparently, genetic tinkering cannot simply change the number of petals that some flower is bound to have by virtue of these constraints. Cell-division processes as well as the overall shape of cells do not seem to have to be coded in the genes either: cell division just works by itself, so to speak (Stewart 1998: 85–7). Here as elsewhere, nature has built on simple physical processes of a very general kind—processes provided free of charge by mathematical design and physical design of the universe. Put differently, cell division is not particularly 'life-like': it exploits given possibilities afforded by physical law.

The mathematical regularity of the Fibonacci sequence in the petals of a sunflower is, at first, a merely descriptive observation—surprising and interesting for sure, but also calling for an explanation. Here, however, we have a case where an actual physical *mechanism* has been offered to explain *how* such patterns in the living world derive from optimality principles such as the geometric principle of efficient packing during the growth of plants (Mitchison 1977). Biological functions have no role in this explanation. Optimality, in this example, is not motivated by functionality but falls out from physico-chemical mechanisms, as in the case of crystal growth (Amundson 1994, section 4, and Stewart 1998, ch. 6).

Stewart also reviews recent work involving a series of 'magic numbers', which happen to be the numbers of identical protein units that can be fitted together in an almost regular way, to form a nearly spherical surface. Viruses instantiate this mathematical pattern. DNA and RNA do too, implying that this pattern may prove significant in explanations of the development of life. While Crick and Watson have called the genetic code (and hence us) an accident—the 'frozen accident'—there is evidence (Stewart 1998: 57–72) that it is not, and that the genetic code (and thus we) are something lawful and expected, with a hidden rationale that is an expression of natural law. Structures deriving from the principle of symmetry breaking are apparently at the heart of much of our understanding of pattern formation in the living world, and also in language (Moro 2000). Insights such as these now provide for a vigorous field of research that continues the tradition of mathematical biology in the sense of D'Arcy Thompson (1917/1966).

Nor does it seem *a priori* unexpected that such explanatory approaches to life would not apply to the mind. On the level of brain anatomy, we certainly find, as already mentioned, patterns of structural perfection (Cherniak 2004); and minimalism finds these in human grammar design, too. Our scepticism about the relevance of the above lines of research as applied to the mind may simply depend on sticking to dichotomies and dualisms that do not make sense. If anything, the essential feature of the kind of 'biomathematics' that fascinates contemporary writers like Kauffman (1993, 1995a), Goodwin (1994), and Stewart (1998) is its generality, which does not only abstract from physiological details of particular species, but from the difference between organic and inorganic nature altogether, given that the same principles are operative in both domains. The aim is a theory of emergent structures no matter whether these arise in societies of interacting organisms, organic systems, groups of cells, or collections of chemicals.[2]

At this level of abstraction, rules for generating a syntactic tree that represents a sentence in generative grammar, and rules for determining the branching pattern in a tree are essentially of the same nature, as Aristide Lindenmeyer's work on the fractal branching pattern of plants makes clear (Lindenmeyer and Prusinkiewicz 1990; Stewart 1998: 130–6). Lindenmeyer, a German biologist pioneering the

---

[2] In Kauffman's case, morphogenetic laws of self-organization in complex systems are not unique to the organic world—aiming as they do at a general theory of life:

ontogeny, the development of a fertilized egg into an adult, is controlled by networks of genes and their products in each cell of the body. If this unfolding depends on every small detail of the network, then understanding the order in organism would require knowing all those details. Instead, I shall give strong grounds (...) to think that much of the order seen in development arises almost without regard for how the network of interacting genes are strung together. Such order is robust and emergent, a kind of collective crystallization of spontaneous structure. (...) [L]ife is not located in the property of any single molecule—in the details—but is a collective property of systems of interacting molecules. Life, in this view, emerged whole, (...), not to be located in its parts, but in the collective emergent properties of the whole they create. (...) The collective system is alive. Its parts are just chemicals (Kauffman 1995a: 18, 24).

computational and mathematical characterization of plant development in the late 1960s, explicitly likens the explanation of regularities in the branching patterns of trees to Chomskyan rewrite rules that build a syntactic tree.[3]

Earlier still, computational biology in this sense was pioneered in Alan Turing's late theoretical work on biological pattern formation through 'activation-inhibition systems' (Turing 1952). Turing demonstrated that two interacting substances with different diffusion rates can generate stable patterns in space, as a matter of mathematical necessity. By now, this theoretical model, which Turing did not empirically attest, has been shown to be real and instantiated in the dynamics of the formation of mammalian coat patterns (stripes, dots, etc.; see Meinhardt 1995, and Kitcher 1999: 203–4). Again, this is explanatory and ahistorical biology, done in abstraction from molecular details.[4]

Human organismic structure may not have *come* to work so well without a measure of utility. But that the latter 'determines' the former appears to be a vision that much current theoretical biology does not support and suggests we should not be satisfied with. The general thrust of the above ideas seems remarkably out of tune with the metaphor of 'genetic programming', or the idea that the 'genes have created us, body and mind' (Dawkins 1976/1989). Why *does* the NDS and the picture it paints of the living world still have such a tremendous influence on our thinking about our own natures? Clearly, that picture of our own nature has much potential to change once ideas like the above are adopted or explored. Whatever a new and future synthesis of developmental biology and evolution may be like, it's unlikely to be regarded as an exercise in history rather than in experiments and laws. As of now, the least we can conclude would seem to be that it is simply premature to draw any large negative philosophical conclusions concerning human nature from current biology, let alone from biology as conceived in the NDS.

3.2 Mind as Function: A Critique

Today, texts such as Dennett (1995) make it appear as if the choice we face is *still* the nineteenth-century choice between 'God or natural selection'. When presented

---

[3] Kitcher (1999) uses Lindenmeyer-systems to argue for breaking what he calls the 'hegemony of the molecular biology', as such mathematical study of development does not depend on specifying any molecular base.

[4] Thus, e.g., ant social life, it turns out, is built on inhibition-activation patterns of the Turing kind as well (Hammerstein and Leimar 2002). Ants intelligently dispose of their corpses in cemeteries without anything like the help of purposeful planning, an architect, or a blueprint. An illustration of the same kind of point is the genesis of the nice geometrical pattern of slime mould aggregations. The slime mould is given no more form of 'instruction' than meant in organizing its behaviour: the order just emerges, spontaneously. We can see that the same explanatory principles apply to pattern formation in cell division, the form of early stages of embryos, and social organizations (Stewart 1998: 76).

by Dennett with a choice between 'skyhooks' and 'cranes', it seems as if we are back in the old nineteenth-century debate between the natural theologians and the evolutionists. Is the living world orderly and purposeful, or does it reduce to the meaningless brute and blind forces which modern physics takes to govern the universe? Post-Galileo, nature was deprived of a purpose, however, and the conclusion that thought is a property of organized matter, essentially drawn by post-Cartesian philosophers such as Locke, Hume, LaMettrie, or Priestley in the eighteenth century, was repeated by Darwin in the nineteenth. What *else*, one wonders, should be the option today (unless, of course, we reinstitute mind-body dualism on some non-Cartesian grounds).

The essence of Dennett's dichotomy is well summarized by presenting the full titles of Paley's (1802) and Darwin's (1859) epoch-making books:

Natural Theology: or, Evidences of the Existence and Attributes of the Deity, Collected from the Appearances of Nature,
versus
On the Origin of Species by Means of Natural Selection, or the Preservation of Favoured Races in the Struggle for Life.

Note that God *as well as* natural selection are explanatory options that fall squarely *within* the *functionalist paradigm* in nineteenth-century biology, which as such opposed the formalist school, with its rather different conception of internalist explanation: this is in many ways a more interesting opposition, and a historically more accurate one, than the one we find *internal* to the functionalist school. I will say more about the formalists in Section 3.3. Let us stay with the functionalists first, scrutinizing problems of functional explanation in Darwinian and Neo-Darwinian evolutionary psychology alike.

The following passage from Pinker illustrates the logic of functionalist explanation, as well as the old 'choice' between God or natural selection:

The 'complexity' that so impresses biologists is not just any old order or stability. Organisms are not just cohesive blobs or pretty spirals or orderly grids. They are machines, and their 'complexity' is *functional, adaptive design*: complexity in the service of accomplishing some interesting outcome. (...) Natural selection remains the only theory that explains how *adaptive* complexity, not just any old complexity, can arise, because it is the only nonmiraculous, forward-direction theory in which *how well something works* plays a causal role in *how it came to be*. (...) Because there are no alternatives, we would almost *have* to accept natural selection as the explanation of life on this planet even if there were no evidence for it (Pinker 1997: 161–2).

Let us first turn to the functionalist catch-phrase '*how well something works* plays a causal role in *how it came to be*.' This, on the face of it, flies in the face of the Darwinian doctrine that neither adaptation nor natural selection are sources of genetic change. Mutations are the sources of novelty, their causes are internal, and they are crucially undirected, hence not intrinsically functional. Functionality helps to explain novel organic forms in the sense of explaining their selective retention or elimination, and the changes in their distribution within a population over evolutionary time. Explaining how new forms arise in the first place on the level of the individual organisms is a totally different matter. As it stands, Pinker's phrase simply conflates function with genesis.

The source of this conflation may be a larger divergence in our understanding of *what exactly* natural selection in Darwinian theory *explains*. The view I am endorsing here departs from the fact that, as Godfrey-Smith (1996: 93) puts it, 'no version of Darwinism holds that natural selection explains how, against a given genetic background, a particular mutation which confers an advantage arises'. Still, this shared agreement leaves open whether natural selection primarily plays a *negative* role in evolutionary explanation (explaining why certain traits cannot or can no longer be found on the evolutionary scene), or whether it also plays a positive role. Neander (1995) in particular has argued that 'natural selection has a creative and not merely distributive role to play' (p. 586). Its role is merely distributive if what it explains is how the proportions of certain traits relative to a population shift over time, without ever explaining why any individual ever has a particular trait. This view will come out as the right one if we adopt the so-called 'statistical' interpretation of evolutionary theory, which contrasts with the 'dynamic' one (Walsh, Lewens, and Ariew, 2002). According to the former, evolutionary theory is a theory about the *structure of populations* only, not a theory of 'forces' acting on *individual organisms*—and hence, crucially, not a theory about any 'creative' forces. Adaptation is the necessary *consequence* of the reshuffling of populations that differential fitness, insofar as it is heritable, automatically engenders. But it is not a *cause*.[5]

---

[5] Walsh, Lewens, and Ariew (2002) compare natural selection to a sorting process of biased coins, as a consequence of which the frequency of the heads-to-tails changes over a sequence of trials (the bias of each individual coin corresponds to the fitness of individual organisms). The systematic bias explains the sorting outcome, but the bias is not the property of any individual coin, being a mean. In the same way that sorting is not a *force* acting on an organism: natural selection does not cause any individual organism to live or die. Sorting is an ensemble-level phenomenon, depending on a *sequence* of trials. Since natural selection does not apply to individual-level phenomena, it can not offer an explanation of them.

As for Neander's suggestion, she appeals crucially to the cumulativity of the adaptive process, in which earlier preservations and proliferations of some coadapted sequence of genes changes the probability of what subsequent variations will arise. Still, natural selection cannot but influence what subsequent variations will '*randomly* arise' (Neander 1995: 586; my emphasis). It still has no hand in how each single mutation takes place, the mechanisms of which remain the ones they are, whether or not they occur with other probabilities on the population level given a changed gene pool in which previous mutations took place. Neander's argument, one might say, depends on mixing two 'cycles of causation'. In a single-step selection process, she argues, there is a 'causal isolation' between each random/select sequence. Here the causal processes invoked are the organism-internal ones giving rise to a random mutation. In cumulative selection, she further argues, one random/select sequence is *not* causally isolated from the next. But, now, the notion of 'causality' has widened and invokes the gene pool in which certain distributional shifts have taken place.

So, again, we should refrain from ascribing to natural selection an explanatory role for evolutionary novelty, or for 'how something comes to be', in the way that Pinker appears to take for granted. For Pinker, an adaptationist explanation in evolutionary psychology starts from specifying a 'goal' to be achieved by the organism for the sake of its survival and reproduction, the likely structure of the organism's 'environment', and the engineering designs 'suited' to attain the goal in that environment. It then requires empirical data showing that the trait in question meets the engineering specifications and manifests signs of complexity, effectiveness, and specialization in solving the assigned problem. But strictly speaking, of course, nature does not know about 'problems' or 'goals', and does not 'create' solutions in the light of them. Talk of 'problems' that are 'solved' makes sense in the light of possible solutions we can envisage for them, but not if these solutions still have to be fabricated by evolution. Irrespective of the organism that 'solves' these problems, we cannot sensibly speak of problems being out there and waiting for a solution to be engineered for them.[6] At least for Darwin, organisms do not actively 'adapt' to their environments in the sense that the environment causes them to have certain designs. Organisms come with whatever structures they have, and then find themselves either lucky—in an environment that gives some of their structures a good use—or not. The environment selects (acts as a 'filter'), but it does not create: it does not craft organisms in its own image.

The metaphor of an evolutionary hill-climbing—with natural selection lifting the organisms to ever greater 'peaks' of adaptive perfection on a 'fitness landscape'—is in many ways misleading. As James (1880) had already warned in his critique of Herbert Spencer's 'Pop-Darwinism', the environment has no concern with design, being more like a cruel and dispassionate spectator watching variants in populations arising, dying, and reproducing.[7] It might seem obvious that the tree tops 'pull' the giraffe's neck higher and higher, but the environment doesn't play this shaping role. Spencer's version of Darwinism seems like the classical locus of perverting Darwin's vision into a form of crass behaviourism and empiricism, with environment alone determining what structure in the organism there should be. With Spencer's application of this claim to psychology and his other claim that progress to ever greater adaptive perfection was not only a meaningful notion but a necessary process, a *distorted* version of Darwinism entered the scene of the philosophy of mind, recently revived by Dennett:[8] the

---

[6] Even what seems like a perfect adaptation for a particular evolutionary 'goal' is as such no evidence for adaptation playing as such any explanatory role in it: even perfect adaptations may predate the problems it solves by millions of years (Lewontin 1990).

[7] I am grateful to Maria E. Kronfeldner for pointing me to James.

[8] Dennett (1995) talks of Herbert Spencer as 'an important clarifier of some of Darwin's best ideas' (p. 393). These ideas, for Dennett, appear to be Darwin's theory of evolution as such, for what he criticizes in Spencer's account are their social-Darwinist *applications*. 'Spencer was a Darwinian—or you could say that Charles Darwin was a Spencerian', we read, and also: 'the modern synthesis is

environment necessarily moulds the mind. Deprived of Spencerism, Darwinism seems as remote from empiricism as one can get.

Pinker's metaphor of the machine raises other problems, as machine architecture implies, and is taken to imply, specialization to some adaptive end. As remarked before, 'optimal design' in the *functional* sense—design suited to a specific 'goal'—is not what we are bound to find in the living world, where nature is a 'tinkerer' and satisficer, making do with solutions which may not work well in some absolute sense, but work comparatively well enough in a specific historical context. The more conflicting constraints there are—and conflict among constraints seems likely to *increase* as fitness does—the more the intuitive category 'optimal design' (when understood in the functional sense) loses a clear content. Optimizing involves *trade-offs*, with decisions being made at points that have unpalatable implications in a future into which selection cannot look ahead. Identifying body parts with an independent evolutionary history or functional explanation is difficult to start with, as the body is not a 'mosaic of traits' that each lend themselves to independent optimization (Gould and Lewontin 1978). If we allow selection to apply at several levels, from the gene to the organism, and from the group to the species (Brandon 1988), the sense of optimization becomes even more opaque. A feature that benefits a group may not benefit the organism within it, just as what is best for Microsoft may not be best for some of its employees.

The problem increases with mental traits. It is hard to *identify* mental traits on the basis of their functions if we mind of these as adaptive functions, for many of them have multiple functions, and solve multiple 'problems', possibly some that do not even yet exist. It remains unclear to what extent we can move from given *behaviours* informally isolated under labels such as 'incest avoidance', 'xenophobia', 'language', or 'cheater detection' to a genetically determined trait with some sort of coherent evolutionary and selectional history (see further Ahouse and Berwick 1998). Particularly in the case of mental traits, we cannot assume *a priori* that they are independent enough for selection to pick them out and optimize them separately, without affecting the others. This assumption requires groups of genes coding for particular traits to assort independently from others. But how would one establish that there are *segregating* genes for particular mental traits, in the sense in which Mendel showed that green and wrinkled peas assort independently?[9]

Spencerian to its core' (ibid.: 394). As a self-confessed 'good Spencerian adaptationist', Dennett assumes, adopting a phrase of Peter Godfrey-Smith, that 'there is complexity in the organism in virtue of complexity in the environment' (ibid.: 395). Apparently, Dennett's behaviourist intuitions lead him to discard a serious and well-established *opposition* between Darwinist and Spencerist thinking in evolutionary biology. See Hinzen (2004) for discussion.

[9] *Some* trait independence there must be on *a priori* grounds, Ahouse and Berwick (1998) concede, crediting the point to James Crow: otherwise evolution would 'grind to a halt, because any change

In this way, if evolutionary psychology starts by making predictions about particular specializations, cognitive subsystems optimized to some function, it is hard to see how it could be right (or promising) without some kind of 'massive modularity' being generally true. Pinker's (1997), Plotkin's (1997), or Cosmides and Tooby's (1992) program would thus do well to establish that architectural assumption on firm grounds, turning the mind into a myriad of modular subsystems lending themselves to independent optimization. This might be attempted empirically, which seems hard, or on *a priori* grounds, which doesn't seem hopeful either.[10] Massive modularity might be just a false assumption, but even *given* a massive modularity, optimization of single traits may be counter-weighted by concomitant difficulties in *unifying* computational products of separate modules so as to arrive at a single and coherent cognitive result.

Regarding the gene-centred adaptationist perspective in general, it is worth reminding ourselves that we do not know of direct causal chains from genes to behaviour, and that even if we had such knowledge, a similarity of phenotypic traits need not correlate with a similarity in the genes. A recent discussion of evolutionary psychology emphasizes 'a new appreciation of the gap between genetic activity and phenotypic outcomes' (see further Lickliter and Honeycutt 2003). Taking this together with the causal independence of developmental, epigenetic processes as described in the previous section, we see that evolutionary psychology inappropriately narrows the focus of evolutionary research to a particular conception of proximate causes of organic development (namely, the decoding of a genetic 'program'), and a particular conception of 'ultimate' causes which basically boil down to functional reasons for changes in this genetic program. But genes have lost their status as independent causes of development, buffered from the influence of extragenetic causal influences. There is no unidirectional chain from genes to organism. As Ho (1984) explained more than twenty years ago:

The classical view of an ultraconservative genome—the unmoved mover of development—is completely turned around. Not only is there no master tape to be read out [by the cellular "slave" machinery] automatically, but the "tape" itself can get variously chopped, rearranged, transposed, and amplified in different cells at different times (Ho 1984: 285).[11]

This evokes the developmentalist challenge again, but Darwin's 'branching tree' model of the evolution of adaptive complexity has come under threat in other, equally drastic, ways too. Genes need not pass 'vertically' from the parent to the

would change all the traits in an organism and so nothing of lasting substance could be built'. See also Schank and Wimsatt (2001).

[10] The *a priori* arguments have been taken on and usefully discussed by Fodor (2000).

[11] For contemporary discussion with relation to evolutionary psychology, see Lickliter and Honeycutt (2003); for recent empirical evidence that although genetic changes initiate evolutionary changes in development, genetic changes can also be the consequence of the latter, see Gottlieb (2002).

offspring, but may also pass horizontally, across species barriers, so as to initiate major genetic changes (Doolittle 2000). There is a *lattice* of life: its form is that of a bush rather than that of a tree; much of life (apparently well over two-thirds of the evolution of life on earth) evolves by means of *lateral* gene transfer, that is, single symbiotic events involving no Darwinian gradualism, competition, and struggle at all (Margulis and Sagan 2002). Darwin also simply assumed that gradual improvement was possible in general, but Kauffman (1995a: 152) calls this assumption 'almost certainly wrong', on the grounds that in a complex system such as an organism, *minor* changes may cause *catastrophic* changes in the behaviour of the whole. It is in this sense simply not clear what it means to talk of 'minor' changes, and how this is to be measured. Even where gradualism *does* hold (minor mutations give rise to minor changes in phenotype), 'it still does not follow that selection can successfully accumulate the minor improvements' (ibid.).

None of this is to say that psychology is not inherently 'evolutionary', or that there should be no further attempts to make functionalist explanations in the Neo-Darwinian paradigm. But it is to say that the availability of such explanations should not be our starting point or default assumption, and that none of these attempts can be heralded as first steps in a 'Darwinian science of mind' that might replace a formalist approach to language structure and function. The latter seeks to understand and characterize cognitive 'anatomy' prior to and independent of understanding its functional utility. Before explaining how something comes to be by appeal to how well it works, we need a *criterion* for 'functional design', 'adaptedness', etc., that is *independent* of actual traits, a causal *theory* of fitness, or how 'well' something functions. Fitness will clearly depend on a myriad of relevant variables, but if the project is to explain future morphologies of life in terms of the fitness values of present ones, we need a way of measuring fitness that does not depend on how it affects future morphological patterns. As a *measure* of well-functioning, fitness should itself be measurable without looking at what functions well.[12]

Wherever actual functions are not what a trait has been selected for, these functions cannot play a relevant part in the explanation of form, as noted. Evolution's tremendous inertia of form (Lewontin 1998: 117) itself, which should not make us expect a perfect match between form and function, would thus seem to recommend making the study of form or structure something *independent* from the study of function and utility, the latter being a contingent matter rather

---

[12] If differential fitness is what we are looking at—the relative fitness that similar phenotypes have with respect to one another—we will in particular have to note that fitness differences are not transitive, so that, if variant B is fitter than variant A in an environment where they compete alone, and C fitter than B, under the same circumstances, the order may be reversed when A competes with C alone, when all compete, and when the environment changes (Sober 2001). So we can't assume that, if B does better than A in some environment on the basis of some change in its genotype, selective pressures will drive it to greater proportions in the population.

than a lawful one. In the case of exaptations, the function follows from the form.[13] While some current exaptations may have been strongly reinforced by some adaptive effect they had earlier in their history (and in *this* sense be adaptations), there appears to be no *general* way of knowing which currently adaptive structures really are adaptations rather than exaptations.

I see no reason, then, to hold, with this generality, that the evolutionary process will 'engineer a tight fit between the function of a device and its structure', as Cosmides and Tooby (1997: 13) put it (implying that the function precedes our grasp of the structure and explains the latter), and that an organism can be 'partitioned into adaptations', which are either (*a*) present because they were selected for (in which case function plays a causal and explanatory role), or (*b*) present because they are causally coupled to traits that were selected for (in which case function again plays a causal and explanatory role), or (*c*) present because they are 'noise', injected by 'the stochastic components of evolution' (ibid.: 14). Non-functional and developmentalist explanations are basically disallowed in this scheme (to the extent that they do not fall under 'noise'). What is missing, in particular, in the statement that 'the evolutionary process has two components: chance and natural selection' (p. 13), is a third component: necessity. A tight fit between function and structure no doubt exists, but this is because whatever structures arise, the environment will select among them, and the appearance of a tight fit is a necessary *consequence* of a sequence of selective episodes that is long enough.

Talking *synchronically* about the function of a particular trait or organ can be an important heuristic ingredient in the analysis of form, but again need not necessarily be joined by talking about function in either a *diachronic* or *explanatory* sense. The synchronic functions are what they are: they or their analysis do not change if it turns out that evolution is not what we think, and our ancestors were imported to earth by extraterrestrials some 30,000 years ago. As Chomsky remarks, if that turned out to be the case, 'the technical sections of textbooks on the physiology of the kidney would not be modified, nor the actual theory of the functions computed by the retina or of other aspects of the human visual and other systems' (Chomsky 2000: 162), and nor, in particular, would the language faculty as described by UG, if the extra-terrestrials had equipped the humans with that system as well. What would change, that is, is history, or material and efficient causes, but not our account of function, making a concern with evolutionary history strangely orthogonal to the actual explanation of function in organic systems.

---

[13] 'Exaptations' are defined by Gould and Vrba (1982) as 'characters, evolved for other usages (or for no function at all), and later "co-opted" for their current role (...). They are fit for their current role, hence *aptus*; but they were not designed for it, and are therefore not *ad aptus*, or pushed towards fitness. They owe their fitness to features present for other reasons, and are therefore *fit (aptus) by reason of (ex)* their form, or *ex aptus*. Mammalian sutures are an exaptation for parturition. Adaptations have functions; exaptations have effects' (Gould and Vrba 1982: 55).

The notion of function employed by Pinker's or Cosmides and Tooby's evolutionary psychologist is, on the other hand, of its essence a *diachronic* one: the function of mental organs *is* to start with assumed to be one that derives from constraints on adaptation or conditions of existence in the course of its history. But then, whether and to what extent the working of the mind *does* in some significant sense reflect the environments and the scarce resources it has had to cope with is exactly what we want to *know*. In the case of anatomy, physiology, or the computational study of vision or language we *have* accounts of internal organismic structure that are ahistorical, and on the basis of those we might then look at history to gain a deeper understanding of why this empirically attested structure is what it is. But in the case of the evolutionary psychologist, the very structure of particular mental organs is *posited* on the basis of an assumption about adaptive history. The dependence of form on function is a matter of methodological principle, and it seems unclear why we can permit ourselves this methodology when studying the mind, though we apparently cannot when studying physiology (another methodological dualism).

In asking about origins and ultimate causes of existence rather than proximate causes of form and function, Pinker's or Dennett's research program is a *foundationalist* one.[14] It is not content with studying the mind and its properties, which Pinker, being a trained linguist, must know is *possible* without inquiring about either adaptive function or reasons of existence first. Generative grammar has not proceeded by engaging in adaptationist 'explanations' while developing its current body of theory. Clearly, the study of adaptation and conditions of existence is *no precondition* for the study of structure. In fact it seems that if generative grammar *had* proceeded by the logic of adaptationist explanation, it would have predicted syntactic structures radically *different* from those that current theory assumes. We should ask then, why, given some natural object, we should be making

> the working assumption that it was designed for some purpose. You dissect and analyze the object with a view to working out what problem it would be good at solving: 'If I had wanted to make a machine to do so-and-so, would I have made it like this? Or is the object better explained as a machine designed to do such-and-such?' (Dawkins 1995: 120).

No amount of intuition about 'purpose' ever *need* play an explanatory role for why the machine is built the way it is; the more crystal-like it becomes, the more the engineering perspective misses the causal forces involved. For an assessment of what sense it makes to inquire about 'the function' of human language in particular, see further section 4.2. To insist that, despite the considerations I list there, language structure *must* have a rationale in functional utility, is to reiterate the dogma that biology must work by a functionalist logic.

---

[14] It is striking that Dennett makes a strong plea for reopening 'why'-questions, which, he suggests, Darwin can answer for us (Dennett 1995: 22, 25; see also the opening question in the first chapter of Dawkins 1976/1989).

In fact, it is arguable that a non-functionalist research program investigating homologies of mechanisms entering into the human language faculty in the rest of the animal world is a necessary preface to a functionalist or adaptationist explanatory enterprise. Before resorting to an adaptationist account that aims to explain how something arises because of how well it works, we should know what trait it is that we actually have to give such an account of. If some mechanism used for purposes of language in humans is found in another species but not used for communicative purposes there, this entails that communication cannot be the adaptation in humans that explains why we have it. If, in addition to such findings, which now abound (Hauser, Chomsky, and Fitch 2002), we provide convincing evidence that mechanisms involved in the generative core of language reduce to a bare minimum (basically, the mechanisms of Merge, as we shall see), we face the consequence that the argument from design is 'nullified', as Hauser *et al.* put it: there simply would not be any intricate and specialized structure there that was especially shaped for its communicative utility in humans, hence would cry out for some adaptationist explanation.

As for shared mechanisms, there is considerable empirical evidence against uniquely human mechanisms special to speech, both as regards speech perception and production. Non-human primates also show an impressive range of conceptual abilities (concerning number, social relations, tools, geometry, etc.), without an accompanying capability to communicate them through some linguistic medium (see Hauser, Chomsky, and Fitch 2002, for discussion and references). It also appears to be true, as noted, that basic mental machinery, such as manipulating variables and recognizing abstract algebraic (non-statistical) relations between such variables are available to other species without having a communicative function there (Hauser, Weiss, and Marcus 2002). Even the basic ability to represent hierarchical structure of the specific kind needed in human phrase structures (Section 5.3) may be present, again in a non-communicative context, in *cebus apella* (McGonigle, Chalmers, and Dickinson 2003). Crucial as regards the infinite productivity of language is the *recursive* property of some of the abstract rules involved in it (the fact that they can apply again to their own result, so that a sentence can contain again a sentence, which can contain again a sentence, and so on). But recursion as such is not specific to the domain of communication either, as it is used in number, planning, navigating, or foraging as well. None of the above is to deny that language may have conferred an enormous advantage on its speakers after it existed, but it throws a large doubt on causally explaining its existence, structure, and function by appeal to that fact.

Natural selection, I have now argued, is not only not all-powerful, but also cannot be properly conceived as 'creative'. That would, given the choice between God and natural selection that Dennett and Pinker confront us with, leave God as in many ways the more sensible choice, but not as an explanatory one either. The next section removes this puzzle.

3.3 God or Natural Selection or...?

In biology, 'functionalists/teleologists' (Bell, Cuvier, Sedgwick, Paley, Whewell, Darwin in the nineteenth century, followed by Fisher, Dobzhansky, and Dawkins in the twentieth) regarded *adaptation* and the 'fit' of the organism to the external environment as the deepest fact of biology and its prime explanandum. 'Formalists', 'structuralists, or 'internalists', on the other hand (Agassiz, Owen, Geoffroy de St Hilaire, Goethe, von Baer in the nineteenth century, followed by D'Arcy Thompson, Goodwin, and Kauffman in the twentieth), focused on organic *form* and commonalities of *structure* as the prime explanandum, leaving their possible adaptive *effects* (qua *consequences* of possible forms) on the side. Importantly, the latter were not generally 'anti-evolution' at all, as Amundson (1998: 159) stresses, discussing the cases of Goethe, Owen, and Geoffroy.[15] It is now recognized, contrary to the historiography of much of the philosophy of biology in the twentieth century, that the dispute between formalists and functionalists in nineteenth-century biology cannot be described as a battle fought over evolution.[16] Evolution in fact played a very minor role in the great 1830 debate between Geoffroy, the arch-formalist, and Cuvier, the arch-functionalist, and the latter in fact had a far greater trouble in acknowledging evolution than the former. Also, while emphasizing the primacy of form over function, and of the 'Unity of a Type' over 'conditions on existence', the formalists did not deny adaptation or the evident utility of most organic structures. They simply argued that it was a secondary and relatively superficial overlay upon the unifying *Baupläne* (homologies) according to which all organisms were built, which constraints on adaptation did nothing to explain. If there is a Unity of Type across otherwise quite radically different organisms and organs, with no accompanying unity of function, we deprive function of a causal role in the explanation of form.

Geoffroy captures the essence of formalism through two mottos (cited in Gould 2002: 304): 'such is the organ, such will be its function', and '*Je me garde de preter à Dieu aucune intention*' (that is: no final causes, intentions, or purposes in nature in an explanatory role). Given some variance in morphology, the formalist will regard it as something to be deduced from some underlying 'generating types' or 'arche-types', an idea most strikingly exemplified in Goethe's morphology of plants (see Gould 2002: 281–91 for an assessment). The primary task and difficulty for any formalist position is the derivation of the vast range of modifications of the same archetype under the varied 'adaptive regimes'

---

[15] Owen in particular ran into problems with his patrons in Natural Theology when he talked about the 'Unity of Type' in a way in which it seemed to lack the *need* for divine underpinnings (see Amundson 1998: 163).

[16] As Gould (2002: 304) notes: 'we will never understand the great antithesis of functionalism and formalism—a subject that has pervaded the history of biology—if we misread this dichotomy in the later light of evolutionary theory'.

encountered by living forms on the planet. For Geoffroy there was, 'philosophically speaking, only a single animal' (cited in Gould 2002: 304), a position interestingly reflected in current discussions on the 'zootype',[17] and also the well-known fact that much of the animal world's morphological types seem to have been produced not gradually and with an unlimited variance, but in one big burst, after which not much genuine innovation took place. As Leiber (2001) summarizes:

> all 20-odd animal phyla appeared within a few score million years in the great Cambrian 'explosion', as if nature were quick to run through all the basic possibilities of the animal type in less than 5% of the time there have been animals on earth. More substantially, it appears more and more likely that all animal phyla use virtually the same *homeobox* 'master genes' and proteins to determine segmentation and segmental identity. (...) *Unity of type* has made an extraordinary comeback (Leiber 2001: 86–7).

While the historiography of biology has quite routinely classified the 'typological', formalist, or structuralist theories of biology as a medieval anachronism that has been overcome by Darwinian population thinking (see Amundson 1998 for a study of many examples), this severely clouds the fact that there is no opposition here: the typologists were simply not *concerned* with an attack on the evolution of species; evolution is a fine concept for the formalist, although he would tend to stress that it takes place within a range of options afforded by an 'archetype'. Defending a Unity of Type hypothesis is a discussion on a different level than the debate between Darwin and the Paleyans, and types are also not the same as species. Mayr's (2000, 2002) identification of 'types' with the Platonic 'forms' is too schematic, as it makes typology come out as a defence of the immutability of species. What Mayr decries as 'metaphysical idealism' in a theorist like Geoffroy presumably was no more than a commitment to a level of biological reality deeper than what was more or less obvious or empirically given, such as how well-adapted organisms are (Amundson 1998: 169–71). Geoffroy's emphasis on non-historical explanation is a stance effectively taken over by developmental biologists who distanced themselves from the NDS. Homology as understood by Geoffroy or Owen is crucially not a concept with an *evolutionary* basis, but a *generative* and *developmental* one. The typologist's systems of homologies were 'generative systems—one basic, simple form gives rise to a diverse range of outcomes, all of which are unified by traces of their origin in the simple form' (Amundson 1998: 172; see also Goodwin's 'dynamic' and developmental definition of homology in Webster and Goodwin 1996: 143–4).

In much that sense, Universal Grammar (UG) as I will present it in the following part of this book is a set of underlying generative principles that give

---

[17] Slack, Holland, and Craham (1993) proposed that all animal phyla shared a particular pattern of gene expression, providing what amounts to 'a morphological criterion for what an animal is'. The hypothesis is not uncontroverted (see further Martinez *et al.* 1998), but has apparently been highly intriguing.

rise to a great phenomenal variety of permitted options, while excluding others, independent of their adaptive significance. It is right here, in nineteenth-century formalism, where, in my view, Chomsky's project has its natural home, not in cognitive psychology (or, therein, the Representational Theory of Mind, a variety of functionalism). Naturally, thus, generative grammar in its Chomskyan shape also inherits many of the problems of the formalist biological tradition. Obviously, when commonalities of form are being explained in terms of an underlying type, the type *itself* needs explaining, and neither invoking a Divine Creator nor functional utility will help. It is no more than a revitalization of this earlier nineteenth-century debate when Dennett accuses Chomsky of not being able to *explain UG*, the type underlying the structure of human languages. Dennett does not presumably *deny* it as such, but would seem to deny its *explanatory significance*, unless it can itself be explained in terms of its functional utility (see Dennett 1995: 397, 384–400).[18] As Darwin remarked on Owen:

It is so easy to hide our ignorance under such expressions as the 'plan of creation', 'unity of design', &c., and to think that we give an explanation when we only restate a fact (Darwin 1859: 482).[19]

But sometimes facts as such are worthwhile knowing, even if they have no explanation themselves. UG as a type is as such an advance in understanding, as it shows how superficially very divergent phenomena quite surprisingly pattern in the same way. No genuine or non-historical explanation of morphological form, it would seem, can begin before one has unified the phenomena into a type in some such fashion, hence knows *what* to explain. Nowhere else in science would the acceptability of a hypothesis unifying a range of phenomena call for the *explanation* of the underlying unity prior to *stating* it. In any case, the sceptical attitude above would have to be questioned the very moment a given structure relevantly showed signs of *non-adaptive* design. In that case, deeper explanations of types than can be given in terms of functional utility must be sought. It should be noted that Dennett, like Pinker and Bloom (1990), makes no attempt to actually trace the effects of natural selection on language design, hence to derive the structural patterns we find from whatever 'function' language is stipulated to have.[20]

---

[18] As far as headings like 'Chomsky contra Darwin' are concerned that we find in Dennett, they make no sense whatsoever, at least as long as one does not turn Darwin into a Spencerian (as Dennett does).

[19] Similarly Bell (1833: 39–40), calling the search for unities of type a 'trifling pursuit'.

[20] Uriagereka (1998) is an elaborate argument that core structural features of the human language faculty have no functional rationale, hence that that faculty is an exaptation (see also Carstairs-McCarthy 1999). Dennett (1995: 390–1) notes this possibility, but misses the point when he argues that even if language is an exaptation, it is still an adaptation:
'No matter how suddenly the punctuation occurred that jogged our ancestors abruptly to the right in Design Space, it was still a gradual design development under the pressure of natural selection—unless it was indeed a miracle or a hopeful monster.'

Given that the formalists argued for their unifying types on empirical grounds, the functionalists could hardly reject them on ideological grounds. Cuvier, in particular, bit the bullet and argued that the *Baupläne had* to reflect broad function, even where none were obvious. Types were not denied, that is, but they had to come out as artefacts of adaptation. Possibly, this is a good example of how within a Kuhnian scientific paradigm data are reinterpreted so as to bring them in line with the paradigm's basic commitments. The formalists' archetypes were also accommodated by Darwin, who used them unchanged, while reinterpreting them: as Amundson (1998: 173) puts it, the archetype 'was well in place, at the root of the tree, in time for Darwin to point to it and declare it an ancestor'. Darwin took the archetype over, that is, while taking it down from its 'Platonic heaven' and transforming it into a 'common ancestor'. But as an ancestor, the archetype is the *basis* for evolution, rather than what the latter *explains.* If evolution is a history of tinkering on a given design, all the explanatory load shifts to explaining the ancestor. Moreover, an explanation of a structural homology in terms of a common ancestor may not be particularly plausible, especially if the same morphologies do not involve the same genes (see Webster and Goodwin 1996: 140–4 for discussion). The somewhat 'Platonist' ontology of the types, also, hardly causes a serious problem for them: if we understand them as explanatory schemes, types are no different in their ontological status than electromagnetic fields, say, and are abstract in the same sense that they are.

In sum, evolution for the formalist is history and selection taking up naturally possible forms for a use. We would clearly not, on this view, be even *tempted* to associate the concept of human nature with an Aristotelian essence, or indeed with the species concept itself. But even if we did, and it is right that species as historical entities have no 'essences', it would not follow that there are no unities of type of an ahistorical nature behind the variation in the world's species. As Amundson strikingly points out, 'Unity of Type *denies* the ultimate individuality of species by asserting real affinities *among groups and subgroups of species*' (Amundson 1998: 173, my emphasis), and as pointed out above, the concept of a homology as the formalist sees it does not have an evolutionary or genetic, but a developmental and structuralist basis. There is simply no implication, in making a claim about human nature, either that the human species is immutable, that 'all humans are the same', or that the members of *homo sapiens* can be described in terms of a set of necessary and sufficient properties. The point is to move up the scale of abstraction, from evolutionary history to explanatory principles in the science of form.

Minimalist Grammar design makes it a concrete possibility that grammar evolution was a sudden event (see Berwick 1997), and has not undergone much external shaping. In a very wide sense, nobody disagrees that everything evolved by natural selection, but that sense leaves open how much looking at gradual shaping lets us comprehend the actual structures we find, and how much it leaves to be explained by chance, constraints, etc.

These principles fit the internalist bill: they restrict the power of what selection can do, and they explain the conservation of form across vast changes in function. It's God *or* natural selection, *or* internal constraint, and we need all three of them, if by 'God' we mean the general design of the universe. We should furthermore insist, as Gould (2002: 256) urges, on the *double* role that internal constraint plays: not merely the negative role of *delimiting* options, given an ancestral form or basic organismic type, but also the positive role of *setting* evolutionary pathways. These are preferred channels of change, 'providing numerous, though ordered, possibilities for modified shapes (including forms as yet unrealized on our planet, but predictable from the channels, and implied by observed developmental pathways)' (Gould 2002: 299).

This simple, sane, and pluralistic position on evolution is Chomsky's, too, whose views on evolution have routinely been presented as 'anti-evolutionary', or as a yearning for skyhooks, in Dennett's (1995) terms.[21] But pretending, on the grounds that God is not an explanatory option, that natural selection is the only or even the major force in evolution, is no improvement over Natural Theology. There is nothing incoherent, Chomsky (2002: 141–2) points out, in being a Theologian and saying that while whatever evolved did so by natural selection, it could not do so by itself: God must have had a hand in it. This is to acknowledge that evolution is a process not depending on a single mechanism alone that operates in a vacuum. Selection requires and depends on a structured environment and given constraints, physical laws at least, but also historical contingencies, within which it can operate (Chomsky 2002: 142).

The power and limitations of natural selection as systematically depending on what the fitness landscape—the structured environment—is like are now subject to scientific investigation. Under certain conditions, if a population were to start its adaptive climb, even locating the highest fitness peaks may be mathematically impossible on the basis of mutations and selection alone (Kauffman 1995a: 183). The population may forever be trapped in an infinitesimal region of the 'design space'. Under different conditions, selection may drive a population headlong into an 'error catastrophe' in which all gradually useful traits melt away: natural selection completely fails. It is not only that natural selection is not the only device to create adaptive design, in many cases adaptive design *must* have a different cause, as selection is unable to achieve it. What seems to be asked for is a systematic investigation of just *when* selection has some power to shape the organism, in the midst of the effects of internal constraints and outer conditions (this is what Kauffman 1995a undertakes).

---

[21] Dennett (1995) overgeneralizes the theory of natural selection to a universal explanatory force and power, a 'Science of Everything' (Orr 1996). Intended as a project in unifying the sciences, and in connecting the realms of life, meaning and purpose with the realm of space, time, causation and physical law, evolution by selection becomes a corrosive 'Universal Acid' that eats its way through everything there is. There is probably nothing 'dangerous' in this, contrary to what Dennett's title suggests, but it may border on vacuity.

If so, as of now natural selection has no purchase on the question of human nature. The question of which explanatory role the latter plays in some evolutionary process is entirely empirical. Rather than engaging in aprioristic stipulations, it seems entirely congenial in the present state of knowledge to focus on proximate causes instead of ultimate ones in the study of a complex trait such as language, to examine how given morphologies fall into patterns, and draw conclusions about human nature from that. The author of *Vaulting Ambition: The Quest for Human Nature* speaks about the 'Herculean labors' that await those who wish to arrive at conclusions about the limits that human nature imposes on the extent to which man is malleable under environmental pressures, and to do so by an equation of human nature with 'the outcome of natural selection' (Kitcher 1985: 28). Kitcher wonders whether the 'quest for human nature' so conceived could ever be proved *right*. But it need not be so conceived. UG is a living example of how it is possible to study human biology quite independently from a concern with historical shifts and selections in the gene pool.

UG is quite simply a posited and empirically attested 'Universal Type'. While it may be hopeless to account for individual behaviours or characters given our genetic equipment (for the same reason that it is hopeless to predict which language an individual endowed with UG will eventually speak, since this is a matter of history, not laws), there is nothing 'vaulting', no super-scientific 'quest' in a science of human nature, as exemplified by the theory of UG. Chomsky's formalist conception of human nature (as I interpret it here), predating that of sociobiology, has been exceedingly *simple*. It is when human nature becomes a Neo-Darwinian concept, with concomitant constraints on methodology and commitments to a functionalist logic of explanation, that our enterprise becomes truly ambitious and speculative.

3.4 Epilogue on Explanation and Necessity

While types, if understood in the sense above, are not species, let alone immutable ones, they prevent arbitrary variance among the members of a species. While variation among the members of a species is expected, it will stop at some point. This is all to the good. If we were to make functional adaptation the cause of morphological form, the biology we would get is an 'anything goes' biology in which everything is possible, because it is solely a matter of history. Mutations could go in any direction at any time. All of our properties would be absolutely contingent: there would be no internal constraints on permissible variation, and the only principle limiting their possible combinations would be the law of non-contradiction. Generalizations we might make would be accidental. Today's humans are such and such, but tomorrow's humans may be different, with no restriction on how different. Could it possibly be right that in this way there are no natures (in the sense of the formalist's types) of members of a species, no *necessities* in the genesis of form?

As I understand it, Mayr (2000) affirms this when he calls evolutionary biology a 'historical science'. But evolution *might* be something else: the theory of what is possible in history and what is not. Critics of Darwinian biology noted from early on that names for species cannot be simply names for absolutely contingent aggregates of independent properties.[22] As such, the search for the possible seems little other than an inherent feature of human inquiry, reflecting an inherent drive in human understanding: collecting empirical facts, stating and describing variation, is not the goal of scientific inquiry. It might of course be that we simply do not come up with an explanatory theory of speciation in biology—it might be that, in some ultimate sense, nothing remains but to narrate the course that evolution took. But short of certainty on that, inaugurating a new concept of 'historical explanation', viewed as a new positive characteristic of a science as such, seems like a theoretical defeat.

While Mayr (2000) claims that 'Darwin introduced historicity into science' and an associated concept of 'historical explanation', the question is whether there *can* be any such 'science' and any such kind of 'explanation'. Plotkin (1997) has no qualms about this, and argues that Darwin changes our very concept of a causal explanation:

Construing historical antecedence merely as a concatenation of events and entities in time is to miss the point that 'where we are coming from' is a *cause* (not an instance) of 'where we are now'. The covering-law model of explanation, which may work in physics or chemistry, just does not fit the case of explanations in evolutionary biology. (...) Causal explanations depend (...) also on the history of selection and other causal events that are stretched out over time and constitute a set of causes unique to any one of millions of species. Antecedence becomes cause (Plotkin 1997: 14).

This observation as such, however, does not make biology different from cosmology, say, where, equally, an ultimate understanding of black hole dynamics depends on history, or what happened after the Big Bang, too.[23] Plotkin, noting this fact, exploits it to impose his historical vision of explanation ultimately on the whole of science. But one need not conclude from the fact noted that the laws of physics are historical in some essential sense. This idea appears to be simply ruled out when we reflect on what we admire about Newton's explanation of why the earth goes around the sun in an elliptical orbit. Newton does not tell us, as

---

[22] Bateson (1894) argued that the 'crude belief that living beings are plastic conglomerates of miscellaneous attributes, and that order of form or Symmetry have been impressed upon this medley by Selection alone; and that by Variation any of these attributes may be subtracted or any other attribute added in indefinite proportion, is a fancy which the Study of Variation does not support.' Driesch (1914) observed that 'the totality of living forms (...) appeared to them [the Darwinian phylogenists] as meaningless as, say, the forms of clouds in their accidental peculiarity. But this at once did away with any deeper meaning for zoological classification. It was settled once and for all; the question had no sense.' Both passages are cited in Webster and Goodwin (1996: 68), where they are affirmatively discussed from a contemporary point of view.

[23] As Wolfgang Gebhardt assures me.

Goodwin (1994) points out, that the earth goes round the sun in an elliptical orbit in this year because that is what it did last year, and earlier still, and so on back to the origin of the planetary system, and because nothing happened to change it. All that is true, yet no one has any desire for such 'explanations'. But it is a kind of explanation, Goodwin points out, that we frequently find in biology:

Trace something back to its origins, point to the first known instance of the phenomenon, and use that as the explanation of phenomena subsequently connected to this event. In biology this origin is usually identified as the common ancestor of some lineage (Goodwin 1994: 79).

Looking at the actual Newtonian explanation that made history, it remains true that laws for the dynamic evolution of the planetary system operate in a historically contingent domain: the initial conditions in which they apply (or whether there are conditions that allow them to apply) is something that the explanation takes as a contingent given. But there is nothing in this concession that changes either our conception of a law or our conception of an explanation. Webster and Goodwin make a case that narrating the story of organismic forms through their selectional histories on the lines of Darwin's theory of descent with modification is not an exercise in *explanation*, and cannot ultimately be intended as such. The theory does not

explain the existence of empirical morphologies but simply takes them as given in the common ancestor. Furthermore, (...) empirical variation between individuals is also taken as given by Darwinian theory; they are brute facts, unanalyzed and unexplained. In terms of the theory, there is no necessity for either stability or variation in the empirical properties of the individuals that comprise a species taxon, that is, a temporally extended population in Darwinian terms. All that is claimed is that *if* variant forms occur and *if* they are adaptively advantageous then they will be accumulated within the population as a consequence of natural selection. There is no *explanatory* basis here for making any claims whatsoever regarding either the necessity or the contingency of properties considered as matters of fact (Webster and Goodwin 1996: 70).

This criticism of Plotkin and Mayr does not imply that the deductivist covering-law model of explanation, which Plotkin rejects for biology, is actually adequate, even for physics. The covering-law model conceives explanation as subsumption of an instance under a law, which itself has the character of a simple empirical invariance, such as 'All crows are black', supposing for the sake of argument that this is a spatio-temporally unrestricted true generalization, as required by the model's conception of a law. If, on this model, we wish to know *why* this particular bird is black, an answer might be that this bird is a crow, while the reason given for its being black is that 'All crows are black is a law'. A deduction of the particular instance from the covering law has been achieved. But does this answer satisfy our explanatory goals? Do we now feel that we know why this bird is black?

Obviously, we would like to know why all crows are black. In fact, the 'all' quantification is not even relevant here. Being told why even *some* crows are black would be an advance over the covering-law explanation just given. But how would we answer that question without appealing to the *nature of crows*? To something that *brings it about* that crows have this colour, spelled out in terms of some kind of idealized explanatory model? Whatever explains that would be a *generative mechanism*, an explanatory principle in the sense of the formalists as described in the previous section: an internal cause that yields the plumage's coloration. What we aim for is a theory from which it follows that the colour of crows is a necessary consequence of their nature.

'All crows are black', by comparison with this, is a summary of instance statistics, as Webster and Goodwin (1996: 75) put it, adding that in today's actual practice of biology it is not empirical invariances of this sort that are deemed theoretically significant. The generalization just discussed contrasts with another one, 'All adult mammals have a heart', which Webster and Goodwin argue is accorded a quite different status in biological practice: it is a 'statement related to a physiological (functional) theory which claims that organisms of the size and complexity of mammals *must* have a heart'. This 'must' is an expression, not of a spatio-temporally unrestricted empirical generalization, but of an explanatory necessity. As far as our given theory goes, an organism with a certain complexity and size *needs* a heart. Just as the nature of water restricts the possibilities of its states and the co-occurrence of certain of its properties, this type of an organism restricts the possibilities for its internal organization.

A counter-instance to 'All adult mammals have a heart' would falsify a presumed law pertaining to the necessary organizational structure of a certain kind of large, complex mammal. It would shake a given explanatory theory. It is relative to such a theory that the members of a taxon are said to have a common nature accounting for a commonality in their morphology. It is in the same relation that one can understand certain coinstantiated properties of an organism *not* to be logically independent, but as constraining one another, and as non-arbitrary. On this view, what unites the members of a kind is that a common nature allows us to derive features of them, given contingent environmental conditions in which they live. Similarly, speaking Japanese or English, but not Fortran, is a dispositional property that human babies have, it is a matter of their intrinsic nature, their 'causal powers' (Harré and Madden 1975), which we then spell out in terms of a mechanism yielding a divergent overt effect.

I have now given my answer to the charge by current philosophers of biology that human nature is a concept invalidated by modern biology, and doomed to be a historical and adaptationist concept if kept at all. Claims about human nature today should have nothing to do with the immutability of species, or with claims that 'all humans are the same', but with a vision of non-historical *explanation* that differs markedly from that of the Neo-Darwinian. While history is not a necessary preface to the study of form, form is a necessary preface to the study of what natural selection may select from. The typologist posits human nature at a higher level of abstraction, with no intrinsic concern with some notion of species uniqueness. For him, the study of nature, including human nature, is not so much a study of what *is* or *came* to be, but of what *can be* and *cannot be*. In a sense this is to reiterate (and substantiate, through science itself) the original Platonic intuition that whatever contingently is—a good deed, a crystal, an organism, or even a table—is what it is as an *instance* of something general, on which it depends for its being what it is. Each thing is the actualization of something that makes it a *possible* thing in the first place.

Part II
Deducing Variation

4

Prior to Function

4.1 Language Growth

Let us begin by recalling and collecting some facts on how the system of language *develops* in the organism, and how it is in fact *used*. Günter Grass tells us about a boy, Oskar, who wills himself never to grow beyond the age of three. This does not work outside the world of fiction, and in a quite analogous way, it would not make sense for a child to refuse to learn a language. Language comes: children acquire a language, and they cannot help doing so. Placed in an environment in the relevant age, children universally 'grow' the language of that environment, and they do it without effort or special instruction. The sort of competence that a 5-year-old child has does not arise from gradually mastering a system of conventions and norms in the sense, say, in which he later learns to write, or to master the rules of traffic. Neither orthography nor traffic rules come naturally to a child. There are children who know neither, or do not know them well, but there are very few children who do not know the sound and meaning of a potentially infinite number of expressions of a language.

The five-year-old also lacks the chemical education to apply the word *water* specifically to samples of H_2O. But he uses it as other children of the same age do. Judging from myself, I have never had any tendency to 'correct' my children's use of it. The use is simply what it is, and I suppose that, although the substance itself may have changed (having become more polluted, say), and our *beliefs* about water have changed, children's use of the *word* (or a translation of it) hasn't changed, in any sense that would be relevant to a naturalistic study of language, in the last millennia—even those millennia that have experienced the effects of the scientific revolution. We are thus addressing the question of meaning at a level where the scientific revolution (and much of our world knowledge) makes no difference. At that level, the meaning (the use) of the word *water* is as strikingly stable as the meaning of *earth*, *tree*, or *person*, to the extent that these have been lexicalized in the languages spoken by populations in the last few millennia. (It is an open question whether concepts—as opposed to beliefs—change *at all* over historical time; for a strong view on this see Fodor 1998.)

As Oskar is exposed to linguistic data, something in his brain responds selectively to it, while in a cat's brain, witnessing the same input, nothing or something else happens. Whatever it is about Oskar that is cognitively responsible in him for this selective response, we have been calling his *faculty of language* (FL), a term meant to be as neutral as possible: the fact that humans have this faculty should raise no controversies. If the mechanisms involved in linguistic performance—the systems that access such cognitive systems for the purposes of speech articulation and perception, or referring and communicating—are not specifically linguistic ones (that is, special to human language), it would follow that what is specifically human about language has to do with the cognitive system—the system of knowledge underlying language—only.

FL undergoes state changes, first being in an *initial state* (IS), say around birth. It can be described through a number of universal *laws*—principles—for the organization of sound and meaning in a human language. The *theory* of these principles is referred to here as *Universal Grammar* (UG). IS grows and matures until stabilizing, at a more or less uniform age, which we will call the *final state* (FS) of FL. The effect of the environments leading to differences in the FSs is captured by letting the principles of UG interact with *parameters*—binary ones in the simplest case, which we assume. A parameter reflects an underspecification of a system for a certain variable, while not affecting the overall uniformity of the computational laws underlying a certain output. For example, the *polysynthesis* parameter (Baker 2001, chapter 4) leads Navajo to have a *word* of the form:

ni-sh-hozh
2s-1s-tickle
'I tickle you'

where English speakers have to use a whole *sentence*, with no difference in meaning. Similarly in Mohawk, we find (to use a somewhat extreme example of Baker's) the complex word:

Washakotya'tawitsherahetkvhta'se'

where, in English, we must say:

He made the thing that one puts on one's body [i.e. the dress] ugly for her (Baker 2001: 87).

But there is no change of syntactic principles here: Navajo and Mohawk simply make different use of an option that UG leaves open, namely that of incorporating nouns into other expressions. Thus, in the Navajo example, the subject and object are both included into the verb, while English does not make use of this option. In ways such as these, languages differ in how they set (or value) parameters reflecting options of UG. According to Yang's (2002) proposal, UG makes available to the child the full range of humanly possible languages, with parameters *already* valued; experience does not play the role of triggering parameter settings, but simply that of shifting probabilities over this given range in a way that increasingly few of them can be used in the light of what grammars are present in the environment. This is a familiarly 'Darwinian' model, in that the environment does not create structures, but plays *a selective* role. It also suggests that although the child moves, due to its cognitive equipment, in a domain-specific space of linguistic principles and parameters, the process of adapting it to an environment works by domain-general (statistical) principles.

Exposure to *primary linguistic data* (PLD) thus leads to switching from one possible language to another, and we may think of language learning as an IS converting PLDs into a particular FS: IS (PLD) = FS, via a number of intermediate stages. We may view these unstable languages as full possible languages in the sense that they conform to UG and could in principle be languages spoken in speech communities. It would not do justice to the child constructing them to talk of it as having, not a full grasp of a language (namely the one it currently entertains or explores), but only a 'partial grasp' of the language of its environment. As Crain and Pietroski (2001) argue, what some would naively (mis)describe as 'childish errors' or 'bad English' are highly creative explorations of alternative linguistic options, possibly realized in adult language elsewhere on the globe, or nowhere on it, for some accidental historical reason.[1]

Evidence for universal principles or laws is there whenever, to our surprise, we don't find temporary violations of them in the course of language acquisition, of a kind that betrays a learning process. Thus, findings suggest that we virtually never find violations of locality constraints on syntactic transformations, of conditions on subject extraction or cliticization, or other effects regimented by UG (Crain and Thornton 1998). UG explains why such violations are not found (if we set up appropriate experimental conditions suitable to our idealizations): finding them would be analogous to a natural object's violating a law of nature. This model of language acquisition suggests that the acquisition of linguistic knowledge is not *data-driven*, i.e., that the formation of inductive hypotheses is not made on the basis of given data. It is more like the free generation of UG-compatible options most of which are then *discarded* in the light of data. The environment selects, but does not create, internal structure—not an unexpected conclusion on more general biological grounds, as noted in Chapter 3.

---

[1] See Crain and Pietroski (2001), section 8, for particularly interesting recent experimental data on language change: English children often speak 'German' for a while, as when using the 'medial-wh' construction, possible in German, but forbidden in English:
*What do you think what pigs eat?
versus:
    Wer glaubst du wer nach Hause geht?
    'Who do you think who goes home?'
Crain and Pietroski convincingly argue that the similarities between the child alternative to English, on the one hand, and German, on the other, run deep; e.g., repetition of lexical wh-phrases is ruled out in adult German:
    *Wessen Buch glaubst du wessen Buch Hans liest?
    'Whose book do you think whose book Hans is reading?'
And in child English we never find:
    *Which Smurf do you think which Smurf is wearing roller skates
        English children would not use the medial-wh constructions where it is disallowed (by UG) in German as well.

Any FS is a mechanical procedure or function that generates an unbounded number of expressions, each with a definite sound and meaning, paired in the right way. We will characterize each FS as made up by a *lexicon* (LEX), containing the primitives of a language viewed as a combinatorial system, and a *Computational System* (CS), which puts two syntactic objects together through its prime combinatory operation, *Merge*, which is the minimal one it needs, hence ideally the only one. CS maps a *Numeration* (NUM), a one-time selection of items from the lexicon (intuitively the *words* figuring in a sentence), to a derivation, the last line of which is an *expression*, EXP: CS (NUM) = EXP.

For each expression that CS derives there must minimally be a specification of its sound and meaning, PHON and SEM, in the right pairing (since in any natural language, any sound is paired with a specific meaning). These specifications get used by the extra-linguistic systems, the sensorimotor (S-M) systems, and the conceptual-intentional (C-I) systems (involving 'thought', reasoning, reference, etc.), respectively. Ideally, by deriving a pair <PHON, SEM>, that is, an expression, a derivation—being a step-by-step construction of precisely such a pair—should explain why the expression *has* that sound and that meaning (in that pairing). That is to say: what is of interest is not the mapping from NUM to EXP as *extensionally* conceived but rather the mapping conceived *intensionally*, as a *sequence of computational steps*. We do not identify a 'language' (state of FL) with a *set of expressions*, which as such does not determine a generative procedure, and could be generated in any number of ways.

So far, no large ontological commitments arise; all we have endorsed is a combinatorial system represented in the mind/brain that *generates derivations*. Constructing some extensional notion of language as an external object or as a set, external to the biology and the mind/brain of a speaker, entails endorsing such further ontological commitments, going *beyond* what we minimally need, a generative procedure.

Available PLDs are primarily *acoustic* in nature—they are audible outputs of language as described in physical acoustics. Any account which sets out to explain how the child determines a language should thus explain how the child does so on the basis of essentially *such* inputs. The SEM corresponding to an audible linguistic output, in particular, which corresponds to linguistically determined aspects of its meaning, is absolutely not visible in this kind of output, containing as it does entirely different primitives and combinatorial principles. If the generative system which computes SEMs allows for variance at all, we thus expect this variance to be severely restricted: the variance, to be learnable, must be restricted as to be reflected in the phonetic reflexes it leaves.

Knowledge of language so conceived consists in an unlimited number of deductive consequences it entails: facts about the sounds and meanings of expressions. This notion of deduction has no normative connotation; it is a purely formal or algebraic notion. The question of how we *arrive* at this knowledge—'Plato's question', in Chomsky's terms—is answered by the theory of principles and parameters, or UG. That leaves open how it is *used*—'Descartes's question', in Chomsky's terms—and also how it evolved—'Darwin's question'. We ignore the latter ones for now, focusing on the first and the proposal that we may describe the attainment of knowledge in essentially the way that we may describe the maturation of a biological organ. Predictably from this point of view, the maturation of Oskar's FL, like organs in the body generally, is *biologically timed*; it has *critical phases* of growth, after which the process stabilizes in a way that we cannot control, and which makes the acquisition of second languages later on a far more laborious process.

Already at birth, infants can achieve remarkable feats like discriminating, by relying on rhythm, among a wide range of languages, including some they have never heard (see Guasti 2002 for an overview, including evidence for the following data). Around 6 months they start babbling (vocally or manually), and recognize the prosodic properties of both words and clauses. Around 10 months they start pairing words with meanings. At 20–24 months already they exploit their knowledge of syntax to derive the meanings of words, particularly verbs, and they experience what has been described as a 'vocabulary burst'. From the earliest syntactically structured productions, children appear to have an understanding of full clausal structure of their native language, of grammatical constraints, rules of movements, and the phrasal grouping of words. An understanding of recursion has to wait until age 3. In the earliest stages of acquisition, when words are segmented in a continuous stream of speech, principles appear operative that are language-specific (specifically, phonological stress patterns in words) rather than domain-general, although statistical regularities (transitional probabilities) seem to be exploited too (Jusczyk 1999; Yang 2004).

In the critical phase, an exposure to external triggers (data) is crucial—again as in the case of other biological organs. If the input comes too late, later teaching and training cannot repair the damage to the system. The necessary input is not tied to one particular sensory modality, however. Selective impairment of one sensory modality, like seeing or hearing, need not as such lead to impairment in linguistic competence. Blind children acquire language in much the same way that sighted ones do, including the vocabulary of sight, which they acquire with remarkable ease and consistency (differentiating *see* and *look*, *see* and *touch*, e.g., and using colour terminology with high sophistication: see further Landau and Gleitman 1985). Similar remarks apply to deaf children, as long as their hearing parents do not make the (catastrophic) mistake of following their empiricist instincts, which tell them that how language is externally *there*—through acoustic or visible articulation (lip movements)—is essential to language. Attempting to teach deaf children spoken language in this way is unlikely to produce good results. Sign languages of the deaf are not *based* on speech, and are not a sophisticated version of a system of 'gestures and mimes'. In their acquisition and expressive power they equal spoken languages, and structurally or syntactically they resemble spoken languages in core respects (Sutton-Spence and Woll 1999). American Sign Language in particular comprises three basic phonological categories: hand shape corresponds to phonetic consonants in spoken language, location or place of articulation to vowels, and movement to tone. Hand shape change is associated with syllables rather than words as wholes. Morphology (word formation) is guided by aspectual inflections, compounding, and derivations (Emmorey 2001).

Sign language research illustrates, not only that sound (physical acoustics) is not crucial to language, but that *phonology*, the component of the language faculty concerned with computing a phonetic representation of an utterance as represented in the mind/brain, is not about *sounds* literally speaking. A phonetic representation that the rules of phonology derive contains what we may call 'instructions' for speech production—for 'articulators' such as tongue, teeth, and lips. But these instructions are nonetheless more abstract, as sign languages also have articulators—hand, eyebrows, eyes, etc. No matter the articulators, the phonology is alike, containing instructions for articulating a given interpretable structure (thought, if you will) in the form of either an auditory *or* a visual signal (Jackendoff 1994: chapter 7; Anderson and Lightfoot 2002: chapter 6).

What about blind and deaf children? Language in a virtually normal sense has been acquired by people 'with no sensory input beyond what can be gained by placing one's hand on another person's face and throat' (Chomsky 2000: 122, and see Mehler and Dupoux 1994). In the light of such data, the 'empty organism' theory we mentioned before seems the least attractive or promising hypothesis to consider for the case at hand: information supplied by the organism itself appears to be very *rich*, contrary to what the intuition suggests that is often taken to be expressed by the Aristotelian maxim that 'nothing can be in the mind that was not first in the senses' (although this maxim may have an interpretation that is consistent with the data above).

We may also say that language is learned under conditions of the *poverty of the stimulus* (POS), but in one sense this should not be regarded as a claim any more surprising than an analogous claim for organic growth in general. In the case of immune responses, as with vision or language, we are quite simply witnessing a process of growth that depends on the internal nature of the organism in question, rather than a process that is literally caused by the environment, not a startling conclusion, one should think.

In the case of language, there are at least four considerations defining the problem that this internal nature—in the case of language the initial state (IS) of FL as described by the theory of UG—must have the resources and design to solve. First, the initial impoverishment is that the acoustic or even the phonetic data do not give many clues on the more abstract principles of syntax and semantics: assuming even that the child knows the specifically linguistic concepts occurring in rules to be learned, learning these rules will further depend on having *negative* data as well—data concerning what expressions violate particular rules—data that appear to be largely absent. We will illustrate this lack of evidence when discussing questions (interrogative constructions) in detail later (Section 5.4).

Second, the PLD on the basis of which languages are acquired are also unsystematic, imperfect, and differ a lot from learner to learner: some parents talk a lot to their children, in other cultures they don't; ordinary language use is full of unfinished or ungrammatical sentences, half words, and slips of the tongue; some parents do not know well the language in which they talk to their children, cannot talk, make mistakes, or are inattentive; children, even if corrected, tend to be resistant to corrections, which they often ignore, and fail to understand; and in some cases a full-fledged language may not be present in the environment at all, as in the cases of Pidgins. These factors do not seem to matter very much. In spite of the haphazard nature of PLD, language acquisition will not fail to produce an understanding of universal principles of human language construction, such as constraints on transforming one phrase into another. Moreover, this remarkably abstract knowledge is achieved largely uniformly and effortlessly, across vast differences in education, intelligence, sensory equipment, and cultural sophistication.

Third, the knowledge attained is not simply a recapitulation of the statistical distribution of the adult input they received. Children do not only produce sentences that are entirely novel, but also make mistakes of a kind that (i) misapplications of non-statistical *rules* would produce, and that (ii) are not likely to have ever been produced by their parents. There are things children learn very late, such as that one must not drop the subject of an English sentence, although every adult English sentence they hear presumably contains a subject; they learn relatively early, on the other hand, what is very rare in the adult input they likely hear, such as the placement of finite verbs in French over negation and adverbs (Legate and Yang 2002).

Fourth, even if imitating plays an important explanatory role in language acquisition, it will not do to imitate actual adult output, since the system of knowledge attained includes an *open ended* set of objects. Abstract *rules*—rules not making reference to the specific *values* of the variables over which they are stated—are to be induced from necessarily finite and limited data, which only result from finitely many *applications* of such rules. As mentioned before, acquiring language requires an *algebraic mind* (Marcus 2001), a mind that, e.g., recognizes that Lewis Carroll's *All mimsy were the borogoves* is an immaculate application of grammatical rules, despite the non-interpretability of its constituents, or the unfamiliar *values* of the variables over which the rules are stated (Hauser, Weiss, and Marcus 2002). Even given such a mind, crossing the huge inductive gap between actual output and rules has taken very smart professional linguists thousands of years of intense linguistic research.

Notice that POS-considerations do not support the idea of modularity—that is, an innate form of knowledge that is specific to the linguistic domain—as appears to be assumed sometimes; what they suggest is the richness of the biological base of language acquisition. This base no doubt exists; moreover, POS-considerations do not quite argue for the *existence* of UG, which is simply the theory of IS, and whose non-existence is thus not in question, but only for *specific structures* it must have and its substantive richness.²

POS-considerations crucially extend to phonology, where they are particularly compelling. Languages employ rather different sorts of sounds, which are described in terms of different sets of *phonetic features* in the sound system of the respective languages.³ Uriagereka (1998: 121), taking a particular phoneme from English, the [t], points out that while we all know what a *t* is, we do not know what it is we know here. It takes a whole system of knowledge to answer the question what kind of thing a [t] is. Within the human system of consonants, it is distinguished by a number of features from the other consonants: like the [p] it is a stop and is voiceless, but unlike the [p], which is bilabial, it is dental and alveolar. A slight change in one of these parameters, and a *t* turns into a *d*. Just as there are dialectical differences in language, no two speakers pronounce consonants in just the same way, although they do stay within the bounds of principles and parameters which determine when one consonant switches to another.

More strikingly, unconscious but systematic rules modify the same phoneme so as to produce objectively different phonetic variants of it (allophones). Thus in many varieties of American English we have the following list of eight *phonetically* distinct pronunciations of the same *phonological* unit, the coronal stop [t] (Kenstowicz 1994: 65–6):

stem	[t]	'plain'
ten	[tʰ]	aspirated
strip	[t.]	retroflexed
atom	[D]	flapped
panty	[N]	nasal flap
hit	[t]	glottalized
bottle	[]	glottal stop
pants	[zero]	zero

In other cases there is no variance objectively, but we hear it (phonetic 'illusions'). For example, we think there is a difference between the sounds *tents* and *tends*. Most of us will claim to be conscious of it and trace it to the consonant. Conscious or not, we are not right about at least these contents of our minds:

---

² See Crain and Pietroski (2001), Laurence and Margolis (2001), and Crain and Thornton (1998) for recent reaffirmations of POS-arguments, and Elman *et al.* (1996) and Pullum and Scholz (2002) for recent critical or negative assessments.

³ Phonemes are not, in the opinion of many, mere 'bundles' of abstract phonological features either, but contain a certain order within them that obeys universal principles (Clements and Hume 1995: esp. 245).

there is no such variance, as transpires on closer perception (the difference relates to vowel length).

Phonological rules of a grammar, which compute phonetic representations (PHONs) from more abstract phonological representations, do not seem to be learned or taught in any intuitive sense. Indeed, most people are unaware of them, hence could not teach them (or, as we have seen, they have wrong views about them). No grammar books used by schoolteachers specify computations in the phonological component. So the POS problem arises here as it did before: just as it is not clear where principles of syntactic computation are to come from, it is not clear from where the child is to learn about the computation of allophones. Learning the sound system of language also seems to be quite unlike imitating whatever sounds are produced in the environment. Children have an unrestricted ability to acquire the possible sound structures of human languages (no normal child is unable to acquire the sound system of Japanese, but not Dutch, say), and their 'learning' appears to be a form of 'forgetting' options that happen to be unused in the environment in question (Mehler and Dupoux 1994).[4]

Given the fact that no child has an apparent concern to repeat witnessed utterances verbatim (or to 'imitate' speech like a parrot, rather than generating new expressions creatively, if not whole languages, on which more below), empiricists have typically made the move that children 'generalize' from their parents' utterances to sentences 'similar' to them. That is, organisms are not quite empty at birth, but equipped with innate cognitive powers to discriminate stimuli that are 'similar' and those that are not. The question, however, is: what is 'similar'? Could children acquire a language, simply by being equipped with an all-purpose capacity to inductively generalize from samples of speech, using judgements about similarity which are then reinforced somehow?

For capacities that have a biological basis, as language has, we would not expect reinforcement to play a large role. One might be tempted to attribute language growth to a superior form of 'intelligence' on the side of the child, but this notion does not explain but simply restates the problem. Anybody taking the idea seriously would have to spell out a theory of the mechanism involved in being 'intelligent', and if the latter is thought to depend on the domain-general notion of being better at generalizing from samples by 'similarity', the argument does not

---

[4] There is interesting experimental evidence suggesting that this principle of learning by forgetting applies to semantic knowledge as well. Hespos and Spelke (2004) report experiments showing that, just as in speech perception, children learn not meaning, but which *distinctions* of meaning the language of their environment makes. Specifically, 5-month-old children raised in English-speaking environments are sensitive to a distinction marked in adult Korean but not adult English, namely the distinction between the 'tight' or 'loose' fit of one object with respect to another. The authors conclude that 'the early development of semantic categories parallels the development of phonological categories' and suggest that 'natural language semantics, like natural language phonology, evolved so as to capitalize on pre-existing representational capacities', much in line with claims of Hauser, Chomsky, and Fitch (2002).

look promising. Judgements of similarity uninformed by linguistic concepts do not seem to play a significant role in language acquisition. Similarity is in the mind of the beholder, as Pinker (1994: 416) notes, and it is this mind that we are trying to explain. What is similar perceptually or mathematically need not be similar linguistically, in particular. As Quine (1969) recognized, if similarity is to have an explanatory function at all, something more than similarity judgements is needed; namely an innate 'similarity space', with a metric that will trigger stimulus generalizations of the right kind automatically, and determine, before the organism undergoes any experiences or receives training, what is similar to what in some domain for the sort of species it is. Without any such 'metric' in place, *John is likely to convince*, which is ungrammatical as a sentence, might look very similar to *John is easy to convince*, which is grammatical, and *John looks good* might look similar to *John looks fish*. Viewed in this way, the Quinean acceptance of innate similarity spaces, when thought through to its logical conclusion and given an empirical substance, leads to something like the postulation of an innate set of mental categories that pre-structure our experiences.

Another fact supporting the same conclusions is *language creation*. Children can create a language where none was before. There are two cases here. First the case of deaf children born to parents who do not know a sign language, and who initiate by themselves the development of a sign system that contains rudiments of grammatical and morphological structure. The parents may use the sign system as well, but 'at any stage of development, the children use a greater variety of signs with a greater complexity of combination than the adults' (Jackendoff 2002: 99, citing Goldin-Meadow and Mylander 1990). The second important case is a situation in which speakers of several mutually incomprehensible languages are thrown together in one spot. Forced to communicate, the speakers develop a 'Pidgin' language, which captures the essence of a rudimentary communication system, as it has been devised to serve a purely functional purpose. It does not have the status of a full human language, having only limited and basic grammatical organization, and lacking morphology and inflection. Children in such a Pidgin-speaking community do *not* grow up speaking Pidgin, a language that cannot be natively acquired, hence an 'impossible language' from the point of view of IS. They rather use the Pidgin as a raw material for constructing, within a single generation, a full form of language called a 'Creole' (Bickerton 1981). The latter may contain grammatical devices not found in the Pidgin or in any of the parent languages from which the Pidgin derives. Most strikingly, however, Creoles share similar parameter values, irrespective of the languages they were built from and of the place and the historical circumstance of their emergence (Pinker 1994; Todd 1990).

A conclusion this possibly invites is that the Creole grammar comes from the child's native expectations as to 'what a human grammar looks like'. Importantly, the Pidgin-speaking parents of these children do *not* learn the Creole, staying with the Pidgin, as they are past the critical age where human biology is fit for language creation. If a drive for communication was what grounded language structure, children would presumably grow a Pidgin, like the adults do, not a Creole, with the specific forms found therein. If children have no specialized neural circuits for human language, but are just general-purpose learning machines, we would not expect a communication system like a Pidgin to be an unlearnable language for them, nor would we expect Sign Language learning children to come up with a far more intricate system than their teachers (interestingly, in an abrupt and discontinuous way).

It is a different question whether the emergence of Creoles through language contact provides some clues or even an ontogenetic analogue for the evolution of modern language from 'protolanguage' some 150–200,000 years ago (as Bickerton 1990 claimed). This suggestion has in particular been attacked in work by Mufwene (2001), who argues that both Pidgins and early child language need not tell us anything about the minds of our pre-hominid ancestors. But Mufwene (2002) makes another important point, more relevant to my present concerns. We common-sensically tend to think that language transmission somehow works in the way that current 'speakers actively pass on ready-made systems to learners' and that individuals 'inherit such ready-made systems wholesale' (Mufwene 2002). I think this conception pervades the philosophy of language, where it often seems as if there is this system of language out there, a public, cultural and rule-governed entity, which somehow enters the child's head through a system of education and norms. On these assumptions, if the 'transmission' is not yet complete, the child does not yet 'know a language'. This conception exerts a rather fatal influence on our thinking, leading in particular to the conception that the formation of Creoles is a kind of *non-normal* language acquisition. Mufwene (2001) is a large argument to the effect that this is not so. Mufwene (2002) points out that

Current speakers "transmit" their languages only indirectly by making available to learners bodies of utterances from which the latter can infer and reconstruct systems similar (but not identical) to those of current speakers. Besides, the reconstruction process never ends before one's death or mental incapacitation.

That is, what we intuitively conceive as a form of passive reception of a given fixed system of public rules or norms involves active restructuring on the side of the child. A 'public language' is on this conception a pattern allowing for much idiolectical variation. Moreover, it is a highly changeable pattern, as processes of language change (as in Pidginization and Creolization) may happen in similar ways *within* linguistic populations, even without any special contact with another population. I return to the internalist consequences of facts about language creation in Section 4.3.

Overall, the above data support the conclusion that 'learning' may be a term quite empty when applied to language acquisition, a process better described as an internally directed process of organic growth or maturation rather than a passive moulding from without. With a certain organic structure in place, a certain function will ensue, given an appropriate environment. In language function, to which we turn in the next section, this essential element of creativity in language growth *prevails*. Thus it seems clear that the use of complex human expressions is not 'learned', in the sense that children are taught when to say or think what, for any possible circumstance. Naturally, 5-year-old children often say extraordinarily inappropriate things on certain occasions, during formal dinners, for example, and gradually learn to be more polite. But such educational efforts only come *after* a genuinely creative use of language has been brought into play, and do not disturb (hopefully) its most basic feature, its *uncaused* and *unconventional* nature: who hasn't encountered young children aged 3 or 4 whose pattern of speech is like a little river, a continuous, creative stream of thoughts of whatever sort that happen to come into their minds and flow out again as soon as they occur. Creativity of this sort is there by nature, and in the absence of mental retardation or very severe totalitarian measures that destroy the human basis itself, cannot be erased either. The principle of compositionality, which we will encounter in the next section, will propose that there is a sense in which the *meaning* of a complex sentence, like its use, is not something learned, the reason being that the meaning of a combination of words can be computed deterministically from syntax and the meaning of its parts.

4.2 Language and Communication

Lots of things can be done with language. It is suited to purposes of reference, the recording of natural phenomena (facts), the expression of one's thoughts, creative imagination, the manipulation of others, the metalinguistic function (using language to talk about language itself, as when saying which expressions are true), the phatic function (establishing and maintaining contact), and the poetic function. Whether *communication* is a distinct function additional to all these, or simply an abstraction denoting one joint overall effect of several of them on certain occasions, is unclear. It is certainly true that we continuously use language without quite literally 'communicating our thoughts' or wanting to do so in talking to others, let alone in talking to ourselves. We may be just talking for social reasons, for purposes of manipulation, or for fun.

A larger doubt arises as to what communication *as such*, an activity that *every* species whatsoever engages in, should tell us about the human communication system *specifically*. Clearly, that system is very special, and its special character does not flow from its being a *communication* system, but from its being a system that involves human *language* (rather than pheromones, say, which are what ants use to communicate). For that reason, it is unclear what its being an instance of a *communication* system should tell us about its unique features, especially its structural ones. Hauser's (1996) comprehensive study of animal communication concedes that much (p. 64). The need to communicate in particular makes no predictions on whether we will find a particular set of lexical categories (four, in human language: nouns, verbs, adjectives, and prepositions), locality conditions on movement, hierarchical phrase-structural organization, asymmetries in argument structure, etc.). Nor does the complexity of human societal organization entail the need for such features: ant societies yield staggering population sizes, and are highly organized as well, while communication is by chemicals.

It is the structural machinery above that explains the specific nature of the *human* thoughts that language allows us to freely express, as opposed to more general communicative contents that one can imagine. These thoughts do not seem to be modelled on a basic capacity to *communicate information about* one's surroundings, a prime feature of animal symbolic capacity: selective pressures on a communication system would presumably have designed a system that does precisely that, rather than a system that is so centrally a capacity *for abstract productive and imaginative thinking* involving a potentially infinite numbers of symbolic combinations, rather than being primarily moulded by experiences or communicative needs. Rather than being constrained in its use by what is *true* in the world (the facts), or by our desires and emotions, it may in fact be *language* that moulds humans' apprehension of the world. Humans, using the infinite resources of language, can 'build worlds' in creative ways, the rationale for which does not seem to lie in *communicating* the results of these activities (Chomsky 2005).

The human communication system is a unique one, then, not because it is a communication system or even a particularly efficient one, but because it makes use of *language*, and perhaps as a consequence of that, does not primarily seem to serve as giving directives for *action*, in the way of communication systems in the animal realm at large. It is equally isolated as a communication system through what is arguably its most important structural design feature, namely its *discrete infinity*: the capacity to generate any number of expressions, of arbitrary length, each falling into a finite number of discrete building blocks (words and phrases). This design feature entails that there is no such thing as a longest sentence, pending accidental and irrelevant limitations such as those imposed by memory, the human life span, or the existence of paper and other material on this planet; and that there is no such thing as an output of the linguistic system that is not a discrete unit, or built on the basis of discrete units: it makes no sense to call half a word, or 10 per cent of a word, or 'slightly more' than a sentence, outputs of the language faculty.[5]

In the 1960s, Charles Hockett listed thirteen primary components or design features of language and studied how they are distributed over communication systems in the animal kingdom (cf. Hauser 1996: 47–8). Most of these features *are*

---

[5] There are things like half-pronounced words and unfinished sentences, but the cause of this is not the language faculty but interference of circumstances, time constraints, an intended effect, or a reduction of speaking effort.

observed in some or other non-human communication system, while occurring in *combination* only in the human system (thus, in particular, a combination of discreteness and infinity seems nowhere else to be found). Rudimentary syntax has even been argued to exist in non-primate and non-mammalian communication systems.[6] Somewhat strangely, however, the Cartesians' feature of stimulus-unboundedness, mentioned above, is missing from Hockett's list; so is the staggering human vocabulary size and the distinction between sentences and noun phrases. Neither of these important features appears to have a rationale in communication (a point to which I return). Discrete infinity also, as Abler (1989) noted, is a design feature very widely found in this universe, in non-communicative contexts. The more general principle behind discrete infinity may be that unbounded diversity of form and function depends on a combinatorial hierarchy arising through the combining and permutation of discrete elements drawn from a finite set. Here these units may be genes, proteins, or chemical radicals, as in biological inheritance, or they may be atoms, ions, or molecules, as in physical chemistry, or they may be natural numbers, as in arithmetic. In this way, while discrete infinity is clearly *useful*, it may have far deeper roots than functional utility in organizational principles at work in other combinatorial systems in both biology and physics, rather than being specifically adapted for language or communication.

In the light of enormous dissimilarities among animal communication systems, the question must be raised whether 'communication' is as much as a distinct topic for inquiry, about which something general and systematic can be learnt. It might be that while one can study various communication systems, the study remains descriptive, lacking interesting theoretical generalizations about communication as such that might let us understand any one of these as an instance of what a communication system in general is. Be that as it may, the test case for the currently fashionable claim that language 'is for communication' (see, e.g., Pinker and Jackendoff 2005) remains whether what it is said to 'be for' rationalizes its universal design features. That is highly doubtful given the considerations above and further ones below.

Chomsky has frequently pointed out that while no one doubts that the language capacity is used, only some *parts* of it are used. Others—either because they are not usable or hard to use—remain unused. Even those that are used need not be particularly *easy* to use:

there is no general biological or other reason why languages made available by the language faculty should be fully accessible (...). The conclusion that languages are partially unusable, however, is not at all surprising. It has long been known that performance

---

[6] A rather striking case, investigated in a large-scale ongoing project by Jennifer Mather, is the Caribbean reef squid (*Sepioteuthis spioidea*). whose skin displays a visual language in which some researchers discern distinctive lists of 'grammatical' components, such as nouns, verbs and adjectives (see Mather 1995).

systems often 'fail', meaning that they provide an analysis that differs from that determined by the cognitive system [of language] (...). Many categories of expressions have been studied that pose structural problems for interpretation: multiple embedding, so-called 'garden-path sentences,' and others. Even simple concepts may pose hard problems of interpretation: words that involve quantifiers or negation, for example. Such expressions as 'I missed (not) seeing you last summer' (meaning I expected to see you but didn't) cause endless confusion. Sometimes confusion is even codified, as in the idiom 'near miss,' which means 'nearly a hit,' not 'nearly a miss' (analogous to 'near accident') (Chomsky 2000: 124).

Chomsky's statement (ibid.), that 'the belief that parsing is "easy and quick," in one familiar formula—and that the theory of language design must accommodate this fact—is erroneous; it is not a fact', seems well-grounded. It is further true that for language to be an adaptation for communication, there would be some expectancy that different languages spoken in the same environments have a tendency to *converge* rather than to remain mutually incomprehensible. While languages mix, however, and change historically, they do not 'blend' arbitrarily into one another, in a way that variation between languages would be continuous, i.e. for any two languages there would be a third one lying in the middle between them (see further Baker 2001: 82). However languages develop and change, they appear to conform to one structural type, characterized by the principles and parameters of UG.

That human syntax should be so highly idiosyncratic and constrained is another surprising finding, in the light of what would seem to be an opposite expectation in a system primarily serving the communicative purpose. If anything, the strange intricacy of syntactic rules makes communication *harder*, by keeping us from assigning meanings to expressions that it would otherwise make perfect sense to assign to them, and that may even effortlessly *be* assigned to them in communication, despite an ungrammaticality that transpires on reflection. E.g., the expression *More people have read books by Marquez than I have* will usually get a meaning ascribed to it (perhaps, *I am not the only one who has read books by Marquez*). But its meaning becomes opaque the moment we think about it. There are strange syntactic constraints on what something can mean that are absent in the symbolic languages of logic. Thus, for example, '2+2=4' might in logic be rated equivalent to 'for all x, 2+2=4'. But in natural language, in *vacuous quantifications* such as this, a quantifier has no variable to bind in the formula that is in its scope, and hence has no effect on semantic interpretation. Since the latter formula is *logically* equivalent to the former, there is no logical or semantic reason and no reason relating to our communication of semantic contents to rule it out. In striking contrast to that, in human languages such semantic vacuity is completely impossible, a correlate of which would be expressions like *Which number is such that 2+2=4?*, or *Which thief stole Jim my watch?* This is a reflection of what appears as a fundamental principle of human grammar design, to which we return:

FULL INTERPRETATION: Expressions must be fully interpretable.

In the above examples, the quantifiers would not be.

If a designer were to fabricate an efficient communication system, it would likely come out dispensing with much of human syntax as we know it today, and with morphology in particular, since rules of complex word formation *in addition to* rules of phrase formation involve dual processing costs, for no obvious reason.[7] Some have tried to make functional sense of syntax by depicting it as a device of *ambiguity resolution*, but syntactic processes may *create* ambiguities where none were before, and it has long since been argued that there is nothing wrong *grammatically* with ambiguous logical forms, even though they seem communicatively of dubious use and nothing like it is tolerated in standard logic (see further Martin and Uriagereka 2000, and Sections 5.5.–5.6 below).

Carstairs-McCarthy (1999) centrally poses the question why it should be that all known natural languages distinguish syntactically between NPs (noun phrases) and sentences—*two* ways, so to speak, in which expressions may 'fit the world', namely through reference (in the case of NPs) and through truth (in the case of sentences). Carstairs-McCarthy argues that nothing in our communicative concerns dictates that all human languages should have any such distinction:

> to a linguistic outsider such as a Martian, the sentence/NP distinction, far from fostering communicative efficiency, could well seem a pointless encumbrance and its universality among humans quite mystifying (1999: 27).

It may *seem* that to make an assertion to the effect that Merkel won the German election we *have* to use a full sentence headed by a verb like *won*. But a linguistic species different from us only in not having sentences over and above NPs as a structural design feature of their language would not have the intuition that a sentence was required here. Even we, equipped with sentences as we are, can simply say *Victory for Merkel*, an NP, leaving the specification of Tense to context, as a newspaper headline might. As Carstairs-McCarthy points out, possible alternatives to languages with the sentence-NP distinction are easily imaginable, e.g., a language arising from English by nominalizing each English sentence. None of them seems intrinsically unusable, or even suboptimal. Again, it may be plausible to say that a *human* NP used for a full assertion is short for a sentence at a deeper level of semantic representation, but for most human languages this is at least questionable; it is less plausible for some human languages that actually

---

[7] More precisely, as Carstairs-McCarthy (forthcoming) points out, artificial languages like Esperanto, while also having morphology and syntax, do not have one aspect of morphology that is found in all human languages to some degree, namely allomorphy: every Esperanto morpheme has only one shape, following the principle 'one form one meaning'. In human languages, the shape changes with context (cf. *foot/feet* or *keep/kept* in English).

feature nominalized constructions as full sentential assertions;[8] still less for any of the non-human languages mentioned above.

It seems deeply problematic as well to blame the sentence/NP distinction on the structure of reality, hence to make relational sense of it, though this time not on a communicative, but on a metaphysical basis. Thus the ontological distinction between things and events, or objects and facts, might be hoped to ground the syntactic sentence/NP distinction. But in the light of the fuzziness of these distinctions the task does not seem a hopeful one, as Carstairs-McCarthy argues, and in fact the causal line arguably runs in the other direction: would a non-sentence-using linguistic creature that is otherwise like us necessarily have the intuition that there are 'facts' out there? Facts are propositional structures, or 'correspond' to propositions, and propositions are what sentences express. The stipulation of an ontology of facts will hardly explain the sentence.

In contraposition to attempts to explain human language functionally or relationally, Chomsky (1966) has reminded us of a number of seventeenth- and eighteenth-century rationalist thinkers who did *not* view human language primarily as a functional system, given its contrast with non-human animal language. That the latter may well be a purely functional system is a conclusion that stands essentially undefeated after many decades of intense study of animal communicative abilities. Descartes noted that what is crucial to humans are clearly not the organs of speech, as the parrot has those as well, nor certain peripheral psychological equipment or sensory organs:

men who, being born deaf and dumb, that are in the same degree, or even more than the brutes, destitute of organs which serve the others for talking, are in the habit of themselves inventing certain signs by which they make themselves understood (Descartes 1637, part V: 122).

Nor was general intelligence of the essence of human language, Descartes notes in the same pages, as no human beings are 'so depraved and stupid, without even excepting idiots, that they cannot arrange different words together, forming of them a statement by which they make known their thoughts'. It is also not the unboundedness of human linguistic output that counts as characterizing the specifically human mind: a machine can achieve this easily by iterating its output indefinitely, or building more and more complex structures recursively. What is crucial, rather, Descartes points out, is *freedom from environmental control* in language use, despite its *appropriateness and coherence*. A man's language is undetermined by 'any fixed association of utterances to external stimuli or

---

[8] Thus, in Gungbe a whole sentence can take a determiner (Det, like 'the'):

hon dee Kofi hon lo
flee that Kofi flee Det
The fact that Kofi fled [with emphasis on fled]

which suggests that the objects to which the determiner attaches have a nominal character. My thanks to Enoch Aboh for these data.

physiological states (identifiable in any non-circular fashion)', as Chomsky (1966) summarized Descartes's position, noting, by contrast, that

> [e]ach known animal communication system either consists of a fixed number of signals, each associated with a specific range of eliciting conditions or internal states, or a fixed number of 'linguistic dimensions', each associated with a nonlinguistic dimension in the sense that selection of a point along one indicated a corresponding point along the other. In neither case is there any significant similarity to human language (Chomsky 1966: 78, fn. 8).

Here we notice a second time, reaffirming our earlier conclusions drawn from the history of science, why we should doubt a relational or referential conception of human language and mentality: in the absence of 'any fixed association of utterances to external stimuli or physiological states (identifiable in any non-circular fashion)', there will be referential acts carried out through language, but the association will not explain these acts. We cannot, without using human language and the concepts it allows us to express, point to objects of reference, and in this way (hence 'non-circularly') explain from these what our words mean. I return to this in Section 6.2.

Descartes concretely and plausibly argued that in contrast to animal language, our words 'make no reference to any passion' (Descartes 1637, part V: 121), excepting cases where we cry out in joy or pain, and our articulations seem directly connected to the passions we suffer. That is, while non-human animal language *can* (perhaps) be studied as a mechanical response system to either external or internal states, the human language system is not in this sense a function of what occurs, or the kind of automatic and mechanical response that the Cartesians associated with the workings of a machine. Despite the absence of stimulus control, human language is not random, however. It is adapted and appropriate to *whatever* circumstance we find ourselves in, and coherent with whatever else we and others say. Only humans, and maybe only in their language use (not maybe in their emotions, their immune system, etc.), have no particular dispositions to react to only *some* possible stimuli adaptively. There is no set of, say, a thousand utterances, or a million, which *alone* I could use as an appropriate reply to something you say when entering my room. Interestingly, the workings of the linguistic system when triggering responses to external inputs does not even seem to depend on the *nature* of the input that sets it in motion, which may be linguistic as well as non-linguistic, like a sunset. In short, we, but not the brutes, have *reason*, in Descartes's phrase a 'universal instrument that can serve for all contingencies'. If, despite the unbounded nature of my responsive capabilities, reason, as manifest in the appropriateness of language use in circumstances no matter what they are like, is *universally* adapted, it is no adaptation at all (which is always dedicated to one kind of task rather than another). It is simply not fathomable, Descartes suggests, that given these facts we could still be machines, in the sense that we are *wired* or *programmed* to react to *any* of the vast number of possible experiential triggers in a mechanical way, rather than being, astonishingly enough, *creative* in responding to them in a stimulus-free fashion.

Animal signalling has now been studied in great detail, but despite the superficial appearance that signals used as alarm calls in vervet monkeys (Cheney and Seyfarth 1990), say, are precursors of human words, such calls may not be referential in the way of human words, and may be quite different in other respects. Monkey alarms are dedicated to a small number of functional contexts, such as the detection of predators or food; the repertoire of such calls in one single species is small, restricted to objects and events in the present, with no hint of any capacity to creatively adapt new sounds to new circumstances. By contrast, even a small child's early word *doggy* is not situation-specific in this sense, and may be used to do various things (comment on the presence of a dog, draw attention to it, call it, inquire where it is, or to remark on the fact that something has a 'doggy' nature (Jackendoff 2002: 239). A primate's call functioning to report on the presence of a leopard, by contrast, is not usable to ask where that leopard is. Most human words, as Hauser, Chomsky and Fitch (2002: 1576) note, 'are not associated with specific functions (...) but can be linked to virtually any concept that humans can entertain', and are 'detached from the here and now'. Child calls, moreover, even in the one-word stage, are sensitive to syntactic distinctions (proper names and common nouns) (Macnamara 1982).

There also appears to be no evidence that alarm calling in monkeys is intentional (or goes along with referential intent) in a sense that presupposes a theory of mind, or takes into account what others believe or want (Cheney and Seyfarth 1997).[9] Combinations of different vocalizations used in particular calls of non-human animals have an iterative character, in that repeating a call may intensify its meaning, in the same way that a repetition of *never* in *I never, never said that* means *I emphatically never said that*.[10] To put this differently, purely iterative structures have what we may call a 'cumulative semantics': as you add more *nevers*, you get more of the same. By contrast, syntactic combinations of words in human languages yield new meanings productively and systematically, a fact that has an explanation in a second fundamental design feature of human language, the property of *compositionality* (for more see Chapter 5):

PRINCIPLE OF COMPOSITIONALITY: Combinations of words yield new meanings, which, although they are new, systematically depend on those of the parts.[11]

---

[9] A limitation possibly linked to human infants' unique ability to imitate, and, unlike chimpanzees, their ability to appreciate referential pointing. For a recent assessment of the available evidence see Tomasello *et al.* (forthcoming).

[10] I owe this example to Juan Uriagereka.

[11] Not all human linguistic expressions can be given a compositional interpretation: the previous example involving *never* shows the opposite, as Juan Uriagereka points out (personal communication). It is not interpreted as *it is not the case that it is not the case that I ever said that*. In that case, it would mean the same as *I said that*, which is not the case.

Human words themselves do not have a 'holistic' nature, like animal vocalizations, each of which is assigned a different meaning, but depend on a system of roughly forty (in English) phonemes that are individually meaningless and have meaning only in structured higher-level units (syllables and words). That is, primate language has no phonology, a generative system of knowledge that organizes a limited set of a few dozen phonemes combinatorially into an intrinsically unbounded set of syllables (subject to universal constraints on sonority), which in turn combine into an unbounded number of words. For example, several phonetic segments concatenate so as to yield the humanly possible syllable *true*, while forbidding a humanly impossible syllable, such as *rtue*.

For several reasons, then, it is questionable at present to what useful extent animal calls can be regarded as precursors of human words. Jackendoff (2002) argues that the severe limits on primate vocabulary that remain even after extensive training suggest a *dedicated mechanism* of word acquisition in humans. While the matter is controversial (see Bloom 2000 for useful discussion), Jackendoff's proposal makes sense of the fact that the difference in vocabulary size (60,000–80,000 words in adult humans, by current estimates) apparently is not due merely to a difference in brain size (Jackendoff 2002: 241–2). Vocabulary growth might be a specifically human specialization, while the apes' vocabulary learning might be more like the way human children acquire reading competence: with effort, requiring motivation and instruction rather than being spontaneous.

Carstairs-McCarthy (1999) suggests a different option, however: bipedalism in savannah-dwelling hominids gave rise to larynx-lowering, and thus enabled humans to emit huge amounts of vocalizations. This in itself tells us nothing about whether all of these sounds would also each *mean* something different, which they consistently do: synonymy in human languages is extremely rare, if existent at all. But this may be a consequence of another cognitive principle, *synonymy avoidance*, 'likely a part of our biological inheritance dating from before the chimpanzee-human split, five million or more years ago', and attestable in chimpanzee learning today (Carstairs-McCarthy 1999: 216). It demands that all contrasts in form imply a contrast in meaning. Given this principle and our early vocalization power, there had to be distinct meanings for the distinct sounds our ancestors were capable of producing.

Interestingly for an internalist perspective, this second model prioritizes sound over meaning in the explanatory order (ibid.: *v*, 132). The vocalization power was *there*, as a new element on the evolutionary scene, and this is what required meanings waiting in the rings to be activated and matched to the sounds, meanings that otherwise would not have surfaced. It also explains why vocabulary size does not seem to correlate with environmental or social factors: the organic prerequisites for a modern vocabulary were essentially there well before 50,000 years ago, effectively independent of any adaptive pressures to have a vocabulary as large as that.

The data I have reviewed leads me to conclude that building either one's theory of words or of sentences on the idea that they are intrinsically action-linked or functionally motivated is inherently problematic. To the extent that words are parts of intentional actions, it appears as if words are a presupposition for such actions to take place, rather than being explained through them. Eagle alarm calls in vervets are causally connected to environmental objects and to an appropriate response-behaviour, but even human *alarm* calls don't function like that, let alone all other human utterances.[12] Of necessity, language use is potentially surprising, like the next sentence I will be writing down here, and your reaction to it.

If the idea of a law connecting environmental state and words is watered down to a statistical generalization, this does not seem to help. A situation consisting of a blue sky and warm weather may prompt me to say 'It's a fine day', but it need not, and it does not give it a certain likelihood either. No matter how fine the day is, I may decide to say any number of other things; and I may use the sentence, with the same meaning, in a situation in which it's rainy and cold, or in which I don't know the weather. If asked in what circumstances I would use this expression, I would say: in a situation in which I think (feel, judge, believe) that it's a fine day, thus re-using the expression in a circular fashion in answering the question (though I only need to re-use its meaning, of course, not its sound, so a translation would do), and I could not fill in the dots in the expression frames 'I say "It's a fine day" when and only when...' or '"It's a fine day" is true if and only if...', in a way that would be non-circular, explanatory, or informative (except for a foreigner who knows a language already). For each candidate one puts in, unless it is the content in question itself, it would seem that it is neither a necessary nor a sufficient condition for my saying 'It's a fine day' or for considering it true.

Can we conceive of a situation in which this sentence could *not* possibly be used in a coherent way? Recall the day need not be fine by other than my standards, I need not myself ultimately think that the day is fine, or have given the matter any deeper thought. I need also not have talked about anything specifically in my environment (the morning, the 12 daylight hours of the day, a 24-hour day, my mood right now, etc.), and I need not even know what exactly I talked about or referred to. There is, again, in this sense no clear one-to-one correspondence, or even any obvious statistical correlation, between actual utterances and specific circumstances in the world (if non-circularly specified).

One might be tempted, when talking about sentential meaning, to introduce the notion of a 'fact' or 'state of affairs' as an independent explanatory notion, so as to supply the notion of sentence meaning with an external or relational correlate in the environment. But independently of the aforementioned problem

---

[12] Thus, if you storm into a room and shout 'Fire!', I may or may not stand up and run out of the room, but ask 'Where?', 'Really?', 'How serious?', 'Are you sure?', 'Did you call the ambulance?', decide to stay and close the windows first, reflect on your reliability, burn, or do a myriad of other things.

that in the absence of language we might not assume such an ontology in the first place, facts and state of affairs are like strange shadows of sentences. How do we know *what* state of affairs is being talked about *without* grasping the meaning of a sentence that 'denotes' it? And which state of affairs *does* it 'denote', as it is used in so many various circumstances? We may have to satisfy ourselves with the fact that while it is true that humans judge various contents to be true or false, it is far from clear that there are conditions under which this happens that could be identified independently of the respective judgement or content (see further Hinzen 2003a and 2006a, b). This is also to say that truth conditions (or states of affairs, specified independently of the relevant content) do not analyze meaning, but depend on it (see further Section 5.5 below).

Also if we analyse meaning in terms of an 'intension', a mapping of words to extensions relative to a context, then before we can know *which* intension to select for a given expression, and which extension to map it to, we need to know the *meaning* of the expression in question: it is *that meaning* on which reference *depends*; only it tells us *when* something qualifies as 'water', say, or that *that substance there* is an instance of it. To determine whether some such substance is water, the concept of water is presupposed. It is in *this* sense *not* an empirical or *a posteriori* matter to find out what the reference/extension of an expression is; reference-fixation is an *a priori* matter.[13]

We will return to these internalist conclusions in Section 6.2. For now we conclude this section by noting that even disregarding problems with functional explanations at large as discussed in Chapter 3, functionality and action-linkage of a kind that we can for good reasons ascribe to communication systems in non-human animals, do not seem to provide good keys for human language. The entire question of the external 'function' of language may be of unclear significance and does not seem to provide a useful heuristic for understanding it. Furthermore, there seems to be little reason to expect that an explanatory benefit for structural aspects of human language will spring from studying communication as such. If an adaptationist explanation of language is taken for granted (perhaps on the *a priori* grounds that the alternative would be 'God'), the important question of whether there are such explanatory benefits would be begged.

---

[13] The so-called 'two-dimensional' framework in semantic theory confirms this point in interesting ways. As Chalmers (1996: 57–9) notes in his lucid exposition of it, '[t]he primary intension of a concept [roughly, it's conceptual content, known independently of empirical findings, unlike the secondary intension [which depends on how the actual world turns out] is independent of empirical factors: the intension *specifies* how reference depends on the way the external world turns out, so it does not itself depend on the way the external world turns out' (Chalmers 1996: 57; and see 78). There is much to recommend the viewpoint here that before we have *any* kind of intension (mappings to referents in dependence on which worlds are actual or counterfactual), we need to know a concept *a priori* which *determines* it and explains how the word–world dependency falls out: intensions *explicate* the content of concepts but do not *substitute* for these. Still, there is no independent ontology of concepts in Chalmers, such as I would advocate.

4.3 Language as a Social Construct

I have claimed in passing that nothing in the empirical study of language requires or has depended on the conception of an external, shared, public, and norm-governed language, which philosophers often regard as primary or at least mandatory, often on grounds deriving from the work of the later Wittgenstein. According to my account, 'languages' in this philosophical sense can only be reconstructed as (non-explanatory) abstractions *from* internal states of an individual speaker/hearer, the degree of abstraction from a given variant being a matter of choice or one's specific interests (hence not reflecting a factual issue). There are dialects distinguished by empirically attestable phonetic and grammatical features associated with single cities in Italy. Should we say there is *one* thing, Italian, or *many* Italian languages? But how many? To some, having many 'languages' will be relevant, to others not. It will depend on interests and concerns, and these may be various. In some cases one can invoke the authority of written or 'canonical' grammar books, but the very existence of such books is irrelevant to human linguistic competence as studied in a naturalistic perspective. There was full linguistic competence before there were any books and schools, and there are many communities today that do perfectly well linguistically without their languages having any orthographic aspect. Swiss German, though not an official written language, could be argued to be a language rather than a dialect on many sensible grounds, and is indeed an important aspect of Swiss identity. Yet some people consider the features of Swiss German to be mere 'divergences' from some normative conception of 'German', which they regard as the 'canonical' idiom. Regrettably, I have heard it said that Swiss German is only a 'primitive' language unsuited for academic discourse. But then, suppose at some point in the future, the Swiss dialect were to cross the German border, and eventually pervade most German federal states. Would not High German then be a 'divergence' from Swiss German? Only prejudice and ignorance about the fundamental structural and expressive similarities of *all* human languages will make us deem the question of the 'canonical' idiom a factual one. What we deem a 'language' and what not is a matter of human values and contingent history. In short, although there is *a* sense in which there are public and shared languages, these notions are shifting and value-loaded, and therefore cannot be the subject of a naturalistic inquiry into the human language faculty.

The way in which there are no imaginable limits on how one might individuate a language is analogous to the sense in which for the Neo-Darwinian the individuation of a species is ultimately a matter of choice rather than fact (there is no way, for him, to 'carve nature at its joints' in this respect). One criterion for individuating the putative 'public' and speaker-external languages might be the degree of *language invariance* in a population, just as one might group individuals together into a species if they are similar enough in some sense. Variance in a population however is what we expect, biologically speaking, and it does not prevent us from identifying and talking about species. No two individuals of one species are biologically quite alike, and if individuals cluster in groups, these will merely exhibit a certain measure of similarity among its members.

The invariance criterion more than any other should make us suspicious in any case, however, as uniformity in a group's language (being the expression of what we may call a language 'norm') depends on an elimination or assimilation of variants that will usually be there, and that may be perfectly acceptable ones, prejudice aside. Throughout history it has been thought that certain languages had some kind of privilege over others: that only these prestigious languages depicted reality as it really was, or depicted thoughts in some pure form. Voltaire said this of French, Heidegger and Nietzsche of German, Herbert Spencer of English. But, although cultural context *may* make a difference to which principles of UG are selected for use, the theory of UG is a perfect empirical basis for the assertion that contrary to what our preconceptions may suggest, it simply makes no sense to call any human language better or worse than any other.

Any 'norm' as what a language is really like or how it 'should' be spoken will have to be enforced in one way or another, through a ruling elite, democratic decisions, schools, etc. The history of modern national languages is a history of chance, political interests, and power, factors through which a certain way of speaking becomes enshrined and canonical. Canonical 'shared languages' for which norms have been put down arise through genocide and invasions, geographical dispersions, or a ruling caste's brute suppression of alternative languages spoken by people judged inferior, minorities, or just illiterates. Twenty-five percent of the world's 6000 or so languages have fewer than 1000 speakers and are threatened by language death (Crystal 2000). By and large, there seems to be nothing desirable, let alone necessary, in a high degree of language uniformity in a population, and there is nothing at all in the biological nature of language that makes any such normatization natural. Even canonized languages constantly shift, independently of 'ruling norms', and unbeknownst to those who speak it. This is why the 'norms' are sometimes *adapted* to a language change that has already taken place. There probably are no laws for how languages change diachronically. It seems good advice from leading theorists of language change today that we should not attribute intrinsic properties or general tendencies to history, but rather we should study language change synchronically and locally, as triggered by a shift in linguistic forms that happen to be produced in some environment (see Anderson and Lightfoot 2002: 161–2).

No matter how shared languages arise, change, and die, the empirical claim made here is that there is something that is unchangeable on a historical timescale, which in this sense is something highly abstract, though not as abstract as the notion of an external public language, which is abstracted even from individual human organisms. The present conception of a language is thus less abstract than, for example, Lewis's (1983) conception of a language as a mapping (in a mathematical set-theoretic sense) of sequences of meaningless marks onto a set of meanings. Schiffer (1994b: 589) notes that languages so conceived exist in possible worlds in which there are no speakers and no brains. The study of *human* language will on this view have to take the form of a characterization of what is called the 'actual language relation'—the one mathematical mapping that happens to characterize a given population of human speakers. This essentially happens by constraining the mathematical mapping by data about how the population intentionally uses language, so as to single out one mapping, the actual one. Lewisian 'languages', Schiffer suggests, though abstract, are abstractions *from* their uses in 'intentional' communicative behaviour.

The present approach reverses these priorities. We do not start with what is *mathematically possible*, but with what is an apparently far smaller range of options permitted by human nature. It is not clear why we have to constrain languages *additionally*, by data on the intentional use of language (as Schiffer does), particularly given the unclear significance of the notion of intention for the study and explanation of linguistic meaning, including lexical meaning. Such data may of course provide *evidence* for possible innate principles of language design. But what does it mean to say that these data *constrain* the human language system? Possibly, having a 'theory of mind' in the sense in which apes may lack it (Cheney and Seyfarth 1997) is a precondition for human word acquisition (Bloom 2000), but this is not the kind of claim Schiffer makes. Structural constraints of human language do not, as I have here argued, seem to follow from the use of language as a communication system. Things are rather the other way around: the intentional use of language is constrained by *language* in the sense that what the language system happens to be like explains certain aspects of how it is intentionally used. In any event, a Lewisian approach depends on the present one, if language acquisition is taken into account: for then we must assume that language is finitely represented in the brain, whence the abstraction from individual mind/brains has to be given up.

Schiffer (ibid.) finds it 'plain' that the meaning of *words* has something to do with the beliefs and intentions underlying our use of them. This might be a claim about human *concepts*, or about which concepts we *pair* with which sounds in the lexicon, but I cannot see why it is plain either way, or even plausible. If the former option is intended it is a substantive claim that having concepts, and applying them in a certain way, has something to do with having certain beliefs and intentions. But if anything, it seems that beliefs *contain* concepts as constituents, and the acquisition of the latter cannot in turn be a matter of acquiring beliefs (see Fodor 1998, 2003). If the latter option is intended, we should observe that the mechanism of the process of pairing sounds and meanings is still in large parts mysterious. There is empirical evidence that we learn our words as infants in a form of learning by exposure that suggests the pre-existence of concepts prior to their lexicalization. Lexical acquisition has been described as 'conventional', in which case beliefs and intentions would enter the picture, if they are used to explicate the notion of convention. But while it *is* a conventional or arbitrary matter—a matter not determined by FL—how concepts are pronounced in a particular language ('chair' or 'Stuhl', etc.), it is not clear what is the empirical basis for assuming that the child's fixation of the sound–meaning link depends on the formation of intentions, when it intuitively does not: the process is intuitively just a matter of growth and maturation. It depends on internal mechanisms of sound recognition, and presumably principles for the assembly of concepts. The latter principles seem almost entirely unknown. By and large, it seems we should dutifully note what the author of *How children learn the meanings of words* (Bloom 2000) tells us in the final pages of his book: 'Nobody knows how children learn the meanings of words' (p. 262).

The claim being made here, then, is that, when taking a naturalistic stance, everything in language development and language change is ultimately the result of processes in individual organisms: 'public' languages change only through changes at the level of the individuals that internally represent them. No external entity, existing somewhere outside the heads of humans is invoked in an explanatory role. At the same time—taking another perspective—nobody would deny that human languages are, essentially, historical and social entities. It seems simply obvious that languages are things which communities invest with values, cultivate, and struggle to defend. Is there a conflict here? Not in the least! When talking about a situation where a community is striving to preserve its language the *naturalistic* basis for this will be that there is a population of communicating humans equipped with a language faculty and a capacity for assessing values, talking in a distinctive way, where 'communicating' and 'distinctive' are a matter of degree. But for a serious inquiry into human struggles of this kind and the social world at large, other theoretical categories altogether will be needed than either the philosophy of language or the biolinguistic framework offers.

These considerations suggest that the dispute between defenders of an alleged 'private language' or 'mentalistic' concept of language in the Chomskyan tradition and defenders of a 'public language' concept is essentially empty. Contrary to a widespread misunderstanding, the choice to focus on an internally represented system of linguistic competence is not an attempt to give a *definition* of language, or to say 'what language is'. Indeed I am not assuming here that there is any 'essence of language' at all. All inquiry is interest-driven, and if one wishes to study human linguistic competence as a part of natural science, it is a consequence of one's methodology that one will not focus on languages as historical and social entities. The fact that languages have a history in populations is a fact acknowledged by everybody; the existence of FL in the present sense is also universally acknowledged; and the legitimacy of a theory of UG describing the state of this faculty at birth, when a child will learn any language on the globe upon exposure to it, should, I am arguing, also be so acknowledged. Problems arise when a philosopher insists on the substantive nature of the dispute and denies the very legitimacy of calling 'language' whatever does not depend on the social-historical nature of language.

In one sense, the present approach could easily accommodate this contention: it would simply be observed that the human language faculty of a single individual does not develop without its developing in a sufficiently similar way in a population, too (minimally, probably, in two individuals). But such a dependency is true for all sorts of other factors. Thus, linguistic development depends on the absence of severe pathologies. That condition should therefore, if we followed the same logic, also be rated to belong to 'the essence of language', but clearly it is not. Furthermore, any such conclusion about social dependence is consistent with a biolinguistic inquiry into the human language faculty, which examines an internal system of mental representations underlying man's social capacity.

Some philosophers would forbid calling such internal representations 'linguistic', but it is not clear why we should obey such strictures on how to use the word 'language'. It would be like saying that the arcane results that physics research on the nature of light has brought to the surface are illegitimate, because they do not meet the intuitions of ordinary people using the word *light*. Consider the following assertion, unabashedly endorsing such an essentialism about language, from a recent paper by Alberto Voltolini:

> the notion of human language, as grasped by conceptual analysts, is essentially social. If something is to be defined as human language it *must* involve a reference to a community: no language-like structure may count as human language if no other individual aside from its present user also actually uses (or used or will use) it. (...) This means that human language can hardly be studied apart from its communitarian aspects (Voltolini 2001: 96).

So if syntacticians investigate the Minimal Link Condition, say, or the polysynthesis parameter, and wish to define these as features of 'human language', they cannot do so without considering their 'communitarian aspects'? Is Jones's understanding of causative verbs really not related to 'language', unless Smith's use of causatives is taken into account, or that of the people of the village in which he lives? *No* level of abstraction, it seems to me, is illegitimate, as long as it yields results of theoretical interest.

Perhaps it *is* essential to our *ordinary* concept of language that it is social. If the 'conceptual analyst' is interested in the structure of this ordinary concept, and the latter had that social content, however, the only thing that would follow is that whatever internal mental representations a generative grammar theory posits to explain human language acquisition, these have no bearing on our commonsense concept of language. This is perfectly possible, and would, if true, be true in just the sense that the physicist's conception of light need have no bearing on the criteria for how we ordinarily use the word 'light'. In turn, the result of the conceptual undertaking would have no bearing on the empirical study of the *natural object* of language, except for initially and informally indicating which object is being inquired about.

'OK,' the conceptual analyst might reply, 'but then the generative grammarian's empirical enterprise should not be said to be concerned with "language" at all.'

But this is bizarre. It remains a fact that grammatical structures and principles (phrase structure, the Minimal Link Condition, etc.) *enter into* the explanation of our human language use, and the explanation of facts of linguistic meaning in particular. These principles may be wrong, of course, but this is not Voltolini's objection.

Like other defenders of the externalist language concept, Voltolini builds his claims on Wittgensteinian assertions concerning the impossibility of a 'private language', and that 'one cannot follow a rule only once', or 'alone'. But apart from the fact that all of these assertions cannot in any easy way be transferred to a contemporary context (the 'cognitive revolution' post-dates Wittgenstein's entire work), I make no claim that we are 'speakers of a private language'. I only claim that my language use, to the extent that it can be explained naturalistically at all, is explained by appeal to internally represented linguistic structures in my mind/brain: in short, by appeal to my human nature. This obviously does not mean that each speaker is a *solus ipse* who controls her language use by some strange operation of introspection alone, and only talks to him-or herself. In fact, as noted, the claim is entirely parallel to similar claims that some internal structure in planets (gravitation, etc.) must be posited to explain their behaviour.

Wittgenstein rejects the very idea that the person who hasn't learned the language of her community, 'knows that he sees Red, but cannot express it' (*Vortrag über Ethik*, p. 50). Now, from one point of view, a person 'knowing' and having the *thought* 'I see Red' simply *is* a person *expressing* it (expressing being not the same thing as *phoneticizing*, so the person may not be using language loudly). Under this interpretation, Wittgenstein's point breaks down. It is directed against the idea of mysterious 'inner objects', as something we could talk about or have an awareness of independently of any language, and that would explain language. With this, the present perspective is in full agreement: one cannot explain language by non-language (a human whose language use is to be explained must possess the language faculty). If Wittgenstein's supposition is one of a person who hasn't learned a language at all, on the other hand, it is not clear that we can make sense of it. There is no such thing as a (neurotypical) human being who 'hasn't learned the language' (foreigners, too, *have* a language, and there is no period of time during which infants do not either acquire or know a language). The (according to Wittgenstein mistaken) idea of a language as something 'external' into which 'internal thoughts, ideas, etc.' are then translated is not even formulable in a Chomskyan frame of mind: the human mind is as such a linguistic one. What remains of it if you subtract the structures of the language faculty, is anybody's guess.

Wittgenstein also argues that if a child had to learn a language by 'connecting' words with certain 'inner impressions' (images, representations in the relational sense, *Vorstellungen*, etc.), it would never learn a language; it could not tell, from the image, and a sound it hears, whether the *right* picture was invoked. But, in one sense, language acquisition as *standardly* understood entails just this

Wittgensteinian conclusion. To *acquire* words, the child *needs* a rich innate endowment already, possibly with a conceptual structure as such, which then is mapped to words (Gleitman *et al.*, 2005). Concepts *are* not learned by extensive comparisons of inner and outer objects. At least *some* concepts must be *there*, waiting to be selected (Piattelli-Palmarini 1989; Bloom 2000; Fodor 1998; Hinzen 2005a). The picture Wittgenstein critiques here is an *empiricist* one, not a rationalist one of the kind that the Chomskyan 'mentalist' is endorsing.

The Chomskyan also makes no claims about 'rule following', in the philosophical sense. Human minds when building syntactic trees do not 'follow rules' or do so 'privately' any more than trees do when they branch in a pattern according to algorithmic principles of plant morphology. Wittgenstein invokes no philosophical problems for law-governed behaviour in the natural realm (as opposed to normatively conceived rule-governed behaviour in human societies), and if human language use is in part law-governed in exactly this naturalistic sense, he need have no objection to the idea of a UG (else a methodological dualism would seem to be adopted). Wittgenstein's objections were to the philosophical invocation of private 'meanings' or other such 'furniture' in the 'inner space' of consciousness in an explanatory role. There is nothing wrong, he notes, in saying things like 'John meant to say such and such when he uttered these words'. But things become non-explanatory if mysterious mental acts of 'meaning something' are thought to be 'denoted' by words like 'John meant (...)', and to bestow 'dead' signs with the 'life' of meaning. Talk about *ideas, thoughts*, etc., I have pointed out in Chapter 1, is *not* to be construed as talk about (either inner, or outer, mind-external) objects, on the model of '"Gegenstand und Bezeichnung"' (object and sign; see PU, §293). This is a model that Chomsky takes pains to *reject* in his critique of referential theories of meaning (Chomsky 2000).

We may usefully think of Wittgenstein's suggestion concerning the explanatory value of inner objects ('seelische Vorgänge', etc.) as a desire—and urge—to stick to a certain *standard of intelligibility*. What Wittgenstein describes in detail when he depicts a shopkeeper in *PU* §1 obeying the order 'Five red apples', are *mechanisms*, algorithmically implemented step by step. Its execution is what we *see*, Wittgenstein claims, it is what lies *open to view*. Something in all of us wishes to go beyond such descriptions in terms of mechanisms, but our invocation of inner 'meanings' or 'intentions' in a causal-explanatory role when going further in this way only leads to irresolvable conceptual puzzles that Wittgenstein spent a lifetime analysing and exposing, by showing how they arise from a misunderstanding of ordinary language—the language that is natural for us to speak, as human beings. In this philosophical vision of how things are made intelligible, saying 'He meant such-and-such when he said...' cannot be a piece of descriptive speech, in the sense of a depiction of some inner process, which can then be accorded some explanatory role in the theory of meaning. Our use of such expressions in certain circumstances is itself the *criterion* of what it is to mean and say. Our use of the phrase illustrates, but does not explain, what it is, in our language, to mean and say something. There is no 'mental reality', but a use of mental *vocabulary* for human purposes. Our common-sensical explanations reach as deep as our ordinary language does, but no deeper. On the other hand, what naturalistic inquiry may reveal about the nature of our minds is an entirely different matter—according to Wittgenstein none that philosophy touches upon.

Note however that Wittgenstein's mechanisms in analysing the shopkeeper's actions primarily serve only a therapeutic and illustrative purpose: they are clearly not intended as empirical hypotheses, and serve to illustrate what a mechanical explanation *is* that does not appeal to mysterious 'meanings', or to things that are 'hidden'. From today's viewpoint, a generative grammar is nothing other than a machine that carries out a sequence of actions, or that computes according to certain principles. The idea of mechanical explanation and the standard of intelligibility it sets are quite the same.

While some have found an explanatory model of human speech behaviour in Wittgenstein—in essence, a behaviourist model—it is interesting that Wittgenstein himself gives good arguments that setting up communal norms and sophisticated systems of training and punishments does *not* in fact ensure that people will follow rules 'in the right way'. (As I would put it, human nature is needed.) For suppose a community convinces a newcomer of 'the right way' to follow a given rule by the brute law of force: *Abrichtung* ('training'), in Wittgenstein's terms.[14] Wittgenstein notes two problems (among others): first, any *Abrichtung* can only use a finite number of samples, say n samples. But no *Abrichtung* on what to do in n cases has the power to tell what the 'right way to go on' in the $n+1$ case is. In fact, just about *any* continuation is consistent with the data provided. Since for an infinite number of algebraic rules (such as 'plus 2') we know or have the intuition that there *is* one and only one continuation, it immediately follows that our knowledge of such rules can't derive from experience or training.

Suppose also, Wittgenstein imagines, you apply exactly the same kind of training or *Abrichtung* to *two* foreign individuals. You give them exactly the same samples, rewards, and punishments. Even so, it may be that one will react differently than the other. Who would then be right? (PU, §206) One of them, when questioned why he 'doesn't get it', might innocently ask: get *what*? 'Well, you know, what I *meant*.' But what is this, *meaning* something? It can't consist in the number of examples for the rule in question that was given, nor in some kind of brain state (any one of which, again, could not determine the 'right way' to go on for an infinite number of examples). Here we are on the familiar course of the rule-following problematic. What you *meant*, ultimately only *shows* in the way you act. There is no way for you to point to 'what you meant' in calling the reaction of your candidate 'incorrect'. The acting explicates the meaning, not the meaning the acting. But the way you act does not interpret itself: it does not wear its interpretation

---

[14] 'Abrichtung' corresponds closest to a behaviourist model of language learning, which Wittgenstein explicitly opposes in PU, §§307–308, or *Vortrag über Ethik*, p. 70.

on its sleeve. It requires interpretation, and there is necessarily an infinite number of possibilities for doing so, as long as we rely on the mechanisms available in a reinforcement model alone, no matter how extensive the *Abrichtung* was.

It seems that an appeal to human nature seems unavoidable if we are ever to get out of the quandary that the rule-following problematic so simply and vividly poses. Wittgenstein here prefigures the very problems we noted earlier for the way in which connectionist nets acquire knowledge on the basis of reinforcements (see Marcus 2001): why do children generalize beyond the training set in a largely uniform and correct way, apparently using algebraic rules that are independent of statistical generalizations over heard input, and why do they *correctly* understand and produce sentences that they have never heard before? The claim has been made that a naturalistic approach appealing to the rationalist idea of human nature could never make sense of the possible 'correctness' or 'incorrectness' implied in the application of a rule.[15] But notice that from a certain age, any child will find that this 'square' is rather imperfect:

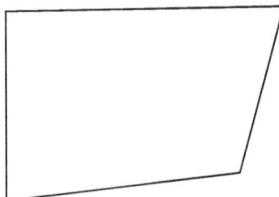

For, quite clearly, it does not live up to the norm that the child's notion of a square provides. It's quite wrong, not because that's what the child 'learned', or because of *Abrichtung*, but because this is what the child's *geometrical capacity*, jointly with her capacity for vision, suggests to her. Somehow, it will seem to the child, the concept of the square and the image do not 'match'. In the same sense, certain sentences sound 'queer' to an adult speaker, are judged 'odd', 'improve' when modified in one way or another, or are 'irremediable'. Normativity comes so naturally here that one wonders where the problem with it lies and what its

---

[15] Note that school grammars might *note* certain violations of syntactic laws, even though most will go mentioned, precisely because the laws are so enshrined in human grammatical knowledge that they go unnoticed. For example, it would be rare for a school grammar to notice, let alone explain, that *Who do you find out how he loved* is ungrammatical, while, surprisingly, *How do you find out who he loved* is perfectly meaningful. Interestingly, if such facts *were* noted, school grammars might formulate the relevant constraints as *norms*: 'You must not say: ....'. Then however normativity would be brought in at a point where we should be talking about syntactic law, since it is that law that *explains* why we have the intuition about wrongness in this instance (we are not dealing with an arbitrary convention here). It's not that 'we must not do' such and such in a language: rather, we (at least if we are native speakers) *will not*, performance failures or explicit intentions aside, make the relevant 'wrong move', if indeed it is ruled out by principles of UG. Here again the *absence* of certain kinds of mistakes in the course of acquisition is relevant (Crain and Pietroski 2001).

explanation might be, if not the inherent structure of our minds.[16] As for grounding normativity by conceiving language as 'essentially social' in the philosophical sense discussed earlier, it is not clear how a community's *Abrichtung*, or simply one's being embedded in it, should possibly yield the single right answers to continuations of rules in infinitely many cases, or how these social parameters could possibly ground the normative force of the intuitions we have. None of us thinks, on reflection, that an ethical judgement, say, that you make becomes right because you make it, or because it is made by your or any community.

Explanation by mechanisms as a standard for intelligibility has always come at a price: things not accessible to mechanisms, such as colour-sensation or subjective experience, will fall outside science thus understood. When Wittgenstein develops what is maybe the simplest imaginable kind of language game—one builder giving short orders to another one using names for well-identified objects in their immediate surroundings (PU, §2)—what we are witnessing is an attempt to narrow down language at large to a maximally small-scale and specialized case. Might we not at least understand what is going on *here*? Wittgenstein falls prey here to the dream of constructing one kind of 'language' that works rather like a natural machine does for the Cartesians: purely mechanically, with no problems of understanding and no need for 'mysterious forces' or something 'hidden' arising. But as our above discussion of *Abrichtung* suggests, even here matters remain too complex. ('How can we make sure that the one builder "understood" the other in quite the way the other "intended", and so on').[17]

What Wittgenstein may be seen to have taught us is that two things should be avoided: the *trivialization* of meaning, in the sense of naïve attempts to reduce it to some reinforcement process, an empiricist learning theory, or a 'causal' theory that is built on the notion of reference that Wittgenstein centrally critiques; and the *mystification* of meaning, in the sense of departures from a mechanistic model of explanation. The rule-following problematic, as I read it, points, on the one hand, to the need to accept that some dimensions in our grasp of meaning are irreducible and primitive. They point to features of human nature, and perhaps we cannot go beyond that. On the other hand, that doesn't mean anything mystical is going on. It just means that with regards to aspects of human meaning, there may be fundamental limitations to the scope of our human scientific understanding.

This chapter has surveyed Plato's problem, the problem of how we know what we do know, on which we have a grip through the theory of UG. Descartes's

---

[16] There also is 'correctness' and 'incorrectness' of a kind that is really not worth talking about: for example, some school teachers in Bavarian schools in southern Germany will call it 'wrong' if a child writes *ischt* rather than *ist*, even though this is exactly how they pronounce the word themselves. On exactly that ground, other school teachers (in Montessori schools) explicitly tell the child and its parents that the former is *right* when it transcribes *ischt* from the phonetics. So who is right? Well, in the end the largest population will decide how things are to be done, and if *it* spells *ist*, there is no chance for the *ischt* to survive in orthography in the long run.

[17] I defend the above interpretations of Wittgenstein in a more elaborate way in Hinzen (2004).

problem, how we come to use that knowledge in the surprising and creative ways we do, on which we have no grip whatsoever, as functional paradigms of explanation that apply to non-humans do not seem to apply here; and Darwin's problem, how we came to have that knowledge, the answer to which does not lie in studying communication, so I have argued. This final section has argued that much in Wittgenstein is consistent with, if not supportive of, the present enterprise focused on language as an aspect of human nature. The following chapter delves into the structures of the human language faculty as such.

5

Beyond the Autonomy of Syntax

5.1 What is Syntax?

The question of this section should maybe have been: what has syntax become? Our technical concepts sharpen as inquiry proceeds; it is not that inquiry adapts to notions as defined independently and prior to it:

> In general, one should not expect to be able to delimit a large and complex domain before it has been thoroughly explored. A decision as to the boundary separating syntax and semantics (if there is one) is not a prerequisite for theoretical and descriptive study of syntactic and semantic rules. On the contrary, the problem of delimitation will clearly remain open until these fields are much better understood than they are today. Exactly the same can be said about the boundary separating semantic systems from systems of knowledge and belief (Chomsky 1965: 159).

What syntax is, then, crystallizes within actual syntactic practice, rather being a matter for a 'theory of syntax', which would lay down once and for all what 'syntax', maybe as opposed to 'semantics', is. Any of my following remarks are prefaced by this remark, and they try to draw some meta-theoretical *consequences* of current syntax rathers than theorize about it. On a *most* general level, we might say this:

SYNTAX
Syntax is the *structuralization of items from the lexicon* (loosely: *words*).

Human linguistic expressions are not assorted bags of words. They even fail to be such bags if we are dealing with a language, such as Warlpiri, in which word order can be freely varied, as opposed to languages like English, where word order is decisive.[1] The point is that in order for an expression to mean what it does, its lexical items must *fit into particular slots* in the syntactic structure of that expression.

Structuralization in this sense is not arbitrary, but highly systematic in human language, which is why syntax is not trivial, and why it is a science rather than a matter for stipulation. A curious fact, for example, is the *impossibility* or deviance

---

[1] What substitutes for word order configuration in English in Warlpiri is a Case-marking system, which indicates by means of affixes attached to words which grammatical function they have. See Baker (2001).

of certain expressions. We would like to know, say, why certain expressions, like *How do you find out who he loved* are grammatical, while otherwise very similar expressions like **Who do you find out how he loved* are deviant. Why should this be? What do such facts about what meaning can or cannot be associated with a sound follow from? It seems in particular that there is no semantic or conceptual reason for this, for there is a perfect semantics we can associate with the starred expression above: *who is such that you find out how he loved (someone)*. But the above expression does not express that meaning.

Note that what we have just considered is an expression that is deviant or impossible *under a particular interpretation*. It is an essential point that there can be many forms of deviance in the expressions a grammar may generate—there is no *general* notion of well-formedness or ill-formedness invoked in generative grammar, indeed there cannot be. What is important here is that expressions are considered as sounds *paired with* meanings, hence that its meaning is a feature *intrinsic* to a human linguistic expression. Certain possible meanings require certain matching forms. We wish to know the reason for the severe strictures that syntax apparently imposes on this relation of matching, which do not seem motivated on semantic grounds.

Nothing in the claim that syntax is 'autonomous', to which we return, should distract from this conclusion: that syntax is a project intrinsically involved with meaning, indeed in exactly the same sense that it is involved with *sound* (though reducing to neither). One may even say that meaning and sound and their relation is what syntax is *about*: syntax is supposed to explain us *why* certain expressions cannot have certain meanings and must mean something else. Take the rather surprising observation that *Mary's mother* does not have the possible meaning of the expression *Mary is a mother*, even though both of these expressions share the same 'substantive' lexical items, namely *Mary* and *mother*, and virtually the same pronunciation. Their other items are 'functional' ones—*s*, *a* and *is*—which do not have a substantive content in the way that *Mary* and *mother* do. On a standard semantic account such as, e.g., Heim and Kratzer (1998: 61–2), the non-substantive items involved in these expressions are semantically vacuous. Hence no semantic explanation seems to be forthcoming for the fact observed. Why then is the former expression not interpreted such that motherhood is predicated as a standard property of Mary?

A good answer is that syntax disallows a predicative role to the noun [$_N$mother] in the former expression, *as a consequence of the nature of its underlying syntactic structuralization there*, particularly its 'functional' (rather than substantive) parts (see Higginbotham 1985: 558, for this example). In a similar way it is an empirical semantic observation that *the portrait of Jay's*, in contrast to *Jay's portrait*, can be used to refer to a portrait painted or owned by Jay, but crucially not to a portrait that has Jay on it. Again the phenomenon we have is that one particular expression pairs one particular sound with a (number of possible) meaning(s), excluding other logically conceivable meanings, in particular the impossible meaning just mentioned. We would like to explain this fact, and the explanation should relate to the nature of the expression involved.[2]

A much more mundane case is *John loves Mary*. Why does this necessarily mean that John loves Mary, while leaving it open whether or not Mary loves John? One answer points to world knowledge jointly with logical reasoning: it so happens, in our world, that the act of loving is not reciprocal, a fact that presumably has nothing to do with language. Thus, when hearing *John loves Mary*, we simply do not infer that it is also true that Mary loves John. But this explanation basically presupposes what is to be explained: the meaning of *John loves Mary*. We have to *understand* this sentence as a description of a possible state of affairs, so as not to infer another state of affairs. The explanation of that understanding, which I adopt here is entirely different, and does not invoke world knowledge, belief, or reasoning at all. There is a fundamental *asymmetry* in the human phrase: human sentence structure is not 'flat':

but 'hierarchical':

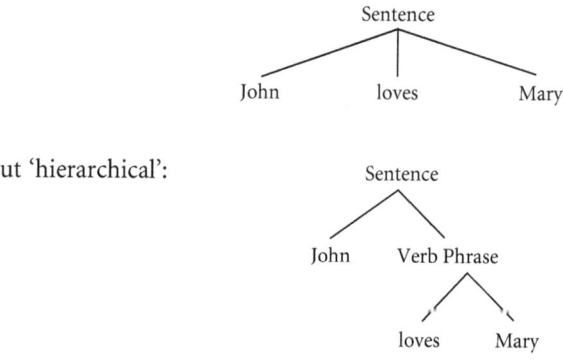

That is, *Mary* is structuralized in a more *local* relation to the verb than is *John*, giving rise to an asymmetry, which together with other syntactic factors (arguments once merged in one syntactic argument position can't be re-merged in the position taken by another argument, see shortly) forbids the arguments to be permuted, so as to rise to the interpretation that Mary loves John. In other words, it so happens in human argument structure that if a transitive verb has two arguments, its *internal* (more local) argument will be the object (the 'Theme' of the activity denoted, or what 'undergoes' a certain action), whereas its *external* (less local) argument will be the agent (what undertakes the action).

In short, *theta-theory*—one *module* of UG—governs that argument position in syntactic structure systematically correlates with thematic position in semantic interpretation. For Mary to be in the position of the lover, it would have to be structuralized as the external argument. But it simply isn't, in the structure in question. To get the impossible meaning, we must violate a law of theta-theory,

---

[2] For the (standard, I believe) explanation, see Anderson and Lightfoot (2002: 47–51). The explanation boils down to the syntactic principle that deletions of elements that are not the topmost items in a complement of an overt, adjacent word are forbidden by UG.

and we cannot do that. We cannot *give* an argument a position in the structure *John loves Mary* simply because we would like it. An expression means what it does, and has the structure it does; we cannot make it mean what we like by making it have another structure. See what happens if we try to give *Mary* the other position, by simply moving it to the front: *Mary, John loves*. This still means—unambiguously—that John loves Mary, not the other way around. In this way, an expression's meaning is not to be tampered with, an example of what has transpired to be a further fundamental principle of human language design:

STRUCTURE PRESERVATION: Thematic relations once built by the syntax cannot be destroyed by later operations.

One has to *change* an expression, make it another expression than it is, to make it mean something else, as far as thematic relations are concerned.

Some structures, on the other hand, have a tendency to switch to another one, without us being much more than observers in this process. The expression *Mary heard Fido bark in the apartment* may, on an occasion of use, either answer the question where the barking took place or the question where the hearing took place. Here again there is a semantic difference that we can trace systematically to a difference in the structure that the language system in our mind 'perceives' when hearing this expression, even though our eyes and ears do not. The semantic difference relates to a difference in the attachment site of the modifying adjunct, *in the apartment*: it either attaches to the matrix verb *heard* or to the bare infinitive *bark*. Structural ambiguities of this sort have a certain resemblance to drawings that our visual system can interpret differently, as in the case of Neckar cubes (cf. Uriagereka (1998: 247)) or the Wittgensteinian Duckrabbit. While there is no difference on one level of representation (the image projected on the retina by the physical stimulus does not change), at other levels different mental representations can be triggered by such an input, and we can switch between them back and forth.[3]

Sometimes we can also switch between two meanings while *no* structural fact supports the difference in meaning, which is indeed illusory: thus the expression *No head injury is too trivial to ignore*, which we contemplated before, is almost unfailingly interpreted to mean *No head injury is too trivial to be ignored (by us)*, that is, we must pay due attention to all. But it means that *No head injury is too trivial (for us) to ignore (it)*, which is to say, *no matter how trivial*, we should ignore it. It so happens that our world is such that, in it, any head injury should be paid due attention. But language is not aware of such facts. It has a mind of its own: its expressions mean what they do, by the dictates of structure.

[3] To say that the ambiguity occurs because the expression just happens to be used in two kinds of circumstances in the population of English speakers is not a proper explanation. The point about usage is simply an observation of a contingent historical fact. Whereas the claim made here that this fact has an explanation in terms of an underlying structure of such expressions that is mentally represented by speakers using them.

Syntax, then, is the science of what I am calling the structures of expressions, and it is a substantive science because these structures are highly constrained, and relate sound and meaning in factual ways which nothing in logic can predict. This is in contradistinction to formal language syntax, where syntax *is* arbitrary and non-autonomous: it is chosen for some purpose in logic, AI, or philosophy, and hence is functionally driven. A 'science of syntax' can be no concern in this area. Logically, nothing forbids *John loves Mary* to mean that Mary loves John, while in human languages, this is an impossible interpretation. The choice of logic as meta-theory is natural from an externalist and empiricist point of view, since as soon as we regard syntax as a factual-empirical issue and as autonomous, we virtually *are* talking internalistically about structures that characterize the human mind as such. Talking about the mind, moreover, is pretty much what modern logic from its inception in Frege purported to avoid. But again, nothing in logic forbids structuralizations that no child will ever be able to learn natively, say grammars built on the idea of numbering words in a sentence, so that the first word must be the subject and the *n*th the verb, or on the idea that the subject combines with the verb into a 'subject phrase', which then is mapped onto a semantic value prior to its combining with the object to form a proposition. Since *no* human language knows of subject phrases in this sense, or is sensitive to number, logic won't explain these universal characteristics.

Talking about the autonomy of syntax means that semantic knowledge does not predict or explain syntactic structures (as far as we know, it doesn't), and that these are whatever they are independently of logic, in particular. The above examples suggest that this viewpoint naturally combines with an explicit stance *against* (even the meaningfulness of) the charge of 'syntactocentrism' as levelled by, e.g., Jackendoff (2002: 107 ff.). There is nothing syntactocentric about seeking to explain certain facts about the pairing of sound and meaning.[4] If this charge, raised by some semanticists, were at all meaningful, it would seem that phonologists could level a similar charge, but they rightfully do not. The explanation of meaning is quite obviously part of our picture; understanding how humans use language meaningfully and understand expressions clearly *depends* and is *explained* by internal mechanisms that make these overt effects possible. Were this not the case, we would have two separate cognitive competences, one 'syntactic', one 'semantic'. But since they are not entirely independent, we will have to connect them in any case and stipulate further 'correspondence rules' to accomplish this, which is what Jackendoff (2002) does. This is to depart deliberately from what would be the 'optimal' case (or would be the best design), namely that semantic relations between expressions can be traced to (or be read off) their syntactic relations as established in the course of a derivation through the

---

[4] Only on a very superficial understanding does the thesis of the 'autonomy of syntax' mean that generative grammar is 'not concerned with meaning'. Chomsky for one never held this view (as he says: cf. Barsky 1998: 157). In generative grammar, it is expressions-under-an-interpretation (forms with meanings that depend on these forms) that are to be derived.

computational system, as suggested above. The optimal case clearly is what should be explored *first*, and evidence that human language is not an instance of it (which Jackendoff 2002, section 5.9, enumerates) must be counterbalanced by claims that human argument-structure *is* in essential respects syntactic, or does fall out from the primitives of, and the relations established by, the computational system (see Hale and Keyser 2002; Baker 1997).

In fact, Jackendorff not only departs from the optimal case, but denies the *transparency* of the syntax–semantics connection, and the arguably basic principle of compositionality as understood in the previous chapter. This principle states that the way in which expressions are composed syntactically tells us how they are composed semantically (e.g., that *Mary* is merged as the internal argument of *loves* tells us that Mary is the thing loved, not the loving thing). Although it is a claim that must be evaluated empirically for its merits, the assumption of a transparent mapping should quite clearly be rejected only if the less optimal case is strongly supported by evidence. But while a strictly compositional mapping from syntax to semantics is challenged by many seeming counterexamples (see Higginbotham 2002 for humdrum examples and Williams 2003: chapter 9, for discussion), I see no compelling evidence to give it up in favour of Jackendoff's *worst*-case scenario, which is to 'evacuate all semantic content from syntactic structure, just as we removed phonological content' (Jackendoff 2002: 124). This suggestion is entirely puzzling if we think of any one of the examples I started out with above, where syntactic structure enters *directly* as an explanatory factor with respect to facts about meaning. Lexical items are here thought to enter the derivation fully *specified* for both sound and meaning (the lexicon being a set of such sound–meaning pairs). Putting such items together in larger, more complex structures is the task that falls to the computational system, which now must explain why particular *complex* sounds are paired with particular complex meanings, and not others.

By contrast to this explanatory strategy, Jackendoff's cited proposal makes syntax 'autonomous' in a somewhat striking and extreme sense, for it makes syntax and semantics two entirely *independent* generative systems. Having made them independent, Jackendoff must then clearly relate them again, since they aren't independent, but the dependence is now stated not directly, but indirectly, in the form of an intervening interface component. The proposal, moreover, burdens us with an independent 'level of thought' (termed 'conceptual structure') that we will now have to assume as simply given and that nothing in the workings of the computational system underlying syntax will explain. To my knowledge, at no time in Chomsky's various versions of generative grammar has an autonomy of syntax in *this* extreme form been assumed.[5]

---

[5] Compositionality/transparency is a property we also lose if we broaden the domain of a theory of linguistic meaning to include all kinds of context-sensitive and pragmatic phenomena, or if we see it as essentially a part of a theory of communication (see e.g. Kamp and Reyle 1994). But this for me is motivation to operate with a properly *restricted* (sentence-based) notion of meaning as the subject of

In fact, if we look at the various models of the architecture of generative grammar since the 1960s, what we see is something striking. Let us first look at the following model, where we start with a given complex, pre-linguistic, semantic level of 'Thought'. This semantic structure is mapped to a 'surface structure', which is of a linguistic character and is then further transformed by narrowly linguistic processes:

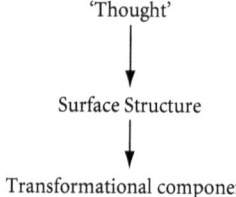

This model was never held by the generative grammar program, which took the course of architectures that is depicted by Jackendoff (2002: 109–10) as follows. In the first (Chomsky 1965), semantic interpretation is read off a level of 'Deep Structure', which was meant to be governed by narrowly linguistic principles such as phrase structure rules operating on the items of a lexicon, LEX:

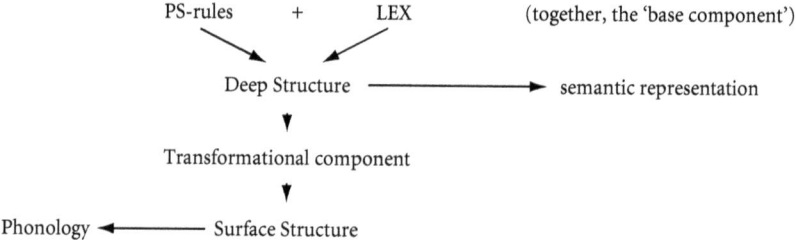

Hence here we see semantic interpretation conditioned by syntactic form. The next model, from the early 1970s, is a reflection of the recognition that semantic interpretation depends also on the *surface* forms derived by the transformational component from underlying Deep Structures:

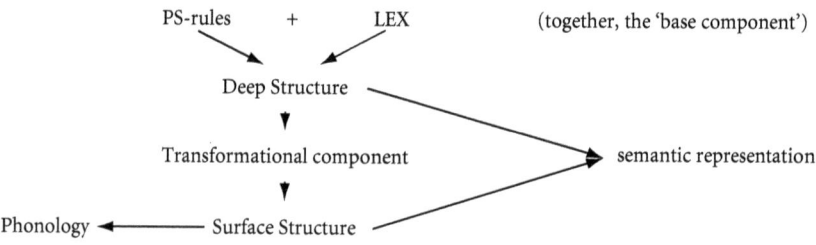

our explanatory ambitions, a notion that will be determined independently of context and other confounding factors. Any such notion will have to prove its fruitfulness in practice.

By the mid-seventies, with the advent of traces (see Section 5.3), it had become possible to read off *all* linguistically determined aspects of semantic interpretation from Surface Structure, and we see semantic representation (the representation of a thought expressed by an expression) again moving one step down in the tree. By that time, also, the phrase structure component had been dissolved into X-bar theory (=X'-theory):

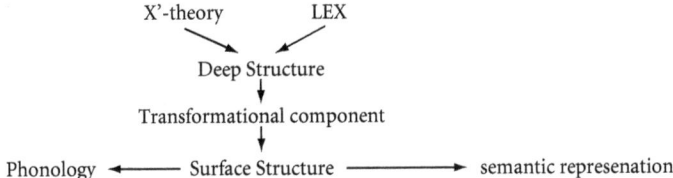

In the early eighties, with the mature Government and Binding framework, the transformational component was largely taken over by the single rule 'Move α', basically allowing the movement of any syntactic constituent anywhere, while the overgeneration this necessarily yielded was filtered by four grammar-internal *levels of representation*, now called D-structure, S-Structure, PF (Phonetic Form), and LF (Logical Form):

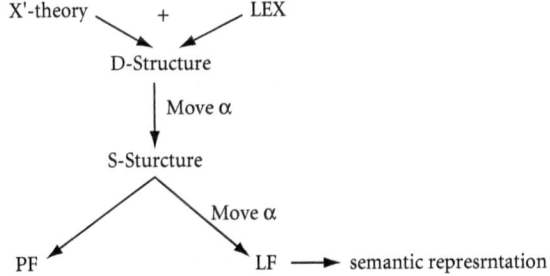

With the advent of the Minimalist Program (Chomsky 1995), the architecture becomes leaner: Move α is replaced by the general structure-building rule Merge/Move; D-structure is dissolved as an independent level of representation; S-structure is replaced by an operation that simply strips off the phonetic features of a representation from its semantically interpretable ones, called 'Spell-Out'; X'-theory is made redundant or 'derived' (see Section 5.3):

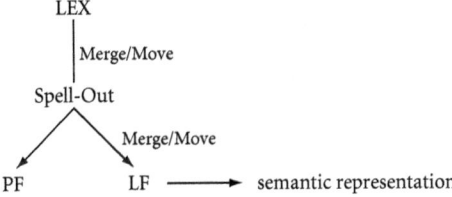

Clearly, what is most noticeable in these transitions is something that Jackendoff (2002: 108–11) does not comment on, namely the consistent *downward shift* of 'semantic representation', corresponding most closely to the philosophical notion of a 'thought'. We began with (the semantic representation of) 'Thought' being at the top, but we finish with it being at the bottom. First, it predates syntax (is an input to it), then it is its product, or something that is at least partially *explained by the derivational process* itself. This shift is central for the general perspective of this book. As a matter of fact, Chapter 6 will end this book with the sketch of a final model, from the current 'derivational' approach to Minimalism, which looks something like this: as a semantic representation is beginning to be constructed, Spell-Out applies several times, as an inherent part of a derivation that itself proceeds in stages or 'cycles', and the interfaces are accessed at each of these points. An LF-representation is never assembled as such; neither are the other old levels of representations, D-structure and S-structure. Instead of such *grammar-internal* levels of representation, we now merely have the semantic interface with the Conceptual-Intentional System, SEM, which, as an interface, is not grammar-internal, and is also accessed several times in the course of the derivation:

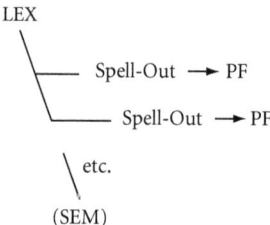

This brings a perspicuous development of over 40 years to its logical conclusion: semantic interpretation is now done as an inherent part of the dynamically proceeding derivation itself.

This development has an evolutionary consequence too: the motivation for the strategy which aims to answer 'Darwin's question' by assuming a propositional level of 'thought', and explaining the evolution of syntax by the need to get this level expressed, disappears (Pinker and Jackendoff and 2005). Specifically, human thoughts *depend* on what the syntax does—the specific syntactic formats that it makes available at the interfaces. This applies to *sentences* to start with: these and only these syntactic items can express propositional thoughts, because nothing other than a sentence (no Noun Phrase, no Preposition) can be true or false, this being a defining feature of 'thoughts' in the philosophical tradition. Even our pre-theoretic notion of propositionality or thought *is* the notion of what can be expressed by a sentence, and it cannot be assumed that the human sentence is something we find prior to or apart from human language. Hence, positing a propositionally structured 'language of thought' prior to human language either raises exactly the same problems as the evolution of human language, or it does not, but then it does not explain human language.

In the absence of a knowledge of just *how* syntactic representations arriving at the interfaces are used and further processed, it is useful to essentially adopt a 'use theory' of meaning, which leaves such questions open. That is, it is assumed that an internal computational system generates structures, autonomously operating, i.e. without being externally or semantically conditioned to operate in the way it does, and these structures then get accessed and used for various human purposes. There is much in the use that is not explained by the present approach, such as why a speaker says what he does, or what communicative goal he wants to achieve, if any. But prior to settling such (much) larger issues, we may be satisfied to study aspects of linguistic meaning that we do see correlating with facts about linguistic form.

Of course, basing structural facts about semantic interpretation on structural facts about syntactic form is to assume that at the lexical level, where syntax does not reign, the meanings are already fully specified, independently of syntax. Clearly, syntax holds no key to the explanation of meanings whose expressions do not manifest any syntactic structure, and hence no question of compositional interpretation in the sense above arises. To take what is perhaps the most extreme case, what would syntax have to say about how we put words to use that are *names*, which we might think of as the simplest of expressions, the 'atoms of language'? Isn't this a matter for an externalist line of explanation *entirely*, the name's meaning being its *reference*, a relation between words and things in the world? My answer to that important question is no, however, and is defended largely in Hinzen (2006a), where it is argued that referential features of names are centrally a consequence of their syntactic form, and their conceptual content is not explained by their reference. Hence, even at the level of the lexicon syntax enters into the explanation of meanings.

Putting the question of lexical meaning aside for the moment, it seems advisable in any case to separate a notion of the *structures* provided by the computational system at the interfaces, where they are interpreted by the conceptual-intentional and sensorimotor systems of performance, from a notion of the *relations* that these performance systems establish to extra-mental structures in physical matter *outside* the human head. The former domain is usefully called 'syntax', and is taken to exclude the domain of external relations, these being 'semantics'. There is a corresponding distinction between the study of how the generative rules of phonology produce phonetic representations instructing the sensorimotor systems for speech production and perception, on the one hand, and the study of the relations between phonetic representations and physical fluctuations in air pressure caused by spoken language in the outside world, on the other. That latter distinction (between phonetics and physical acoustics) seems uncontroversial. On the meaning side, an analogous distinction between what's inside and outside the head should be as well.

This implies that the label 'semantics' is not usefully employed for semantically interpretable structures accessed by performance systems *inside* the human head, contrary to what is proposed by Jackendoff, for example, for whom 'conceptual structures' are an internalist matter. Clearly, saying that what Jackendoff calls semantic/conceptual structure 'does not *have* a semantics, but *is* the semantics for language' (Jackendoff 2002: 279) will cause heavy protests among all those who think that semantics is relational and not internal to the head by definition. The present usage of 'semantics', which reduces it to mind-world relations or to how internal structures get *related* to outer objects on an occasion of language use, does not induce this problem.

We may also note in this connection that the syntactic notion of LF has become much richer in content in recent generative grammar than Jackendoff assumed when laying the foundations of his system. In Jackendoff's system, the assumed *poverty* of these semantic representations within syntax is part of what motivated the new level of 'conceptual structure' (cf. remarks in Baker 1997: 126–7). But because the syntactic notion of LF is richer than assumed, there is motivation to say that syntax *does* structure our very thoughts, and does *not* reduce to the task of *expressing* them in a language, as Jackendoff (2002: 278) proposes. The Jackendoffian picture, that is, assumes language-independent thoughts with logical forms in a non-grammatical sense, which then get translated into language. But there is a *syntax* of logical forms too, and it is part of UG, hence in this sense, it is, while being universal, language-*dependent*. This is good, for it means that there *is* an available and systematic theory of important structural and logical aspects of human thought, namely syntax, and one does not have to presuppose a far more *abstract* level of 'thought', with structures provided by an unknown and unrelated system that then would somehow have to be related to the structures provided by syntax.

The situation thus appears to me to be this. Either we propose a more ambitious and substantive notion of syntax (alias the 'computational system') as something that explains sound-meaning relations and how the meaning of complex (and perhaps even simple) expressions systematically depends on their form. Or we go for two (or more) independently operating computational systems, one generating 'thought', the other generating 'syntax', and supplement our two-pronged generative architecture with a richer interface component that does indirectly what the first approach does more directly: account for form–meaning correspondences. Form–meaning correspondences which simply seem to be there would have to be captured on both accounts, but they are captured more directly on the first, as meaning on the second view is not specifically linguistic and is in fact enriched with all kinds of non-linguistic information, making it a much more difficult formal object to study. As noted, the second strategy also loses force the more we see that a word's argument structure is actually syntactically conditioned.

5.2 Explanation in Linguistic Theory

The child has IS, the initial state, but no theory of it. The linguist has both FS, the final state, and a tentative *theory* of IS (and various FSs). A theory of any given FS in a person or population is what we call *a grammar*. A *generative* grammar that correctly characterizes the properties of a language's sound, meaning, and structural organization, is called *descriptively adequate*. For example, a grammar that derived something on the lines of a structure relevantly like *John is unlikely to forgive* for the expression *John is impossible to forgive* (lexical differences aside) would be descriptively inadequate. *John* is the logical object (the thing not to be forgiven) in *John is impossible to forgive*, but the logical subject in *John is unlikely to forgive* (the thing that forgives).

It is important not to *mis*understand this goal of descriptive adequacy as the goal of devising a machine, or a set of rules, that is capable of generating 'all and only the grammatical sentences of a language'. This latter picture is based on the following idea: any language is characterized by an infinite set of formulas, or sentences, which partition into two sets, the set of well-formed sentences and the set of ill-formed sentences. The task is then to find a set of rules which allow the derivation of all and only the former ones, a task similar to the logician's or philosopher's task of devising an axiomatization of a logic, or a system of inferences. An axiom set for such a system is a system of rules generating all and only the valid inferences. This is crucially *not* how the goal of descriptive adequacy in early generative grammar should be understood, which was rather the goal of correctly describing 'the intrinsic competence of the idealized native speaker' (Chomsky 1965: 24), hence a *cognitive state* of the speaker and its contents. Put differently, our grammar must make sense of what it is to *know* a language. A theory of that competence is not evaluated in terms of whether or not it generates all and only the grammatical sentences of a language (in fact infinitely many machines that could achieve this can be devised for any such set, whereas our mind presumably only uses one of them). It addresses an *empirical* task, not a task for computer engineering.

To rephrase this simple but important point, the task of a generative grammar cannot be formulated thus: 'Here is a set of well-formed expressions. Give me a rule system that generates it mechanically!' This task is simply too easy to achieve, as was clear after early achievements of the generative enterprise. Particular generative rule systems for given languages had been devised as instances of the general scheme for a human grammar imposed by UG. But the theory of UG imposed few constraints on what a possible rule of a human language was: to allow for the derivation of the wide variety of diverse surface forms found among the world's languages, early generative grammars allowed for and posited a wide variety of ever more complex rule systems. If a new construction was found in a language that could not be generated, one would simply design a new rule for it.

These rule systems became powerful enough to describe human languages in the sixties, where a vast generative literature with full-length generative grammars came into existence.[6] But while these early grammars correctly mechanized the formation of particular constructions, they fell short of the explanatory power that generative grammar was centrally seeking. As Chomsky summarized the problem in 1972, in a statement recalling Descartes's worries about the too large deductive power of his theoretical models:

The gravest defect of the theory of transformational grammar is its enormous latitude and descriptive power. Virtually anything can be expressed as a phrase marker, i.e., a properly parenthesized expression with parenthesized segments assigned to categories. Virtually any imaginable rule can be described in transformational terms. Therefore a critical problem in making transformational grammar a substantive theory with explanatory force is to restrict the category of admissible phrase markers, admissible transformations, and admissible derivations (. . .) (Chomsky 1972: 124).

To illustrate, early generative rules systems were *construction-specific*: they would have rules for forming a question; different rules for forming a reflexive, or a relative clause, or a passive. This causes a seemingly insurmountable problem for the child learning any such language on the basis of the PLD: it will have to suppose that the rules for one such construction do not constrain those of any other, and can freely co-occur with them. All of the construction rules were in turn specific to one particular language, not generalizing to others. Thus there were rules for questions in Japanese, relative clauses in French, etc. This, if true, clashes with the assumed universality of the IS.

The problem noted by Chomsky for such systems is *not* a problem of 'psychological reality', but explanatory deficiency. The range of possible human transformational grammars is too large, and to achieve explanatory adequacy, it has to be restricted. Finding the relevant constraints (*conditions* on transformations) will alone allow us to make sense of language acquisition, i.e., the way the child arrives at the relevant cognitive state that a theory of grammar describes. Given its IS, as characterized by such constraints, certain logically possible rule systems will then not even have to be tested by the child.

Importantly, looking back at the history of how the above problem was solved, as noted in Section 2.3, a movement *up* the scale of abstraction was required. The earlier construction-specific and language-specific rule systems were replaced by more general generative principles *encompassing* the earlier rule systems which now became redundant.

A new task for generative grammar emerged from these insights. The enterprise could not now begin by splitting the 'set of the expressions' of a language into those that are 'well-formed' and those that are 'ill-formed'. While generative grammar remained oriented towards descriptive adequacy, the latter notion no

---

[6] Interestingly, one of the earliest full-length generative grammars seems to have been written up not for English but a native American language of North America, Hidatsa (Matthews 1961).

longer meant getting all and only the grammatical sentences right. If a cognitive state rather than an output is the object of inquiry, there is no pre-theoretical notion of *grammaticality* (or 'well-formedness') on which we can rely. The primary descriptive category will not be grammaticality, but a speaker's judgements of *acceptability*, judgements with regard to whether a particular sentence sounds 'odd', is relatively more acceptable than another, or is inappropriate in a particular circumstance. Data such as these allow conclusions (though never *direct* ones) to be drawn about the system of knowledge underlying the generation of such data. These judgements are crucially *graded*: thus *Sally kills Bill* is perfect, as is *Who kills Bill*, but *Who kills Sally Bill* is worse, while *Who kill Sally Bill* is worse still, and *Yasll llik rG Illb* is worst.

The last example is virtually unrecognizable as a sentence of English, but our knowledge of English clearly *extends* to even the third and fourth examples, about which we still know a great deal: we know the topic of this question (a particular event of killing), or that Sally is the subject and Bill the object in the act of killing that is being thematized. But these expressions are not sentences of English, viewed as a set of all and only grammatical expressions. Hence, this notion of English as a set does not capture our judgements in such instances: our knowledge of English is witnessed in intricate and differentiated psychological reactions to *ungrammatical* sentences, too. It does not help to *include* degraded expressions in the putative collection, as then even the last example will have to be included (about which we still know something, say that it has words and a verbal phrase), and the very idea of having such a collection becomes opaque.[7] No such problems arise on the intensional conception of language as an internalized generative procedure that assigns structural descriptions to an indefinitely extensible set of expressions.

Grammaticality, then, is a *theoretical* notion rather than a descriptive one; it depends on the insights of a developing theory of native competence, and cannot be extracted from the data or a native speaker's *intuitions* of grammaticality alone.[8] Let us assume then, in what follows, that the *extensional* notion of a language as a 'set of well-formed formulas', familiar from formal language theory and computational linguistics, is not the relevant notion for the present enterprise. The 'intensional' notion of an internally represented generative procedure

---

[7] In other words, there is no clear way (and no theoretical point) to identify things like 'English' or 'Japanese' as certain sets of expressions. The misunderstanding of Chomsky's program as being concerned with generating 'all and only the well-formed sentences of a language' and hence an extensional notion of language, remains pervasive and is at the root of much traditional and contemporary criticism.

[8] It takes *thinking* for a native speaker to make a judgement on some kinds of data, and in the course of this thinking many errors (performance failures) may occur, a kind of 'noise' in the experiment that may have to be cleared away before we know what any such 'experiment' actually tells us. Note that while judgements of acceptability are data for the theory, they are not what the theory is *about* (they are the outcome of what the theory is about).

is a subject of inquiry of a different kind, comparable to procedural models of the workings of the immune system or plant growth, as in computational biology.

The leading ideal of an *explanatorily adequate* grammar now became to have a theory of IS, hence a theory of how a particular FS *is attained*. This is the task of tracing back the surface variance of languages and idiolects to the unity of the IS; the task of showing that 'the apparent richness and diversity of linguistic phenomena is illusory and epiphenomenal, the result of the interaction of fixed principles under slightly varying conditions' (Chomsky 1995: 8).

The aim is to reduce the language-specific options that UG allowed to an absolute minimum, the ones that are still necessary to achieve descriptive adequacy. Parameters interacting with fixed principles should be few, and the way they take values depending on a particular environment is an instance of chance interacting with law. Since, as noted, the child is exposed to input having primarily a *phonetic* form, what we expect to be parameterized is only what can be detected in data of *that* kind, hence not the syntactic or semantic component of the linguistic system. In this vein the following principle should be understood:

PRINCIPLE OF UNIFORMITY (Chomsky, DBP:2): In the absence of compelling evidence to the contrary, assume languages to be uniform, with variety restricted to easily detectable properties of utterances.

Note again that the move from the earlier rule systems to the later 'Principles and Parameters' that occurred in this way had thus nothing directly to do with a move from something that is 'psychological' to something 'more naturalistic' or 'biological', as Rey (2003: 125) alleges, but with a simple and natural drive towards deeper explanation. Ontological notions (what is 'psychologically real', as opposed to 'linguistically or biologically real') do not enter. The framework also, more so than its precursors, clashes with the idea of the child as 'theorist', or as an inductively generalizing device representing theories as the contents of its mental states. Again the environment merely selects, among a range of restricted and preset parametric options in the child's development. The other options are discarded, and cease to be available after the critical phase of language growth. Theory formation, belief revision, etc., plays on part in this at all. The predetermined options from which the environment makes its selection are not 'about' anything, or theories 'of' something, theories that could be 'partial', or 'partially erroneous'. The child is no 'representational medium', as there *is* nothing in its environment 'of' which the principles of UG in its head could be 'true'. The environment's selective task is not that of making some kind of propositional 'content' 'true', or 'matching' an inner reality of mental representations against an outer one, which these representations represent. The notion of *truth* does not enter into the analysis of linguistic knowledge as we analyse it here (for some epistemological consequences of this, see Section 6.2).

The computational modelling of the human language faculty in terms of a system of principles and parameters will predict that in the mind of the child only certain structures will form (others being impossible for a brain like ours), giving a basic answer to Plato's question: not through saying *how exactly* it happens that the child arrives at the system of knowledge it does, but by saying how it *can* happen, or how what the child factually does is *possible*. In other words, each and every one of the principles actually proposed could be wrong, but we can claim to have a model of the *general format* of a theory that *would* answer Plato's question.

All this leaves, in the presence of each particular theory of principles and parameters that we may propose, a basic question, which is the most central from a philosophical point of view: *why* are these principled and parameterized structures of the human language faculty the ones they appear to be? This is not a question about laws. The laws are what our best theory of UG suggests they are. What we now ask is why there are those laws and no others. Is there a rationale for them? What *sense* do they make? It would surely be a surprise if there was an answer to this rather breathtaking question. Still, suppose grammar theory took the form of an attempt to vindicate assumptions of *what* design optimality, given a certain assigned task, would be, and was successful to some relevant extent. Then we *could* make some deeper sense of the structures of language: we would say they reflect (a certain measure of) *perfect design*.

In this case, there is no such question as *why* design is perfect. If something *is* as we rationally expect it would be, given what task it performs, nothing asks for a special explanation. If light travels in a straight line between two points, this is what we expect. If it is deflected, this is what we seek to explain by looking at further conditions or forces in play. With the vindication of perfect design, nothing calls for further explanation. Perfection, as noted, is something we expect in the *physical* world and mathematics only, but the more we vindicated it in the realm of human language and the mind, the less we would be justified in our assumption that different principles must hold in human and non-human nature, and that standards of explanation must be different too.

Suppose now that we start with an assumption about perfect design in language, so as to see what comes out of this assumption. Then more likely than not, the assumption would immediately crash. We will find imperfections all over the place—properties of the language faculty we simply can make no deeper sense of, or that seem unmotivated. But imperfections are of different sorts, and what is an imperfection in a functional perspective need not be one in a non-functional one. That a garden-path sentence like *The horse raced past the barn fell* is hard to process does not mean there is any structural imperfection to it. Only one kind of design is design-for-a-particular-use. If we try to rationalize human language as an instance of the latter, it will most likely come out as a paradigm of *bad* design (recall Section 4.2). On the other hand, design-for-a-particular-use is not what we are after. It is design-for-having-a-use-at-all (usability), or for satisfying minimal design specifications; perfect design as we may find it thus may have as little to do with utility as the intricate design of the sunflower petals (Amundson 1994).

Not that our notion of a 'task' above is entirely non-teleological: the task of light may be that of travelling through space and time, that of the language faculty to pair sounds with meanings. It is true that the notion of design optimality only makes sense with respect to some function to be performed (some 'purpose' of the system). So it might seem as if there is an assumption here that we must be asking a factual question as to what the 'function of language' is. But this is not so. *Whatever* the 'function' is that we wish to ascribe to language, it is a pairing of sounds with meanings: if we let that be the basic function with respect to which we ask what perfect design would be, then perfect design should deliver and relate representations of meaning and representations of sound, which then get accessed or used by other cognitive systems.

More specifically, nothing *other* than representations having an interpretation in terms of either sound or meaning should exist in the system (all representations should be interface representations). Moreover, *all* representations we find should be fully *interpretable* at their respective interfaces (recall 'Full Interpretation'), and there should also not be *operations* internal to the computational system that make no sense in other terms than the reaching of interface representations. *Everything other than* mechanisms ensuring the pairing of sound and meaning will have to be especially motivated; as long as the system works so as to produce sounds and meanings, everything is as expected, and we will have explained these workings in a more principled way.

Again, looking for perfection may be hopeless for a natural object that was subject to the vagaries of evolution, but then again it may not, since a program emerges, in essence the Minimalist Program itself, to *show* that imperfections that would not be found in a more perfect system, but seem empirically attestable (such as apparent violations of Full Interpretation) are (i) merely apparent, or, if they are real, (ii) reflect *a best possible way* of meeting extraneous conditions imposed on the system by virtue of its interfacing with other systems in the mind (see Section 5.5). If (i), the assumption of design imperfection has been shown to be an artefact of our description or theoretical perception; our *theory* was imperfect, not the object. If either (i) or (ii), a move towards a more principled explanation has been made.

Pursuing the program in this fashion, what looks like a purely aesthetic move at first turns into something quite different. We wish to say that we find the laws we find because nature is perfect (all imperfections must be ours). But this works only if the laws we hypothesize in our theories *are* perfect. So we attempt to *make* them perfect, hence to re-analyse given data that may on the face of them suggest opposite conclusions; we fit the data to a theory rather than vice versa. If we succeed, while crucially preserving descriptive adequacy, we say that the reanalysed data and the more perfect principles are the good ones, for the perfect ones are the ones we expect in a perfect nature.

Of course, only under the *assumption* of natural perfection is the perfect theory more adequate, but this simply reflects the idea that nature sets a *standard* for perfection. There is nothing here that would in principle forbid that the human language faculty be 'ugly'—full of redundancies, say, or violating interpretability of representations at every step—and hence nothing can forbid a theory of grammar that depicts just these ugly realities: such a theory could not, obviously, be regarded as *ipso facto* wrong. But then suppose we *have* a theoretical depiction making for a perfect grammar—a theory that, by respecting only *minimal* design specifications, would still be descriptively adequate, and also be adequate with respect to extra empirical tests, such as explaining acquisition, meeting neurological constraints, constraints on processing, and so on. Then it would *thereby* also be *explanatorily* superior. Since it says the system has *just* the structure that it absolutely needs to be usable, another theory saying it has additional structure that would have to be justified on independent grounds, would be ruled out.

In this way, the assumption of perfection in language has an inherent drive towards its own vindication: the assumption of natural perfection leads us to design minimalist grammars; but then, once we have those, and we have shown them, with help from nature, to be descriptively adequate, nothing else will do. This is a 'self-vindication' of the Minimalist grammar, in the sense that its very *existence* or *possibility* will tend to prove it also *right*.

We moreover have a strong incentive to *start* with the assumption of perfection in the engineering of the sound–meaning connection, or to make it our default hypothesis. Empirically, again, it might in principle be that the sound–meaning connection is badly designed. In a worst-case scenario, the language faculty might be deprived of meaning altogether and would produce only complex sound structures, while the meanings would accrue to these sounds accidentally, say by whatever one happens to be thinking at a certain moment, or by whatever games a speech community happens to play; it might be arbitrary whether to interpret *John is impossible to forgive* relevantly like *John is unlikely to forgive*; compatibility of sound and meaning might fail entirely, so that *John goes home* could mean *I believe that John goes home with his umbrella*; and so on.

But little in this worst-case scenario is at all plausible. The connection between form and meaning seems amazingly systematic. Compatibility for example appears generally satisfied, in that semantic interpretation accords with a given choice of lexical items that enter a derivation. Hence *John goes home* could not mean *I believe that John goes home with his umbrella*. And there is not a shadow of a doubt, on reflection, that *John is impossible to forgive* can*not* be interpreted analogously to *John is unlikely to forgive*, since *John* is the logical object (the thing whom we forgive) in the former expression, but the logical subject (the thing that forgives) in the second. On analysis, it turns out that the surface similarities that suggest an analogous interpretation do not match its underlying structure, making form match with meaning perfectly again. The underlying structure *explains* why the interpretation is not the same in the two cases. Full Interpretability, the demand that syntactic representations must be fully legible (interpretable) at the interfaces, seems substantially correct as well when applied to the semantic interface. There are linguistic features that are uninterpretable, but Full Interpretation makes the prediction that if there are such features, the computational system should act so as to regard them as foreign to the system and needing to be eliminated: in technical parlance, they must be 'checked' for the derivation to proceed.

For example, suppose the system first computes the structure *is a bachelor* from *is* and *a bachelor*. T, the head of the node in the clause encoding tense, then has a nominative *Case feature* to 'check' against that of a Noun that will be its subject. That Case feature is uninterpretable semantically and appears to serve a purely syntax-internal function.[9] Assuming we have *John* available in the derivation, we get *John is a bachelor*, and together with a Complementizer, *that*, we get *that John is a bachelor*. Suppose the string T *is believed* is then merged with this, where T is the matrix Tense node. Then, this T has a nominative Case feature too, and needs to check it against that of a Noun. But *John* cannot do this job, as he has *lost* his nominative Case feature in the embedded clause already. So there is a feature in the matrix T that remains *uninterpreted*: in the absence of checking against the Case feature of another Noun, the structure should crash at SEM, the semantic interface. However, suppose *John*, despite having lost his Case feature, hence violating the economy principle that all moves should be for a reason (or forced), *moves* into the matrix subject position, leaving its original position empty. Then from the assumption that the grammar is economically designed, we would again predict that the derivation would *crash*, which it does: **John is believed that e is a bachelor*, where e is the position, now empty, from where *John* is moved. This example illustrate how economy principles are predictive for how the system works. See further Section 5.4.

Suppose now the sceptic were to insist: beautiful as the design of the grammar and the sound–meaning connection may become, how can that tell me that it describes an aspect of (psychological) *reality*? I have responded to this charge in Section 2.3, but there is now a more striking and powerful response (see Chomsky, MI, version of 2000: 97). With the present approach it seems that there simply can be no such constraint as 'psychologically reality', even supposing we could make sense of the spurious dichotomies in play here ('mental' as opposed to 'physical', 'linguistic' as opposed to 'psychological' evidence, etc.).

---

[9] Thus, e.g., compare (i) and (ii) below:
(i) We thought him to suffer.
(ii) We thought he suffered.
where the pronoun plays the same role semantically in both cases, the role of the person that suffers, even though it bears overt accusative (ACC) case in the first example, and nominative (NOM) case in the second. Languages differ in the extent to which Case is overtly marked, English being particularly poor in this respect, Latin or Russian being richer. On the standard assumption that all languages have Case abstractly nonetheless, it is surprising that there appears to be no direct semantic motivation for it.

The point is that the system might be *exhaustively described* by the way it meets the interface conditions optimally—conditions that *must* be satisfied—and has no more internal structure besides. If you have perfection, what more can you expect from 'reality'?[10]

This is not to say that we might not learn more about neurology, processing, or language evolution. But we would expect that our theory of *language* to be essentially finished: with the vindication of perfect design, the grammar satisfies all 'psychological' tests that might be imposed as *further* constraints on the theory as well. Instead of saying that we are doing 'linguistics', or 'psychology', we will not care about such academic labels any more and simply say: we investigate properties of a natural system, one crux of which is its satisfaction of interface conditions.

Notice again what happens if we give up on the idea of certifying 'psychological reality': we essentially have lost the 'mind', in the old sense of something we distinguish from nature, a locus of 'mental states', propositional attitudes, and so on. But we have won it back in another sense, as an autonomous and abstract structure in nature which to study means to study us, as natural objects. Looking at these ideas, the original goal of linguistic theory, descriptive adequacy, has naturally lead, via the notion of 'explanatory adequacy', to the more ambitious minimalist project of 'principled explanation'. The latter goes beyond 'explanatory adequacy', which aims to explain how the child reaches a stabilized (final) state of the language faculty from an initial one, IS (S_0, in the quote below):

the initial conditions on language acquisition fall into the categories (i), (ii), and (iii):

i. Unexplained elements of S_0.
ii. IC [interface conditions] (the principled part of S_0)
iii. General properties [of organic systems, such as general principles of computational efficiency]

Principled explanation, going beyond explanatory adequacy, keeps to (ii) and (iii) (Chomsky, BEA, version of 2004: 106).

To the extent that we can keep to (ii) and (iii), language will be rationalized as a solution satisfying conditions on usability (interface conditions, 'bare output conditions') in conjunction with general principles of computational efficiency not specific to language (principles of locality, of structure preservation or conservativity, and so on). The implications for language evolution are immediate: to the extent that principled explanation is achieved, not much of an evolutionary explanation is *called for*: human language design will be rationalized as a mapping between interfacing systems that are already given, hence are not

---

[10] One sceptical doubt concerning 'psychological reality' (Devitt and Sterelny 1987: 142–6), moreover, was that theories of the computational system on offer (in 1987) had too many alternatives. I claimed this was true but irrelevant, and didn't prevent any such theory from having empirical content. But now we see: a perfect grammar has no alternatives.

specifically shaped by natural selection for the purpose of language. Principles in category (iii) are domain-general as well, hence no longer involve natural selection as a designer of the language faculty specifically. It is category (i) that will demand special explanations and the search for extraneous factors, such as fortuitous accidents of evolutionary history, contingent features of brain physiology, genetic tinkering for some function, or whatever else, which one will then see as interacting with natural necessity, or law.[11] Indeed it is a coherent possibility at this moment of inquiry that there is *no* mechanism within human language use that is unique to language and unique to humans, *including* the crucial element of recursion. If so, all that is new in humans is how these mechanisms get *integrated* into a system serving some novel function, in which case the need for adaptationist explanations of the mechanisms involved in that system falls apart: the 'argument from design' would be 'nullified', in the terms of Hauser, Chomsky, and Fitch (2002).

5.3 Human Phrase Structure

The fundamental assumption of phrase structure theory is that words in human sentences group into abstract units, namely *phrases*, which fall into a number of *types*, indicated by so-called *labels*. Thus, suppose the computational system of language has 'merged' *destruction* with *of Syracuse*, to obtain the syntactic object *destruction of Syracuse*. Then because of the *recursive* character of the Merge operation, this very object can enter into further computations, or be merged again. This object moreover contains information that will have to be accessed in these computations, and will play a role at the interfaces (where nominal constructions are interpreted differently from verbal ones, for example). The idea of having labels is that this information is contained in only the *label* of the syntactic object, which specifies its type: in our case, that it is of the *nominal* type, like the lexical item *destruction* itself. It is because of this that our object will play a certain role in the further computation. Hence, if labels are not assumed, a generalization

---

[11] Note that if a feature that falls into category (i) involves historical accidents, we cannot automatically exclude the possibility that we find both principled and internalist explanations here as well. Take the sentence/Noun Phrase distinction. I have mentioned that there may well be no principled explanation for it in terms of bare output conditions: the conceptual-intentional systems putting linguistic structures represented at the semantic interface to communicative use (category (ii)) do not seem to necessitate such a distinction. But it also does not seem to fall out from principles in category (iii). Thus it falls into category (i). But then, there is Carstairs-McCarthy's (1999) suggestion that the distinction derives from the exaptation of an evolutionarily prior physiological trait, the lowering of the human vocal tract. This allows vocalizations with a syllabic structure, which is then 'exapted' for syntactic structure, which will mirror the structure of the syllable. Is Carstairs-McCarthy's explanation for elements such as this 'unprincipled'? No, it is just that the principles are more akin to those applied in palaeontology than to those applied in physics or mathematics. There would be, given vocal tract lowering and syllabic structure, a principled (and internalist) explanation for why sentence structure is what it is. My thanks to Andrew Carstairs-McCarthy for conversations on this topic.

will be missed. Accordingly, a mind capable of phrase structures must have *symbolic representations*: its transitions from one stage in a computation to the next stage depend on what abstract type of symbol it is dealing with, though not on its context of occurrence or derivational history.

That implies that for labels to be useful at all, they should be relatively few: if there were as many labels as there are lexical items in particular, they would be trivialized. And few they are: with the generative tradition I will here assume that the primary *lexical* category labels are limited to four, namely N(oun), V(erb), A(djective), and P(reposition), with the first three being clear instances of the natural kind 'lexical category', in contrast to the fourth, which has a somewhat dubious status (Baker 2003). Each of these categories has an *open class* of members, each with a substantive content, contrary to the functional categories, like T(ense), D(eterminer), *v* (transitivity marker), or C(omplementizer), to which we return later, and which determine 'closed' classes of expressions that universally contain only a limited number of (short) morphemes, if they are phonetically overt at all.

Phrasal types are not physically manifest in either the phonetic or the orthographic form. But we unfailingly perceive them, or 'impose' them on the acoustic input we hear. This is what explains why *I love chasing cats* is likely to be uttered by a cat-chasing child, while *I hate chasing kids* is uttered by the child-chased cat.[12] For what we perceive (and interpret) here (in this context) is really *I [love chasing] cats* and *I hate [chasing kids]*. Syntactic transformations respect such phrase boundaries, or are 'structure-sensitive': thus, when moving the noun phrase [*chasing kids*] in the last example, we can obtain [*Chasing kids*] *I hate*, or [*Chasing kids*] *are hated* (*by me*). By contrast, something like [*Chasing...*] *I hate* [*...kids*] or [*...kids*] *are hated by* [*chasing...*] *me* would be ungrammatical.

We might now start characterizing various phrases and specifying rules for generating them, but that, as noted, raises the problem of construction and language-specific rules. Early phrase structure rules moreover seemed redundant, in duplicating information that had to be there in the lexicon already and anyhow, particularly information about which other lexical items a given lexical item *selects*, or can co-occur with, which follows from its meaning (e.g., *give* requires an NP and a PP, as in *give* [*the gift*] [*to Mary*], while *persuade* selects an NP and a clause, as in *persuade* [*Mary*] [*to give birth*]). The old rules also missed a clear pattern in how human phrases can be internally constituted. Thus, in old-style, construction-specific phrase structure rules for, say, the formation of VPs, APs and NPs, there were 'rewrite' rules like VP→V, AP→A, NP→N, or VP→V PP, AP→A PP, NP→N PP, where the arrow indicates that the label on the left can be rewritten as the respective labels on the right. But here, clearly, a common pattern transpires, revealing that a generalization has been missed. The first group of rules says that a VP, AP, and NP may bottom out, respectively, as a V, an A, and

[12] A nice example from Uriagereka (1998: 175).

an N, while the second specifies that we may rewrite a VP as a V with a PP (as in [vp *walk* [pp *in the dark*]]), and similarly for an AP and an NP. These rules are very permissive: there is nothing in a phrase structure component so conceived which forbids on principled grounds, say, a phrase structure rule like NP→D A.

X-bar theory (Chomsky 1970, Jackendoff 1977) did exclude such options on principled grounds and captured the noted generalizations that are possible between different construction-specific phrase structure rules by viewing phrases as subject to *headedness* (endocentricity): every phrase arises with a *head* taking arguments and projecting, in line with its lexical semantic (selectional) properties, a phrase, which then *contains* its dependents: thus, a V like *kill*, when applied to an N like *Bill*, results in a phrase, [*kill Bill*], that bears the category label of the V, or 'is a' VP, not an NP. That a lexical head *projects* its label to the phrasal level in this sense holds *cross*-categorially, hence phrase structure rules should not mention category labels at all, and we should instead assume that a head 'X' will project a phrase headed by it, in line with its selectional requirements as listed in the lexicon. These demand that the head *kill* should take a second argument, *Jill* say, and project again, to obtain [*Jill* [*kill Bill*]], a maximally projected verb.

It is, then, a universal scheme that a head, X, if it takes an argument, projects, and, if it takes another argument, projects again. This creates two phrasal layers, an intermediate one (X'), and a maximal one (XP), the former containing the head's *complement* (cpl), the latter its *specifier* (Spec):

THE X-BAR SCHEME

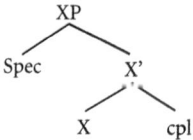

While early phrase structure rules of the rewrite type would also capture *linearity* (the linear order in which words are pronounced), this is irrelevant now. For we may permute linear head–complement order in the above scheme, for example as follows:

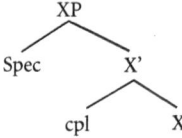

In this case, we would get a language in which the head follows the complement, and *Jill kills Bill* comes out as *Jill Bill kills*, as in Japanese. But importantly, the *hierarchical* order in the syntactic object would not change in that case, as *Bill* is still the complement of *kill* and *Jill* its specifier/Subject. In short, human language is at least two-dimensional, despite the one-dimensional (linear) output that it has in physical terms, and phrase structure as such has no inherent directionality, capturing hierarchy only (for complications, see Fukui 2001).

Possibly, moreover, linear order even *follows from* (or is determined by) hierarchy, through a one-to-one correlation (Kayne 1994), reducing variation even further, a point to which I briefly return in Section 6.1.

So far we have looked at X-bar theory as constraining a level of representation dedicated to lexical categories and the *argument structure* they project in their complements and specifiers. Abney's influential (1987) thesis argued on empirical and conceptual grounds that it was implausible to view determiner elements such as the definite article as specifiers that do not head any projections themselves:

OLD NP

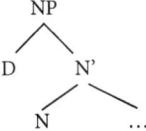

Abney inaugurated the idea that Nominal projections are much more similar to clausal ones. For him, there are both 'category projections'—projections of lexical heads to the phrasal level—and 'semantic projections', viewed as a path of *further* functional nodes along which the substantive or 'descriptive' lexical content of a lexical head is 'passed along', while no new content is added. Thus the structure of nominals in effect becomes this:

NEW NP

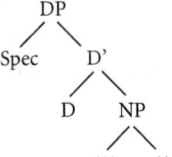

That is, Ds project their own functional projections, DPs, and take NPs as their complements; their specifiers can, for example, be occupied by a possessor.[13] The DP is thus the 'semantic' and maximal projection of the lexical head, the Noun, just as IP, the phrase projected by the inflections of the verb, might be viewed, following Chomsky (1986: 3), as the 'semantic' projections of the lexical Verb. IP is the functional domain immediately above the VP in the structure of the clause, where Tense morphemes and agreement affixes (indicating number, person, etc.) are encoded.

In the influential tradition emanating from Pollock (1989), IP was soon itself split into distinct functional projections, a Tense Phrase (TP) and an Agreement Phrase (AgrP) (Belletti 1990), just as CP was split into separate Finiteness, Topic,

---

[13] Although the co-occurrence of a possessor and a determiner is impossible in English (witness *John's the book*), it is acceptable in many other languages, and in English too the DP construction makes good sense in other respects: for example, we can say *John's every concern was his wife*, where *every* heads the DP and *John's* is in its specifier.

Focus, and Force projections in the highly influential work of Cinque (1999) and Rizzi (1997). On the other hand, many linguists today follow Chomsky (1995: 377) in not coding agreement relations as separate projections (AgrPs), on grounds that they serve no interpretive end, in contrast to the other functional projections mentioned above. If they serve a purely syntactic function that can be taken over with no descriptive loss by already assumed projections (possibly with extra specifier positions), this would clearly result in an advance in the attempt to vindicate a notion of economy of representations such as we are seeking from a Minimalist point of view.

I will here follow another standard assumption that the old 'VP'-label is internally decomposed, splitting into the old VP-layer and an outer verb shell, which licenses a second (external) argument position for the V-head and codes aspectual properties of the verb (e.g., Hale and Keyser 2002; Chomsky 1995; Baker 2003):

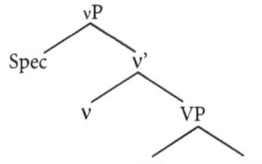

With Grimshaw (1990), functional projections became known as the 'extended' projections of their lexical complements. Grimshaw pointed out that functional heads do not 'select' any *arguments in* the way that lexical heads do and should therefore not be regarded as projections in their own right. In other words, a DP is not quite the projection of a D, which takes (selects) an NP as its argument in the way a verb takes (selects) an NP as its argument. It must be *relationally* understood, rather. That is, DP, e.g., is not quite a category in its own right, as it is the functional category 'for N'. Even at the top of a syntactic tree, that is, in both the nominal and the verbal domain, we remain intimately related to the lexical categories N and V.

This is, as Chametzky (2003: 215) notes, a *relational* kind of information that is not capturable by classical phrase-structural hierarchies, and hence requires independent explanatory elements. In other words, while Grimshaw's idea seems quite intuitive, the mechanics of how this happens is far from clear, especially under recent conceptions according to which a lexical head is inert beyond its maximal projections, and cannot exert its selectionist powers there (Chomsky MI, DBP). Clearly, the generalization of the X-bar scheme is not quite as innocent as it may look. Chametzky (2003) points out that there is still no actual theory of functional projections around, the deeper reason for this being that there is not much of a serious theory of *lexical* projections around either, a point I agree with and return to below.

Perhaps the solution is to think of both C and T as selecting substantive categories, after all: C would select T (whose status as a substantive category may have independent support, see Chomsky, DBP), whereas T would select a verbal element. Both provide a specifier position: Spec-TP in particular is the position where the verbal subject, base-generated in Spec-vP, gets ultimately dislocated, attracted by formal features encoded in the head T, such as its EPP-feature (for 'Extended Projection Principle', demanding that sentences must have subjects). This happens through a movement or displacement process, the subject of the next section, and results in a structure that yields the *sentence*.

The latter, under the X-bar theoretic generalizations we are pursuing, is now no more than a descriptive artefact: a sentence is simply the extended projection of the verb that heads the sentence, an IP, and appears to share much of its internal construction principles with the nominal domain. The bare bones of the human sentence are thus, if we were to ignore phrasal projections and look only at the heads, as follows:

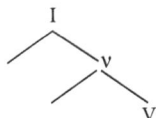

When we look at the morphological structure of single words, what we see is an exact mirror image of this (Brody 2003). Using a Hungarian example from Brody, where ASP stands for a morpheme encoding verbal aspect:

THE 'MIRROR':
    olvas-hat-om
    V   -v -I
    read-ASP-1SING. PRESENT

The Mirror indicates a possible redundancy in our descriptive apparatus, a prime example of the kind of fact Minimalism looks for, when searching for a minimalization of our descriptive apparatus.

Given that the human clause seems essentially warped around two lexical domains, Nouns and Verbs, and phrase structure is not category-specific, we might also suggest that, in a perfect world, the way they project their extended projections should be the same: or that, structurally, the very distinction between N and V that we are making is epiphenomenal, hiding an underlying uniformity. To some extent that seems to be the case (see Szabolcsi 1994; Bernstein 2001; Svenonius 2004), perhaps to the point that DP splits in much the way that CP does, containing Topic and Focus layers as well (Aboh 2004). Surely at the bottom of both domains there is, to start with, a *thematic layer* in which the N and the V distribute all and only their *thematic roles*. The verb *destroy*, say, would assign the theta-role THEME to its complement, say *the city*, and once that has happened, the theta-role AGENT to its specifier, say *the enemy*. All that would be internal to the vP. Similarly, the noun *destruction* would, internal to the NP, assign the role THEME to its internal argument, again *the city*, as in *destruction (of) the city*, and assign the role AGENT to its specifier, say *the enemy*.

The construction of the vP gives us *the enemy destroy the city*, where a Tense specification, which does not exist internal to the vP is as yet missing. The construction of the NP gives us *the enemy destruction (of) the city*, where again functional structure is missing, in particular the genitive Case marker '*s* (which I assume to head a DP) and an analogon to *v*, called 'small-N' or '*n*', may also be involved (Svenonius 2004; Borer 2005). For vPs to get tensed, their respective heads must *adjoin* to the tense morpheme and form a morphologically complex word: *destroy+s*. This is an instance of *head movement*, as the head of the vP moves to the head of the TP.

After the verb has moved to T, the argument *the enemy*, although it has obtained a *thematic role* from the verb, has not yet checked its (NOM) Case, hence must 'A(rgument)-move' into the domain of the inflection, I, where this can happen, landing finally in Spec-IP:

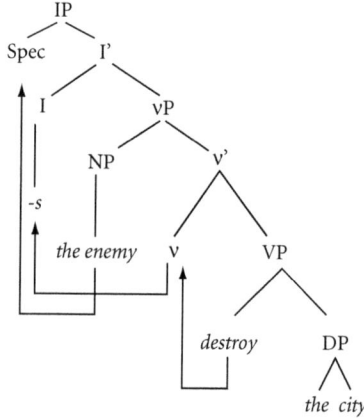

IP may finally itself become the complement of a clausal operator or Complementizer (C) such as *that* in *that the enemy destroys the city*, which selects the IP and projects in turn a CP. While head movement does not bring us beyond pure phrase structure yet, in the sense of and insofar as the mirror generalization holds, A-movement for Case, agreement, and EPP reasons does. There is a further layer of complexity still, the quantificational one, which crucially involves the specifier position of CP, and gives rise to new semantic effects (see next section).

Note a sense in which head movement in the IP correlates with a specific semantic effect: while a VP is as such purely *predicative* (Szabolcsi 1994), it strictly comes to be *about* something only once it gets, in the process of building up structure, tensed: this is the 'deictic' function of Tense. On analogy, D would also comprise the 'deictic element' in the nominal domain, where again NP itself would be purely predicative: *city* does not refer to anything specifically, but *the city* (in a particular discourse) does. A philosophically intriguing simplification, Kantian in flavour, would be that T locates in time where D locates in space.

Note that without movement of heads and arguments, we would have only *thematic structures*. A creature stopping right there could relate heads to their arguments but would not have sentences. Increasingly more powerful creatures could relate heads to heads, bring arguments to agree with the relevant functional heads, and be capable of locating judgements in space and time. But without transformations needed for *quantification* ('A-bar'-movement, see next section) there would be no such thing for this creature as asking a *wh-*(who, what, which, etc.) questions, or saying something *about properties* (say that some property holds of all individuals in some domain) instead of merely *about individuals*.

Prior to *all* of these layers of structural-semantic complexity, however, is a more primitive or archaic one, where there is not even such a thing as arguments bearing thematic roles: the *adjunct system*.[14] Adjuncts are things that are 'not needed'. While this is a sad statement to make about adjuncts, it captures their essence. Any lexical verb has a number of arguments, and it needs each and every one of them. This argument system is extremely *limited* in human languages. Virtually no verb with more than three arguments exists in any language, with most lexical verbs having only one or two. Again, we wish to rationalize this design feature, and it seems likely that the reason is an internalist, not a semantic one: limitations on argument structure fall out from limitations on syntax, if Hale and Keyser (2002) are right. If this is the case, syntactic constraints explain how our concepts, or at least those we lexicalize, are constrained. Correlatively, it is interesting to note that while a verb does not *need* to have any of its adjuncts (does not select them and assign no thematic roles to them), it may have an *infinite* number of them: *Jill killed Bill with great satisfaction, with her bare hands, at dawn, looking down on him, with contempt* (. . .). This asymmetry seems crucial, and an initial reason for not assimilating arguments and adjuncts, whose syntax indeed is entirely different. Adjunction, as an operation more primitive than argument-taking, does not require the apparatus of hierarchical syntax as given through projection, and perhaps has no significant syntax at all.[15]

---

[14] Prior to having an adjunctive system there is of course already something semantic, namely the lexicon. But there is nothing here that productively creates new meanings. We only have a *conceptual mind* here that cannot engage in anything that demands the structuralization of lexical items—at the very least adjoining them—as in any complex thoughts or judgement.

[15] Thus, Chomsky (BEA, version of 2004: 117–8) plausibly speculates that adjuncts exist due to requirements of the semantic interface, specifically that 'an operation of predicate composition' is in place there, which we may see mirrored in the adjunct system. As Chomsky notes (ibid.), the adjunct construction behaves as if the adjunct isn't there in the syntax 'apart from semantic interpretation', or as if it 'ha[s] no syntax', as Chametzky (2003: 206) puts this observation. This makes good sense of the fact that adjuncts do not take part in the kind of movement processes studied in the next section, or do not seem to be visible for the syntax (see also Chomsky 1995: section 4.7.3).

Overall, thus, we seem to be facing a hierarchy of possible human thoughts, thanks to structural complexity induced by the computational system in increasingly complex layers. Adopting the idea of adjunction as a form of pure predicate conjunction championed by Paul Pietroski (2002), we may say that a linguistic creature having only adjuncts will only have one semantic type, predicates, and one operation, conjunction: it will note things like *edible-fast-white*, with a semantics like *there is here something edible and fast and white*, and *run-fast-quiet*, with a semantics perhaps like *running be fast and quiet*. A creature with arguments, on the other hand, will have a notion of *singular* events and event *participants* rather than merely types of events, noting things like *John run*, an event of a certain type with an individual participant playing a *thematic role* in it. Here we have a distinction between two semantic types, individuals (event participants, and perhaps events as such, if these are ontologically also individuals) and predicates (*properties* of events and individuals, expressed through verbs and adjuncts).

What I will be calling a *judgement* requires more than argument structure, namely the human *sentence*, which captures the verb's association with Tense. Association with Tense is required on the assumption that all our judgements *are* intrinsically tensed. In order to judge that something *is true, is a fact, has a point, is blue*, etc., we must *anchor* our judgement in time (we cannot, now, make a judgement tomorrow, say). Introducing in the place of the notion of a judgement the metaphysical category of a 'fact' for what sentences express, and saying that a 'proposition' 'denoted' by a tensed VP (or an IP) corresponds to a 'fact', obscures this: a fact does not contain Tense, and neither does a proposition (though it is hard to tell, as that notion, as a purely technical one, will depend on how it is defined). To illustrate our notion of a judgement, consider (1a) and (1b), the first a verbal structure containing a Tense specification, the second a nominal structure lacking Tense:

(1) a. (that) Syracuse was destroyed
    b. (the) destruction of Syracuse

Despite their differences these are, in an intuitive sense, about the same event: they involve the same lexical concepts, in the same thematic relationships. How do we properly describe the identity as well as the differences between these two expressions? I will say that the identity holds at the level of *conceptual information*, while the difference relates to discourse-related aspects of *reference and quantification*, which I will summarize under the label *intentional information*, typically coded at the 'left edge' of the clause. Concretely, (1a) contains reference to a time encoded by the Tense, at which the event took place; but (1b) refers to the process itself that *Syracuse* underwent at this time, namely the destruction process. We might paraphrase (1a) as quantifying over and referring to a time as determined by the Tense and associated to the event (see 2a), but (1b) as quantifying over the destruction itself (see 2b):

(2) a. There is a time, such that the destruction of Syracuse happened at it.
    b. There was a destruction, such that Syracuse was a inherent part of it.

Quantification and a difference in reference thus do not affect the basic predicational relations established at the level of *pure conceptual structure*, while presupposing them. A difference in quantification is a difference that is brought out post-transformationally in representations of expressions at the level of LF, lying at the *end* of the derivation. LF tells us nothing specifically about the event as such, which is assembled prior to it through a head's satisfying its basic thematic requirements, and which does not involve any operator-variable structures, quantification, reference, or Tense. In other words, pure conceptual structure encodes events *as such*, without a specific way of referring to them, while intentional structure encodes specific ways in which these events figure in judgements of truth and falsehood, and are referred to under certain perspectives.

A crucial philosophical question that arises is why syntactic tree-growing in the nominal domain finishes at the DP level, and in the verbal domain at the CP level. Why is it that we cannot pile up further projections on top of the CP? Why do we rather have to begin from scratch and assemble a new clause from the bottom up? Apparently there is something special about the CP level (which, although it perhaps correlates with the DP level in the nominal domain, as noted, does not correlate perfectly, and seems to be something in its own right). We might try to motivate the restriction functionally, by saying that the CP gains its prominence from its ability to express some truth-bearing proposition, supposing we had some empirical conception of what these entities are, and could identify them non-circularly, i.e. without *using* a sentential structure (an IP/CP). On this externalist suggestion, the need to map language to truth would be what gives prominence to the CP, which alone can be mapped to it. But this not only seems circular, but cannot be right for other reasons, since it seems that we could communicate our thoughts quite efficiently in terms of DPs only (Carstairs-McCarthy 1999), as in fact some languages do (see the discussion in Section 4.2). There is in this sense no intrinsic connection between the uses of language, in particular the fact that we make assertions and CPs. We cannot look at the performance systems that the syntactic system interfaces with to understand why there are CPs, and why they are structured in the way they are.

Although there may be no non-circular way to use mind-and language-independent 'propositions' to rationalize the existence of the human sentence, I see no reason why we should not go the other way and try deriving certain empirical properties of thought contents from an insight into the structure of CPs. Could the very structure of a CP perhaps explain, for example, why propositions, in the sense of what (*that*) *Brutus killed Caesar* is used to express on an occasion, are the units of semantic analysis? The latter fact would then be explained from the *structural* fact that the human linguistic system simply does not produce structures that systematically relate meaning and form beyond the clausal level (whatever the evolutionary explanation of *that* fact is). This direction of explanation would clearly be desirable, given that our knowledge of syntactic structure is empirical and better grounded than our knowledge of 'propositions', of which there are no empirical theories at all (there are metaphysical and normative ones). Propositions are strangely intermediate entities between what's in the head and what's out there in the physical universe. It would be nice to get rid of them and to effectively 'deflate' them into the notion of a CP.

Let us for the rest of the section take a more detached view and look at the status of phrase structure and X-bar theory as a component of human grammar.[16] What exactly does the X-bar scheme explain? And can its strictures be explained as following from more general and fundamental principles in the workings of the computational system? Or must we take it as an ultimate syntactic template that follows from nothing at all, accepting notions like headedness or projection as primitives? I have taken phrase structure above as an inherent part of a theory of how the computational system interfaces with the conceptual-intentional system, and the ways in which that interface is internally *differentiated*. In particular it linguistically constrains pure conceptual (or thematic) structure, assembled independent of and prior to any transformations (movements, dislocations), and not distorted by them. However we might explain X-bar theoretic constraints from deeper principles, I see no way to eliminate *this* role it plays—its role in configuring this particular kind of semantic information, and hence satisfying interface requirements.

Perhaps, though, the right way to think of the basic X-bar theoretic relations is that they fall out from the dynamics of the derivation itself. Perhaps we can think of bar-levels as deriving from relations in which heads stand to elements in their local environment. On this view, we can only tell from its place in an ongoing derivation what the categorial status of some lexical item is. At the stage of the derivation where α, the head, has been saturated by its argument, there is no option of its being a head and unsaturated any more: the *context* of the derivation decides whether we have a minimal or a maximal projection. As long, however, as this 'derivation' of X-bar theoretic principles does not entail the *elimination* of bar-levels, the proposal does not and should not entail that they don't exist.[17]

It may also be that no extra X-bar theoretic stipulations are needed to make it the case that the *second* argument merged to a head has to be a specifier as opposed to a complement. That is, the notion of specifier may lack an independent theoretical status, simply being an instance of 'second Merge'. Consider the

---

[16] The following discussion has been greatly inspired by Chametzky (2003).

[17] Consider in this context that e.g. Brody (2003) claims that projections and projection levels do not 'exist', while going on, in the very next sentence, to say that a 'head X in a syntactic tree should be taken to ambiguously represent both the X and zero-level head and the phrasal node' of X's projections. One cannot represent what does not exist, I take it.

situation in which we have the head take its internal argument, and want to merge another syntactic object with the result of this. There is then a question of why we don't take the *complement* from inside the projection and merge it externally to the projection (the root of the tree). In other words, why is second Merge not a form of 'internal Merge'? Why does it add a specifier rather than a complement? But, we can now say, the complement is a maximal projection, and the verb, after taking it as its argument, is a maximal projection and saturated, too. Hence if there is another argument position in the verbal domain, a *new* unsaturated item, *v*, must first be merged externally to it (or at the root of the VP), thereby extending it. Its argument will then become the *specifier* (a non-complement) from the perspective of V.[18]

Internal Merge operations on this picture can only take place when all thematic requirements, in the lowest layer of semantic complexity, are satisfied. If the complement were to move from down under the tree, this could only happen by *preserving* the already established thematic relationships of the head. It is possible, say, when we have a passive *John was seen*, where John is moved from under the VP *see John* (see next section), but where he nonetheless remains the complement and the THEME (the thing seen), despite its fronted position in Spec-IP. But we do not have **Bill kills*, with the interpretation that Bill kills himself, hence plays the roles of both the AGENT and the THEME. The indicated derivation would 'tamper' with the thematic information already contained in the base, the information about what is the THEME, which is necessarily prior to and presupposed at the time of the specification of the AGENT (Chomsky, MI, version of 1998: 27). In this way, the precedence of external Merge over internal Merge follows from the way in which semantic information is built up.

In a case where internal Merge is forced due to some kind of defectiveness in the base, as in passives, the complement XP apparently must also be merged at the root, again necessarily *extending* the tree, leaving it internally unchanged, as considerations of computational efficiency would entail:

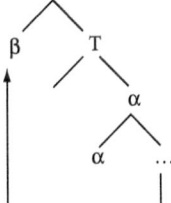

This extension condition, a conservativity requirement that appears to be operative, virtually forces a conclusion discussed in the next section, that if an item is *internally* merged to a tree, there must be a sense in which the moved item

---

[18] See Hallman (2004) for discussion, and a proposal for 'eliminating' specifiers.

is still *present* in some sense in its base position (in the form of a so-called *copy*): nothing *else* can get into this position once it has occupied it.

If X-bar theoretic relations come to hold automatically by virtue of the way the derivation proceeds, it would in particular be wrong to think of the assembly of pure phrase structure prior to any transformations as a *level of representation*, that is as satisfying specific constraints on well-formedness. That these constraints would have to be satisfied would simply follow from the workings of the computational system, rather than having to be stipulated explicitly. Note that this would not have to mean that the dynamics of the derivation does not begin with building structures reflecting thematic relations between lexical items only, as one layer in the construction of a complex human linguistic meaning.

Still, there are difficulties in this project of making X-bar and phrase structure theory redundant. Let us return to Chametzky's (2003: 196) worry that relational notions, like adjunct or head, cannot in fact be captured in phrase structural or X-bar theoretical terms. To be so captured, the relational notion would have to be stated or defined in terms of *configurational* position in a phrase structure tree, that is, part-whole or 'immediate containment' relations of constituency. One *point* of having phrase structures was not to have relational notions as primitives, but to reduce them to configurations. Thus, for example, Chomsky (1965) defined Direct Object (DO), equally a relational notion, as the thing immediately contained in (or dominated by) the VP, a configurational notion, in contrast to Subject, which was immediately contained in the (then existing) category S(entence).

But indeed, it would seem that adjuncts express a kind of *dependency*, not a kind of configuration. Under X-bar theory, DOs would be immediately dominated by X' (DOs being complements), subjects by XP (being specifiers). But adjuncts are prima facie neither specifiers (under XP) nor complements (under X'). There is simply no natural place for them to be in the X-bar scheme. But then, we might ask why all dependencies should *have* to be captured by phrase structures, if indeed the adjunct component is a more primitive, and perhaps more archaic ingredient of language, in the way I have suggested above. As for the notion 'head', why *should* phrase structure capture it, if the question of which of two lexical items that are merged becomes the head is decided by the *lexical* properties of these heads?

This however is to push the phrase-structural notion of headedness to the lexicon, where it does not belong: no explanation is really offered. The *empirical* motivation for headedness is that *not* having headed phrases would mean to miss a descriptive pattern, and to make languages seemingly unlearnable, due to the total unrestrictiveness of the rules a language. But an empirical motivation is not enough to derive headedness on principled grounds. One might argue, though, that, *conceptually*, a lack of headedness would be an extremely undesirable property for a grammar to have: the category immediately dominating two syntactic sisters would not be necessarily related to at least one of them; information at the mother node would be new information, or go beyond information present at the daughter nodes. Ideally, Chomsky has argued, the syntax should be *inclusive*, or not yield any objects that are not lexical items or constructions from their features:

INCLUSIVENESS: Outputs consist of nothing beyond properties of items of the lexicon (the syntax does not add new entities of its own).

Together with Chomsky's further assumption that lexical items are nothing but feature matrices—sets of sets of different linguistic features specifying their semantic, phonetic, and formal (uninterpretable) properties—Inclusiveness entails that 'the interface levels consist of nothing more than arrangements of lexical features' (Chomsky 1995: 225, cf. 228). This would be another example for a strong *conservativity property* in the grammar: all information that a derivation explicates is already contained in its lexical base.

Still, desirable as Inclusiveness in this sense might be from a Minimalist point of view, it has not been established, and hence the necessary headedness of phrase structures, if we make it depend on it, has not been either (cf. Chametzky 2000: 146–7). On the other hand, one might content oneself with the idea that it is a typical 'best design' feature reflecting an economy of organization, hence should be assumed in the absence of evidence to the contrary. Moreover, Inclusiveness has been a fruitful heuristic for research, at least on the meaning side of the grammar, in contrast to the phonetic side, where Inclusiveness is standardly denied.[19] This asymmetry we precisely predict if language is not 'made for' communication, so that the phonological component would simply use the system in a direction that was not its original function, this being, say, the expression of thought.

But even if we let Inclusiveness be our null hypothesis at the LF-side, then we *still* would not know how to express headedness in phrase structural terms. Inclusiveness suggests that the syntactic object created from merging two syntactic objects X and Y, including its label, should be entirely constructed from them. This alone does not quite give us the crucially asymmetric notion of headedness, which depends on only *one* of the sisters projecting and determining the label. As such, Inclusiveness allows for *both* X and Y to project, or for *neither* to do so. But the latter option can be ruled out on empirical grounds, for then there simply would not be such a thing as projection or headedness at all. But phrases just seem to be of certain types. Interface constraints might be seen to determine this property, if

---

[19] The phonological component of the grammar takes syntactic objects constructed by the computational system and converts them to representations legible there by performance systems dedicated to speech processing. This conversion involves the introduction of new elements such as prosodic structure and intonational contours. Possibly, phonological features of lexical items are not even interpretable at this phonetic interface, so that the phonological component has to convert one kind of vocabulary into another. In the latter case, the requirements that all and only lexical features of expressions should be interpretable at the interfaces would be strongly violated on the phonetic side of the grammar, and the inclusiveness/interpretability requirement in its strongest sustainable form be entertainable only for 'narrow syntax', the process in which the computational system constructs representations readable at the semantic interface (Chomsky MI, revised version 2000: 100, 118).

indeed the interface imposes constraints on their being both arguments and adjuncts, and argument-taking involves headedness and projection. Moreover, even though, on this option, there would ultimately be only lexical items (though no projection or phrases), perhaps an attractive conclusion minimalistically, it would have to be assumed that these lexical items stand in certain *relations*, such as theta-theoretic, Agreement, and sub-categorization relations, and these *are* asymmetric. A relation-based account dispensing with phrase structure would have to take these as primitive, and we would be clueless as to how they *come about*, or what specific configurational structures they are associated with.

As for the former option—labelling as involving features from *both* X and Y—this can also be ruled out, Chomsky (1995: 244) reasons. In particular, the label might arise as the set-theoretic union of the features in X and Y, but this would likely give rise to 'contradictions' between opposite values of the same features (say both a + and a − value on features determining whether some constituent is 'verbal', as in a V-N compound). Or it might arise as their intersection, but this will often be null. Chomsky's conclusion is that features do not intermingle at all: the label is either the one of X or the one of Y itself. This Inclusiveness-driven reasoning crucially depends on the set-theoretic assumptions it makes, which alone suggests the options of union, intersection, and identity in the first place. One might well question this on the grounds that lexical items have a unit in their own right, which they would not have if they were sets, given that these reduce to their members.

The minimalist reasoning above *does* give us a form of headedness: at least, we have got a phrase being *labelled*. This is attractive, but it also seems as if nothing like hierarchical phrases ever appear in this system, given that XP = X, if X is the head. Perhaps it is too minimalist, then? Recall the above suggestion that human phrase structure is primarily a matter of *argument* structure rather than adjunction, and that in argument structures there is a crucial asymmetry between functions (heads) and arguments. Phrase-structural hierarchies build this asymmetry into the syntactic object, since the result of projection (or what the label captures) is not the X itself, but an X'/XP, something different. The reality of phrase structural levels, if the radically minimalist analysis were to deprive us of these, would speak *against* the minimalist analysis.

Consider an additional argument, put to me by Uriagereka. Function-argument relations are (categorially) labelled by assumption, but it is arguable that head-adjunct relations are not, and cannot be. Adjunction is unbounded, but if it is unbounded, then either there is an *unlimited* number of labels to distinguish all adjunctions, or adjunction to X does not *modify* the type of X. In either case labels are pointless (in the first because lexical categorial labels must be few, as otherwise they are computationally vacuous or redundant.[20] Again, then, we see that it is with arguments and them only that the need for labels (hence projection, head-

---

[20] As Uriagereka points out, this makes good sense of the fact that while we know that syntactic operations target labelled constituents, not unlabelled ones, we do not see empirically that we can distinguish between syntactic operations on the basis of whether adjunction has taken place to a given

edness, and phrase structure) arises in the first place. But then, there should be a reflection of the fact that labels involve and indicate argument-taking: they must be relational notions, which they aren't in Chomsky's proposal (I return to some of the latter's technical aspects shortly).

Collins (2002) is more radical still than Chomsky and aims to 'eliminate labels'. Collins claims that labels are not needed to capture what the syntax essentially has to do: establish various kinds of *relations* between lexical items that enter into a derivation. Once one has the relations established, the claim is, the part-whole structures (constituent hierarchies) of X-bar theory are a theoretical redundancy that should be dispensed with. This approach however would not be inherently more 'minimal' or 'economical' than an approach dispensing with relations in favour of configurations. Take the thematic relation Theta(X, Y), 'X assigns a thematic role to Y', where X and Y are lexical items. For that relation to be established, X, say, has to *assign* one of its theta-roles, and Y has to *bear* one. Say it has to be the THEME. Now, why state, Collins asks, in *addition* to that, that Y is immediately contained in some X' hierarchical object? But one can turn this question around: once having hierarchical phrase structures, why have, in *addition*, relations? Maybe 'THEME' *is* essentially configurational, relating to being in a part-whole structure of the right sort.

Consider also the 'is a' relation, that *kill Bill* 'is a' VP, *Bill* 'is an' NP, or *Jill killed Bill* 'is an' IP. If *kill Bill*, with its specific sound and meaning, is to be generated, it must be the result of thematically structuring the lexical items *kill* and *Bill* in such a way that we can understand why the result is mapped to a meaningful semantics: in particular, Bill has got to become one-who-is-being killed (or made dead); indeed, when the killing is finished, Bill is no more. This is what it means to be the Theme of a killing, it means to be an inherent *part* of it, and to last as long as it. If phrase-structuring lexical items is to yield thematic relations, *this* is what it has to yield.[21] That is, as hierarchical complexity is being built into the verb phrase, further dimensions are being added to our mental representation of the object, Bill: a time dimension in particular, and a 'goal' which makes the event inherently bounded. In this sense, a VP is 'dimensionally higher' than an NP. Even having *Bill dead*, where a dynamic dimension is missing, is more than having just Bill: now we have him together with a property or aspect of him.

---

targeted syntactic category. Consider the following example, from Uriagereka, in which the VP *conquer Gaul* is preposed in front of the subject of the embedded clause, *he*:

Caesar said he would conquer Gaul [in one year] ...
a. ... and conquer Gaul [in one year] he surely did
b. ... and conquer Gaul he surely did [in one year].

During this transformation of preposing, the (bracketed) adjunct behaves as if it wasn't there.

[21] Nothing as trivial as an arbitrary mathematical function's applying to some argument is required here. What we express by function-application in a formal semantic theory is a relation between Larry and blueness in, say, the sentence (judgement) *Larry is blue*. What we claim here is set-membership of Larry in the set of the blue things. This is not what we need for a thematic relation.

If this talk about dimensions (Uriagereka 2002, Chapters 14–15) is to be more than merely verbal, a more substantive notion of phrase-structural 'containment' has to be sought that yields the needed part–whole relations, a point to which I return at the end of this section. Becoming the phrase-structural sister in the course of the operation of merging a head and its first argument will equally then not be comparable to having anything as trivial as *concatenation,* as Chametzky (2000: 127–9) correctly notes and argues at length. The latter operation does not yield hierarchically structured syntactic objects: 'sticking strings next to one another to make a new, bigger string does not provide the means for analysing sentences as hierarchically structured objects' (Chametzky 2000: 158). Again, syntax is not as minimal as that, apparently, providing a richer structure for purposes of semantic interpretation. Phrases *are* needed, particularly if the external theta-role (Agent) is assigned 'compositionally', i.e., by first composing *kill* with *Bill* so as to reach the saturated expression *kill Bill,* which is then composed with the external Agent argument. If it is an XP, not an X, which takes the external argument (see Marantz 1984), the very asymmetry that exists between arguments thus depends on having labels which encode it. The syntax must 'see' phrasal projection levels, and α in its role as head and α in its role as label or as a projection must be marked as distinct. In this way, given compositional theta-role assignment, Collins's notion of the relation Theta(X,Y)—X assigns a theta-role to Y—*depends* on notions he claims to derive or eliminate.[22]

Collins also suggests replacing the old X-bar theoretic notion of a head with the notion of a derivational *locus*. The latter is meant to differ from the notion of a head in that a head is a 'representational' object that *persists* as such throughout a derivation, whereas a locus exists only at the moment in the derivation when an unsaturated expression (like a V-head) is not (yet) saturated. Once saturated by

---

[22] There are other empirical arguments that the syntactic relations figuring as primitives in Collins's project of eliminating labels and bar hierarchies depend on what they deny. Thus Collins appeals to a relation EPP(X, Y), Y satisfies the EPP-feature of X, where, again, that is a hypothesized feature on a functional projection demanding that sentences have a subject (merged in the specifier of TP). But as Boeckx (2004: 30) notes, EPP is not a featural requirement, but a specifier requirement, hence depends on a notion of 'specifier' (and XP) that is not available on a label-free approach. Boeckx (2004) further argues that the same applies to the relation Agree (X, Y), feature X matches feature Y, as required for purposes of Case and Agreement checking; and to the relation Subcat(X, Y), X subcategorizes for Y (say, a V-head subcategorizes for a complement with an N-feature).

On the other hand, Boeckx (2004: 32) also calls labels a 'stipulated mechanism of the grammar', which suggests they are in principle pointless, at least semantically. He conjectures that 'maybe they help to reduce computational load'—but why should we care about such a reduction if projection does not intrinsically yield semantic effects (or phrases are distinctively interpreted)? Boeckx appears to assume this, suggesting in particular (p. 35) that projection does not change the head (whereas I would prefer to say that it *values* it, so as to create a new complex semantic object, see below). I do not regard reduction of computational complexity is an *intrinsic* feature of design optimality. What matters is the form–meaning connection, and if that takes computations of an abstruse complexity, these could still be 'minimal' in the required sense.

an argument, it ceases to exist. But if projections are *interpreted*, as I have claimed, they capture one kind of (thematic) information that *must* persist throughout the derivation (the content of the so-called 'projection principle', or PP). It is not clear how, say, a *v*P projection could *not* persist, given that it is a maximal and saturated object, which does not take or demand any other arguments.

While Collins's proposal regarding phrase structure may be far too austere, I have already indicated in what way Chomsky's seems to be, too. Chomsky views the basic structure-building operation, Merge, as what any recursive combinatorial system will minimally need. Merge takes two syntactic objects α and β, each possibly complex and equipped with labels LB(α) and LB(β) indicating their syntactic type, and forms a larger unit from them, which is simply the (unordered) *labelled set* of them: Γ = {γ, {α,β}}, with γ the label. The notion of a *syntactic object* (SO, see, e.g., Chomsky 1995: 243), is recursively defined on the following lines:

A POSSIBLE SO is
(i) either a word (lexical item), or
(ii) a set ('bare phrase marker') of the form C={LB, {A, B}}, with A, B SOs, and LB the label of the set.

As noted, Chomsky further stipulates that the label is necessarily one of the two merged syntactic objects itself; moreover, which of α and β projects and becomes the label is not determined by Merge, which itself is entirely symmetric, but by the lexical properties involved. Let us assume that because of these properties, Γ = {α, {α, β}} rather than Γ = {β, {α, β}}, which is, in graphic notation, the following syntactic object:

RESULT OF MERGE:

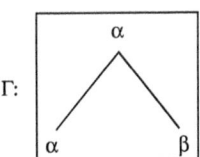

Γ:

If now a new syntactic object δ is taken and merged to Γ, and it projects, what we get is the object Δ, which contains Γ as a proper part:

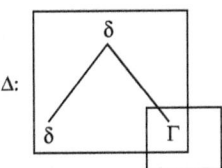

Δ:

Since the result of α's projection is α again, and α as such gives no indication that anything has been merged to it, the result of the Merge operation is as if no Merge operation had taken place. On the other hand, the projection *is* distinct if we look at its *context of occurrence*. In its lower occurrence we think of it as a head, in its higher as a label of a set. That difference thus carries the entire explanatory burden: it must explain now why a *thematic structure* has arisen, in which the internal argument has become the *theme of the killing* and an inherent part of the event that an object such as Γ may encode. In one sense, the part–whole relation *is* there in the Chomskyan proposal above, as Γ *contains* β; on the other hand, there is absolutely no indication of the *relation* in which β has come to stand to α. Perhaps Γ could be set equal to α, but this is excluded by the definitions, and also contradictory, as Γ properly contains α, and α cannot properly contain itself.

Consider also Chomsky's (1995: 247) definition of a 'term': for any syntactic object K, K itself is a term of K, and if L is a term of K, then the members of the members of L are terms of K. Taking Γ for K, this definition will make Γ a term of K, as well as α and β. Now, when the specifier combines with XP, say, this is an object in which, in classical phrase structural terms, the complement β has become a constituent part of (or is contained in) the head α, which has projected. But that XP object, in Chomsky's terms, would be the *label* of the set Γ = {α, {α, β}}, and labels are not merged. Instead, in the example above δ is merged with Γ, which *is* a term according to Chomsky's definition. But this result, that δ enters into no relationship with the label, is *built* on having labels as things separate from the object itself that is the result of the Merge operation, namely Γ, and defining 'term' so as to deprive labels of termhood.

There is also *a relation* connecting all and only the terms that are merged with one another in the course of a derivation: *derivational c-command* (Epstein 1999). δ could then never stand in that relation to the label of the set Γ: instead it would stand in that relation to Γ itself, to α, and to β. These are the terms or the 'functioning elements', which labels are not. But again, this result, which makes labels syntactically inert while not doing so for the sets they label, begs the question against the idea of having a substantive notion of label and projection.

What we may rather want to say, if the notion of projection is to make the substantive sense it does, is that the syntactic object resulting from the projection is, not the head all over again, or the complement all over again, but some *value* of some function lexicalized as *kill* and applied to *Bill*, who becomes the 'killee' as a consequence of that application. That does not mean we violate Inclusiveness: no new lexical features are introduced. The novelty that has arisen in the compositional process is of a *structural* nature, not a lexical one: it concerns the relations in which lexical items come to stand to one another by embedding one another. We may compare this to the emergence of water molecules, whose substantive content is also merely that of H and O: but as a structural pattern, H_2O has emergent properties that are not traceable to either H or O, and only arise from the dynamics of their interaction.

Note that while an object α cannot properly contain itself, there is a sense in which the value of a function applied to some object does contain that object. Let the number 2 be a shorthand notation for the value of the successor function applied to an initial object, O, in the natural number sequence, which we may set equal to the number 1. That is, it is really the object s(O). Viewed thus, the result of applying the recursive operation of successor formation is a 'projection' that contains the head, and its relation to the non-projected head is *not* identity. Just as we would not say that the foot is in some plain sense *contained* in the leg, or the leg in the body, but that the foot is a part of the leg and the leg a part of the body, we might say that a derivation creates integrated wholes, which, when the derivation continues, become parts of larger integrated such wholes. Intuitively, when inserted into the derivation, *kill* is inherently deficient, like a whole lacking one of its essential parts, such as a leg without a foot. As such, *kill* simply makes no sense, just as a leg doesn't that lacks a foot. By contrast, *kill Bill* begins to make sense. *Bill* has repaired the deficiency, and the machinery of sense generation begins to work.

Chomsky (2005: 14) emphasizes that a head–complement structure is a *pure* set, hence has as such not even as much structure as an *ordered* pair. He notes the rather common view that *linear* order should not be captured by Merge, given that the need for linearization only arises in the mapping to phonetic form, hence inside the phonetic component. But hierarchical order is a matter of narrow syntax if anything is. And in Chomsky's austere bare phrase structural framework, it strangely seems to be the *label* α which is contained in {α, β}, not the other way around, as should be the case, if we want VP, say, to contain NP, in the way the number 2 contains the number 1, and its formal representation, s(O), contains both s and O. What is missing is a mechanism that somehow 'lifts' α, when it projects, to its new categorial status.

That said, there is, I think, a way of more positively appreciating Chomsky's austere framework. The point is that it gives us, in pristine purity, the core of narrow syntax: the mechanism of recursion itself that is its generative engine. Even though projection does not follow from Merge as thus conceived, we might now ask: why necessarily *code it into* the operation Merge? Why not code it separately? Consider that it is also true that Merge yields *binary* constituents, but this also does not follow from Merge as such, but from whatever explains that human phrase structures branch binarily, as has been assumed since the early 1980s (perhaps reduction of memory load, semantic constraints, the necessary linearizability of phrase markers, etc.). If we viewed Merge as primarily capturing the abstract and domain-general property of *recursion* itself, Merge as such need not even be binary. It only happens to be so when generating the combinatory structure of human languages, and it has as such—as simply a form of set formation—nothing in particular to do with labels or other *linguistic* objects at all.

If Merge were restricted to be a *unary* operation, for example, as Chomsky (2004: 16) interestingly notes, it 'yields the successor function, from which the rest of the theory of natural numbers can be developed in familiar ways'. Thus, take von Neumann's theory of ordinals, in which ordinals are built up recursively from a single object, say the empty set, Ø={}. Applying Merge qua set-formation to this single object, it yields the singleton set {Ø}, a set different from the empty set in containing exactly one object, the empty set itself. Since Merge is recursive, it can be applied again to that second object, {Ø}, to yield a set that contains that very set {Ø} plus its single member: {Ø, {Ø}}. Applied to that object once more, it yields the set {Ø, {Ø}, {Ø, {Ø}}}, and so on. We may then think of this series as being associated with the series 0, 1, 2, 3,..., which goes on *ad infinitum*, until it meets the first limit ordinal, the infinite ordinal ω. Any object O' in this set-theoretic series, as the reader may check, is related to its predecessor, O, by being the union of O and its singleton set. If we set O'={O ∪ {O}}, we may call O' the *immediate successor* of O, a terminological choice justified by the way in which O' and O relate (see Machover 1996: 61).

In this example we see what Merge can do for us: it is the recursive engine of a system, creating all by itself an infinity of discrete objects in containment relations to one another. As such we can view it as well in the case of labelled *binary* sets, which happens to be the ones Merge constructs when operating in the linguistic domain and in a lexicon that contains more than one single lexical item. Note how Merge in this beautifully austere picture is *domain-general* in exactly the way that the program of evolutionary explanation tied to Minimalism seeks to establish. Again, no substantive notion of projection, I have claimed, arises from it. Yet, we might as well keep Merge so conceived and ask what has to be *added* to Merge to get projection as well.

I want to suggest that what has to be added at the very least is thematic roles, which means that we actually need a *theory* of thematic roles. We suggested earlier that projection is an issue only in the argument system, not the adjunct system, in which there are no labels. The job of theta-roles would be to do what we said is needed, to lift the head up to something expanded that can properly contain its zero-level projection. Recall now Pietroski's proposal that the semantic contribution of binary branching (syntactic complementation) in general is predicate conjunction, for some given event, e.[23] On this proposal, the *adjunction* structure [*Jill killed Bill*] [*by strangulation*], whose (simplified) syntactic structure is

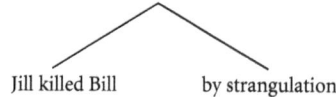

Jill killed Bill   by strangulation

---

[23] In what follows I am indebted to conversations with Cedric Boeckx, Paul Pietroski, and Juan Uriagereka.

means that 'there was an event e of killing, of which two predicates hold: *Jill killed Bill* is true of it, **and** *by strangulation* is true of it'.[24] Now suppose the same method of interpretation is true of an *argument* structure, like this:

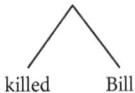

Then we face the problem that this will have to mean the meaningless 'killed **and** Bill' (there was an event e such that it was a killing **and** it was Bill). There are two problems here: where the boldfaced conjunction, which appears in the semantic paraphrases, comes from, and how 'killed and Bill', which makes no sense, can make the sense that *killed Bill* makes.

As for the conjunction, it is plainly not a component of the sentence or phrase in question. So where does it come from? Pietroski answers that last question, as noted above, by proposing that it is the semantic contribution of the *syntax* itself, or of binary branching: 'the syntax itself contributes the conjunctive aspect of meaning', it bears this 'semantic load' (Pietroski 2002: 106). This is a nice instance of the general direction of semantic explanation I am pursuing in this book.

To the second question, how it can be that argument-taking is adjunction, and how *Bill*, a name, can be a predicate, Pietroski replies in a fashion that, as I will conclude, effectively nullifies his assimilation of argument-taking and adjunction: the system, designed to blindly combine predicates, *turns* the argument NP *Bill* into a predicate, essentially the predicate 'Bill is a THEME of e', or [THEME (Bill)] (e). This amounts to the thesis that theta-roles are 'type-shifters': they lift a symbol for an argument from the type of *individuals*, to the other type available in the system, that of *predicates*.

Thematic roles thus allow Pietroski to preserve the assimilation thesis in the light of plain differences in the way arguments and adjuncts combine. Note however that although in *killed Bill*, for Pietroski, the verb crucially does not express a function applied to an argument—since what we have here are two conjoined predicates—there *is* a function in play here, after all, which is applied to an argument, namely the theta-role THEME. But then, as in the case of the conjunction, we have to ask where we get it from, and Pietroski's answer is the same as in the case of the conjunction: they are determined by the syntax, in fact trivially by the *syntactic position* of the respective argument. Syntactic position corresponds one-to-one, Pietroski (2002) argues, defending a proposal of Baker's (1997) (and see Hale and Keyser 2002), to 'thematic role'. That is, we can *read off*

---

[24] I am here presupposing the Neo-Davidsonian idea that all verbs come with an event argument of which they hold as predicates, and that these semantic representations of quantifications over events must be 'thematically separated' by having extra predicates such as 'x is the AGENT of e' and 'x is the PATIENT of e'. See Parsons (1990) and Pietroski (2002, 2003).

from the configuration, or from *Bill* being the internal argument of transitive V, that it will have to be the THEME (indeed, in no language would the internal argument be the AGENT, or would the external argument of transitives be interpreted as THEME).

This is yet another paradigmatic instance of an internalist direction in semantic explanation. Syntax, an internalist science, is invoked to explain aspects of the syntax–semantics mapping. That is, once we have a *syntactic* schema that we can extract from a transitive construction like *Jill kills Bill*, namely [α [Φs β]], translate brackets (branching) to conjunctions and add theta-roles, and allow ourselves an existential quantifier ∃ to bind the event-variable, we get the *semantic* form:

∃e such that AGENT(α) is true of e and [e is a Φing and THEME(β) is true of e].

Pietroski (2002: 111) concludes, on essentially this basis, that syntactic form determines semantic form. This internalist conclusion I strongly endorse.

I want to make two comments however. The first is that the above analysis of thematic roles *compromises* both the conjunctive analysis that is the centrepiece of Pietroski's proposal and his assimilation of adjunction and argument-taking (although none of this disturbs the internalist conclusion he rightly suggests, if implicitly). For although it is true that both of the latter now come out as forms of predicate conjunction, it will now sometimes be the case that the syntactic object

means 'α & β', while sometimes it will mean 'α & θ(β)', where θ is a thematic role. But θ comes from the syntax, by hypothesis, so the syntax is different in both cases. I thus prefer to say that while in adjunction there is *no* projection at all, theta-roles give us a grip on just that: projection. But that kind of difference in dependency must then be *built into* the syntactic object, which must express functional relationship between phrases and constituents, wholes and parts. The syntax must guarantee that the argument-NP truly becomes a *participant* in the event, not just a further aspect or feature of it that we add conjunctively to its description. To put this in another way: the argument-NP must *stay* an argument; lifting it to the status of a predicate is the wrong move unless it *preserves* that information; in which case we may ask why it is lifted at all.[25]

One way of building appropriate whole–part relationships into the syntactic object interpreted, replacing Pietroski's proposal of building conjunctive

---

[25] On a common view, in fact, an argument NP is not an NP, but a DP, and D is what turns the NP, an essentially predicative expression, into an argument, an essentially referential expression (parallel to the way in which T, a deictic-referential expression, is associated with the VP, a descriptive expression; see Longobardi 1994: 634; Szabolcsi 1994: 181). Type-shifting this argument back to the status of a predicate strangely *reverses* that process.

predication into the syntactic object but retaining its spirit, is to view syntactic objects not only as hierarchical, but as *dimensionally* different, in the sense that number-theoretic representations are (Uriagereka 2002, chapter 15). Thus, rational numbers necessarily 'contain' or 'entail' the naturals, and the reals the rationals, in such a way that the mappings of the formal objects involved to the right part–whole relations do not have to be stipulated, but follow from the dimensionality of the formal arithmetical system itself. The right 'entailments' in the clausal domain—that a VP contains an NP, and a *v*P a VP—might follow in a similar fashion.

The second remark is that a modified Pietroski-analysis may give us a more principled explanation of why there are *labels* in the grammar at all, although I present this as a very tentative suggestion. For Pietroski, it is theta-roles that license conjoining verbs and arguments that are names, hence not predicates. The only way for the system to recognize the names, if it works in the simple way Pietroski assumes (conjoining predicates), is to *turn* them into predicates. But the result of that—the creation of new part–whole structures not possible in a purely adjunctive or, in Pietroski's terms, 'concatenative' system—may be that the system must now explicitly mark representationally the difference between symbols bearing the *two different semantic types*. Perhaps it is as a result of this very fact that labels arise.

This brings me to the end of my introduction to and discussion of phrase structure: it is the locus of recursion and compositionality in the grammar, where hierarchy is established, irrespective of linear order. Nothing happening further in the derivation can change the hierarchical and thematic relations once they are established there. The attempt to 'minimalize' the phrase structure component has made it so bare and flat that it is hard to see how a substantive notion of projection could come about, which however seems independently needed for a meaningful mapping of syntactic objects to emergent semantic interpretations. A 'bare phrase structure' that has 'no projections or other violations of inclusiveness' (Chomsky DBP: 6) and gives labels a status that positively invites the project of eliminating them (Collins 2002), may effectively deprive us of phrase structure. Maybe, though, what happens is that the pristine arithmetic and set-forming recursive routine of Merge as such is joined by operations logically independent from it, inducing the right hierarchical cuts into a derivation. Perhaps theta-roles force the system out of its dump conjunctive routine, and into the use of labels. I have also introduced the idea that semantic content is built up in layers, a fact that Chomsky's own bare phrase structure project by no means denies but claims *to derive*, by assuming a preference of external Merge (phrase structure) over internal Merge (transformations), a point to which I return. No violation of Inclusiveness needs to ensue from building functional relationships into the architecture of phrase-structural syntactic objects, or from building them in layers of function-argument relationships each of which contains previously built ones as parts.

5.4 Transforming the Phrase

We have looked at basic X-bar theoretically constrained phrase structures capturing 'is a' and thematic relations, and mentioned the Case and agreement systems associated with functional layers in the human clause and triggering movements of arguments to suitable specifier positions. We have also mentioned the movement of heads for the sake of adjoining to heads just above them in the phrasal hierarchy. These systems are all involved in human judgements of relatively simple types. We will now encounter more complex judgements, which cannot be described as phrases, as lexical items standing in X-bar theoretic relations, or as syntactic objects in the sense of the above definition of external Merge. Transformational operations of the kind we encounter now require a different kind of mind. As we noted, a phrase-structurally characterizable mind will have symbolic representations—it will have labels, or represent structures as NPs or PPs, but it need not ever relate *two phrase structures* to one another or keep a *memory* of how a label came about derivationally. Arguably, to do the latter things, it needs not only abstract internal representations but the power to *represent an internal representation*, hence have a symbolic capacity of *higher order*.

We begin with the derivation of the 'interrogative construction', i.e. questions, thereby taking up again our earlier discussion concerning the problem of construction-specific rules in the process of the child's acquisition of language. A plausible (and already reasonably complex) inductive hypothesis for the construction principle of the English *wh*-question might be that it starts from a structure like (2), where the position occupied by *Gustav* in (1) is filled instead by a *wh*-element:

(1) you are looking at *Gustav*
(2) you are looking at *who*

In one respect, *who* is in the right position here, as far as interpretation is concerned: it is in the place of the object of the verb, the thing looked at. On the other hand, there is a plain sense in which there is no thing we are looking at in (2). That is to say, there is an element here that is *uninterpretable* in that position. Thus there is another interpretive strategy to which English resorts: something along the lines of *who is such that [you are looking at him]* is generated, with *who* and *him* necessarily interpreted as the same person. What we notice here is that *who* crucially appears wholly outside the original clause (or takes *scope* over it), while, as just noted, still being intimately connected semantically to its original position in that clause. The question is how we *get* the kind of structure underlying our paraphrase of the question's meaning, which, on the surface of it, is rather different from what we see in (2). English points our way in this instance, however, as (2) is indeed only marginally well-formed, the correct surface form being (3), where the *wh*-element appears fronted (or has 'moved'), and where we have marked its original position (where it in some sense still *is*, being the direct object of the verb), as *t* (for 'trace'):

(3) who are you looking at *t*

The rule of generating a question thus seems to be that *wh*-expressions, although interpreted, as far as argument structure is concerned, in their original position, move out of that position, to the left edge of the clause that contains them, somehow taking that whole clause as their argument.

The ordered pair consisting of the moved item itself and its trace (or traces, if it moves several times) is called a *chain*. It is interpretively relevant in forcing a coreferential interpretation of *who* and the variable element *t*, spelled out phonetically as *him* in our rendering of the meaning above: *whichever* person is substituted for *who* must be substituted for *him* (if it's John, then John is such that you are looking at John; if it's Gustav, then Gustav is such that you are looking at Gustav, etc.). Intuitively speaking this interpretive consequence is precisely the reason why the *wh*-element moves from its base position: there it cannot control the interpretation of any other element, which appears to be in its nature as an operator to do. This indicates that the creation of a chain is nothing as trivial as changing the order of the words of a sentence: it involves changing hierarchical order, not merely linear order: an entirely new object arises that wasn't there before, a long-distance link between the head and the tail of a chain, which effectively repairs the semantic deficiency of (2). It is an object that cannot possibly arise in the course of projecting a clause from the lexicon, but only after that is accomplished, giving again rise to a kind of 'layered semantics'.

If we now were to try formulating a question-formation rule, then a rather trivial one depending on linear order only would be 'Move the *wh*-item to the front'. That rule works well in an unbounded number of cases, such as (4) and (5):

(4) a. you are thinking that you are looking at **someone**
    b. you are thinking that you are looking at **who**
    c. **who** are you thinking that you are looking at?
(5) a. you are saying that you are thinking that you are looking at **someone**
    b. you are saying that you are thinking that you are looking at **who**
    c. **who** are you saying that you are thinking that you are looking at?

But it falters quickly in others. Thus in (6) something different happens: although (8) might be interpreted and intended with the coherent meaning (9), it is in fact impossible:

(6) you are looking at a man whom you just asked a question
(7) you are looking at a man whom you just asked **what**
(8) *****what** are you looking at a man whom you just asked?
(9) what is the question such that you are looking at a man whom you just asked that question?

The example raises paradigmatic questions for any approach that regards language acquisition as a form of hypothesis testing and theory formation. For an expression like (8) is never tested by language-acquiring children or uttered by them, and they will never hear it uttered as a counterexample to the rule (Crain and Pietroski 2001). If (8) is an exception to the rule, and nobody tells every English child that it is one, how do children unfailingly know that it is? If language acquisition is a form of theory formation, children would have to 'decide' whether a given sentence type is only accidentally absent from the corpus of utterances they have heard, or whether it is actually impossible (ungrammatical), and it is not clear how they would. Suppose, similarly, that a child comes up with the rule that to form a question out of

(10) The man is my friend

you take the 'first auxiliary (AUX) after the subject' and move it to the front (this is to suppose that it knows what an AUX and a 'subject' is, notions that are already not definable in linear terms). This rule falters in an example like the following:

(11) [[The man [who is my dad]] [is also my friend]],
    since it yields
(12) *Is the man who my dad is also my friend?

Here we notice that the 'first auxiliary after the subject' is, as it were, opaque to the transformation. It is contained in a unit of higher order, the NP 'the man who is my dead' and the relative clause therein, which forms a so-called *island* to extraction, just as the relative clause dependent on *man* does in (6). As a consequence, the first auxiliary cannot be touched. Importantly, that transformations are sensitive to phrase-structure boundaries and islands in this fashion has nothing specifically to do with questions: it is a general feature of transformations, whether employed in the service of asking a question or for some another purpose to which we put language.

The learning child thus minimally needs a notion of hierarchical structure plus an understanding of transformations and constraints on them. That notion of phrasal structure might seem in (11) to be something like a 'subject phrase', but there really is no such thing as a subject phrase, and it is, in fact, the wrong notion entirely: thus the 'subject' (in square brackets) in example (13)

(13) [The man who is my dad] is called by my Mom

is really the *object* of that sentence, the thing that is called by someone. The notion needed is that of a *matrix* (main clause) *Inflectional Phrase* (IP), which in (11) is the phrase [$_{IP}$ e is my friend]. This notion enters the following rule of question formation:

(QF) 'Move the auxiliary in the matrix IP.'

This rule would make the child discard the *is* contained in the 'subject', which now unpacks as really being the Specifier of the matrix IP. But where would the exotic concepts entering into the formulation of this rule come from? If (12) were available to the child and available at the right moment, for example, the first conclusion we would expect it to draw is not QF, but that *any* AUX can be moved to the front. Moreover, numerous *other* rules are compatible with (12). As Lasnik and Uriagereka (2002: 149) point out, all of the following rules would be consistent with the data and world be predicted more than QF:[26]

A: Front the first AUX, unless there is an intonation change, in which case front the AUX after it.

B: Front the first AUX, unless there is another one after the first complete constituent, in which case front it.

C: Front the first AUX, unless there is another one after the first semantic unit I parse, in which case front it.

This problem of how to restrict the hypothesis space will not only arise here but for *any* grammatical construction over and above questions and the abstrusely complex rule systems originally stipulated for them: without a principled restriction on *which transformations of a given structure are possible*, the options left open for the child to check are too vast.

Given the facts of language acquisition and the very limited testing that children engage in, the options should be few. At best, there should not *be* a construction-specific 'rule of question formation'. Rather, there should be *general* principles of how constituents in a sentence can be moved around in it, irrespective of whether we are talking about questions or not. Example (14) in particular illustrates a 'raising' construction, and (15) a passive construction:

(14) The lion seems to be likely to roar.
(15) The lion was beaten.

To consider (14) first: here *the lion* is the subject of *roar*, roaring being what he does, as in *the lion roars*. The paraphrases in (16a, b) suggest this, too:

(16) a. It seems that it is likely that the lion roars.
    b. It seems to be likely for the lion to roar.

The initial *It* in (16a, b) carries no semantic or referential role—it is purely pleonastic. This raises the question of why *the lion*, which *does* carry a referential role, can appear in a position in (14) where a semantically vacuous item like *it* can appear, too. Note further that the verb *roar*, by contrast to *seems*, absolutely needs

---

[26] All of these rules, they argue, would account for most examples likely to be available to the child, and hence, in order to be ruled out, require explicit negative evidence to be brought to the child's attention (i.e., counter-examples to these rules marked as such). Negative evidence and correction is known to be scarce in language acquisition, however, and the counterexamples required here are likely never to be produced at all (or, if produced, not corrected, or, if corrected, not attended to by the child, or, if attended to, too complex to process, or if attended to and not too complex, not *robustly* available *often enough* to all children). In short, the determination of the correct rule QF does not appear to happen on the basis of available data. Note that, as the qualifications made were meant to indicate, this argument does not suggest that the data needed to rule out the wrong hypotheses are not available (contra the line of argument run by Pullum and Scholz 2002); rather they must be available in sufficient quantity (see Legate and Yang 2002).

a *non*-pleonastic subject, as we see from the fact that in the phrase *it roars*, the *it* does refer to some contextually specified lion or other animal, hence is not pleonastic. We may thus suggest that at an early stage of our derivation of (14), *the lion* is indeed the subject of the infinitive *to roar*,

(17) [the lion [to roar]]

But by the same reasoning, *the lion* is also the thing that is likely to roar, that is, the subject of *to be likely to roar*. If this suggestion is true, another intermediate representation is (18a):

(18a) [the lion [to be likely [the lion [to roar]]]],

where in the phonetic output of (14), the lower occurrence of *the lion* gets erased—we don't hear it—crucially leaving its semantic interpretation as the subject of the roaring unaffected:

(18b) [the lion [to be likely [t to roar]]].

Adding *seems* gives us

(18c) seems [the lion [to be likely [t to roar]]].

As a final step, *the lion* moves again, and its previous occurrence is again erased in the phonetic component. Then the derivation stops:

(18d) The lion seems [to be likely [t to roar]]

We thus have a sequence of movements to the edges of clausal boundaries that have been transgressed, illustrating the idea that in human languages long-distance movements are broken down into a number of shorter or 'successive cyclic' movements, each of which cross a minimal unit of structure. Similarly, *wh*-questions have been commonly assumed to obey this requirement, so that

(19) Who did you think the lion thought he should roar at

comes out as

(20) [$_{S'}$ Who [$_S$ you think [$_{S'}$ t [$_S$ the lion thought [$_{S'}$ t [$_S$ he should roar at t]]]]]]

where 'S' informally indicates clausal (sentential) boundaries and 't' is the trace of *who*. This assumption about the necessary *locality* of movement would explain why examples like (21) are out, the idea being that more than one of such boundaries is crossed, which the so-called *Subjacency Principle* forbids:

(21) *[$_{S'}$ Who did [$_S$ you wonder [$_{S'}$ whether [$_S$ John knows [$_{S'}$ why [$_S$ I adore]]]]]]

Here, but not in (20), subjacency is violated since the positions where we see the intermediate landing sites of successive cyclic movement in (20) are already *occupied* in (21). As a consequence of that, movement cannot be local. But it must be. Hence we understand why (21) is structurally impossible.

On the other hand, each of a number of short or local moves cannot be too short either. If we imagine a real lion for the moment, then, when crossing a distance there is, given its physiology, an optimal way to cross it: jumps cannot be longer than they can be, and they also cannot be shorter, two forces that pull in opposite directions. There will then be a number of landing sites that will correspond to what is, everything else being equal, the perfect way of filling a distance:

START   END

Analogously, mixing the necessary locality of movement (Collins 1997), which demands that a minimal distance is crossed, with its necessary anti-locality (Grohmann 2003) which demands that the distance is not too short either, we should in principle be able to understand where moving items land and why. In the instance of (14), one explanation for having the locality in question might be that moving arguments are in some intuitive sense bound within derivational 'phases' (here basically clauses): a connection *to* them can only be established from a higher point in the tree if they move from their base position to a position at the 'edge' of each phase in which they are contained. I return to phases in Section 6.1.

As for the passive construction (15), *the lion was beaten*, we notice again that what is beaten is the lion, hence that *the lion* is the object (the THEME, or PATIENT) of the verb, despite appearing in initial position. To account for this interpretive fact, we may thus suggest that the initial structure was

(22) beat [the lion].

But since the verb is deficient in some sense, related to its lack of a second argument (the AGENT of the beating), the object moves to the front, leaving a trace behind. This gives, after insertion of *was*, the surface form (15), whose underlying form is [the lion [was [beaten t]]].

We also notice that the relationship between passives and their active counterparts is perfectly *systematic*, a generalization that independent phrase-structure rules for both would completely miss. Whenever we have a structure NP_1+V+NP_2, as in *Paul beats the lion*, we can also have a structure $NP_2+be+V\text{-}en+by+NP_1$, as in *The lion was beaten by Paul*. Moreover, in the latter, unfailingly, *beat* will remain a transitive verb, NP_1 will still be interpreted as the AGENT, and NP_2 as the PATIENT.[27] On such grounds, we may conclude that there simply is no such thing as the 'active' and the 'passive' construction, each with their own rules, but that there is *one* underlying phrase structure here which can be *transformed* by moving its constituents, leaving thematic relations projected from the lexicon intact.

[27] For a more detailed reconstruction of the Chomskyan original argument for the passive transformation, in the context of the development of generative grammatical theory, see Boeckx and Hornstein (2005).

Note that it is presumably *possible* to generate both constructions by purely phrase-structural rules rather than transformational ones, and thus to state their restrictions by independent rule systems. The point made is not that such a task could not be achieved, but that it would miss a generalization and have no explanatory power. Clearly we would prefer a theory that accounted for questions, 'raising' constructions, *and* passives: an overarching and cross-constructional theory of movement whose intrinsic constraints made no reference to such constructions themselves.

Let us now look at quantificational constructions like (23), which, we shall see, exhibit abstract structural similarities to the *wh*-questions we began with above:

(23) Every man stared.

Every man is a *quantified noun phrase* (QNP): in (23) we are not saying anything about some particular individual, but about all individuals in a particular domain, as long as they are men. Thus we are not saying, about some individual such as Fred, that he stared. There is no thing, called 'every man', to which the property of staring might apply. Rather, we are saying something about this very property of staring: namely, that it applies to each one in an entire domain of men. We are ascribing a property to a property. Now, a property of its nature *applies* to something, x, which an individual like Fred does not do: Fred does not 'apply' to anything. So we must distinguish properties applying to some individual x, from properties applying to properties. *Every man* thus applies to the property or function *x stared*, saying of it that x can be every element in the domain of men. This function is called the *derived argument* of the QNP, because it is the argument that this QNP, which is that function itself, takes after it assumes a position outside the phrase expressing that function. In that phrase, x is interpreted variably over the domain of men: if it's Fred, then Fred stares, if it's Victor, then Victor stares, etc.:

(24)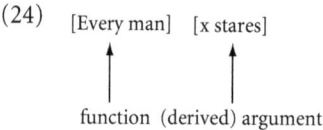

Since the derived argument is, as such, also a function applying to an argument, namely x, the function *every man* is a *second-order* function, applying to a first-order one. The form of the resulting structure, in a diagrammatic notation, is basically this (where the sub-tree *x stares* is the syntactic *sister* of the QNP):

(25)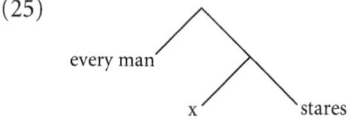

This leaves us with the task of finding corroborating syntactic evidence for the movement of the QNP in (24) now postulated on semantic grounds: our grounds were merely that the structure generated by the movement would make syntactic sense of an interpretive property of the expression in question. Put differently, syntactic evidence is needed for the tight fit between syntax and semantics that a certain structural assumption allows. We will return to this problem several times, noting here that movement transformations correlate with and apparently enable specific semantic effects: without transformations, no quantifying or variable binding. Consider now expressions like (26):

(26) Jack kills no one.

The QNP *no one* takes as its argument the property of *being an x such that Jack kills x*. (26) tells us that whatever such x we take, the predicate expressing this property does not apply to it. Note however that this predicate is not, syntactically, the sister of the QNP, and that it is thus unclear in what way the QNP can take it as its argument (see further Fox 2003: 84):

(27)

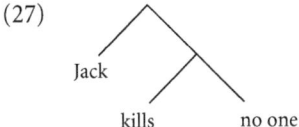

This may lead us to the suggestion that the underlying syntactic structure is in effect different: the QNP is in a position where its derived argument *is* its sister. This would result in the following structure, which one might paraphrase as saying: no one is such that Jack kills him (in this paraphrase, *him* phonetically spells out the trace of the moved QNP):

(28)

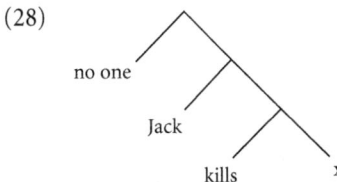

In this structure, as in our structure for (24), the QNP is in a position where its argument, 'Jack kills x', is precisely its sister. What we need to postulate, to get this desirable result, is that in this construction, too, where the QNP is in object rather than subject position, a transformation will bring it into a position where it does take its whole sentential argument as its sister. The theoretical cost is equally clear, however: we must postulate that in instances such as this, nothing for the true underlying structure of an expression follows from its phonology: the QNP is heard in the position of the variable x in (28). But it is semantically interpreted at the highest point in this tree. If so, semantic interpretation is potentially read off syntactic structures generated by (covert) transformations. This hypothesis (May 1997) is the *quantifier raising hypothesis*:

(29) QUANTIFIER RAISING (QR):
Quantifiers raise to attain their proper scope position.

The proper scope position is the position in which the quantifier is outside its derived argument (its 'scope'), its internal argument being its *restrictor*.

(30)   No   man   (x is an island)
        ↑   ↑   ↑
        Quantifier restrictor scope

Evidence for the QR-hypothesis would be the demonstration that in other languages than English, QNPs in object position actually move *overtly*, i.e., *with a phonetic reflex* (see, e.g., Kiss 1991). We might then say that whether QNPs move overtly or not is a *parametric* difference with respect to which different languages choose different options, whereas the principle (30) as such, that QNPs move to their proper scope position, could be kept as a universal principle.

In English, it may actually be that one of two quantifiers contained in the same clause stays overtly in its base position, or *in situ*, as in (31):

(31) Someone read every paper.

While this is perhaps most intuitively interpreted as saying that there is a person, x, who read every paper, the claim might be made that it can also mean that for every paper, y, there was someone, x, who read it, and not necessarily the same x. The latter interpretation, by the reasoning above, would require that the internal quantifier takes scope over the external one, as in (32):

(32) [every paper [someone [x read y]]]

Put differently, QR, which would have us move the QNPs mechanically into a position where they take the predicate *x read y* as its argument, predicts that this may happen in two ways, depending on how the two quantifiers turn out, after being moved, to be ordered. If the lower quantifier crosses over the upper one, or takes scope over it, we predict the less common reading. If the upper quantifier takes scope over the lower quantifier, as in (33),

(33) [someone [every paper [x read y]]],

the more common reading will ensue, or be its semantic consequence. Consider now further evidence for QR, in (34):

(34) John liked everyone that Bill did.

What exactly did Bill do here? What he did is like everyone that also John liked. How do we explain that?[28] Suppose that elliptical structures like (34) proceed by deleting some material in the sentence under conditions of parallelism. Thus in (35),

(35) John liked Sally and Bill did, too

what we understand, but do not hear, is the material indicated as (phonetically) deleted in (36):

(36) John liked Sally and Bill did, too, ~~like Sally~~.

The deletion is phonetical only, since semantically this verbal phrase is clearly *there*. It is interpreted as a predicate holding of Bill. Call the heard 'higher' VP the *antecedent*, and the deleted, or 'lower' VP its (anaphoric) *dependent*. Now, this explanation of why (35) can mean what it does fails to work for (34). The antecedent VP in (34) is *liked everyone that Bill did*, and if we copy this into the gap after *did* in (34), we get a structure that has a gap at the end once again:

(37) John [liked everyone that Bill did] [like everyone that Bill did] GAP

Clearly, repeating the copying operation one more time will give us an infinite regress (ever more gaps will appear), and never what (34) actually manages to mean. Given QR, however, a solution suggests itself: somehow the quantifier phrase internal to the antecedent can be *moved out from under* this VP, so as not to depend any more for its interpretation on an antecedent *that itself contains it*. In other words, the surface appearance that the QNP is *contained* in a VP that at the same time is its antecedent must be wrong or structurally misleading. Suppose then we take the QNP and move it out of that VP into a position where it takes scope over the entire sentence (the arrow indicates a movement of the whole QNP):

(38) [$_{QNP}$ everyone that Bill did], John liked [$_{QNP}$ everyone that Bill did]
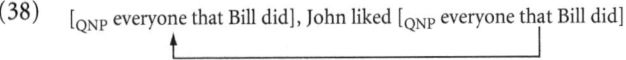

Apparently, as noted, our language faculty allows only one of the occurrences of a moving phrase to be pronounced. So it can be that, although it is necessarily in the occurrence in the displaced position that the quantifier is as such *interpreted*, either *that* occurrence is deleted in the phonetics, or the *original* occurrence is. Our example is an instance of the first case, since (38) is heard as (34). We may say that (38) is a more abstract 'semantic representation' of an expression, of which (34) is a (less abstract, phonetic) representation.

---

[28] My way of phrasing the issues here foreshadows my later account of 'syntactic meaning explanations' in Section 5.6.

How does that solve the regress problem above? In (39) the elided part in (34) is indicated with a gap, an empty category, a VP:

(39) John liked everyone that Bill did [$_{VP}$ e].

The problem was that this elided VP was *contained* in a larger VP that was, at the same time, its antecedent: [$_{VP}$ liked everyone that Bill did [$_{VP}$ e]]. The result of QR now yields (40), in which we have moved all that comes after *John liked* in (39), leaving a gap [$_{QNP}$ e] in its original position behind:

(40)   [$_{QNP}$ everyone that Bill did [$_{VP}$ e]], John liked [$_{QNP}$ e].

Now the elided lower VP is no longer contained in its antecedent VP: it has escaped its influence and is structurally on top of it. To fill the gapped VP, [$_{VP}$ e], in (40) with a semantic content, we copy the overt verbal phrase [$_{VP}$ liked [$_{QNP}$ e]] into this gap, obtaining

(41) [$_{QNP}$ everyone that Bill did [$_{VP}$ liked [$_{QNP}$ e]]] John [$_{VP}$ liked [$_{QNP}$ e]],

in which *e* is interpreted as a pronoun that co-refers with everyone: Everyone, x, such that Bill liked x, is also such that John liked x.[29]

In short, transformations of given structures explain their attestable interpretive properties through more abstract 'semantic representations', not necessarily reflected in phonetic ones. The typological virtue of this solution is that languages which differ on the surface need not therefore differ in their underlying semantic structures. If we constrained our grammar to contain only movements that leave a trace on the phonetic surface, we would predict, for languages where *wh-*expressions or QNPs do not move overtly, that semantic interpretation would obey radically different principles. But this seems hard to sustain. To start with, it would cause problems for acquisition, given that we concluded parametric differences have to be detectable on the surface, which seems difficult for more abstract principles of semantic interpretation. The solution, namely, that parameterization affects not which transformations take place but which of them are heard, looks attractive.

In some respects, *wh-*movement in English is an analogue of QR. *Wh-*questions may be fundamentally similar to quantifications, in that both constructions are built through an operator-variable structure, and the construction of a structure containing a long-distance relationship, generated by a transformation,

---

[29] For recent analyses of 'Antecedent-Contained Deletions' (ACDs) of the kind just discussed see Fox (2003), on which I have drawn, Johnson (2000), and Hornstein (1995). The last (ch. 5, esp. section 4) argues that the phenomena are better accounted for without QR, and more in line with NP movement of the kind witnessed in passives (*A-movement*), but the essential point in the text, that quantifiers move out of their base positions without a phonetic reflex is left unchanged.

between two items in the structure of an expression. In questions, too, a movement creates a syntactic object that did not exist before: in our example (3) above, the object [*you are looking at t*]. This is, equally, a function, and it has a 'hole', as it were, which makes it an impossible syntactic object. It becomes a possible syntactic object only if either its hole is filled by an argument, such as *John*, as in *you are looking at (John)*, or if the whole function with its open place becomes itself an argument of a second-order function, namely the *wh*-expression *who*, as in *who (you are looking at (t))*. In the second case, we are getting an object that can be used as a question.

As noted, movement of *wh*-items is often held to pass through a number of intermediate positions in the clause. These intermediate positions of the moved item do sometimes become *overtly marked*, as for example in Spanish and Irish, providing for something like a 'visible trail' of the item's path. Long movement over several intermediate positions does not seem to *require* this visibility, though—certainly not if our analysis of English was right. If language was 'made for communication', we would expect items in their trace positions to be spelled out, so as to aid the hearer's reconstruction efforts. On the contrary, however, human language obeys an economy principle of a quite different sort: if there are two copies of one (moving) item, it can be heard only once. Moreover, in languages like Chinese, *wh*-items *never* move overtly. But there is striking evidence, not only that these differences in phonetic visibility are not accompanied by interpretive differences, but that there are very similar *locality constraints* on (covert) long-distance moves of *wh*-items. This would be an interesting result, for it would show that if a movement goes via intermediate positions and an overt trace is left in each of the latter, this is not because the long movement is too long to be *processed*, and hence must be supported by an overt trail: locality constraints movement *no matter* whether the movement is overt. In other words, the overt marks of movement that we find in some languages have no functional rationale, such as a rationale in the facilitation of processing, or the use of language (see further Lasnik 1999).

To illustrate, Chinese *wh*-items stay put or *in situ*: there, to ask whom you love, you do not say (42) but the Chinese analogue of (43):

(42) whom do [you love ~~whom~~]
(43) [you love who].

In fact, though, that does not seem to be too different from what happens in English, where, as briefly noted, although single *wh*-phrases must move overtly, in multiple questions one of them can also stay put, as in

(44) Who asked what?

English is thus a mixed case, as French is, in contrast to Chinese, which settled on the *in situ* option. There is also the other extreme, of languages where *all wh*-expressions move overtly, giving us structures like (45), from Serbo-Croatian:

(45) Ko koga vidi?
 who whom sees
 'Who sees whom?'

It is thus a very attractive conclusion typologically that the overtness of movement is again not a principled difference but a parametric option in human language, in which movement works otherwise uniformly.

By way of example, it has long been observed that an adverbial adjunct introduced by *because* cannot be extracted from its local configuration, as examples like (46) suggest, where x and y indicate the (phonetically deleted) base positions from where the *wh*-items *what* and *why*, respectively, are moved:

(46) *What$_x$ did you wonder [why$_y$ [I bought x y]]

The word *what* questions the thing, x, that was bought (a coke, say). The word *why* questions the reason, y, for why I did this (because I was thirsty, say), so that the base clause from which the question is formed is *I bought a coke because I was thirsty*. Now, while (46) can be interpreted in the way just indicated, it is clearly grammatically deviant. Even worse however is (47), where again the *why* questions a reason for the act of buying (not the act of wondering):

(47) *Why$_y$ did you wonder [what$_x$ [I bought x y]],

There is a common reason for these ungrammaticalities: locality constraints on movement. Once the derivation has constructed the structure (48),

(48) [why$_y$ [I bought a coke y]],

the operator *what*, generated in the position of *a coke*, must, to reach its wide-scope position in (46), cross the clause boundary where *why* is located. But this is to move too far: again, the embedded clause forms an island from which no extraction of an operator can take place. A similar account holds for (47), which however is worse than (46) because adjuncts (in the position of y above) are generally harder to extract than complements (in the position of x).

Now, the interesting is that that the Chinese question, where nothing moves overtly, obeys constraints of the very sort that we just saw for languages in which *wh*-movement is overt (data from Huang 1995: 152–4, whose discussion I follow):

(49) Ni xiang-zhidao [wo weisheme mai shenme]
 you wonder I why buy what

Although (49) allows the interpretation *For which x do you wonder why I bought x*—where *which* has widest scope and corresponds to the complement position—it disallows the wide-scope interpretation for its embedded operator, *why*: *for which reason, y, do you wonder what I bought for y*. This is interesting, for if Chinese *wh*-operators were not to move, there would appear to be no reason why

(49) should be uninterpretable in the way indicated. By contrast, if they do move, though covertly, then we would expect them to be subject to the same constraints. If this prediction is born out, this is evidence for our assumption of semantic uniformity at SEM.

The impossibility of (50) illustrates locality constraints on extraction from another kind of island, in this case the sentential subject:

(50) *Who is [that John married t] a real pity?

Again, Chinese obeys the same constraint. (51), if possible, would mean something like *who is such that the fact that Zhangsan married that person is a real pity*:

(51) *[[Zhangsan tao-le shei], zhen kexi]
     Zhangsan marry who real pity

Again, this ungrammaticality is expected if English and Chinese were essentially alike in what moves where, and the same locality constraints prevented transformations from crossing the boundaries of islands (for discussion see Culicover 1997: 301–3).

With locality constraints we have now encountered a surprising instance of a kind of *economy* in language design, which nothing in logic, utility, natural selection, or communication predicts. Nothing in these domains predicts that movement must take place within minimal amounts of structure. But the complexity of syntactic computations is thereby reduced: and it seems that we are looking at a generic design principle of computationally efficient systems in nature here, not something that has specifically to do with language. From the viewpoint of language as a natural object obeying constraints found in other dynamic systems in the physical world, constraints of this very general nature are not surprising at all.

In this section, we have surveyed a great variety of constructions. What do *wh*-questions, raising constructions, passives, and quantificational structures have in common? The explanatory problem for early theories that we noted was that they have nothing or too little in common: rule systems devised for each of them did not speak to one another. Now they have in common that when starting from a base structure—in which the question is not yet formed, the NP not yet raised, the *wh*-expression or the QNP not yet moved to its scope position—the relevant 'construction' emerges through the displacement of items in the generated phrase structures: the *wh*-expression, the NP, or the QNP are moved in a right-to-left direction, subject to locality and other constraints, thereby creating new semantic possibilities and impossibilities.

Crucially, the constraints on displacement are *general* overarching principles and do not mention rules for specific constructions or categories, just as with the advent of X-bar theory, principles of phrase structure ceased to be sensitive to construction or category. Since the transformations are not language-specific, moreover, a natural hypothesis transpires that human languages do not differ with respect to phrase structure and transformational operations, nor to constraints on either, but rather as to whether these operations leave a phonetic reflex, a property of languages presumably detectable from their overt output. In the specific case of *wh*-movement, in particular, where they may differ is with regard to the *location* of the 'spell-out' point in the syntactic derivation from the lexicon to the final semantic representation, SEM, below which all transformations take place covertly. In Chinese this point will be early, as none of multiple *wh*-expressions moves overtly. In languages like Bulgarian or Serbo-Croatian it is late, as all such items move, leaving a middle ground for mixed languages like English or French. This gives us a model of the following sort, in which different languages are arranged along of spectrum of options for when the cut off point for phonetic visibility occurs:

(52)

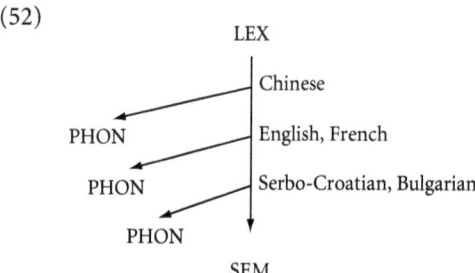

5.5 Why is there Movement?

Nothing in the above answers the question of *why* syntactic objects get transformed. Maybe we should reject this question. A transformation is a 'warping' of a phrase marker (a phrase structure generated by the base component), in a topological sense, and just as there is no 'reason' for a topological operation in an *n*-dimensional mathematical space, there is maybe no basis for looking for one in our case. Things in nature, or in the spaces of mathematics, do not move or get transformed for a reason: as Galileo argued, answering why-questions is not part of the scientific endeavour.

Still, minimalism is centrally the question of why language is the way it is, and thus we should ask why the architecture of human language is such as to have the displacement property. Now, it has been argued, especially in early Minimalist syntax (Chomsky 1995), that displacement is a *prima facie* 'imperfection', on the grounds that things would be more perfect and as expected if expressions were generally heard in the places where they are interpreted. This assessment, so formulated, seems ungrounded however. Note that although a QNP is interpreted in its base position for one of its features—being thematically the PATIENT or THEME, say—it is *not* interpreted there *as* a binary quantifier or as an operator. It has no derived argument (scope) as its sister in this position, hence cannot operate as a binary quantifier there.

This invites several other conclusions, as already noted in the previous section. First, *higher-order structures* created by transformations—namely, chains—are *objects of interpretation*: without such objects, no quantification will take place. Second, semantics is *distributed*: the meaning that a lexical item has in the sentence in which it occurs comes about in stages during the derivation, rather than being there from the start, or coming about in one fell swoop in the end. Third, the trace of a moving QNP, while being identical in form with the moved QNP (and in this sense a 'copy' of it), is not interpretation-wise equivalent to it, as interpretation depends on the structural configuration in which it occurs. I return to these conclusions.

As Chomsky (1995: 252) suggests, the formally identical links in a chain may be distinguished by their syntactic *contexts* or *occurrences*, i.e., their immediate neighbours (sisters) in their respective configurations. Thus in (53), (53)

Every man was killed

the immediate syntactic context of the QNP (its *sister*) in its lower site is *killed*, the VP. In its derived position, the QNP's immediate syntactic context is the sentence *x was killed*, an IP:

(54)

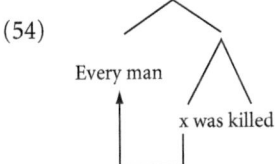

The chain has thus the form:

(55) CH = <<every man, IP>, <<every man, VP>>.

Factoring out *every man*, we may identify it as the object: CH = <IP,VP>. As we see here, to get structures lending themselves to quantificational purposes, we minimally need syntactic objects that are not phrase markers but sets of them. What is semantically interpreted is not a configurational position, as in thematic interpretation, but a pair of positions.

However, this proposal clearly does not go far enough, or is somewhat too 'minimal'. Chains are not *mere* sets either: one of these is *contained* in the other, or is a part of it. Containment itself moreover is not trivial by any means, as noted, since it involves function-argument relationships of increasing orders. The moved QNP leaves what I have called a 'hole', licensing it from its derived position, since the expression *x was killed* is obviously deficient and cannot stand on its own. The hole cut into a given phrase gives us a first-order unsaturated object, which, when targeted by the transformational operation, becomes the saturated argument of a second-order unsaturated object, the moved QNP. The hole is the sister of a first-order predicate, which itself is the sister to the second-order predicate. At each order, sisterhood indicates function-argument relations; only their orders differ.

The function-argument dichotomy, which we first discussed in relation to argument structure in Section 5.2, is probably the most basic asymmetric relation in grammar, corresponding semantically to the two semantic types that are minimally needed to get a semantics of the kind found in human language going. At each level or order, this asymmetrical relation seems to re-establish itself.

There is a consequence of this, however, which we should not miss. As I said, the activity of killing, say in the sentence *Jill killed every man*, takes two participants, which must be present in the verbal domain, hence are the arguments of *kill* together with its outer shell, the transitivity marker, *v*, although they finally end up in the subject position internal to the TP:

(56)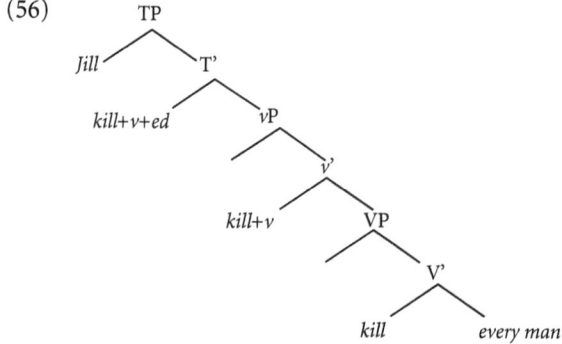

After re-merging the QNP, the structure is (58), in which now a question arises about the label that the root of the tree bears:

(57)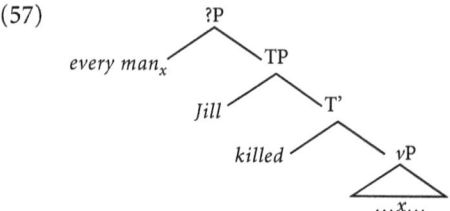

Traditionally, QNPs are maximal projections moved to a specifier position. From this point of view, the root of the tree, the ?P in (57) is not a projection of the D-head of the specifier that this QNP forms: ?P is not a DP. However, we might also argue as follows (see Larson and Segal 1995: chapter 8). Semantically speaking, a binary quantifier establishes a relation, not between individuals, but between sets or pluralities of individuals: in our example, that of the men and that of those who are killed by Jill. What (57) claims is that the former set is contained in the latter. 'Weak' quantifiers like *some* or *a* denote a relation too; thus the relation claimed to obtain between the two sets in question in *some man was killed* is that the intersection of the men and those being killed is non-empty. However, if it is true that *some man was killed*, it will also be true that *some of those who were killed were men*. Hence the arguments of a weak quantifier *are* not intrinsically ordered. By contrast, those of a strong quantifier like *every* are intrinsically ordered, as witnessed by the fact that *every man was killed* does not entail that *all those who were killed were men*. But if a (strong) binary quantifier must *order* its arguments in the way that a verb does too, creating an asymmetry between them, it would seem that both arguments would have to be in the *scope* of the determiner in the first place. Suppose then that argument-taking of determiners is parallel to argument-taking of verbal elements that we are by now familiar with. That is, both take an external argument after having been composed with an internal argument:

(58) THEMATIC STRUCTURE: V + internal argument (external argument)

STRUCTURE OF BINARY   D + internal argument (external argument)
QUANTIFIERS:

But then, the result of attaching the QNP to *Jill killed x* must be a DP after all: the entire sentence must be headed by D, in order for D to impose an order on its subject and object arguments. That is, the *internal* argument of D in (57) is the Noun *man*, and its second, or *derived argument* becomes the predicate *Jill kills x*. By consequence, after its move *every man* cannot be a DP or a fully projected phrase any more, but must be a *non-maximal* projection or D' again that only *now* projects to its full categorial status, thereby in turn demoting its sister to a maximal or saturated projection that does *not* project further. In short, the semantic consequence of binary quantification is plausibly only possible if *re-merging* an item from within a tree to the tree that contains it involves *re-projecting* that item (see further Uriagereka 2002: chapter 6). This gives a more vivid sense to my earlier remark that containment relations that get established as a part of chain formation are not trivial: they do involve *changes* in the object from under which the moved item is taken.

Keeping this analysis of how movement happens in mind, let us return to the question of why movement happens. I have already argued above against the idea that displacement must necessarily be an 'imperfection' on minimalist assumptions, since chains are *interpreted*, and the relevant interpretations that they enable are impossible without the formation of chains. For that reason, we can rationalize displacement through its semantic consequences at the interface, making it a 'principled' element in human language design. But Chomsky appears to have a slighlly different view of the matter (see, e.g., Chomsky 2000: 12): his prime suggestion has been that it is an imperfection *only when looked at in isolation*. Thus, Chomsky has suggested that when taken together with *another prima facie* imperfection, *both* disappear, because they are now predicted from the need to meet interface conditions and optimal ways of meeting them. This other imperfection is the existence of grammatical features of expressions that are uninterpretable semantically or phonetically.

The latter design feature is surprising as long as we assume that the human linguistic system is geared towards matching sounds with meanings: on the idea of a tight form–meaning correspondence, uninterpretable features in the system appear like a kind of noise in it that, other things equal, should not be there. But clearly enough, there are Case features, which seem uninterpretable semantically, and so-called *phi-features*, specifying person, number, and gender, which like Case need not be overtly visible: thus e.g. in English, the pronoun *you* is overtly second person, but only covertly either singular or plural. These features make an obvious difference to our semantic interpretation of the nouns or pronouns that have them in their morphology. But we also find them on *verbs*: English verbs in particular mark number, too, and it is not clear what phi-features such as number do on verbs. In a similar way, we may find Case-features on determiners such as *this*, as in Russian, wheras we expect them only on nouns.

We see, however, that the number feature on the nominal and the verb, or the Case-feature on the determiner and the Noun, must *agree* (**she fly* is not well-formed in English, and **this-[NOM] book-[ACC]* is not in Russian), hence we see the phi-features entering into the syntactic process. There appears to be an operation Agree that is driven by morphological features in the syntactic object triggering it, which is called the *Probe* in Chomsky's system MI. Satisfaction of the demands its features make is necessarily prior to continuing the derivation by merging further lexical items to the syntactic object constructed so far: in short, Agree has to happen first (a cyclicity requirement), which may depend on *moving* (or internally re-merging) some constituent within a given derivational cycle. The Probe thus 'probes down' the syntactic tree in which it is contained, limiting its search locally to the constituents (terms) in the domain of its syntactic sister. If it finds a *Goal* with a matching feature in this local domain, the Probe can be neutralized (erased), and the derivation continues (Chomsky MI, version of 2000: 122–3; 132). Thus, e.g., in

(59) T-was promoted a bad student

uninterpretable phi-features in T probe down into T's sister, hitting upon the phi-features of *student*, in this case requiring it to overtly *move* to the specifier of T. Once that happens, and the features match (are identical), they can be erased and will prevent the derivation from crashing (as it would if there was a plural feature on the Goal, and a singular one on the Probe, say).

While something like theta-theoretic structure (who did what to whom) is, as Chomsky (ibid.: 127) notes, a property of any language-like system, inflectional morphology is not (artificial languages created in logic for communicative purposes lack it, for example). They seem specific to human language. Moreover, they appear to constitute a major source of overt linguistic variation, while not having a rationale in the form–meaning connection. But once morphology is there, it may require agreement or checking, which in turn may require displacement, which we argue *has* a semantic consequence. Uninterpretable features then *have* a rationale for existence, at least an indirect one, in conjunction with the movement they trigger: even though uninterpretable features when appearing at SEM would not be 'legible' there, once triggering movement they lend themselves to deeper and more interesting uses, as in quantification.

On one way of looking at this story, movement was 'made' for uninterpretable features (in order to erase them), and viewing the story thus it has a certain 'teleological' flavour: *prima facie*, a movement is said to take place because, if it did not, uninterpretable features would appear at the interface and the derivation would crash. But then of course, one might ask: why should it not crash? And how can the derivation, prior to reaching the putative interface, know what demands will be made there, and arrange itself accordingly? Even assuming it can somehow do that, it remains unclear why, if movement exists for the sake of eliminating uninterpretable features in morphology, such elimination should systematically give rise to new and higher-order semantic effects, such as those seen in binary quantification.

Suppose, however, that the external interpretive systems accessing language do not only demand interpretability or legibility *as such*, but also make a distinction between *two kinds* of semantic information and demand it to be *marked* in the surface forms of language. One kind of information, we have seen, is *thematic information*: what are the arguments of the verb, what is its subject, interpreted as the agent, what is its object, interpreted as the theme, what is its indirect object, perhaps interpreted as its goal (as in $Annie_{Agent}$ gave the $book_{Theme}$ to $Mary_{Goal}$). This information is delivered by a distinctive semantic layer, without transformations, as we have suggested. The other kind of information is discourse-related information, typically involving the left edge of the clause: topicalization requiring fronting, focus, presupposition, scope, force, etc. Call this the dichotomy of 'deep semantics' versus 'surface semantics'.

Given this external demand on the syntax, Chomsky (2000: 13, MI, version of 2000: 121) reasons, the syntax may now be forced to meet it as well as it can; and maybe it uses the other putative imperfection for that, the existence of uninterpretable inflectional features. These then suddenly make principled sense again. Now, though, it appears that uninterpretable features are 'made for' movement, not that movement is 'made for' uninterpretable features, as before. Displacement is the systematic function to be achieved, as it is externally imposed on the system; uninterpretable morphology is the mechanism implementing it; and given that on closer inspection the *kinds* of features that we find operative in morphology seem actually to be just what is needed to implement displacement, the factual solution to the problem of meeting the external condition may even be a perfect one after all.

But this suggestion *still* has a teleological flavour, and the externalist motivation for displacement is now more direct than on the first line of reasoning. Darwin, as noted, opposed suggestions to the effect that internal complexity is induced by external function: just because external systems make certain demands on a system, that system will not simply come to satisfy them (as it might on a more Lamarckian construal of evolution). One might say of course that if an internalist explanation of some organismic property is not forthcoming, then there is nothing wrong in seeking an externalist one. But that presupposes that an internalist explanation cannot be found; and even if the external systems cared about different kinds of information, and this explained a distinction between a base component and a transformational component in some sense, this would not say anything about what is cause here and what is effect: maybe the 'discourse-related' functions are what they are because there are syntactic transformations generating certain kinds of structures, arising as a kind of side-effect from them.

Can we even identify the former functions without reference to the latter structures? Do 'discourse-related' properties form a domain unified by anything other than the syntactic fact that they involve transformations? As Chomsky himself notes, the surface semantic properties of human languages that depend on displacement are not found in all language-like systems, not formal languages, say, which only care about 'deep semantics'. But if surface semantics is indeed specific to human language, it seems that nothing short of human language would explain it. In any case, binary quantification, say, does not seem particularly 'discourse-related'.

It seems that even if there had been such a thing as independently identifiable 'discourse functions' prior to the transformational component, which could have shaped the latter, this would not yet be the beginning of an explanation of how structures get arranged in the syntax in the intricate ways they have to be to obtain something like questions or binary quantification. If we imagine a transformation to be a complex topological operation, building a higher-order object from a lower-order one and embedding one in the other appropriately, then, surely, again the necessary topological structures do not come into existence because certain external demands are made on the system. The opposite conclusion seems invited, rather: that there are certain operations that the structure of our nervous system, perhaps by virtue of deeper principles of a mathematical and physical nature that it instantiates, makes available; and that these lend themselves to certain uses, as in discourse or quantification.

How could we see displacement as falling out internalistically from intrinsic features of syntactic objects as constructed in the syntax itself? Moro's (2000) proposal is one rather more in this vein, in that it regards movement as the result of a *symmetry-breaking process*. Ultimately, for him, this process reflects output or interface conditions too, however, although now it is the *phonetic interface* (PHON) that imposes anti-symmetry as a condition on well-formed structures appearing there: this is said to be because the phonetic channel is linear, whereas linear order does not seem to be a structural requirement on thoughts and the syntax that structures them as noted. In other words, hierarchical order must be of the type that can be linearized at PHON. Since order is not intrinsic to hierarchy, movement may have to reorganize the phrase marker so as to make it possible to read linear order off from it, and this might be the rationale for displacement.

This is yet another example of a functionalist logic, however. Although we know more about sensorimotor systems that access PHON than we know about the systems accessing SEM, from where Chomsky's argument regarding two kinds of semantic information is drawn, and linearity *does* seem to be a fundamental condition imposed on PHON, it must still be established that PHON is *essential* to narrow syntax and can actually and has actually shaped structure-building processes in it. Particular sensorimotor systems could have become accidentally related to the core syntactic system in evolution. Maybe it is true that grammars deprived of a transformational component would not necessarily generate linearizable structures. But then, who said that they have to? If they did not, language in its full generative power would perhaps not have become used in the way it is—SEMs would simply never be sent to PHON, or PHON would not exist, who knows? Worse accidents have happened in evolution.[30] And if linearization were to blame, why should we not have a narrow, one-dimensional syntax in the first place? If it is more than one-dimensional (has at least linear and hierarchical orders), as it seems to be, linearization does not explain that.

Maybe we could say that the functional demand of linearizability is not after all what shaped movement transformations in narrow syntax. Rather, it just *happened* that narrow syntax had these independently, and that when language came to be used via PHON, only those structures would be usable that *were* linearizable. But this conclusion would be equivalent to saying that PF-linearity does not explain movement. On purely conceptual grounds we are thus driven to the conclusion that externalist or interface explanations for movement should be treated with care, and maybe used as a last resort.

An internalist explanation might be that, for whatever reasons, the human system of meaning is organized structurally into layers, such as a thematic, an Agreement, and a quantificational layer. In particular, the basic structure-building operation that builds the thematic layer, external Merge, could, once a syntactic object has been constructed that is fully specified in thematic respects, apply further: only now it takes objects from *within* the tree constructed, targets them, and merges them at the root (see further Section 6.1). This form of 'internal Merge' would be nothing other than Movement. In other words, the only novelty that arises with transformations would be that, while in external Merge α and β are separate objects, in internal Merge the targeted object β is a part of α. Chomsky (BEA, version of 2001: 8) remarks that it would be surprising if a

---

[30] Movement, Moro (2000: 29) says, is a 'blind mechanism, an automatic by-product of the process of linearization. The "task" of movement will be simply that of rescuing those structures that would fail to be linearized at PF'. Although the metaphor of blindness is paradigmatic in evolutionary theory to denounce a teleological mode of thinking (the 'blind watchmaker'), and the intentional term 'task' appears in inverted commas, the line of reasoning in Moro remains teleological in ways that compromise its explanatory appeal.

system, once having external Merge, would not use it in this other fashion as well. Displacement is natural, that is; it comes 'for free', and no externalist or functional motivation for it is needed (looking for one, as in Chomsky's MI and DBP, was the mistake). Chomsky describes the relation of that insight to the duality of semantic interpretation used earlier to motivate displacement externally, as follows:

> 'There are two kinds of Merge (external and internal) and two kinds of semantic conditions [at SEM] (the duality noted earlier). We therefore expect them to correlate. That appears to be true. Argument structure is associated with external Merge (base structure); everything else with internal Merge (derived structure) (BEA, 2001b: 8; cf. version of 2004: 110).

Crucially, there is now no suggestion that the duality of semantic information, considered as independently given, 'forces' the system to engage in certain transformational processes. Instead we have structural conditions on the one hand, and interpretation facts on the other, and 'we expect them to correlate'. This makes it unclear however, why we should still also want to argue that the semantic interface 'imposes order at PHON and duality of semantic interpretation at SEM' (Chomsky, BEA version of 2004: 110). In fact, that the structural conditions are 'made for' the semantic conditions with which they match so well appears to be something now denied by Chomsky: for the duality in the structural conditions is said to simply fall out from the fact that once we have Merge, we can freely apply it externally and internally. Once the structural conditions were in place, they simply lent themselves to a dual use, a much more attractive suggestion. But it seems to be in full conflict with the idea that displacement is motivated by interface requirements or semantic legibility conditions.

On the reading now envisaged, Chomsky pursues a fully internalist line of explanation, even though many further remarks remain that require extensive interpretation.[31] A crisp and unambiguous statement of an internalist conclusion is the following:

---

[31] Thus, in BEA, version of 2001: 10, Chomsky starts talking again about the application of internal Merge being 'motivated by the nontheta-theoretic C-I conditions' (i.e. SEM); on p. 15, the application of internal Merge is said to be 'determined' by interface conditions; and on p. 16 the existence of a special operation introduced to account for adjunction is said to be 'required' for the sake of a sufficient 'richness of expressive power' at SEM. Read literally, I have no clear idea what the second remark could mean. As for the third, one can object by asking what would be wrong about a system not having such richness of expressive power; and one should react to the 'functionalist' overtones of this remark as Chomsky himself does later on: we can think of the formal feature triggering the application of internal Merge and providing an extra-specifier position for the item moved there as 'having "the function" of providing new interpretations', although 'in the analysis of any process or action (the operation of the kidney, organizing motor action, generating expressions, etc.) such functional accounts are eliminated in terms of mechanisms' (for similar remarks see Chomsky, MI: 17). That makes his internalist commitment, in my terms, clear, even though one may quibble about the fact that the functionalist might agree that ultimately one is talking about mechanisms alone: he would just say that all of these mechanisms are selected because of the functions they perform, hence

(60) SEMANTIC BLINDNESS:
'Movement is blind to semantic motivation, although it is not immune to semantic consequence' (Uriagereka 2002: 212).

A rather clear statement of this view from Chomsky himself is in DBP. Talking about Object Shift (OS) constructions whose details need not concern us here, he writes:

> Sometimes the operation is described as driven by [the semantic properties of the object that undergoes OS] (...). That is a questionable formulation, however. A 'dumb' computational system shouldn't have access to considerations of this kind (...), typically involving discourse situations and the like. These are best understood as properties of the resulting configuration, as in the case of semantic properties associated with raising of subject to [Spec, T] (...). One might also say informally that in (55) the phrase *the men* is raised in order to bind the anaphor.
> (55) the men seem to each other to be intelligent
> But the mechanisms are blind to those consequences, and it would make no sense to assign the feature 'binder' to *the men* with principles requiring that it raise to be able to accommodate this feature. We may also say informally that he's running to the left to catch the ball, but such functional/teleological accounts, while perhaps useful for motivation and formulation of problems, are not be confused with accounts of the mechanisms of guiding and organizing motion (DBP: 32).

In other words, while we can *look* at the computational system as tuned to fulfil interface requirements, this way of looking at it has no explanatory status.[32]

Nothing in this commitment precludes finding empirically that form and meaning are perfectly matched, and nothing precludes finding such matching even for expressions that are not readily *usable* by the performance systems we are equipped with. Moreover, there is no necessity to the correlation, as Chomsky notes. That is, once one has both external and internal Merge, nothing in principle *demands* that the former is mapped to argument structure and the latter to discourse-related properties. One *could* have arranged things so that whenever an argument has to pick up a theta-role, it has to move; or so that discourse-related properties are marked by extra features on heads. In a derivation, discourse properties would be settled first, and then the thematic layer

---

depend on the functions for their explanation and rationale. In any case, the last quoted remark invites us to drop the very common (in the minimalist literature) talk of 'motivating' properties of narrow syntax from interface conditions, or seeing the syntax 'answering' to 'output conditions' imposed by the 'semantic component'. Why still talk about uninterpretable features such as the mechanism 'for' displacement at all (ibid.: 15)? A notable exception to this trend is Brody's version of Minimalism, which precludes all 'externally induced imperfections' (see Brody 2003: especially chapter 9).

[32] Philosophically, this conclusion seems to contrast with e.g. Fox's principle of interpretive economy: the idea that UG has principles 'designed to ensure that *a particular* interpretation ('desired' by the outside system) is achieved in an optimal manner'. Fox's economy principles are 'designed to ensure that a given truth-conditional interpretation is achieved with "no more effort than is necessary"' (Fox 2000: 2). If truth conditions are involved, which are relational, this seems to make the grammar (stupid, blind mechanisms, in Chomsky's terms) sensitive to what is beyond grammar.

would be dealt with. *Semantically*, that mapping might be equivalent to the actual one and not better or worse than the other. But if semantically the mapping could in principle have gone the other way around, we cannot *explain* the actual mapping that seems to obtain between the structural conditions and the external semantic ones by deriving the former from the latter.

That means we can't derive either form from meaning or meaning from form. But they correlate. So what can we do? Could it be that they are *identical*? That there simply are two ways to look at the same structural conditions, a syntactic and a semantic way? The only thing there would then be is an *interface*, and whether we call its internal differentiation 'syntactic' or 'semantic' would not matter very much. The whole issue of correlation would not arise. I return to this suggestion when discussing SEM in more detail below in the next section.

That still leaves us with the question how this structural dichotomy came about, which opened to humans a whole new domain of information. And I think that it is too easy to say that once we have external Merge, we have it applying internally. Arguably, the most important discovery in early generative grammar was that natural languages have a complexity level that phrase-structure grammars do not adequately describe. That is, with transformational grammars having 'internal Merge' we reach a complexity threshold that involves cognitive feats not available before, and certainly not available just because one has external Merge. In particular, the Probe-Goal system requires the system to keep a *memory* of the derivation, as noted in the previous section. But memory is *representational*: a given phrase-structure tree has to be represented, and its dominance hierarchies be preserved, when the Probe searches for a Goal (even if not much of it has to be represented, under a conception of the Agreement system as severely constrained by locality).

Now, as Piattelli-Palmarini and Uriagereka (2004) emphasize, there *is* another biological system that evolved so as to equally cross that complexity threshold: secondary RNA sequences create loops of a kind that, if modelled computationally, must be modelled in terms of 'grammars' as complex as transformational ones (Searls 2002). In other words, 'memory' in the sense that these devices demand is in principle there in nature, independently of the purpose to which we put it in language. The workings of the immune system provide other suggestive analogies. Antibody-construction requires in a remarkable way what the Agreement system demands: identification of the intruding antigen by matching its categorial type, and deleting it. Could we view movement as analogous to an immune response to a viral infection? This 'virus theory' of the origin of displacement has the advantage of crucially not employing any 'interface' in the motivation of movement. In the virus model, movement would not be caused by uninterpretability, a property only determinable in relation to some interface, but a 'viral infection', an alien element entering the system, requiring it to activate inherent resources to match it.

Taken together with 'reprojections' in QNP-movement of the sort mentioned in the beginning of this section, one can perhaps see the seeds of a naturalistic explanation of binary quantification in this analogy of movement with immunization. Let me explain. Note that a strong transparency requirement on the syntax-semantics mapping lies behind Larson and Segal's (1995) determiner analysis, which Uriagereka's (2002) reprojections in QNP movement exploit:

STRONG COMPOSITIONALITY: R is a possible semantic rule for a human natural language only if R is strictly local and purely interpretive (Larson and Segal 1995: 78).[33]

Such a rule is *purely interpretive* if it does not create structure on its own, but passively tracks the structures given to it by the syntax. Human semantic interpretation is *read off* a syntactic phrase marker, interpreting its constituents in a piecemeal fashion: the meaning of a whole sentence then comes out as directly determined by the meanings of its parts and the way they are combined syntactically. The semantic interpretation rule would be strictly *local*, furthermore, if, when accessing a category for interpretation, it can only make its interpretation dependent on that category's sister, hence exploiting a minimum of structural information. Arguably Hornstein and Uriagereka's reprojections of D-heads in binary quantification structures provide for precisely such a transparent syntax–semantics mapping: they give a mechanism explaining why semantic dependence *can* be local (restricted to sisterhood), and how the most essential features of binary quantifiers come about: their conservativity and the orderedness of the arguments of their D-heads.

These two properties are related. Conservativity means that if all whales are mammals, it is also true that all whales are mammals that are whales. In short, one can intersect the superset of which the set of whales is claimed to be a subset again with the set of whales, and the claim would be the same; the claim does not depend on whatever properties non-whales might have.[34] As Larson and Segal (1995: 300) point out, conservativity in binary quantification is an apparent semantic universal in human language that nothing in logic predicts; non-conservative determiner relations, they note, would be 'neither conceptually inaccessible nor somehow unnatural or unuseful'. Conservativity depends on an asymmetric relationship between the arguments of a (strong) binary quantifier like *all* or *every*, making them non-permutable, as noted. It entails that if a quantifier's first argument, X, is its restriction, and its second, Y, its scope, then what is applied to the second argument Y is necessarily D(X), the result of composing D with X. Reprojections explain how this order comes about, providing a syntactic basis for a semantic universal.

---

[33] Pure interpretivity in a related sense was an early assumption of generative grammar: cf. Chomsky (1965: 75).

[34] Formally, if Q is the quantifier, X is its internal argument and Y its external (derived) one, then $[[Q\ X]\ Y]$ iff $[Q\ X]\ Y \cap X$.

This would relate to the virus story in language evolution as follows. What movement does is to create new local relations between elements that could otherwise not interact: specifically it gives, by reconfiguring a given tree, a head a derived argument which it otherwise could not have. Thus in *Every man was killed*, the move of *every man* from the object position of *killed*, triggered by the need to eliminate an infectious virus on the T-head, has as a by-product that the VP *killed* comes into construction with the D-head, which it was not in construction with prior to the move. A chain is created, identified by the set of sisters of the moved item, <T′, VP>, which in the virus theory of Piattelli-Palmarini and Uriagereka (2004) is compared to a 'hyperlink' between T′ and VP. It is now possible that the men are all the *men who were killed*. The 'warping' of given tree relations that arises through movement for the sake of eliminating a viral element creates new links between constituents formerly too far away from one another. Binary quantification, with its compositionality and conservativity properties, arises as a semantic consequence.

In sum, unless one wants to give up on the autonomy of syntax as expressed in the law of 'semantic blindness' (60), and postulate properties of the syntax because the semantics 'demands it' or 'forces it', one might rather explore the other direction, and let interpretive properties follow from, or at least be enabled by, form, as derived dynamically. What correlation facts between syntax and semantics suggest is on this picture no less and no more than that the sound and meaning connection that the computational system establishes is very tight, up to a point where one may identify the cause of semantic principles in syntactic terms. This brings us to a final meta-reflection on the material of this chapter, the actual natures of LF and SEM.

5.6 The Proper Interpretation of LF/SEM

In Section 5.4 we presented arguments suggesting that aspects of semantic interpretation are read off, not from phrase structures, but from transformations of them. Moreover, phonetic forms are not necessarily suggestive of an expression's semantic structure, which is something 'deeper', first called 'Deep Structure', then seen as something that is itself derived by transformations yielding an LF, which is then mapped to the interface SEM.[35] This rather immediately suggests both that syntactic transformations deriving such semantic representations are *part* of the explanation of linguistic meaning, and that meaning is not given independently from the linguistic system, at some pre-or non-linguistic and external level of 'thought'.

---

[35] The following discussion will mainly be carried out in terms of LF, in the Chomskyan (1965) sense of a level of representation with conditions on well-formedness imposed on it that act as filters on ungrammatical expressions. This discussion is preliminary to that of SEM in section 6.1, where arguments are provided that LF does not exist in its own right, and can basically be eliminated in favour of SEM alone.

On the opposing conception of generative semantics and functional grammar, semantics is independent from syntax: in principle, syntax may be ignored if we turn to questions of meaning. Pursued to its limits, this position contends that in the best of linguistic designs, syntax should not exist, or should be trivial: there should be a level of non-linguistic 'thoughts', and there should be surface forms of language (phonetic forms); and while there must be transformations converting the former into the latter, there should not be transformations in any more substantive sense. In particular, there should not be levels of representation such as LF in the linguistic system in which semantic information is coded by means of narrowly linguistic principles and constraints. This attempt to bypass syntax on the way from thought to language was one of the founding ideas of *generative semantics*. As Postal and Lakoff put this same idea in the early 1970s:

because of its *a priori* logical and conceptual properties, [the vision of an optimal and direct mapping between the semantic level and surface structure] is the basic one which generative linguists should operate from (Postal 1972).

Syntax and semantics cannot be separated, and the role of transformations (...) is to relate semantic representations and surface structures (Lakoff 1971).[36]

In the latter quote 'semantic representations' are representations of the putative 'thoughts'. But in the terms of the previous sections, that has the cart before the horse. We did not start with an independent level of thoughts; on the contrary, whatever thought an expression expresses is something to be *explained*, and its intrinsic syntax *is part* of that explanation. The derivation does start from meaning, but *not* that of structured thoughts: it starts with *unstructured* lexical items, or words, fully specified for their (lexical) sound and meaning. The meanings of complex structures then emerges in the course of a derivation in which these structures are built. On the present view, transformations do not 'mediate' between thought and language: they build the former.

Generative semanticists would also suggest that, just as we may have to abstract from phonology to get to the underlying semantic structure of complex expressions (the thoughts coded in them), we may have to abstract from *morphology*, or the form of words, to get to the *meanings* of words. What looks on the surface as a word, typically is, at the putative 'semantic level', something complex, or something generated by the computational system of language. On this view, there is no deep and categorical distinction between the lexicon, the locus of simple and unstructured words, and the syntax, the locus of complex structures with meanings predictable from the meanings of the words they contain and the way they are put together: words themselves may code whole complex thoughts.

Brutus kills Caesar, for example, was said to really have the underlying structure of *Brutus causes Caesar to die*, which in turn was meant to 'derive' from *Brutus causes Caesar to become not alive* (for a modernized version of these ideas see

[36] Newmeyer (1996) is a very informative historical account of generative semantics.

Jackendoff 2002: 338). All of these expressions were said to be equivalent 'at the semantic level', that is, on the putative and presupposed level of 'thought' (or 'conceptual structure', in Jackendoff's terms). Similarly, *break* was thought to come about through *cause+comeabout+be+broken*. In this way the syntactic 'deep structures' postulated by generative linguistics at the time became very similar to the 'semantic representations' of thoughts familiar from logic and truth-conditional semantics, to a degree that the deep structures as an independent level of grammatical representation were abandoned entirely in favour of semantic representations in the logical sense. In this way, generative semantics deflated syntax, or the study of form, as an interesting subject in its own right.[37]

By contrast, Fodor argued from early on that linguistic form teaches a lesson on linguistic meaning: if a meaning is expressed by a word (a structural atom), its meaning is an atom too (an unstructured concept) (see Fodor 1998 and Hinzen 2006a). Also on the presentation above, the extent to which the productions of syntax are similar to the semantic representations of logic is an entirely empirical question. A particularly interesting illustration of this fact is Hornstein's and Pietroski's (2002) discussion of Quine's famous sentence,

(61) Ralph believes that the richest man is happy,

which hundreds of logic courses around the world have used to convince students of quantifier scope ambiguities. The ambiguity is meant to relate to whether the speaker of (61) is committed to the existence of a particular individual who is the richest man... (paraphrase: 'There is a man who is the richest such that Ralph believes of him that he is happy'), or not, in which case the speaker simply reports on a belief of Ralph's that there is someone that Ralph thinks of as the richest man and who he believes is happy (paraphrase: Ralph believes that there is a man who is the richest and who is happy). This in turn—if this is to be a linguistic observation—will have to do with whether or not the embedded NP *the richest man* can take scope over the matrix verb *believes*, resulting in the interpretation *the richest man is such that Ralph believes of him that he is happy*. This is a purely structural question, and an empirical one. More than one's semantic intuitions are needed to decide it: in particular, can the NP escape the clause in which it is contained? Hornstein and Pietroski say no, on empirical and theoretical grounds. It need not concern us here whether they are right. The point is that if they are, one can of course *associate* the wide-scope reading to the Quinean sentence, but one will not have stated a linguistic fact, a fact about linguistic meaning as depending on linguistic form.[38]

The case has many interesting implications, e.g., in the light of prevailing intuitions in philosophy (long after generative semantics) that it is semantics that powers syntax, or that the meaning of a sentence falls together with the

---

[37] Judging from Newmeyer's (1996) historical account, indeed, generative semantics made syntax *too trivially* determined by thought (or semantics) and it was this that led people to lose faith in it.

[38] It may then be a fact about interpretation, e.g., or contextual inference.

'thoughts' assigned to it. For example, it has been assumed that LF is essentially a level of ambiguity resolution: if there are two distinct thoughts expressed by a sentence, syntax somehow *must* provide two distinct LFs for it (syntax, to be good at all, must satisfy functional needs). But there seems no reason to believe that anything like that must be true, a point to which we return below.

In these respects, also current discussions about the 'individuation' of the 'contents' of 'propositional attitudes' come to mind. Ever since Frege there has been a question of whether the *sentences* 'Hesperus is Phosphorus' and 'Hesperus is Hesperus' express different meanings. The motivation for asking this question is transparent: there is every right to say that there are different *thoughts* expressed by these sentences, as is clear from the differential way in which we *ascribe* thoughts to people by using them (in suitable contexts, having the one thought is intuitively not the same thing as having the other, no matter the co-referentiality of the terms involved). If so, the reasoning goes, something about the two expressions must *tell* us why this is so (or why *Hesperus* and *Phosphorus* do not mean the same). Some have been led to propose that names are, well, not quite *names*, but rather complex *descriptions* at some 'deep level'. But to make such a claim is to make a claim about *syntax*—in particular, that names have internal structure or are quantificational expressions (assuming descriptions to have QNPs in their LFs). One needs *syntactic* plausibility for positing the syntactic structures that one's semantic intuitions concerning 'semantic equivalence' yield. For general arguments that syntactic atomicity (structurelessness, as in the case of names) maps to semantic atomicity see Hinzen (2006a). I will assume here that there is, in the human linguistic system, a quite radical split between what is semantically simple and pristine—lexical atoms—and what is syntactically complex, or constructed from these atoms.

I will equally assume for now what was the major conclusion after the downfall of generative semantics, that syntactic structures cannot be directly motivated by some such level of 'thought', or logic.[39] Instead, I will assume that writing up

---

[39] For a presentation of the empirical reasons for abandoning generative semantics for the position of 'lexicalism', see Webelhuth (1995). As a consequence of that, the linguistic theory of semantic representation or SEM became much leaner, as lexicalism deprived it of much of the information that generative semantics had coded in it. This in particular included pragmatic information, or the use of language in discourse. By and large, the 'appropriateness' or 'felicity' conditions on the use of an expression are one thing, its linguistic meaning quite another. It is worth recalling Katz and Bever's diagnosis of the reason for the downfall of generative semantics, and the conclusion at the time that grammar theory cannot include a 'full theory of acceptability': 'This assimilation of the phenomenon of performance into the domain of grammaticality [in generative semantics] has come about as a consequence of an empiricist criterion for determining what counts as grammatical. In almost every paper Lakoff makes explicit his assumption that the explanatory goal of a grammar is to state all the factors that influence the distributions of morphemes in speech. On this view, any phenomenon systematically related to cooccurrence is *ipso facto* something to be explained in the grammar. Since in actual speech almost everything can influence cooccurrence relations, it is no wonder that Lakoff repeatedly discovers more and more new kinds of "grammatical phenomena"' (Katz and Bever 1976, quoted in Newmeyer 1996: 122).

truth conditions for natural language sentences in some logical notation provides *data* for a theory of human language, while having no explanatory status: data about conditions under which we would consider an expression true are things to be explained, and at best to be derived on syntactic grounds. The data do not determine LF-structures, but are their overt effect: the syntactic explanation of the conservativity of binary quantifiers mentioned in the previous section is a case in point. This direction of explanation is highly desirable, as we are otherwise left with no explanation of why *there are* the semantic or truth-conditional intuitions there are, or else some such 'explanation' as that we have whatever semantic intuitions we have because of the 'conventions of a speech community'. The apparent systematic dependence of meaning-theoretic facts on structural–hierarchical ones, and the universality of these structures, do not seem to make this latter option a likely one.

In the light of this it is not surprising that the major empirical evidence for the existence of LF as a level of representation had nothing to do with some level of 'thought' and ways in which the syntactic system would 'represent' it. As one pioneer of the LF-hypothesis summarizes the evidence (see Huang 1995: 128):

(i) quantificational expressions have various semantic properties that distinguish them empirically from non-quantificational ones (generality rather than singular reference, scope properties, etc.);

(ii) these special properties can be best captured by purely syntactic generalizations, such as the generalization that a QNP must move into a position commanding its original site;

(iii) the syntactic representations capturing these generalizations can be derived by essentially the same computational rules that one is familiar with from the overt part of the grammar. Hence the new representations fall out from the grammar at no cost.

In other words, LF was motivated by the finding that specific kinds of observations informally or pre-theoretically classified as 'semantic'—observations about inferential properties, truth conditions and referential properties of expressions—are actually captured by *syntactic generalizations*, or *fall out* from the syntax. They have explanations in terms of operations that are assumed to be part of the grammar on grounds independent of the semantic facts for whose explanation they are now shown to be apt. Far from depending on a specific theory of what goes on in the semantic component, they *derive* various empirical observations about the meanings generated in it. In short, LF was a piece of syntax with a purely internalist and empirical rationale. (Note that SEM, the interface to the conceptual–intentional interface, into which we will suggest dissolving LF in Section 6.1, is by contrast primarily motivated conceptually: minimally, it is reasonable to suggest, there must be such an interface. All the same, its motivation remains an internalist and architectural one.)

Hence also, Huang elaborates, 'LF is not to be equated with the level of semantic structure any more than PF is to be treated as a level specifying the sound waves of any given utterance.' PFs (PHONs) are internal representations defined to encode instructions to the speech articulators, hence to performance systems inside the brain. But they do not mysteriously reach outside the organism. They say nothing directly about air, waves, or motions of molecules. In the same sense, LFs as such have no intrinsic connection with mind-external propositions, states of affairs, commitments of thought or speech, and so on. Neither semantic observations about a 'thought expressed', nor observations about ambiguity in the linguistic encoding corresponding to two different thoughts, can as such provide motivation for a level of representation of LF in the grammar. If that was one's starting point, Huang points out, one could as well

> devise mapping rules that convert S-Structure representations directly into semantic structure, without the mediation of LF. No appeal to semantics *per se* can provide a real argument for the existence of this level of syntactic representation (Huang 1995: 130).

Thus, suppose some standard truth-conditional semantics given, a theory allowing you to derive sentences of the following Tarskian form, where S, for example, could be the French expression *La neige est blanche*:

T-SCHEMA: 'S' is true if and only if S.

Suppose also you have an *overt* syntax (a syntax without covert operations or LF, which one surely needs). Then it is clear that such a semantic theory is not as such a *reason* to hypothesize *other* kinds of syntactic representations generated by *covert* transformations, corresponding more closely to the logical forms in predicate logic. For one might devise some mapping or 'correspondence' rules that transformed the overt syntax of S to semantic representations in the truth theory *directly*. In fact, that option would seem to be more optimal, in line with Postal's remark, quoted initially above. The fact that truth-condition-bearing propositions can be *associated* with language is as such no reason to say, of a language, that its grammar has mechanisms for computing such propositions or their logical forms.

It falls into place on this account that LF need not capture all aspects of the logical forms that we teach in logic courses and use to codify rational beliefs, but may be perfectly acceptable meaning representations all the same.[40] A grammatical theory deriving LFs need not meet either the demands of ambiguity resolution (which virtually any logician imposes on formalization), or even of logical interpretability.[41] And while it is belief-theoretically and metaphysically relevant

---

[40] Hence that the 'work of logicians and grammarians' is *not* 'nicely complementary' (Devitt and Sterelny 1987: 89).

[41] This point is made in a general way in Huang (1995: 130). Martin and Uriagereka (2000: 14) offer *Smith's murderer is insane* as a factual example for a sentence that is ambiguous between two well-known readings but only has one syntactic representation at LF, hence as an example for the fact that

whether a name is a *fictional* one or not, it is not clear why the difference would matter *linguistically*.

Thus, consider the fact that some philosophers have been led to analyse fictional but not real names as descriptions. But no language seems to morphologically mark the difference that existence makes. Indeed *Mary would like to marry Hamlet* has a reading where the fictional name *Hamlet* designates as much *de re* as a non-fictional name does.[42] Wide-scope reference is a universal property of proper names—a linguistic fact—and real world denotation appears to be irrelevant to it. There are no *syntactic* reasons to analyse *Hamlet*, but not *Mary*, as a description. The differences between *Mary* and *Hamlet*, rather, are an *interaction effect*: a matter of how one cognitive system, the linguistic one, happens to be embedded in another, a system of beliefs. Again, from our concepts alone, or our understanding, nothing follows for existence: conditions of existence are a matter of experiment or interference with nature, not theory, or representation. Existence is not a matter of thinking or talking, but doing. Language and the meanings it determines will necessarily leave the question of existence open.

Other familiar doubts arise in this connection about the explanatory status of the Tarski scheme above. If 'S' is to be used to derive the equivalence that the Tarski scheme states, that derivation would seem to depend on understanding the meaning of S: those who did not know that *La neige est blanche* means that snow is white could only figure out from a translation comprehensible to them that it meant that snow is white (cf. Larson and Segal 1995: 50–2). Even in 'homophonic' cases, however—where we simply pass from *mentioning* an expression (on the left hand side) to *using* it (on the right hand side), with no translation or other language being involved—that use will depend on understanding the meaning of the expression S. If that is not assumed, that expression is viewed merely as an arbitrary *noise*—perhaps syntactically structured, but not relevantly structured in respects of meaning—and there is no way to map noises to meaningful sentences unless one already understands the noises as these sentences, in which case the T-schema presupposes and does not explicate that grasp of meaning. In particular, that mapping will depend on knowing things like which phrase in S embeds which, which projection re-projects, what is the internal and external argument, hence the THEME, GOAL, and AGENT, and so on. A meaning-theoretic approach built in one way or another on the T-schema appears to use a notion of expression as an entity that is *not* a sound-meaning pair, but somehow deprived

---

ambiguity resolution is not a sufficient condition for the existence of a grammatical rule. Since it does not seem to be a necessary condition either—the application of grammatical rules can cause ambiguities where none where before—it does not seem that the grammatical process is driven by some such principle as ambiguity resolution. Examples for LFs that are not even logically interpretable might be those of *I don't exist*, or *This man that you just pointed out to me does not exist*. These sentences are used (or could be), and they are perfectly fine products of your language faculty, grammatically speaking.

[42] Cf. Longobardi (1994: fn. 32) for relevant further remarks.

of meaning, though it is 'mapped' onto one. What I have been saying is that without understanding it (the concepts involved, in their structural arrangement), we would not know to which meaning to map it.

Let us consider a final example to illustrate the explanatory status of LF as regards semantic interpretation, and the explanatory redundancy of mapping LFs to mind-external propositions. Consider the following syntactic generalization:

INVERSE LINKING PRINCIPLE. If two quantified noun phrases, one of which is contained in the other, both have sentential scope, the containing one must have *lower* scope than the one it contains.

On the face of it, this principle contains no semantic terms. But it explains, with nothing to add, why an expression with two QNPs, like

(62) Pictures of everybody are on sale

can mean that everybody is such that pictures of him/her are on sale (individual pictures), and that pictures are on sale that have everybody on them (group pictures), but *cannot* mean that for some pictures of everybody, everybody is such that these pictures are pictures of him/her.[43] For, to generate the impossible meaning, a structure would have to be derived that violates two independently motivated laws of UG: (i) every variable in language must be properly bound; (ii) every quantifier must bind a variable.[44] These in turn follow from deeper principles, such as that a variable arises from a movement and cannot arise otherwise, and the economy principle of full interpretation, which forbids vaccuous quantification. In formal languages violations of such constraints do not need to have any significance. To violate them in human languages is to violate entailments deriving from hierarchical relationships. It is like wanting an apple to fall upwards. There is no reason why it shouldn't fall upwards, other than the design of the universe. There is no reason why the impossible meaning is impossible, other than the design of the human language faculty.

The Inverse Linking Principle is thus an example of a purely syntactic generalization that captures and explains semantic properties that we find certain kinds of expressions to exhibit empirically. For the inverse linking phenomenon, at least, syntax carries the explanatory burden. Suppose we thought it did not, and some philosopher were to impose the constraint that a 'semantics' was to be

---

[43] More perspicuously: for some pictures, x, of everybody, y, everybody, y, is such that x is a picture of y and x is on sale.

[44] The impossible derivation begins with the larger QNP moving to a position commanding its trace t_j in its original position:

[pictures of ...]$_j$ [t_j are on sale]

But by assumption, the smaller QNP also has sentential scope and binds a trace from there. That leads to the following LF, in which the containing QNP has wider scope than the contained one:

[[pictures of t_i]$_j$ [[everybody]$_i$ [t_j are on sale]]].

Here [everybody]$_i$ does not bind any variable/trace, and t_i looks in vain for a binder (see Huang 1995: 132–5). I see no semantic motivation for this semantic consequence here.

added to our account, a 'representational relation', a mapping from expressions to 'thoughts' or 'contents' endowed with truth conditions. The question is what explanatory problem this would solve. If the structure of the alleged thought contents was to explain what we took our LF-principle to explain, it would have to be isomorphic to our LF-structure (as long as our explanation, and the generalization it appealed to, was itself correct). But then it is redundant. Or it was not isomorphic, and it is not clear how it does its explanatory work in the light of the generalization that we have got.

In fact, it seems to me that the proposal only introduces new explanatory problems. Different predicate-logical forms we ascribe to 'thoughts' expressed by sentences like that in our example do nothing to explain why such expressions *have* those logical forms, and how a child knows, without effort or instruction, that the expression *can* have its two possible meanings, but *cannot* have a certain other one. The solution to these problems suggested by a syntactic generalization like the Inverse Linking Principle is immediate: those two logical forms can be *derived* by independently motivated syntactic processes, which *build up* the structure underlying the expression step by step, and thus *make it have* the structural properties it has.[45] I could imagine various purposes for 'propositions', 'truth conditional contents', but my present point is that invoking such entities for explanatory problems like the one we started with above adds nothing to syntactic meaning explanations like the one given. All it could do is to trace the hierarchical relations and chains that our derivation has created and spell out their semantic consequences.

One objection that has been put to me (by Gabe Segal) is that if you have a LF-representation of an expression like (62), you haven't explained anything 'semantic' yet: you could even map your structure to the proposition that John loves Mary. But this is a very peculiar suggestion. Of course, you can map any mental structure in your head to anything: your wastebasket, the Empire State Building, or *John loves Mary*. But there is no empirical reason to posit such mappings. And there is reason against it. The explanation of the meaning of why *John loves Mary* means what it does is that it contains the lexical concepts that it does, paired respectively with the sounds *John*, *loves*, and *Mary*, none of which are contained in the other expression, *Pictures of everybody are on sale*; and that it contains a different hierarchical structure, in particular no quantifiers. Due to these differences, the two expressions will play a different causal role in our mental life and behaviour. We could express the differences in semantic terms using a more or less fancy meta-language, but if explanatory, they would have to restate what the structure gives us for free: in particular, the scope relations between the two embedded quantifiers.

[45] If one does *not* follow this strategy, it is not clear what kind of explanatory scope one's theory of meaning will have. To be sure, it clearly *need* not have one: consider Davidsonian meaning theory, which is not aiming at explanation in the way that natural science does, and exploits decision theory essentially, interpreted as a normative enterprise. Or consider standard formal semantics, such as dynamic semantics: here explanatory ambitions are clearly different from standard naturalistic ones, often explicitly so, and they may be non-explanatory (and explicitly normativistic) in the very same sense in which logic itself is. I discuss these matters more fully in Hinzen (2003b).

I entirely agree that even when we have explained what structural property of *Pictures of everybody are on sale* accounts for its possible readings, we haven't said anything yet about what happens on the other side of the interface with this expression. But for all I can see, introducing a further ontology of 'propositions' or 'thoughts' sheds no light on this dark issue. (And as far as I can see, any further mechanisms one introduced would have to be more *internal* mechanisms still, and hence be a matter of syntax in the broad sense.) The objection we are facing is thus true in something like the sense that you can map any DNA sequence of an organism to bottles and pancakes. The question is why you should. The DNA codes for the proteins it codes for, playing a particular causal role in an organismic process, which, while depending more directly on the proteins, depends ultimately on the DNA. An LF/SEM is, equally, a particular organismic structure, used and transcribed into various other structures with other constituents, but not understandable in terms of them. To develop this line of thought, consider, e.g., Larson and Segal's (1995: 249) discussion of the

PROPER BINDING CONSTRAINT: A referentially variable expression α can be interpreted as a variable bound by a quantified expression Q only if Q c-commands α at LF.[46]

The authors remark that this is a purely syntactic constraint and as such an unexplained 'axiom'. Taking in conjunction with their semantic theory, by contrast, they claim it *follows* 'from the way in which meaning is related to form'. But the constraint follows independently. It states that quantificational binding is under c-command. But, plausibly, establishment of a c-command relation is a by-product of how the derivation proceeds: thus, in Epstein *et al.*'s (1998) system, what an item is merged with in the course of a derivation is whatever it c-commands. Thus, in particular, an argument merged in second position (a specifier) will c-command the head and the complement, though there is no such relation in the other direction. For the same reason, a quantifier re-merged in Spec-C will c-command its trace. Moreover, that the moved QNP will control the interpretation of its trace is a natural consequence of the fact that it *is* in the position of that trace, in the form of one of its copies. No semantic explanation seems needed here.

On the contrary, the semantic explanation the authors offer (pp. 249–50) arguably depends on *exploiting* syntactic information, such as that the QNP is re-merged as the sister of its derived argument; or the economy principle that the semantic interpretation of a constituent never looks deeper into the syntactic tree that contains it than its sister.[47] The latter principle is a form of locality

---

[46] In phrase-structural terms, a phrase X c-commands another, Y, if X and Y do not dominate one another and the first node dominating (containing) X dominates Y.

[47] The explanation also seems to depend on indices relating the moved item and its trace, a device that is non-explanatory and captures information that must follow from the way the phrase marker is built: in particular, the head of the chain and its tail must be the same lexical item (in different occurrences).

constraint, which nothing in the semantics demands; thus, semantically, nothing in principle speaks against semantically composing just those items in a categorial domain which stand in a maximally *asymmetric* relation: specifiers and complements, say, or specifiers and heads.[48] But that appears wrong. It so happens that semantic composition, as an operation that is driven by features of the head, applies exclusively to the head and its immediate sister. This makes sense derivationally, in that one might propose that a head can only take up semantic relations with syntactic objects it is in construction with, i.e. merged with. If sister is a derivational notion, a constituent cannot have as sisters or depend on what it has not been merged with. If minimalist work suggesting that human syntactic computations obey constraints of maximal efficiency is on the right track, then the principle that heads are first composed with the arguments that are their sisters falls out from a simple principle of *minimal search*: do not look further down the tree than the complement.

Similar remarks apply to Larson and Segal's (1995: 252) claim that the following principle is an unexplained axiom in syntax but follows from the putative syntax–semantics mapping:

SCOPE PRINCIPLE: An expression α is interpreted as having scope over an expression β just in case α c-commands β.

That suggests, e.g., that if in *Ralph believes that the richest man is happy* the embedded NP is interpreted as having wide scope, it follows that it c-commands the matrix verb *believes* at SEM. But this is to beg the question against the empirical issue raised by Hornstein and Pietroski (2002). On the contrary, it would seem that it is *only if the embedded NP has wide scope over the entire sentence* that it has the meaning in question. The interpretation follows from the c-command relations that get factually established in the course of a derivation; it is not that the c-command relations follow trivially from the way an expression is interpreted (as in a version of generative semantics, in effect). Put differently, Larson and Segal's semantic theory explains why it is that an expression is interpreted as having scope over another if the former c-commands the other, only by begging the question: nothing in principle forbids writing up other semantic axioms, and assigning widest scope to the lowest QNP in the tree, say. The result may not be compositional, but then, why should it be (especially on the assumption that syntax entails nothing about the semantics)? Compositionality

---

[48] As noted in Section 5.1, we may or may not 'map' the expression *John loves Mary* to the logical formula 'loves(John, Mary)'. But while it is a matter of pure convention to map that formula to the proposition that John loves Mary rather than that Mary loves John, it isn't a convention that the linguistic expression means the former and not the latter. In this case it is our mental apprehension of the hierarchical structure of *John loves Mary* (the asymmetry between the arguments *John* and *Mary* or the fact that *Mary* is embedded in a VP while *John* is outside it), and only it, that leads us not to 'map' it to *Mary loves John*. Possible worlds, and truth conditions defined in terms of them, do not enter in this process.

gives us the right interpretations only once it is conceded that syntax carries an explanatory burden for semantics: semantic interpretation traces out c-command relations established independently.

On the other hand, note that the syntax–semantics correspondence in the other direction of the Scope Principle quoted above also does not follow: in *John loves Mary* it does not follow from the fact alone that because *John* c-commands *Mary*, it must be ordered as the second argument and be interpreted as the AGENT, having scope over the THEME. *If* syntax does not entail an interpretation, *then* nothing can forbid mapping sisters of heads to AGENTS and specifiers to THEMES. What excludes this on the present account, rather, is a stronger assumption about the hierarchical organization of syntax: the asymmetry of the interpretation must be built into the syntactic object itself, and THEMES must be inherent *parts* of (and presuppositions for) the full event encoded by the verb in a sufficiently strong sense of 'part' (see Section 5.2). AGENTS will simply be mergeable only in a layer of structure higher than THEMES, where a VP meaning has already emerged. Once this is the architecture of the syntactic object, the fact that events caused by agents entail THEMES follows.

Larson and Segal's (1995) enormous achievement may thus lie in having made plausible the feasibility or at least desirability of developing an account of the syntax–semantics interface under the constraint of Strong Compositionality, or the 'transparency' of semantic interpretation with respect to syntactic form. But this does not support their philosophical interpretation of this framework for semantic theory. Here the authors take an approach to syntactic form that is wedded to externalist assumptions about the determination of linguistic meaning or 'content'. I have argued here that it adds nothing to our explanatory apparatus of syntactic forms to map these forms to mind-external propositions or Fregean 'Gedanken', if these are to have an explanatory status. A mapping *inside* the mind to performance systems seems to be what is required to make sense of how LF matters to interpretation, not a move beyond the confines of the head, and hence beyond what computational operations over mental representations can accomplish. The logicality of thoughts in particular makes as such no predictions for the structure of the language faculty and the LFs generated by it, nor does the existence of thoughts, if thoughts are construed as truth conditions or sets of possible worlds, in which case they have no intrinsic linguistic structure at all.

If anything, I wish to have created a feeling for the *reality* of these syntactic and hierarchical structures, as something which, if we look at them, seems to have virtually nothing to do with what beliefs and other propositional attitudes we have, or what we know about the world on non-linguistic grounds. An LF/SEM is a natural object in the real world, like DNA, not an artefact, like logical forms used in philosophy. It is crucially not the *representation* of an expression, or of its 'semantic content', but *that expression* itself, viewed at one of the levels where it is hypothesized to appear in our linguistic minds. An *expression* in the present sense is *never* a 'symbolic expression' that has no meaning intrinsically, and for this reason has to be mapped to one, to which it then relates externally.

Again because LFs are natural objects, with no purpose, they will not serve for all objectives a theorist may have, such as obtaining a full theory of truth conditions that addresses the meaning properties of an expression as interpreted in a situated context. But this is not our goal if we address meaning as a biological property of human organisms, and may in itself not be a feasible subject of naturalistic inquiry. In philosophical inquiry into language, as we have seen, it is precisely this natural aspect of human language and mind that tends to fall ouside the picture, as it is what is to be 'regimented', given a divergence between 'grammatical and logical form', as Wittgenstein put it in the *Tractatus* (4.0031). But the grammatical form is an empirical matter to determine, and though unconstrained by principles of logic, generative grammar has found it to actually harbour principles of logic and rational inference. Empirical arguments for the identity of the LFs underlying English and Chinese expressions, e.g., which we mentioned, moreover, confirm, a fundamental unity of LFs that we expect on independent grounds: can the logicality of a Chinese mind differ from that of an English one? With the support of a substantive theory of UG, we derive that unity on internalist grounds.

LFs cannot of their essence be 'normatively constrained', in the way that 'regimented languages' are. It is interesting to ask, on the other hand, where our intuitions on what the normative commitments of our thoughts are come from. This question has puzzled philosophers for millennia: the question how we can know *a priori* the necessary truths of logic is as puzzling as the question of how we can know the truths of geometry or arithmetic. But if our logical intuitions come from language itself—that is, if human languages on a deep and more abstract level are much *less* messy, vague, and illogical than the Fregean tradition takes them to be—then this suggests one answer to the question of where some of our *a priori* knowledge of logic comes from: it comes from human biology itself. Our mind, we will say in the next chapter, is a *rational* one.

Frege's 'psychologism' objection—that the human mind is the wrong place to look for logicality—then rests on a false empirical claim about the human mind. The mind may set a standard for what logicality is, even though it may be that we only have a blurred view of what these structures in our minds are, which reveal themselves only through reflection. The mind is not how we 'happen to think', crude and uneducated until the canons of reasoning are imposed as 'norms' upon it; it is an expression of rational laws that organize its intrinsic structure, laws that may be grounded themselves even deeper in natural law.[49]

---

[49] For some evidence suggesting that this conclusion has a much wider significance with respect to animal cognition, see McGonigle and Chalmers (2002).

If aspects of logic were to have a grammatical origin, there would also be little support from contemporary linguistics for a conventionalist analysis of logic. If logical forms were conventional, Quine's (1972) conclusion—that there is no such thing as *the* logical form of a natural language sentence—would be entirely correct. According to Quine, to provide a paraphrase in a regimented language of a sentence which is treated as its logical form is 'to put the sentence into a form that admits most efficiently of logical calculation, or shows its implications and conceptual affinities most perspicuously, obviating fallacy and paradox' (Quine 1972: 452). If so, there is no factual question about what the logical form is. An indeterminacy in the analysis of LF/SEMs, on the other hand, is purely epistemic: there is a fact of the matter, even if we may never come to know it.

In a naturalistic project, there is no scope for the anti-naturalism implied in Quine's conventionalist analysis, and it is unsurprising that, as we noted, Russellian conceptions of logical form (Russell 1914, Lepore and Ludwig 2002) go in this anti-naturalistic direction too. Russell argued that different-looking sentences, in the same or different languages, can have the same logical form, concluding that this makes sentences 'impure' expressions of thought, and that logical forms are by necessity forms of *propositions*, not sentences (Lepore and Ludwig 2002: 58). My present concern is of necessity with expressions, not with propositions, as propositions are not natural objects having whatever properties they have, exactly as Russell believed (although Russell took this to *recommend* them). In any case, if different-looking sentences such as English and Chinese ones *have* an identical and non-language-specific analysis at LF, no recourse to mind-external propositions is needed to get the 'purification' of language that Russell sought. His argument for propositions, which depends on the language specificity of the forms of sentences, will not go through.

Note that if one takes Russell's line, and leaves out LFs/SEMs in the present sense, one will have to ask what *mediates* between the 'grammatical' forms of expressions and the 'logical' forms of propositions to which one maps them. One approach is to say: 'Conventions do it!', meaning that PHONs of a language (or its external acoustic manifestations, which would not even be PHONs, which are internal mental representations) are mapped by means of conventions to a logician's logical form.[50] On this view, 'expressions obtain their semantic properties from conventions governing their use. These conventions are themselves explained in terms of regularities involving beliefs, intentions, and so forth, of speakers of the language' (Loewer 1999: 108). But such regularities turn out to have no explanatory status when we look at concrete semantic phenomena and explain them in terms of such things as the locality of movement, the nature of chains, or phrasal hierarchy. That it *is* conventional which sound a concept is

---

[50] A different approach is to define a precise algorithm for transforming surface structures of a language into a logician's logical form, the project of Hans Kamp's Discourse Representation Theory (DRT) (Kamp and Reyle 1994). For discussion, see Hinzen (2003b).

paired with in a particular language, is no argument for the fact that *once a lexicon is fixed* (arbitrary sound–meaning pairings are established), the complex expressions generated from these words by the syntax are arbitrary in the way *they* pair sounds and meanings, too. Indeed it seems that given the lexicon, Inclusiveness, and the fact that syntactic operations apply if they must, one may conclude that the meaning of the resulting expression as represented at SEM is a natural necessity.

Despite all this, the view that a meaning is not intrinsic to an expression, and that it is meaningless to say of an expression, taken by itself, that it has a meaning, clearly prevails in philosophy today. On that view, if you subtract the relations that some internal state or some external symbol has to something in the world, all content properties are gone. Francois Récanati remarks that what's left when subtracting content relationally understood, is the 'bearer' of content, the meaningless 'syntactic form'.[51] By 'syntactic form', it seems Récanati has in mind the physical shape of a symbol, or the acoustical properties of a linguistic sound, not an expression in my sense. But neither shapes nor sounds are even relevant to language, let alone to syntactic form, not at least if the latter relates to such things as phrases, lexical items, chains, empty categories, SEMs, phonemes, etc. Clearly, if expressions *were* physical entities in Récanati's sense, they would have neither sound nor meaning intrinsically. But they do seem to; even the phonological properties of an expression cannot be defined in terms of its external physical properties (air pressure waves, movements of molecules).

Récanati's view appears to be endorsed by all those who believe in 'propositions', whose independence from their mental encoding is part of their definition (see e.g. Schiffer 1994a). On this view, the meaning (proposition) associated with an expression may change, and the expression may remain what it is. But this is incorrect, since if you change the structure of an expression (eliminate a trace, move a constituent, say), you can see it becoming meaningless, or meaning something else. If expressions are deprived of meaning and propositions are introduced to supply it, it seems they simply give some meaning a name. The immediate question will then be how the *proposition* gets the content it is meant to encode. Maybe we should map the proposition to something else, again (a set of possible worlds perhaps)? It is simply not clear how these various mappings, constrained perhaps by various homomorphy constraints, are ever to help with the basic meaning-theoretic problem. Once more, the insight is Wittgenstein's: when seeking to explain meaning, it's no use introducing *Vorstellungen*, mental images (*Muster*), or mind-independent propositions with which we are getting

---

[51] See Récanati (1993: 211). In the formal semantics literature we find similar views. Stokhof argues that the meaning of an expression and an expression itself are 'utterly different entities': 'expressions are physical entities, written signs or spoken sounds (...) meanings are not like that at all' (Stokhof 2002: 8). This again, apparently, is to assume that an expression as such reduces to something like a shape (a non-linguistic notion).

into some epistemic contact, as exactly the same questions will arise for these entities which arose for expressions in the first place.

To conclude this discussion and this chapter, it is not that semantics does not exist, a meaningless claim, but that we must take it seriously as a domain whose phenomena we have to *explain* rather than merely state formally. Semantics should be viewed as a natural science, not as applied logic. In the best case, semantic phenomena fall out from the way a syntactic object is built. Syntactic analysis would then explain something about the constraints imposed on possible human sounds and meanings, and how these relate. Syntax could not do this, if it was itself a matter of meaning, and it is not clear how it could be, unless we made question-begging presuppositions on which structures were there prior to language, so as to be capable of moulding human syntax. As of now, the best bet seems to be to grant that the human language faculty provides *forms* that a possible human structured meaning may have, leaving a residue of non-structured meanings (concepts), a substantive amount of which we share with other animals that lack syntax (or at least do not use it, or do not use it for purposes of language). These forms are autonomous as structures in nature that we can study as such, even though we see them, somewhat miraculously, systematically condition properties of linguistic meaning that we can empirically attest.

The only real doubt that I can see arising for the present kind of approach to the naturalization of meaning—quite radically different from the causal-referential one that has been pursued in the philosophy of language for many decades (Loewer 1999)—is what the *scope* of syntactic meaning explanation is. How *much* of meaning does syntax explain to us? I have reviewed evidence here that it extends to the syntax of arguments (a prime claim of the tradition of Hale and Keyser 2002, and Pietroski 2003; see Hinzen 2006a for discussion), and to the syntax of quantification and scope (the tradition of LF as understood by Huang 1995). I have argued elsewhere that it applies where one would least expect it, too: to the syntax of reference (Hinzen 2006a) and the syntax of possession, including predications of truth (Hinzen 2003a).

Part III
Rational Mind

6

Good Design!

6.1 Phases and Cascades: Beyond LF

So far we have been implicitly assuming a universal set of human linguistic features F, and selections F_L from it, partially separate for each language, L. We have also been assuming that we cannot proceed from here to characterize the set of derivations that L determines directly. Rather, there is LEX, too: the features in F_L are further assembled into words (lexical items, LIs). Furthermore, there is the numeration, NUM, a selection from LEX, not F_L. Computation is from NUM to EXP=<PHON, SEM>, with no further access to F_L after the assembly of NUM, given Inclusiveness. That is, lexical access in the course of a derivation is only once: a derivation does not 'carry along' the lexicon on its path, but only NUM, a one-time selection from it. This again, Chomsky argues, is a way in which the system obeys conditions of optimal design: it respects constraints in the reduction of 'operative complexity' (Chomsky, MI).

One would nonetheless like to know why then we need even LEX, as Uriagereka (DDS) points out, rather than having NUM access F_L *directly*. Wouldn't this be less complex than having an extra LEX layer in-between, and hence be a more minimalist conception? This idea has the flavour of generative semantics: words are a relatively superficial aspect of language design; deeper down LIs are not atomic or non-structured at the semantic level of representation, and the simplest assumption about their internal structure is that they are sets. If what recommends having a LEX prior to a NUM is a reduction of 'operative complexity', then as Uriagereka notes, this moreover raises questions, if the place where considerations of derivational economy and computational complexity come in is *after* NUM, in the mapping to EXP. It is here that derivations in Chomsky (1995) are said to 'compete for optimality', so that, for example, derivations with fewer computational steps win over those with more. To justify LEX in terms of computational efficiency, on the other hand, is to assume a pre-lexical syntactic process, and to effectively deny LEX. Not to do that, however, is one of the main points in Chomsky's 'lexicalist' critique of the generative semanticists! Moreover, to view this point from a different angle, if the existence of LEX is justified on simplicity/complexity grounds, it is not clear why there should, in the end, be anything else *other* than the lexicon: instead of a recursive syntax we would simply code any structural expression as a word.

The point is: more has to be said to justify LEX. There should be a deeper rationale to it than reduction of complexity, as it is not obvious how to measure how effective this reduction really is. As I argue in Hinzen (2006a), LEX makes better sense if we see words as having a specific and unique semantic correlate, which nothing in the syntax has, and which is not captured by viewing a lexical concept as a set of semantic features: for any lexical atom there is a semantic atom, a non-structured concept, and it is here that the decompositional process in the combinatorial system of language stops (Fodor 1998, Fodor and Lepore 2002).

Let us now turn to NUM, and consider how it is structured. This as well, from a minimalist point of view, is a descriptive/explanatory device one would in principle like to dispense with. On the other hand, starting out with a NUM will prevent the computational system from having to access LEX at all points in a derivation, a desirable result if operative complexity matters to how derivations are set up in the linguistic system. Still, as Chomsky (MI, DBP) emphasizes, whether the linguistic system reduces computational complexity or not is precisely an empirical matter to determine, and one of the major issues in the Minimalist Program. Examples like the following are offered as evidence for the former alternative:

(i) there is likely [$_\alpha$ to be [a proof discovered]]
(ii) *there is likely [$_\alpha$ a proof to be [~~a proof~~ discovered]]

where strikethroughs mark phonetic deletion of traces (or copies, in the launching sites of the movement in question). Why does (i) outrank (ii) in acceptability? Economy yields an explanation, assuming the existence of numerations. For suppose both derivations have reached the step in which the structure (iii) below has been built, and (iv) is what is left in NUM:

(iii) [to be a proof discovered]
(iv) {there, is, likely, ... }

Then a derivation departing from (iii) can continue so as to Merge *there*, which afterwards moves to the front, yielding (i). In (ii), by contrast, before Merge the operation Move takes place, displacing *a proof*. As Move is arguably more complex than Merge, (i) is preferred at this stage of the derivation. One might argue that this does not matter because in the end both derivations end up making use of Move, but it is precisely this consideration that does not matter in a 'derivational', as opposed to a 'representational', approach: the preference of Merge over Move is a *local* one at a stage in a derivation. If the grammar has no look-ahead properties, as it should not if complexity matters to it, what happens *later* in a derivation should be of no concern to it. The existence of a NUM is crucially assumed in this line of reasoning: it is only because the lexical item 'there' is *available* in the NUMs for both expressions that (ii) should prefer merging it to moving *a proof*. Consider (v) and (vi), however, also taken from Chomsky's discussion:

(v) I expected [$_\alpha$ a proof to be [a proof discovered]]
(vi) *I expected [$_\alpha$ I to be [a proof discovered]]

Now here it seems at first as if the previous conclusion is refuted, for the grammar apparently *prefers*, at the same stage of the derivation, an early Move of *a proof* to a Merge of *I*. This seems to reverse the preference we just saw and explained in (i)-(ii). But no, Chomsky argues, for here another condition is operative, according to which an argument cannot *move to* a theta-position (such as the subject position of *expect*), but must be *initially merged* in such a position. This condition would follow on principled grounds if theta-structure forms an interface with the semantic component, in something like the way that D-structure did: if semantic interpretation is first read off from pure phrase structure, then merging the thematic arguments of a head should happen prior to all movement. Minimalism, on a derivationalist approach, would simply capture this old idea, not in terms of a constraint applying to a level of representation such as D-structure, but in terms of a derivational condition (cf. Chomsky, MI, version of 2000: 104–5):

CONDITION ON THETA-ASSIGNMENT:
Arguments must be initially merged in theta-positions.

If then, at α, this condition is operative, (v) and (vi) will fall into place. The 'decision' for Move over Merge in this instance is again dependent on *local* determinants only: given the derivational condition on theta-assignment, the derivation need not look ahead to its eventual 'last line' to check whether an earlier step can be made or not. In sum, if Merge is preferred over Move unless other conditions intervene, and a NUM determines available options for continuing a derivation, a nice account of the above data can be given.

A general assumption about NUMs then is that they are first assembled arbitrarily: the generative theory, after all, is about what mechanisms operate once some combinatorial materials are *there*. If it happens that a given NUM is insufficient for a derivation (material is missing that is needed to check features of elements contained in NUM), the derivation will crash; and if it contains material that contains unusable elements *after* the derivation converges (NUM is too large), we do not get a convergent derivation either. Chomsky in MI leaves it open whether we get a *crash* if a NUM is only partially used up, or whether we get merely a *cancellation* of the derivation. Still, note that if the former option obtains, this would mean that we will not know before convergence (or a crash) whether our arbitrarily selected NUM was a valid one or not. As Chomsky puts it, 'convergence determines whether NUM is too large' (MI, version of 1998: 11). I come back to this rather undesirable conclusion (or imperfection) at the end of this section.

On a most general level, NUM encodes a *conservation law*: it encodes the limited amount of material for a derivation to work with, to which nothing can either be added (given Inclusiveness), or subtracted. If the derivation converges by exhausting NUM, we may select a new NUM, to construct a new syntactic object, which may either extend the given one (leaving it intact), or be a separate one. This entails another form of 'compositionality', in the sense that a derivation from a NUM is first finished and sent off to interpretation before selecting a new one.

In MI and DBP, Chomsky significantly *extends* the complexity-theoretic reasoning underlying the justification of NUM (and LEX, on his account): NUMs are accessed 'cyclically'. That is, just as a complex discourse is split into a number of separate NUMs, each NUM is now split into a number of separate derivational *phases*, each exhausting a sub-array of items within a given NUM that is placed in active memory while its phase proceeds. Consider the following examples for illustration of cyclic lexical access in this sense, taken from Uriagereka (DDS: 7). At first, they seem to speak against constraining derivations by the form of conservatism encoded into NUMs:

(vii) And the fact is that [$_\alpha$ there is a monk in the cloister].
(viii) And there is the fact that [$_\alpha$ a monk is in the cloister].

Here we have a local Move of *a monk* in (viii), and no such Move in (vii). Two questions arise: Why is the expletive *there*, contained in both NUMs, not equally inserted in the subject position of the embedded clause in (viii)? And given the preference of Merge over Move, why is (viii) not *less* acceptable? In answer to that, Chomsky in MI argues that in (vii) and (viii) the derivation is semantically evaluated at the stage α, up to which a proper part of NUM (a sub-array) has been driving the derivation, and that part is *not* shared between the two derivations at this point. Hence the derivations at this stage do not compete on grounds of economy, and the Merge over Move principle does not apply. Each derivation converges in its own way at α before proceeding.

The question then, however, is why this analysis should not apply to (i)–(ii), where equally, one might think, there are distinct phases of the derivation depending on different sub-arrays of their NUMs. Chomsky suggests that the difference is that here convergence is not at the level of the embedded clause, but only the matrix clause. The complementizer *that* in (vii)–(viii) makes a difference: CP with finite TP is a separate derivational phase, while a non-complemented and non-finite TP is not. The principle 'first converge' does not apply. This raises the question *why* TP as such is no phase or possible sub-array of a given NUM. Chomsky (DBP: 12) suggests that this is because phases are in some sense 'propositional': for something to be interpretable, we need 'verbal phrases with full argument structure and CP with force indicators, but not TP alone or "weak" verbal configurations lacking external arguments (passive, unaccusative).' That derivational phases are 'propositional' then, comes, in essence, down to the idea that they will be CPs and verbs with full argument structures, including external arguments in the outer *v*-shell of V. Phases are meant to be independent units of interpretation, and it is access to the semantic interface in fact, as a consequence of Spell-Out, that is cyclic. This implies a further reduction of computational load, on the assumption that one phase, once its NUM is used up and it is interpreted, is gone from the derivation. Syntactic operations cannot target this phase any more, which has become 'opaque' to transformations, except for its top, consisting of features of the head, and its left edge, a specifier position. Moreover, cyclic access to SEM seems to be coordinated with cyclic access to PHON—e.g., CPs appear to also mark prosodic boundaries—and thus we face the option of actually reducing two cyclic mappings to one, i.e., a *single* cycle.

This is clearly very interesting, but the appeal to 'propositionality' is problematic. Note that assuming NUMs provides us, from a Minimalist perspective, with an empirical burden of proof: we are postulating an object that, if existing, would presumably reduce operational complexity, but must be shown to exist, by way of some inference to the best explanation. For this reason alone, we want NUM to be as simple as possible (Chomsky, MI). Now, as simple as possible means, in particular, that we posit no structure internal to NUMs; the more we did this, the more they would resemble the old D-structures, levels of representations that Minimalism wants centrally to do without. But now, we are told NUMs *are* structured into sub-arrays, and by no means in an *arbitrary* way, but in a way that is sensitive precisely to the kinds of thematic and interpretive properties that D-structures was meant to capture![1] Minimalism's priding itself on being able to 'eliminate' things might once more have been premature. But note that on a proper understanding of Minimalism, a more minimal structure is not *per se* good, and the failure of a particular minimalist analysis should provide us with the positive insight that we have found a surplus of structure that may be interpretively relevant, or may tell us something about the structure of human meaning.

The idea of derivational 'phases', all containing at least one C and *v*, raises other conceptual and empirical problems. It again appears here as if an external semantic property—what is interpretable in a particular way and what is not—exerts an influence on the organization of syntax. The computational system seems to be set up so as to be sensitive to particular interpretive conditions imposed at the semantic interface: something smaller than phases won't be legible there. But then, why would legibility matter to the computational system? What distinction can *it*, purely formal as it is, make between things that are interpretable and things that are not? How can it look to the other side of the interface prior to reaching it? How does it know that at some point α, it has to send the derivation off to the semantic component, and at others not?[2]

---

[1] I owe this insight to conversations with Juan Uriagereka.
[2] As Epstein and Seely (2002: 78) put it, referring to Chomsky's calling phases 'relatively independent' in semantic and phonetic respects: 'How can we know that they are relatively independent *at the*

Note that propositionality corresponds to a particular way in which we use language: only propositions can be used in assertions, in particular. But we haven't endorsed the commitment that language is engineered for use; moreover, as noted, it is simply not clear what access we have to such notions as propositionality independent of what syntactic structures the computational system fabricates; or whether the *use* of language would make any predictions on which syntactic categories a language would have (probably it would make none, as a language deprived of CPs and *v*Ps might have much the 'propositional' uses that our language has: see again Carstairs-McCarthy 1999). In short, either we understand the notion of propositionality traditionally, that is as a semantic one, and then it does not explain us why the syntax should be organized in one particular structural fashion rather than another one; or it is a syntactic notion, in which case it does not explain the sub-structure now posited in NUMs.

Given the stance taken in Chomsky (2000) against mind-external propositions and externalist accounts of meanings generally, it is clear that the notion 'propositional' has to be treated with caution. But if it is a purely technical one, what exactly is it? And do we have a grip on it independently of our understanding of CP and *v*P? Propositionality does not seem in fact to have much to do with the independently understandable notion of a *sentence*, because fully developed argument structures of verbs (not being sentences) are said to be phases, and some speculate that DPs are phases as well (Svenonius 2004). Epstein and Seely (2002) note that both some *v*Ps and some CPs are not intuitively propositional, offering *who bought what* as an instance of the former: prior to *wh*-movement, these *v*Ps exhibit vacuous quantification (no variable is bound); after movement, these *v*Ps have variables in the place of the *wh*-operators, hence are 'open sentences' rather than propositions. In turn, some propositional structures, such as small clause structures like *[John smart]* as in *I consider John smart* are probably neither *v*Ps nor CPs (for these examples and a host of further empirical problems with the Chomskyan notion of phase see Epstein and Seely 2002, especially section 5).

It seems interesting that, on the one hand, 'propositions' include force-indicators, and on the other hand correspond to the verbal domain with a fully projected argument structure. These kinds of interpretable product differ pretty much, it would seem, in the way that D-structure and LF were thought to differ, prior to the 'elimination' of D-structure: the latter had been thought to encode verbal argument structure prior to movements and LF as understood here is the level where intentional information relating to an utterance in the discourse context is coded: information like what the force of the utterance is, together with

---

interface if Spell-Out applies *before* the interface is reached, and without access to the interface properties? It is a potential architectural paradox to hypothesize that *v*P and CP are spelled out *cyclically, internal to the narrow syntax* by virtue of them having the property of being, "later," relatively independent *at the interface.*'

information about scope, topic, and focus. From this point of view, the cutting of NUMs in separate sub-arrays leading to their own convergent derivations might be a contemporary reflex of the older insight that the semantic interface of the grammar must be assumed to be internally differentiated. Again, human meaning, in my previous terms, may be layered, each layer having its distinctive semantic characteristics. Pursuing the minimalist program, the insight would be: the lexicon aside, there are at least two such layers, and nothing much is won in claiming 'minimality' for a coding of all semantic aspects of an expression 'at LF', that is at one single level of representation.

None of this means that we should resurrect the architectural assumptions of the 1980s, regarding D-structure and LF as levels of representations where linguistic representations are scrutinized for satisfying certain constraints. Letting the derivation proceed in phases or cyclically, with semantic and phonetic evaluation after each, means in effect never having a LF in the old sense, i.e. a unified syntactic object that is interpreted only after it is fully assembled, and that is subject to specific constraints (Chomsky, BEA, 2005). Moreover, if the dimension of meaning captured by the old D-structures—in essence, theta-structure—is taken care of by a derivational condition (the above condition on theta-assignment), then D-structure need not exist as a *level of representation* either. The logical goal of this strictly cyclic and derivational conception of grammar would be to dispense entirely with the need to assume representations, over and above derivations.

Epstein and Seely (2002), having argued that there simply are no two privileged points in a derivation (like CP and *v*P) where Spell-Out takes place and the derivation is mapped to the phonetic and semantic components, respectively, provide an argument that Spell-Out in fact *cannot* apply to a single representation at all, at a particular point in the derivation. Recall that one major rationale of the derivation in minimalist theorizing is the satisfaction of Full Interpretation as an interface condition: uninterpretable lexical features must be gone from the representations that the derivation constructs by the time it reaches the interface. Spell-Out is the operation removing SEM-uninterpretable features from the syntactic object constructed so far, which after Spell-out can be shipped to the phonological component. One problem Epstein and Seely note (Epstein and Seely 2002: 68–70) is how the derivation knows, at a point *earlier* than the interface, which feature will be uninterpretable *there*, information involving a form of 'look-ahead' that we do not wish to assume.

In DBP, Chomsky replaces the interpretable/uninterpretable distinction with another one, the valued/unvalued distinction, but problems remain. The need for feature checking and deletion is now said to apply to features that are not yet *valued*, and it is a local configuration to the attracting feature (the Probe) that is needed to value it through matching with a corresponding feature. But consider what Spell-Out would 'see' when contemplating a derivation before the valuation of the unvalued feature takes place: obviously, an unvalued feature. If Spell-Out applied to the representation containing it at this point, it would be too early: the derivation would crash at the interface. Suppose then, as Chomsky (DBP: 5) in effect does, that Spell-Out applied shortly *after* feature valuation has taken place. But clearly, it then would apply too *late*: after is after, and what Spell-Out is by assumption sensitive to is the interpretable/uninterpretable distinction, now further assumed to be reflected in the valued/unvalued distinction. After valuation, the relevant distinction is lost.

Epstein and Seely (2002: 75) take this paradox to lend support to a derivational conclusion: if Spell-Out can neither operate on a representation before feature valuation, nor after, there is no single representation to which it applies. Instead, they assume that Spell-Out applies *internally* to the derivational step in which feature valuation takes place: given a derivational rule that leads from one step of the derivation to the next, the rule's input are the unvalued features, while in its output they are now valued. The null hypothesis should now be that *whenever* a feature's being unvalued triggers a rule application, evaluation at the interface takes place, a form of cyclicity requirement that is now entirely independent with respect to stipulations concerning CP and *v*P. In effect, 'each transformational rule application constitutes a "phase"' (ibid.: 77).

Like Chomsky's, this is a 'level-free' approach to the architecture of the human language faculty That is, there are no levels of representation. There used to be D-structure, but its rationale can be shouldered by external Merge. There used to be S-structure, the level of representation where the derivation splits into a phonetic branch on the one side, and a narrowly syntactic component on the other, where more movements take place that then fail to leave a phonetic reflex. Now we need only say that, for the sake of satisfying interface conditions, there must be *something* that plays the role of this level, but it can be a *point*, a moment of 'transfer' of what is semantically uninterpretable to the phonetic component. On Chomsky's (2005: 13) approach, following Nissenbaum (2000), both Transfer and Merge take place at the phase level: if Merge is internal and takes place before Transfer, the movement will be overt; otherwise it is covert. If covert, the lower copy has already been spelled out when internal Merge takes place. If overt, a choice on which copy to spell out is now a matter of the next phase. The old contrast between an 'overt' and a 'covert' component separated by a level of S-structure disappears. On Epstein and Seely's line, Transfer applies in the course of *each and every* transformational operation. In *both* approaches, an LF is never assembled as one single syntactic object. As in the case of D-structure and S-structure, the semantic effects captured by LF are there, but with less descriptive technology and fewer stipulations: we maximally exploit the effects of a single operation, Merge, whose existence in itself is conceptually necessary in a recursive system, as well as necessities deriving from the need to satisfy interface conditions, such as the elimination of uninterpretable features through transformational operations in the course of which Spell-Out applies.

This same basic architecture can be interestingly obtained on other grounds, however. Recall we have been assuming that while phrase structures are organized around hierarchical relations, they are as such free of linear order. Thus for example there is no order among the terms of the SO $\Gamma = \{\alpha, \{\alpha, \beta \ldots\}\}$, where α and β are syntactic objects, and α is the label as well. Linear ordering however is a representational condition imposed by the phonological component, given the linearity of speech. Hence there has to be a procedure, call it *Linearize*, which maps hierarchical relations into linear ones. The same is true if we merge the independently constructed SO γ as well, getting SO $\Delta = \{\alpha, \{\gamma, \{\alpha, \{\beta \ldots\}\}\}\}$, where α is again the label of the whole object. But now note that successive applications of Merge produce c-command relations that hold between all and only the syntactic objects merged. A natural suggestion would then seem to be that the linear ordering will *mirror* the way that the command relations came about derivationally. Hence tracing the derivational order backwards, in our example, the ordering will be that γ precedes α, α precedes β, and β will precede whatever terms it contains: that is, $<\gamma, \alpha, \beta \ldots>$.

If Linearize can exploit in this way the already given hierarchical relations, the following axiom, originating in the work of Kayne (1994) and taken up in Chomsky (1995), tells us how unordered bits and pieces of meaning are transparently mapped into *ordered* such bits and pieces:

LINEAR CORRESPONDENCE AXIOM
If α c-commands β in the syntax then α precedes β in the phonetics.

Let us now say, following Uriagereka (2002, chapter 3), that a *Command Unit* (CU) is an SO generated through a sequence of continuous applications of Merge. The looming problem in the above lean picture is that not every SO is built by a successive application of Merge to the same SO. Thus take the Merge of two separately assembled SOs, like $\{\alpha, \{\alpha, \{\beta \ldots\}\}\}$ and $\{\gamma, \{\gamma, \{\delta \ldots\}\}\}$, to yield the SO

$\{\alpha, \{\{\gamma, \{\gamma, \{\delta \ldots\}\}\}, \{\alpha, \{\alpha, \{\beta \ldots\}\}\}\}\}$,

or, in tree form:

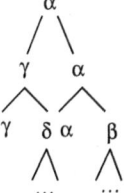

This object is not a CU, and γ, δ, do not c-command α, β. It did not arise through continuously merging new SOs to the same object. Hence it cannot be linearized by means of the above elegant axiom: any such linearization would lead to a crash at the phonetic interface. But then, this will hold only if we assume that Spell-Out and Linearize can occur only *once* in the derivation, rather than multiply. If Linearize applies *at every point* where Merge becomes *discontinuous*, the above axiom can be maintained. That is, the above object, which cannot be linearized in the simple way above, is not linearized *at all*, because only smaller chunks of structure—CUs—that *can* be linearized in the simple way *are* ever linearized. Again, now, derivations become intrinsically dynamic, or split into 'derivational cascades', and we arrive at a notion strongly reminiscent of Chomsky's cycles or phases—except for the crucial difference that they are structurally or geometrically rather than semantically grounded in some notion of 'propositionality'.

When the derivation continues after one linearization, the SO/CU sent to the interfaces is gone from the derivational workspace. That is, it has been converted into some sort of phonetic symbol, and its internal structure is no longer phrasal, or 'visible' to the syntax. In this sense, it is not 'penetrable', a condition imposed by Chomsky on phases as well, though on Uriagereka's approach it now simply follows from not having an SO in the derivation any more (a linearized and 'flattened' phrase not being an SO in the technical sense). Given this 'impenetrability', cascades might be thought of as 'words', that is possibly giant but *non-syntactic* 'frozen compounds', somewhat like idioms. Being words, however, they *are* SOs, and can again *merge* with other separately assembled structures, despite the opacity of their internal structure.[3] Note that in this way, if the interpretational component is accessed multiply in this way, and each chunk of structure that gets interpreted is a word, interpretation is of its nature on the word-level. Again, what was formerly an LF, a representational object in the linguistic system that intuitively corresponds to a structured proposition, is now a descriptive artefact, an abstraction from the dynamics of derivations.[4]

Having dropped an LF-level from the grammar—whether by resort to phases or cascades—we are now ready to drive the idea, mentioned above, that meaning is a natural necessity, to a surprising conclusion. In Principles and Parameters

---

[3] A process that predicts the need for such a thing as Agreement, viewed as a procedure that 'links' a spelled-out chunk of structure (CU) to another that is active in working memory, so as to obtain a final, linearized object. This makes good sense of the fact that Agreement is not manifested in complements, but only in non-complements, such as subject–verb: it 'glues' separate derivational cascades together that Spell-Out has split (Uriagereka 2002: 51). On the other hand, it may be that spelled-out and linearized chunks of structure are gone from the syntax entirely, and are unified with other such chunks not in the syntax but in the post-syntactic performative component. On this latter model, human syntax is fundamentally paratactic.

[4] 'Multiple Spell-Out' generates a rich set of empirical predictions, for example that semantic phenomena at LF will be sensitive to command relations as established in the course of building up a CU, or that phonological domains will mirror syntactic ones, to be mention but two. To illustrate the latter prediction, a pause or parenthetical phrase should sound natural between a non-CU, like subject and predicate, or between phrases and adjuncts, as in the following examples, but not within a cascade. It sounds natural to say: 'Michelangelo ... painted those frescoes', or 'Michelangelo painted those frescoes ... in Florence', but less natural or emphatic to say that 'Michelangelo painted ... those frescoes', or 'Michelangelo painted ... those frescoes in Florence' examples from (Uriagereka 2002: 55).

theories, a meaning is the outcome of the necessary operation of certain mechanisms, subject to representational constraints: but this is not to say that whenever the grammatical system gets into action, something meaningful is produced. Meaning is a necessity once we have a derivation of it that does not violate the principles of UG and of the particular language of which it is a part. But this is not the case for all derivations. Some derivations start, but only in order to crash later on. This is bad design, in a quite obvious way: the latter derivations should optimally be cancelled on the way, rather than going on in a futile way in order to crash at the interface. Optimally, that is, a derivation should fail through certain *derivational conditions*, without any need for *representational conditions* to sieve them out later, after further and needless computational steps. Put differently, it should fail *locally*, through constraints operative at steps in the derivations, not *globally* because it yields nothing meaningful in the end (we should not have to wait to see a derivation fail at one interface if we know, at an early point in the derivation, that it must). In an optimal system, an impossible meaning would never be produced, and syntax would be 'crash-proof'.

This optimal solution may well be the actual one (Frampton and Gutmann 1999, 2002): that is, the products of locally correct steps of a derivation are *always well-formed*, and meet the interface conditions. To take one of Frampton and Gutmann's examples, suppose we begin a derivation of *men arrived* with *arrive* and merge the Tense head 'Past' to it, obtaining [$_{T'}$ arrive-d [$_V$ t]].

Then this derivation is doomed to crash, no matter how long it goes on, as the verb's argument cannot now be merged any more: merging it now that the VP and TP are built, would be a counter-cyclic operation. The argument has to be merged in the VP. But in the crash-proof model, the above object is simply impossible (underivable). In that model, each introduction of a new head introduces a new cycle, in which the first thing that must happen is the satisfaction of selectional features of the respective head. For this reason, *men* must be introduced first, since itself it does not select anything. The V *arrive* must be introduced next, since T does not select N but V and there is no V yet; furthermore, V, which selects N, must select *men*, nothing else being available. This completes the cycle initiated by the merger of V, since there are no features on V to be satisfied by Agreement. Then T is merged, and Agreement comes into play. As this example illustrates, the automatic order of selection of heads makes a crash impossible (see Frampton and Gutmann 2002 for similar proposals on how to account derivationally for the necessary satisfaction of representational conditions, such as the Case filter, demanding that all NPs must have Case at LF).

On this radically dynamic model of grammar, like on the previous one using Multiple Spell-Out, points of representational stability in a derivational dynamics arise each time that an interpretable object is constructed during a derivation, but there may be a large extent to which we can understand these as emergent ones: they won't be representational objects in their own right, on which we could impose conditions of well-formedness that they might fail, as we did with levels of representation. This makes it all the more important to determine which *representational residues* there are in such a radically dynamic system (in particular, can basic lexical categories be regarded as 'emerging' derivationally?).

If this line of thought is carried to its limit, the notion of representation ceases to play the explanatory role it used to play, in a very transparent sense: there are no longer any conditions that representations have to meet in order for them to be meaningful. At least intuitively, a *derivation* does not represent anything, it just proceeds. When syntactic mechanisms operate, they don't 'know' about the meanings they eventually produce, a theme discussed earlier under the heading of 'semantic blindness': while there are interfaces, they play no direct role in the process of generation. The conclusion we can now contemplate in the wake of the crash-proof program is not only the startling one that syntax may indeed be blind to meanings; it is also that, to the extent that the program succeeds, human syntax is organized so as to produce them with maximal effectiveness. As Uriagereka puts the same idea, it is 'as if syntax carved the path interpretation must blindly follow' (2002: 275). Some such idea may ultimately turn out to be true or not; but if true, this idea would likely be the philosophical essence of the Minimalist Program.

6.2 Epistemology For Mental Organs

To draw some epistemological consequences from the lean picture of human grammar that we are now looking at, we may begin by breaking the epistemology of human concepts into two parts: the epistemology of complex concepts constructed by the computational system, and the epistemology of simple ones. This distinction presupposes that in the human conceptual system a categorial distinction between complex and simple concepts *can* be made, something that would not be the case if that system was not a 'particulate', but a 'blending' system (Abler 1989): but recall that in human languages, when concepts are combined they preserve their independent status by becoming independent *constituents* of the complex concept constructed. This is another instance of a conservation law operative in language, and would not be the case, for example, if concepts were to be identified with distributed patterns of neuronal activation in which one could not discern subpatterns corresponding to the concepts entering into the complex concept.

As for the epistemology of complex concepts, we have now explained the sense in which the meaning of an expression as represented at SEM may be a natural necessity. But what about the epistemological status of the syntactic structures entering into these complex representations? We could say, if we wanted, that the structures emerging in syntactic processes are 'structures of organized matter', in something like Priestley's, LaMettrie's, or Locke's sense. Such a claim would be perfectly empty, were it not for the fact that it could serve to emphasize that the present undertaking is not 'mentalistic' or 'psychologistic' in a sense that takes the mind out of the physical world.

The knowing mind *consists* of certain natural patterns. These are as such abstract, but by their nature depend on physical matter in the sense that it could perfectly well be that they would not grow or emerge in any *other* physical matter than that of our universe, or in any other life forms not obeying the laws governing the specific life form of which we are an instance. Again this is to say that the study of the human language faculty has nothing specifically to do with the *principled* form of abstractness that we find in traditional functionalism, with its vision of psychology as an autonomous, special science with its own ontology of 'psychological' states and 'propositional attitudes' that 'represent' certain 'mental contents'. Principles of the Initial State as described by the theory of UG characterize profoundly abstract structures, but abstract in no less a legitimate sense than those characterized by explanatory principles in physics, such as electromagnetic fields.

Once that has been accepted, we can investigate empirically how rich our theory of UG will have to be to account for the facts of acquisition, and the way in which human languages can usefully be mapped onto the same structural type. Generative grammar has steadily converged on the view that there is a principled uniformity to human language which nevertheless allows for a great surface variation. We seem to be facing a remarkably homogeneous pattern, with some disturbances caused by a tiny part of the lexicon, the functional one, leading to interlinguistic differences in how inflections are morphologically expressed. Beyond that, there are selections from universal systems of substantive phonetic and semantic features, arbitrary pairings between them on the level of LEX, and a fundamentally uniform computational system that structuralizes these items from LEX.

Could we say that the abstract structures postulated as structures in the Initial State—say the profoundly abstract X-bar schema, in conjunction with a very general theory of movement—are taxonomic artifacts, bloodless and non-explanatory abstractions that exist only in the head of the theorist? This would be to take a nominalist and empiricist stance: we would give our credence to what is there on the *surface*—constructions such as passives, questions, relative clauses, etc.—different among themselves and among languages, learned one by one, while everything else that seems 'deeper' is *abstracted* from them, existing in our *minds*, but not in *reality*—'linguistic reality'. As noted, that latter distinction is in itself a curious one in the case of language at least, since language becomes *language* only *through* a mind like ours. That aside, however, the various theoretical notions we have reviewed and defended were posited for reasons of *explanatory power*, which means we cannot consistently take them to be the empiricist's 'abstractions', which cannot of their nature carry explanatory power. From an empiricist point of view, it seems, we are left with mere variety, deducible from nothing.

Idealizations in Galilean physics crucially depended on a *non-empiricist* (in this context, non-Aristotelian) account of abstraction. An abstraction in the empiricist's sense would be an abstraction *from* something—something supposedly *more* basic epistemologically and ontologically, from which the former abstraction will then be said to *derive*. But from *what* have we abstracted, exactly, when we talked about the X-bar schema, say, or locality-constrained movements? The proposal above was that given an apprehension of the X-bar scheme (or of more fundamental principles it may follow from), language-specific constructions such as NP or VP, passive, etc., are not strictly speaking even *perceived* as such by the child, being artefacts of *our* theoretical description. The actual direction of explanation taken by the field in the 1970s was that those specific constructions were *explained away* as having an independent reality in the grammar. *They* were instances (possible variants or transformations) of an abstract schema, rather than the schema being an abstraction from the constructions.

The paradigmatic instance of an empiricist operation of abstraction is the *intersective* operation that strips off from various constructions the features that are not common to them, such as stripes from Zebras, leaving the horse part (Hornstein 2005). This is because, for the empiricist, the mind's operations cannot add more content to that given by our experience of the world. All the mind's content is what it has experienced and inferred from its experience inductively and deductively: in short, what has happened to it, and what followed from that. In this case, there would be various different grammatical constructions, different from language to language, all corresponding to contingent descriptive observations, with nothing common to them and to explain them. If the X-bar schema were *derivative* from this theoretical 'mess', rather than being its underlying organizing principle, it would be powerless to *explain* the fact that children unfailingly find their way through all of this apparent (but ultimately quite illusory) complexity.

Generative grammarians would *like* to see all languages falling into one pattern, but *why* languages do so is a different and further question. Put differently, the theory as such gives no rationale for *existence*, for ultimate causes or origins—except that, in the form of the Minimalist Program, it now explores a completely new direction in answering 'why'-questions, which do not appeal to 'what something is for' except as a heuristic, and turns instead to extremely general design conditions of organic systems together with various kinds of conceptual necessities. One may contrast with this functional explanations, which are centrally devoted to rationalizing the *existence* of some mental structure, and why it functions in the way it does. While it is true that generative grammar analyses mental functions, the functions as such play no explanatory role (there are mechanisms that explain *them*). The approach is content with the Galilean intuition that science gives a mechanical model, and does not concern itself with 'reasons' for its operations. Given a starting condition, a law (UG) allows us to calculate a final condition (the Final State) from a starting one (the Initial State), no matter 'how it works', or for what ultimate reason it does so.

What then becomes of the philosophical enterprise of 'epistemology'? Traditionally understood, it addresses the question of what entitles us to claims of knowledge, the question of when mere 'belief' (or claim to the truth) has further properties that convert it to knowledge (actual truth). It should be clear that this question cannot be posed in the present framework, at least not with respect to knowledge that we naturally, or by our nature, have. We *are* here concerned with an aspect of human knowledge, in the simple sense that humans know languages, or have linguistic competence. But in its drive towards models with ever greater explanatory power, the generative enterprise has been driven towards models that give 'beliefs' no more of an explanatory role to play in the process of such knowledge acquisition than the idea that the acquisition of linguistic knowledge is carried out in a fashion that we might call 'justified'.

Nor is the knowledge attained by the child 'true' in any sense I would know how to explicate. The structures that grow in the mind in the course of the child's development converge with those of its environment, but this does not mean that they represent them or become 'true of' or confirmed by them. It so happens that the child has the right organismic structures for its environment to select an option that these structures allow its brain to diversify into. This sort of study of human knowledge is thoroughly internalist: while recognizing that the cognitive system of language is embedded in a much wider cognitive space allowing its use in a social environment, it makes no appeal, in analysing that cognitive system itself, to how it relates to the world. While it is embedded, its being so embedded does not explain its (initial) internal structure, nor, obviously, do the internal structures possibly explain or predict how they get used.

As Rey (2003: 125) notes, this internalist picture is somewhat analogous to the way in which the immune system responds to antigens with antibodies: '*immunity* is not a state that is *confirmed* by the antigens that may nevertheless be required to trigger it'. But the question of *confirmation*, he notes, is precisely the kind of relation between a state of the external world and a state inside that is checked against the former, which fuels thinking underlying the Computational-Representational Theory of Mind (CRTM), and much of current philosophical epistemology. It follows immediately for Rey that *if* representations generated in the language faculty are not evaluated in terms of their contribution to the probability of *truth*, we should not be talking of internal mental 'representations' *at all*:

it is the rational relations of, e.g., *evidence, inference* and *confirmation*, involving truth-valuable *contents* that largely motivate [the CRTM]. If a child is not confirming hypotheses, then perhaps there is no reason to regard the states as 'structural descriptions' or 'representations' of anything. Maybe they are *just structures* (e.g. tree structures) that are realized by the brain without being represented in it, in the way that certain complex structures are realized without being represented in, e.g., crystals, molecules, genes, plants and antibodies (ibid.: 125).

One might agree with precisely this suggestion, were it not for the fact that we need to posit internal structures of a more intricate sort inside the language faculty than we need to in the case of crystals, planets, magnets, or other objects satisfying the laws of gravitation or electromagnetism, and explainable in terms of these. Clearly, even in the modestly complex phrase-structure grammar component we have looked at, the system must internally represent symbols such as TP or V' that it uses to represent phrase-structure hierarchies. But this is still a purely internalist use of 'representation' which would not satisfy Rey, who concludes that on Chomsky's approach to internal representation or the one adopted here,

> the result would cease having a claim on *psychological* reality. Again, a *mental* state *qua* *mental* state involves a relation to a *content*. (ibid: 126).

I agree that concepts are individuated by their contents, but to postulate as internal representations only what is syntactically or physically individuated, leaving all content to relations to the environment or posited mind-external constructs, does not advance our understanding of how they end up having those contents. Here a methodological dualism shows up again: it is what prevents us from positing simply what it seems we have to: concepts in the mind itself. From the viewpoint of a methodological monism, the fact that 'grammaticality' is not a state checked against some external reality it is 'true of' is only reassuring: for this would mirror precisely the way that '*immunity* is not a state that is *confirmed* by the antigens that may nevertheless be required to trigger it'.

While Rey thus sees an eliminative materialism appearing on the horizon once the present viewpoint is adopted, the opposite conclusion appears to be warranted. What we study when we study syntax is a mind building structures, embedding, warping, and collapsing them, enabling humans the creativity that is our most characteristic feature as a species. All of that may happen on the basis of some pristine atomic meanings that we begin with in a derivation, and which we take from the caverns of the lexicon. That entire *mental reality* is obscured if we adopt instead the functionalist and externalist attitude that Rey defends, in many ways representative of a widespread misperception in philosophy that Chomsky's program is an instance of functionalism and the 'computer model of mind'.

If the present analysis of grammatical knowledge could be generalized to other domains of human cognitive competence (arithmetic, morals, art, etc.), the fact that millennia of epistemological reflections have not yielded firm answers as to what turns mere belief into knowledge is just what we would generally expect. As noted in Section 2.2, there is a sense in which according to the Platonic-rationalist tradition our knowledge is 'ungrounded': we cannot reconstruct it from some more primitive basis, in a way that we could talk about its justifiedness or trace it to its origins. The knowledge is there by (human) nature, and even though it takes years of maturation and development, we basically find ourselves having it.

Also noted by Plato is the sense in which a *speaker* is also a *thinker*—or in which someone who merely *speaks Greek*, as Socrates makes sure before questioning the slave boy in the *Meno*, would *as such* be capable of knowing basic truths of maths. We have mentioned evidence above for an intrinsic *logicality* of the linguistic mind. If it wasn't the case that certain logical aspects of semantic interpretation were read off from the structures that are generated through syntactic transformations, its logicality would be *external* to the mind (maybe it would be an imposed *norm*), in the sense that the language system would not intrinsically determine aspects of utterances that enter into the logical and inferential roles they play in human thought. But transformations do seem to determine aspects of semantic interpretation, hence are not a mere 'input'-system at the periphery of the mind, in the sense of Fodor (1983). Language appears to be a *part* of a (presumably richly structured) 'central' system, a part that is itself devoted to making infinitely many structures available for use at the conceptual and intentional interfaces.

Language was understood as an aspect of human reason also by the logicians and linguists of Port Royal in the seventeenth century, although in a different sense: they distinguished 'particular grammars' (of German, French, etc.) from 'rational grammars' (also called 'philosophical grammars') (Chomsky 1966). The latter focused on an underlying pattern relative to which a seemingly arbitrary surface variance gives way to something more 'rational'. It shows itself amenable to human reason and explanation. I take this to be an instance of the general way in which the structure of the world, or of human experience, comes to be seen to *be* the structure of human reason in rationalism, and vice versa: the world as it becomes understood *is* the world as amenable to human reason, but for it to *be* so amenable, or to *be* intelligible, it must itself *be* rationally organized. Rationality is no fiction in our head (the way we 'happen to think'), or a theorist's abstraction, but rather reflects the theorist's *domain*, a certain structure in nature.

In this way, the Fregean 'psychologism' objection—that it is a conclusion of subject matter to look for logicality in contingent human psychological processes—seems misdirected against a rationalist enterprise as here understood. We are not talking about contingent psychological processes, but the remarkable finding of the intrinsic logicality and rationality of the human cognitive mind, if not the primate mind as such (McGonigle and Chalmers 2002). The rationalist conception of the human mind and human thought, while being naturalistic, is fundamentally *non-psychologistic*. From a rationalist's point of view, the mistake in the study of human thought and reasoning is not psychologism, but to think about the mind in narrowly psychologistic terms. The objection of psychologism relies on an empirical claim about the human mind which we have reasons to reject.

'Rational' then, is, firstly, the structure of the human *mind* which allows us to think, and secondly the structure of the *world* as conceived by our minds, in (by and large surprisingly fruitful) theories. Compare Goodwin's conclusion that there is an 'inherent rationality to life that makes it intelligible at a much deeper level than functional utility and historical accident' (Goodwin 1994: 105). What 'rationality' here means, apparently, is that some phenomena that seemed to lack any deeper explanation than that accorded by historical accidents and functional utility, now reveal themselves to have some intrinsic lawfulness and intelligibility for a mind structured like ours. To 'rely on the principle of reason' has in this sense nothing to do with proceeding in line with some stipulated and conventional canons of reasoning, but is, again, to hold that the rational structures of thought *are* in themselves the rational structures of nature.

Invoking another familiar metaphor, human reasoning conceived as a psychologistic process would be a 'process going on behind the walls of our skull', or maybe in the 'inner space' of consciousness, and nothing would follow for reality from what goes on in there (a point of view also leading to an anti-realistic stance). This would be why what goes on inside our minds has to be *externally evaluated* and 'justified' in the first place: only then can it claim to capture the external reality. In this way we are accustomed in philosophical disputes to a strict dichotomy between what is 'inside' the head and what is 'outside', as the debate about whether meanings 'are in the head' illustrates. The idea of what is merely 'inside the head' awakes a deeply rooted philosophical horror of idealism, and the 'Cartesian theatre', a space in which ideas float around in a solipsistic fashion, dangerously losing contact with what is outside (Rorty's 'epistemological problematic' again).

But the rationalist can make no sense of this dichotomy. What we don't find out there in the world or in our experience—perfect geometrical forms, say—is not thereby 'subjective' or 'unreal'. The human mind, being a part of nature, happens to be structured by certain systems of knowledge, and its neural hardwiring happens to allow it to tap more deeply into the nature of the real by using these systems of knowledge and the categories they involve, to whatever extent the world is patterned in line with these categories.

Consider one such 'category', an IP. It seems like a mystery how a child gleans the category of an IP from, say, air pressure changes as we see them on an oscillograph. As we have seen, if a child has no exposure to linguistic data at the critical age, it will never experience anything like an IP, and telling it about it will be to no avail. Nothing in the external world is an IP, no physicist has ever discovered such a thing, just as nothing in the external world is the Kantian category of a substance (although many external things can be analysed by using this category). But nothing in the 'internal world' of a child can be quite said to be an IP either, certainly not in the total absence of linguistic experience. Still, IPs are as 'real' as it gets, being empirical phenomena attestable in (presumably all) human languages. While the environment determines whether a child will speak English or Japanese, it is not the environment which decides whether there can be something like English or Japanese, or whether there is something like an IP.

Our categories of a Verb or Noun allow no other conclusions. Our (universal and tacit) notion of a Noun is not what we get when we tape-record all the world's phonetic pronunciations of instances of it, and compile a list of them. Nor does looking at the 'referents' of specific Nouns help to deduce this category, as these referents may be anything ontologically speaking, from persons like *John* to events like *Christmas*, physical objects like *pencil*, abstract objects like *2*, states such as *poverty*, and social-political entities like *France*. This is a set so heterogeneous that it tells us little coherent about the theoretical notion of a Noun or of nominal reference. Instead, these categories are plausibly defined in syntactic terms (Baker 2003), in which case their understanding presupposes a grasp of abstract phrase-structural principles. These can't be obtained from sensory input under an empiricist learning theory, for the reason noted: empiricist learning can only give us weaker or lesser contents in the course of intersective abstraction, not qualitatively new concepts.[5]

A human mind makes sense of its experience or of whatever is out there in the light of a category of its understanding, such as that of an IP. A cat's mind does nothing of this sort; it may make sense of the same phenomenon in terms of a catish category, or in terms of no category at all, in which case the relevant phenomenon will simply not be a phenomenon for it. The difference between us and a cat when facing linguistic utterances is one of *understanding*, of making *sense* of our experiences. On the basis of this difference, we will relate differently to the world, but how we so relate won't explain the difference. Our category of an IP does not 'denote' or 'refer to' anything out there, in the sense of something that can be identified independently of a particular category of our mind and the way we use it. It is a *form* under which an experience (a 'content', if you will) enters human understanding. What does a form *denote*? Surely not the content, which simply is what appears *under* that form. One could stipulate that the category of an IP 'denotes' some kinds of air pressure waves and moving molecules, the ones that the cat, under a different category, perceives as well, or that it is causally affected by. But it is not clear what the point of the stipulation is, and it seems to be a mistake: those air pressure waves as such are categorized in terms of acoustic phonetics, not categories of syntax.

Note I am talking about *the category of an IP* here, which we assume is internally mentally represented somehow, but not some external *content of* such a mental representation, in the externalist's relational sense. I assume there are categories in the mind, but have no use for representations (internal to the mind), of categories (viewed as mind-external). An IP is not a 'mere form', in the sense that a logical symbol is, which *is* a more form in the sense that its content is

---

[5] There is also recent evidence from aphasia that Noun and Verb, as well as Consonants and Vowels on the phonological side, are indeed discrete internal representations rather than bundles of features arrived at in an associationist process. They seem to be primitives of the human linguistic system, which cannot be derived from something else more primitive than them (Caramazza and Shapiro 2004).

external to it. An IP is an actual and contingent feature of reality, not a representation of a feature of reality.[6]

It may be harder to accept that what seems to be true of IPs might also be true for garden-variety lexical concepts such as *chair*, *house*, or *freedom*. It is not clear, however, how to motivate this asymmetric treatment of syntactic categories and substantive lexical concepts. While we can learn by experience whether there are houses in some place, it is not clear how we, when *lacking* the concept of a house, should acquire *it* by looking at the world, or exposing ourselves to causal relations within it.

Whether an expression contains the concept *house* or the concept *hut* makes a difference to the interpretive systems accessing the structures into which these concepts enter. That is, once these structures are computed in the faculty of language, systems in the mind accessing these outputs will react differentially to *house* and *hut*, just as articulatory systems react differently to the phonetic features [stop] or [continuant]. Ultimately, we may expect that this differential treatment shows up in human actions, too, as when I use *house* more often for something big, and *hut* more often for something small, by some evaluative standard. In this fashion, lexical items like *house* and *hut* 'relate to the world': performance systems accessing the outputs of the language faculty play a causal role in differential behaviour during language use.

There is, then, in this sense, a 'language–world relation'. But I see no other sense in which we could say that an item like *house* 'has semantic reference', or why this new technical concept is needed. It seems misleading because it induces the picture that the language–world connection we have just claimed to obtain is somehow 'direct': for any one word there is one thing in the world that fixes its (referential) meaning, and from which we can understand what it means, and possibly learn it. But what sort of thing is this? A set of houses, an abstract object? A mereological sum, a concrete object, though a rather strange and unintuitive one? Or a single house on each occasion of its use? These questions are not answered in any easy way. Clearly, from a set of objects *falling under* the concept to be explained—in this case, houses—we could not *obtain* the concept of a house, if we lacked it. Natural language makes this nicely perspicuous by making the word we use to refer to houses—the complex word *house-s*—morphologically *more* complex than (hence dependent on) the concept expressed by the word *house*.

Saying that *I have a blue house*, I make reference to my house, under a perspective crucially involving the outer side of its walls (whereas I would talk of something with reference to the inner sides of these walls when saying *I have a blue room*). The outer walls will be irrelevant on other occasions where I talk

---

[6] On the other hand, of course, the conventional sign 'IP' refers to or represents an IP, a mental structure. Like other scientific categories, we hope that an IP captures an aspect of reality which is independent of common-sensical or native human interests and concerns.

about my house, say when I refer to *my empty house*, where I now (exclusively) refer to its interior. And if I say that *I will have a blue house*, I use the same expression *a blue house*, but this time I refer to what? To a house that I will have (this being what)? To a house that I think I will have? To an idea? To an *actual* blue house that I once saw and is like the one I imagine to have? It seems unclear which *physical properties* the external thing has to which I allegedly refer, or whether it needs any for me to be able to refer to it. None of these questions becomes easier if I say *I had a blue house*. For what is the supposed thing referred to here? A thing stored in the past? A memory? All this is not to argue that I do not use the expression to refer, but that it is not clear how this relation of reference can be understood as a relation between some word or some inner object, on the one hand, and some outer represented (and independently given) object, on the other, described in physical terms not presupposing the human concept in question.

Some assertions, it seems, can be made, though. Thus it is crucial to the individuation of what I am talking about when I talk about *my house* or *the city of London* that it is not a place (cf. Chomsky 2000: 37). The house, removed and rebuilt elsewhere, may remain *my house*. If it was a place, this could not be so, contrary to fact. It is also no concrete object, as in saying *my house is gone* I refer to the same object, my very house, though now no longer existing. My house is my house even if it has been destroyed by a bomb, for then I say *my house has been destroyed by a bomb*. My house may also never have existed, contrary to what I always thought. It will still be my house that never existed, for I can say *I now realize that my house has never existed*, referring to my house.

All this is again to say no more than that there is a dissociation between our human concepts and external conditions of existence, the latter being, once again, not a matter of conceptual understanding, but of action and practical interference with external states of affairs. It is not my conceptual understanding of the expression *my house* which tells me anything about the external object I am referring to. What that object is actually like, and whether it exists, and where it exists, is something I have to *find out*, and language tells me nothing about it. This is parallel to the way in which I have claimed that the grasp of an explanatory hypothesis in science, or the discovery of a new concept or theory, says as such nothing about the experimental process in which these figments of our mind are shown to be useful or not.

Language–world relations exist, then, but they seem to be rather indirect and complex. Lexical uses have to be looked at carefully on a case-by-case basis to figure out how precisely we use a lexical item to refer on an occasion, and what we actually refer to. One day we might understand more about how performance systems operate in accessing the outputs of the language faculty for the sake of language use. It seems no advance over current ignorance to stipulate that 'there is a relation of reference between a lexical item like *house* and some external object in the world' (see further Chomsky 2000; 2003, Replies to Egan and Ludlow).

As we pursue this line of thought, the conclusion we reach for lexical concepts like *house* or *chair* is the same then as the one that we reached before for syntactic categories like *IP*: not that human categories or concepts are 'independent of experience', but that human concepts are categories which minds like ours employ to interpret their experience, and through which it is the experience it is in the first place. We cannot look at the experience, describe it in terms not depending on the concepts of human common sense, and then simply assume that these concepts will spring out of our description. There is no point in arguing with a cat about the *thing-in-itself*, part of the reason for assuming that *existence* is not a property of things (such as houses, as we think about them), but of concepts, as Kant taught.

An epistemological consequence to be drawn from this is analogous to the one reached earlier for integrated systems of knowledge, such as language: that they are not true or false in some relational sense, or 'of something'. For a simple concept to be 'correct' or 'incorrect', or 'true' or 'false', it would have to be comparable to the thing it is meant to be 'correct' or 'true' of. But it is hard to see what this could mean, especially in the case of simple concepts. In general, experience does not confirm or disconfirm *concepts*. If we make *judgements*—which *use* concepts as parts—to say that some thing described as an X is a Y, there is a sense in which we may let experience correct us: X may not be a Y, as an experiment might suggest. The sense in which this is so is not *very* clear, to be sure, as even a plainly empty space under your table need not cause you to concede that there is no rhinoceros there, as Wittgenstein famously noted against Russell. Nonetheless, there is such a sense: it would be exceedingly difficult, for example, for you to try construing your visual experience as you look under your table right now as a rhinoceros.

Even here, what we notice is, not that your experience shows your construal correct or incorrect, but that, in a practical and non-theoretical sense, your mind simply *fails* in the assigned task. In a similar way, you might *find yourself failing* in the attempt to construe a genocide as morally justified (you simply can't convince yourself of that, as much as you try and tolerance would ask you to succeed), and again it is unclear whether there should be *any* talk here about 'correctness with respect to a norm' or something external that confirms or refutes your judgements, except for a norm that follows from your moral *concepts*, which may simply make it rationally *impossible* to construe your experience in a certain way.

Even if we grant that a judgement that X is Y *can* be confirmed or refuted, nothing is yet said about whether X and Y taken singly can be so confirmed or refuted, or be checked against a reality. Note that if that was indeed not so, we could not be right or wrong about concepts we have or grasp. Indeed, if I hear a foreign language that I partially speak, I will form hypotheses about which *sounds* are attached in that language to my *concepts*. Experience may confirm or disconfirm any such hypothesis. If a scene I witness in the French countryside disconfirms my hypothesis that the sound of the French word *chasser* means the same as my word *hunt*, this is, it seems, *because* of the fact that I *have* the concept of hunting something, and have used it to classify the scene in question.[7] If a scene confirms such a hypothesis, it is equally because of the way I myself have classified this situation. The confirmation and the disconfirmation *presuppose* the concept. The concept itself is not confirmed or disconfirmed at any point. For experience to confirm or disconfirm something, it seems we need, in the least, a *predication* (this is a..., this is called a..., this sound expresses...). If truth and falsehood arise, as Kant held, through a 'synthesis', this is a way of saying: it arises with *syntax*. This recalls again the importance of separating *intentional* from *conceptual* information.

The conclusion on the epistemology of concepts now reached reveals an inherent affinity to the one that I earlier ascribed, in the beginning of this book, following Yolton, to theorists of ideas in the seventeenth and eighteenth centuries. I quoted Yolton's statement that the world of ideas *is* the world *as known*. Common-sense ideas or concepts thus understood have no rationale in terms of what is outside. Stimuli we receive lead to concepts infinitely richer and different than the stimuli themselves.[8] With our eyes and sense of touch we may (perhaps) explore how an object is coloured, smells, feels, and sounds. But the idea that such an object awakes in our minds may be that of a *person*, an infinitely richer and completely different idea, to which smells, sounds, and physical properties are also quite inessential, as they may be missing in something we might still call a person.

Our senses do not individuate persons, which we have no conceptual difficulty in tracing through a series of amputations, plastic surgery, or even reincarnations, in the course of which the physical shape of what is the same person (for us) continuously changes, or even ceases to exist. Clearly, just as we can imagine angels, we could fancy some technological advance—perhaps depending on a slight change in actual physical laws—that would lead persons to be disembodied for some time (say, they could 'buy' some 'disembodied time', and a whole industry grew around that). There seems to be no question at all that under these consequences, the name of your friend John, who undergoes this transformation, would still refer to the same person, hence that his physicality is quite inessential to him, in the sense of being no conceptual or logical necessity.

We may thus quite follow Hume, who calls personal identity a 'fiction'. Currently, philosophy's favourite fictions tend to be things like phlogiston, or Santa Claus. But this is not what Hume means. He thinks that persons are fic-

---

[7] This, precisely, is the situation of the language-learning child according to the so-called 'informational change' hypothesis of Gleitman and her co-workers: the child gradually learns which sounds mean things it already understands. It does not lack concepts, but information on when to apply them, and which sounds to link them to (see Gleitman *et al.* 2005).

[8] For interesting applications of this kind of internalist conclusion to visual perception see Mausfeld and Heyer (2004).

tions in exactly the sense that houses are (or animals, plants, and ships). We can call a ship the 'same' ship, even if all its parts, or a considerable part of them, have been changed, he points out. Ships, animals, houses, etc., 'endure a *total* change, yet we still attribute identity to them, while their form, size, and substance are entirely alter'd' (Hume 1739–40/1978, I: 257). No amount of *looking* at a situation in which we discern different personalities in a single body, Wittgenstein suggests as well, helps us in our judgement about whether there is one person here, or two. It is a matter of choice: 'Wir können sagen, was wir wollen',[9] though again we should emphasize here that *given* our concepts and what they mean, it's not that 'anything goes': there are conceptual *impossibilities* as well. It is just that the *world* will not tell us about them: it does not tell us how to use the notion of a person, as our notion of a person is what helps us to make sense of the world.

We bestow the identities, and how we bestow identity and unity on *persons* is not special in this regard. It is in this Humean sense that a house remains a house if it is moved, painted, bombed, or displaced. We cannot look at the world to find out what houses are, contrary to what the reference theorist of meaning does, since a physical description of the world would be fully consistent with the fact that my house, if it is bombed or painted green, is not my house any more, facts that my concept of a house, however, rules out. Hume also adds, as I would, that the fictions of everyday understanding are *natural* fictions: we make them by our nature, in contrast to various philosophical or 'metaphysical' fictions, which do not come naturally and are in fact not adequate (see Mijuskovic 1974: 112 for discussion).

How then do we arrive at our concepts? For complex concepts, the matter is quite clear, if the system is as we have described it above: assuming a compositional system, no complex concept will have to be learned, and their meanings are all known *a priori* (though implicitly). As for simple ones, I have now made the negative claim that we do not arrive at them by standing passively in certain environmental or causal relations, that no empiricist process of 'abstraction' will yield them, and that no physical description of the world would give us them. Rather, organisms, instead of being externally conditioned, actively and creatively respond to their physical conditions by using their internal resources, which include a certain set of concepts. As noted, it may be that learning in the animal kingdom at large does not work by classical conditioning, and that there is no 'unitary learning process at the computational level of analysis' at all, as Gallistel (1990) claims:

the process of association formation—as traditionally understood—is not involved in any form of learning that has been experimentally investigated, including classical and instrumental conditioning (see Gazzaniga 1997: 81).

[9] Wittgenstein, *Das blaue Buch*: 99–100.

That is, the remarkable computational abilities of lower animals may not be based on learning by associative binding and generalization by similarity. Apparently it is hard even in the case of the most classical conditioning experiments to explain the learning involved in terms of associative processes, even though here the learning does at least intuitively involve them. If so, although an informal sense remains in which animals learn (acquire knowledge), there is another sense in which 'learning' may not denote a natural kind, i.e. a single phenomenon for science to study, contrary to what common sense suggests.

Similarly problematic then would be the related common-sensical view of learning as caused by *instruction*. This is the view that teachers and experiences tell us what we ought to think, and that we adjust our cognitive state in the light of the evidence, or in mere obedience. But what we 'see' here is merely that the instructor does something, and that the pupil does something. No doubt what the teacher does plays a causal *role* in what the pupil comes to do. But we do not know about the actual processes that go on, or the learning mechanism that actually operates, when we are, as we say, 'instructed' about mathematics, say. Talking about 'instruction' is no more than a redescription of a process to be explained. In particular, the label 'instruction' may hide any amount of creative activity on the side of the pupil.

Over and above the empirical problems with associative learning, there are well-known *conceptual* difficulties with learning by instruction. According to Socrates, learning is a conceptual impossibility. Either, Socrates argued, the idea to be learned (say the idea of a *house*), is already present in our minds. Then we have no need to learn it. Or the idea is not already present in our minds. Then we cannot learn it, since, if it reached our mind from the outside and entered, we could not recognize it, or know that *it* was the concept we were looking for. In a nutshell:

ARGUMENT FOR THE INNATENESS OF CONCEPTS:
You cannot ask for (or think about) a concept you lack.

But we do learn, as is obvious to all. Hence we adjust our notion of learning in the standard rationalist fashion that experience *occasions* innate ideas, but does not create or shape our minds, as in the metaphor of the wax tablet (or learning by imprinting). On the wax tablet model, an external object imparts its physical shape on the malleable substance of mind. The mind attains whatever physical form the input had. The mind is formed by the experience, not awakened by it. But the perennial rationalist response to this picture I have pointed to above: there is a radical *dissimilarity* between the external trigger and the 'idea' that it awakes. Notions like 'person' or even 'physical shape' are in the mind of the beholder, and our insight into the necessary truths of geometry does not derive from the various shapes we 'see' out there. On the contrary, that we perceive a table as a rectangle has a rationale and explanation in our concept of a rectangle.

Is there something wrong with Socrates' conceptual argument against learning by instruction? This question has been discussed throughout the history of philosophy and psychology, and we still don't know (cf. Carey 2004). The most promising reply to Socrates' problem may well be that concepts are (semantically) structured, or have parts. Say it's the concept of a cow that you lack. On this idea, we acquire the concept of a cow because this concept contains *other*, more primitive concepts, which *can* supposedly be learned by dint of experience. But of these concepts, what, other than 'here brown now', might qualify as notions derived from 'direct learning by seeing'? Indeed, colour concepts themselves pose many kinds of problems, given that their contents are not specified in psycho-*physical* but *psychological* terms (no one would acquire the concept of RED, if he lacked it, by being told about wavelengths and brain processings: we really would have to tell him about RED; see Mausfeld and Heyer 2004 for discussion). But even assuming colour concepts to be obtainable from experience, whatever that means, no matter how much logic we add to such sensory concepts, the concept of a *person* or an IP, it seems, will not spring up in our minds.

So at the very least, the option above must assume a sizable number of primitive concepts, and it is worth noting that the basic problem of the origin of concepts is therefore not solved even on this empiricist approach.[10] This sizable number of concepts granted, problems will also now arise from their necessary *means of combination*: this much structure, too, has to be contributed by the mind. On empiricist grounds, we expect this mode of composition to be something like logic, for on empiricist and externalist assumptions, the mind must not contribute any contents to its mental representations: the content must come from an exposure of the mind to the world *alone* ('reference exhausts meaning'; see Fodor 1990, 1998). Hence if the mind were to contribute anything *else* but contentless logic, the mind would determine contents by itself. But this would be no less than saying that mental representations by themselves are *semantically* individuated, which is what I am overall committed to assume in this book, but which to reject I take to be one of the basic axioms of functionalism and the philosophy of mind (see Fodor 2000).

Indeed, the whole point of introducing internal mental representations was to combine an anti-behaviourism (the black box should become open) with a physicalism (don't posit internal structures in the organism that are not only individuated in terms of their physical, say causal, properties). Hence mental representations must supervene on their syntactic properties, even if a semantic content is *correlated* to them. 'Syntax is not semantics', one reads in any

---

[10] In what follows I will not deal with theories that are prototype or statistical theories of concepts, which are variants of a decompositional approach to the lexicon. On this approach, a complex concept C will be structured in the manner of a prototype if its constituents correspond to properties that things falling under it *tend* to have, under some interpretation of *tends*. I have little to add to Fodor's (1998: chapter 5, and see Fodor and Lepore 2002) points against prototype theories, but will not discuss this approach in any detail.

philosophy of language introduction, and maybe this view now shows its true colours as the most direct expression of an empiricist and externalist learning theory: the content *must* come from the outside. There is nothing inside except for what is not content-determining (logic, mechanisms for associating given contents, etc.). But then again, the old problem is that concepts individuated in terms of their content simply don't seem to emerge from a specification of physical properties of their referents, or physical properties of brains that process them; and that even if we grant logic as a means of combination, it is not clear why adding it would give us new complex concepts.

Note that logic will contain its own primitive concepts, such as the concept of AND (conjunction), and as Fodor has argued in a recent paper (Fodor 2004), it is not plausible that having this concept means having a disposition to draw certain inferences, say. As long as this inferential behaviour is not merely physically described (as a mechanical manipulation of certain symbols with no understanding of them at all), engaging in this behaviour presupposes rather than explains our possession of the notion of conjunction (the inference rules that govern the behaviour of this concept *contain* or *mention* it, and cannot be understood or seen as justified in its absence). Clearly, then, the concept of conjunction does not supervene on a symbol or a syntactically individuated mental representation and its causal role. Even assuming that we arrive at that concept without presupposing it, we should recall from Section 5.3 that combining two concepts is not generally a form of conjoining or associating them (recall the case of KILL and BILL that we discussed). Our understanding of the verb phrase resulting from this combination does not supervene on its constituent concepts and logic, but crucially requires *grammar*, which is not logic.

Ignoring all of these objections, the implausibility remains that the concept COW should *be* another, more complex, concept, like MATURE FEMALE ANIMAL OF A DOMESTICATED BREED OF OX. The concepts occurring in this decomposition are clearly no less complex than the concept to be explained.[11] Moreover, this analysis—and any other I can think of—looks like an analysis of what somebody *having* the concept of a cow happens to know about it. An *analysis* of a concept need not *substitute* for it. It remains to be shown that somebody *lacking* the concept of a cow,[12] but knowing a number of such subconcepts, comes to acquire our concept of a cow. This seems unlikely, as we call things *cow* that are not female (e.g., we could imagine a surprising sex change,

---

[11] A general problem that tends to reoccur with all kinds of lexical decompositions, particularly of abstract (non-sensory) concepts such as BELIEF. As Leslie (2000) shows, current proposals for how this concept 'decomposes' into other concepts either *presuppose* an understanding of that concept, in which case they don't help to explain how a child would acquire it, or they *don't* presuppose it, but then they fall short of capturing its actual content.

[12] Note we are not of course talking about someone (like a foreigner) lacking a *word* for the concept, a trivial case that raises far fewer problems.

which might draw the comment: 'This cow is not even female!'). For *any* possible combination of other concepts, it seems we could logically have *them* but *lack* the cow concept; it is conceivable that we could think of certain entities as COWs, while not having the concepts of what it is to be domesticated.

What we would really need, then, is an *essential* property of cows. This would be a property that, if an exemplar lacked it, would make it something other than a cow, and which, if it had it, would thereby make it a cow. But centuries of discussions of essential properties have not clearly yielded any. Nothing as trivial as the cow genome, for example, is a necessary or sufficient property for us using the concept of a cow: even if we knew that something was a mutant, this would not necessarily make us judge that it is not a cow—not for example if we saw it looking and behaving like a cow. In turn, a cow looking like a cow, behaving like one, and having the genome of most other cows, need not make us judge it to be a cow. We might judge it a fake, a mere machine, or a reincarnation of your grandmother, but not a cow, even though it may look like one.

A famous attempt to *define* a human concept—the concept expressed by the transitive verb *paint*—in terms of a number of jointly necessary and sufficient conditions was made by Fodor (1981). The attempt falters badly, even though Fodor *allowed* himself to use the concept expressed by the Noun *paint*. Suppose we start by saying that the verb *paint* means the same as *X covers Y with paint*. But no, an exploding paint factory would not count as *painting* something! So you need at least, it seems, *x is an agent and x covers the surface of y with paint*. But then again, suppose you are an agent and kick over a bucket of paint and thereby cover your shoes with paint. This still wouldn't count as painting them. This suggests that your agency must affect the *intentional* covering of the surface, a further constraint. Hence let us say: Michelangelo *paints something*, Y, iff he is an agent, intentionally covers the surface of Y with paint, the primary intention being to cover Y with paint. But now consider Michelangelo's dipping his brush into the paint. He agentively covers its tip with paint, and has a primary intention to do so. Does he *paint the brush*?

Given sufficient imaginative power, it seems we could proceed further indefinitely here, studying ever new cases where we would use or not use the word *paint*, reaching ever more convoluted definitions of *paint*, all of them driven by, it seems, and presupposing our knowledge of what it is to *paint*. There is similarly no way, it seems, to compress our knowledge of the concept of a *chair* into a definition so as to be able to anticipate in principle what kinds of things we might be calling chairs. Fodor's point, thus, is that no matter how much we go on analyzing a lexical concept, that concept will not *consist* in that analysis, which will never exhaust the concept's content. We *may* analyse a concept, but this won't tell us what concepts *are*. Whatever the analysis we provide of *cow*, *paint*, or *chair*, our knowledge of this analysis, as long as it does not *contain* the concepts to be explained, is logically consistent with our lack of knowledge of the concept analyzed.[13]

This is the *typical* case in the analysis of human concepts: a mounting intricacy as we dig deeper. Our knowledge of the meaning *entails* all of the judgements we have made in the course of the above analysis of *paint*, yet no dictionary definition of the verb *paint* goes even remotely into such details, and no parents ever explains them to their children. Somehow, a child comes to know that if a cow breaks a leg, the herd that it is a part of doesn't; or that if a cow is cut in two halves, it is still *a cow*—though in two halves, which are the halves *of* a cow—not two different entities. But if it is cut, not in two pieces, but in a large number of small pieces collected together in one big bucket, it is not *a cow* any more, but *cow* (a mass of cow meat). It also knows that if a wizard turns himself into a lion, the lion has the personality and the identity of the wizard (although he will roar, and look like a lion). One does not have to explain such facts about psychic continuity to a child, who simply appears to 'know' that a person need not, and typically will not, become a different person in a given plot by changing shape.

We might think that it cannot be so hard a problem to define what a *chair* is, say, but its designer need not have had an intention of making a chair; it need not be material (think of holograms); it need not be possible to sit on it. We feel no trouble, in art exhibitions say, to talk of a *chair* even where it hangs from the wall, where sitting proves impossible, temporarily or forever. Neither do children, who may excitedly point at such a chair, remarking to their parents: 'You can't even sit on that chair!', unhesitatingly using the concept of a chair, without usually being corrected, or being told that it's a lesser example of a chair.[14] At the same time, not everything is a chair: with certain scattered objects, we will find it impossible to conceptualize them as a chair; and if a chair was consistently used by a dwarf as a bed, it might not occur to us to call it a chair.

There may be typical 'clusters' of properties associated with any one concept at any moment in time, but again I see no reason that this cluster would *be* the relevant concept, rather than being associated with it. In the absence of concepts over and above the clusters, it would seem that nothing in principle would prevent two concepts blending into one another. But it is not clear whether one concept ever becomes another concept. Clearly, even if there is something that under one perspective is a chair and under another one is a bed, this does

---

[13] Jackendoff's decompositionalist reply to this Fodorian problem (Jackendoff 2002: section 11.2) seems to evade this issue. Jackendoff points out that decomposing concepts into primitives is descriptively useful, yields fruitful generalizations, need not provide definitions, and need not give synonyms. All of this is not the issue, however, which is that our knowledge of a concept won't *consist* in (or reduce to) any analysis we will provide.

[14] Rare would be a parent that 'corrected' his or her child's remark in such an instance, 'instructing' it by saying: 'Look, you have made a mistake: this object is not...'

not mean that our concept of chair is our concept of a bed, or that any one concept could be another concept, a possibility perhaps as absurd as that I might be my brother.

We arrive at the position that, ultimately, what makes a chair is that it is, well, a *chair*—that we can think of it in these terms—without being quite able to explain to a non-human creature lacking that concept, say a Martian, what it means to think of something as a chair. In other words, spelling out 'possession conditions' for any one concept—conditions jointly necessary and sufficient for one's having a concept—probably results in circularity (for a similar conclusion, see again Fodor 2004). But if lexical decomposition fails, it seems as if there are not many ways around the above conceptual argument for the 'innateness' of concepts.[15]

I think this insight conveys a very basic point: while we make *judgements* about what is true in a way that has *some* kind of connection to our experiences, there are *concepts* occurring in these judgements whose possession by us is, on the face of it, some kind of mystery. We would like to trace their origin, or the origin of our knowing them, to our dealings with the world. But it seems we cannot make sense of our dealings with the world without *presupposing* that we have the concepts required to do so. We may stomp our feet and say there *must* be a causal line running from experience to concepts in our head. But the modern scientific investigation of our possession and acquisition of concepts has by and large not lifted the mystery from the origin of our concepts.

Plato's view that concepts (ideas) do not derive from experience and that the world is organized according to ideas and ahistorical formal principles, may indeed be the least attractive option to try. Leibniz had already suggested cleansing Plato's theory of the 'error of a pre-existence' of the soul (Leibniz 1686/1996, §26: 374). Today the Platonic metaphor of 'recollection' has been replaced by the idea that it is *genes* which predate our physical existence, and direct organismic growth. Hence the knowledge we recollect from an earlier existence is our ancestors'. But, again, to what extent our conceptual system is a result of genetic tinkering is an open question, as it is in the case of syntax. If the above point is right that no exposure to physical features of an environment will determine human concepts, then no exposure of our ancestors to the physical structures of an environment will yield that feat. I have also noted that it is not clear whether the idea of explaining our conceptual system as a functional adaptation is particularly promising. What makes having our concept of a person (consciousness, mind, etc.) necessarily adaptive in an ecological context where our conspecifics lack it? If laws of form, as opposed to genetic tinkering

---

[15] For discussion of Fodor's 'ontological' solution in Fodor (1998)—which is externalistically inspired and, I hold, ultimately falls prey to the same objection of circularity that Chomsky (1959) levelled against Skinner's semantics—see Hinzen (2005a, 2006a).

due to changing selective pressures, are as relevant for the structure of language as they seem, a similarly non-historical explanation may hold for our conceptual system too.

Contemporary empirical research on the acquisition of linguistic sound and meaning suggests no opposite, that is empiricist, conclusion. It is noteworthy that much research in language acquisition does not even attempt to address the problem of the origin of concepts, and seems largely directed towards a completely different problem, the problem of how children *map* unknown sounds to known concepts (the 'mapping problem'; see Gleitman *et al.* 2005). Recent work in psychology on the origin of concepts suggests that Socrates' problem might be overcome by 'bootstrapping' the relevant concepts from other, already available, ones, say by mapping between them in a new fashion (see, e.g., Carey 2004 on the acquisition of the concept of number). But either these other concepts are *as* powerful (have as much content) as the one to be explained, in which case the origin of such powerful and abstract concepts itself is not explained; or it is not, in which case the mapping will leave the original problem unsolved. Other approaches appeal to the non-linear dynamics of a learning neural network in which phase transitions occur through ever denser patterns of connectivity (Molenaar 1986), but it seems unclear to start with how neural network dynamics accounts for the origin of concepts rather than (merely) their ontogenetic development: in the absence of an eliminativism about concepts, concepts are, as noted above, individuated by their content, not by psycho-physical properties they are correlated with (just as a symbol is not essential to the concept it expresses) (see also Hadley 2004).

Chomsky (2000: 120), points to

> the rate of lexical acquisition (...), with lexical items typically acquired on a single exposure, in highly ambiguous circumstances, but understood in delicate and extraordinary complexity that goes vastly beyond what is recorded in the most comprehensive dictionary,

leaving little room for the notion of 'correction' to play an explanatory role in word acquisition. Nor have developmental psychologists found 'good evidence that a word's meaning is composed, component by component, in the course of its acquisition' (Carey 1982: 47). Concepts come whole, it seems, and the empiricist idea of composing more primitive concepts into larger ones does not seem to depict what actually happens. Furthermore, the child does not seem to classify in terms of overt or salient *perceptual* similarities, but in terms of stipulated *essences* that may not be observable at all. In the case of artefacts, say, she will not judge them from their superficial outer appearance, which may vary a great deal, but from hidden functional, social, and psychological properties (e.g., in the case of *house*; cf. Bloom 2000: 161). The same is true for adults, who do not make their concept of a chair superficially dependent on its having four legs, or even on its serving the function of sitting.

Just as in the case of syntax, word learning takes place without significant 'negative evidence', i.e. explicit evidence concerning errors relative to the parent's lexicon (Bloom 2000: 8). Bloom notes that most of the 60,000–80,000 or so word meanings an American child acquires by the time graduating from high school are not explicitly demonstrated to them, and acquired without extensive tutelage or feedback. The number of words alone is breathtaking, as it depends on learning about ten new words, each with an immense complexity, per day (Pinker 1994: 151). It is naive to suppose that word meanings are acquired by a knowledgeable person's *pointing* (a conclusion again prefigured by Wittgenstein's discussion of 'ostensive definition'). Intercultural experimental evidence suggests that ostensive naming is unneeded for word learning (Bloom 2000: 8), and not necessarily helpful if it does occur.[16] As Quine (1960: 29) already noted, my pointing to the galloping rabbit and saying 'Gavagai!' is consistent with virtually any hypothesis you might fathom (I might refer to the time-slice of a rabbit, the fur, the skin, the ears, the category of an animal, or, why not, 'rabbit—but only during daytime; else food'). The child's situation is if anything worse than that of Quine's anthropologist, as children need to extract the stimuli pertinent to speech from what is simply a confusion of noises, a mixture of the rustling, whistling, buzzing, roaring, and gushing of miscellaneous objects around them.

Thus, facing an instance of 'Gavagai' (or its equivalent in a downtown London environment), the child will first have to be clear, not only that it is facing an instance of *naming*, but—more basic—an instance of a *word*, or maybe several words, as the linguistic sound might be segmented into different phonetic word-level units. Thus some initial phonetics would seem to be required, which may in turn demand some phonology, which we are assuming is intrinsically related to syntax. Even if the child has figured out that it was witnessing an act of naming a rabbit, how would it know how the concept it has acquired is to be applied on *future* occasions? All that it knows so far is consistent with applying the rabbit concept only to rabbits running, or to rabbits against the background of a forest. *Of course* it is 'entirely natural' for us—or the 'simplest hypothesis'—not to perform these generalizations, but this 'naturalness' is exactly what needs explaining.

Little in the acquisition literature, then, points to 'learning by instruction' as opposed to mere 'selection' of innate, abstract structure characterizing human nature. It remains a plausible guess that what we *call* 'concept learning' is no more than an association of phonetic labels with innately known concepts. In the light of this we might postulate in this domain a 'WAD'—a Word Acquisition

---

[16] Many verbs and abstract nouns cannot be pointed at, or are not observed as co-occurring with an utterance, and in the case of concepts of concrete objects the child is not attending to the referent of the word up to 50 per cent of the time. Most of the time that adults use verbs, the actions corresponding to them are not currently taking place. The child is not, contrary to what one might suppose, somehow concentratedly scrutinizing the scenes while hearing words that describe them (see Bloom 2000).

Device—just as we postulated, for the domain of syntax, a LAD, and ask what its structure is. Its structure will have to be rich enough to make the data we have just reviewed fall into place. It will impose constraints known to the learner about what a *possible lexical item* is, and thus dispense with the need for the child to test an abstruse number of hypotheses logically compatible with the data. Several such constraints have already been proposed.[17]

It may be very hard to come up with a solution to the Gavagai problem, if one conceives it, in an empiricist fashion, as an induction problem whose structure is exclusively logical or statistical. If one sticks to an empiricist bias, a thesis about the 'indeterminacy of meaning' will be the logical conclusion. *Logically*, that is, Quine's problem is probably unsolvable. But the indeterminacy thesis is surely unintuitive and undesirable: our thoughts just *seem* to have a determinate content, an intuition that I consider worth preserving. The rationalist will thus recommend giving up the empiricist bias, rather than the determinacy of human concepts. If there are innate biases, Quine's problem need not be solved, as nature has solved it for us, by giving us concepts so as to pre-structure our experience, leading us to 'expect' certain structures to occur in it.

In conclusion, a 'rational mind' is not necessarily a 'well-founded' one, in the sense that we can tell a coherent story about how our knowledge is built up constructively from non-knowledge, or how our concepts derive from something that was not a concept. In any case, an internalist inquiry into our possession of concepts seems called for. The hypothesis should be taken seriously that simple concepts are primitive entities in their own right, written into the structure of our mentality, if not this world. As for the construction of complex concepts when using syntax, the previous section has suggested, weird as this may seem, that human mind design might be the best imaginable design, and hence be 'rational' in just this sense. The extent to which we can hold on to this hypothesis is very much worth considering as a defining question for a new philosophy of mind.

---

[17] See e.g. Markman (1989); Spelke (1994, 2000); Hauser (2000).

Conclusions

In the wake of the scientific revolution, the 'natural philosophy' emerging with Galileo builds methodologically on a combination of an (essentially Platonic) notion of idealization, on the one hand, and a notion of experiment as interference (see Chapter 2), on the other. A century later, British philosophers begin the project of a science of human nature, an extension of the science of the day to mental aspects of the world, using an encompassing notion of 'matter', crucially without the kind of materialism that has been a founding assumption of the contemporary philosophy of mind.

As modern philosophy develops, this idea shifts; eventually, with the advent of the nineteenth century, it comes to be regarded as dubious. Metaphysical dichotomies arise, and philosophy is set on another foundation, a basis for the methodological dualism that we find in some of it today. Whatever the reason for this shift, a seemingly sound and uncontentious idea becomes a controversial metaphysical assumption: the idea of a human nature, as something to be explored internalistically rather than to be viewed as a reflection of outer conditions of existence. A human nature in this sense is an inner cause that yields aspects of how humans behave as overt effects, there being no implications that this inner cause is unique to them as a biological species. Such a notion of human nature, which might *a priori* have turned out empty, but has not, gains an empirical content through specific structural hypotheses formed to explain behavioural data.

Methodological dualism prevents a naturalistic perspective on human nature in this sense, but it seems ungrounded, as it places a roadblock in the path of an empirical inquiry that should be judged by its fruits. Normative conceptions of language forbid it too, but this is no threat either, if we dispel the persistent empiricist intuition that we must individuate languages as external entities whose regularities are explained by imposed norms, rather than letting some of the normative aspects of language follow from its lawful type, and other aspects be conditioned by sociological and political factors from which naturalistic inquiry will abstract. Much thinking in biology is inconsistent with human nature, too, but again this idea goes unscathed if we accept that a search for the natures of things may require higher levels of abstraction than the functional perspective allows. In a formalist perspective, there is both another explanandum and another concept of explanation, the search being for generative mechanisms in the origin of biological form.

The study of the human mind is then simply another chapter in the study of nature, namely human nature. I have offered no theory of mind, of 'what the mind is', and in fact I consider the idea that there could be one as problematic as the idea that there is a theory of 'matter'. The 'nature' we have unearthed, reflecting on the path that generative grammar took, holds a number of surprises: not only do we have, in Otto Jespersen's terms, a 'sense of structure' that underlies our use of language (and perhaps our concepts, if these are structured), but it is a structure in which little appears left to chance: we find features of design that is optimized relative to minimal design specifications for a novel organ in the brain interfacing with others. Unexpectedly, syntax precisely is as it should be if the language system is geared, not to the optimization of communication, but to a linkage of sound and meaning, without having more structure besides.

In one sense this means that descriptive technology used in earlier approaches to generative grammar can be dispensed with without loss, and in some cases with an increase of theoretical insight, descriptive adequacy, and empirical coverage. A prime example would be the elimination of multiple independently operating derivational 'cycles', from NUM to D-structure, from D-structure to 'S-structure' (the 'covert' cycle, feeding the phonological component), and from S-structure to LF (the 'covert' cycle, feeding the semantic one), and from LF to SEM, in favour of a *single* cycle mapping NUM to <PHON, SEM>, with no levels of representation at all. 'Overt' and 'covert' of movement become side-effects of operations of Transfer to the interfaces in the dynamics of the derivation (Chomsky, BEA, 2005).

In another, more spectacular sense, what minimalism reveals is not only the possibility of simpler redescription, but that descriptions depicting the human linguistic domain as messy, complex, and convoluted, are actually *misdescribing* it. Thus the structural complexity (in rule systems, explanatory principles) that was the basis of early generative approaches to the language faculty and even of early Minimalism (Chomsky 1995) is simply not there, opening quite different prospects for evolutionary theory. The structure-building apparatus might in essence boil down to the very simple recursive operation Merge. Combining separately assembled trees (labelled sets) or lexical items (atoms) into new trees (other labelled sets which embed the former), it builds all possible syntactic objects, sometimes in conjunction with the operation Agree. In a Probe/Goal framework, Agree requires feature matching in a particular configuration, which may depend on applying Merge internally. If so, moving items must leave a copy in their original position, due to the 'law of conservation' that no initial structure can be destroyed as the derivation proceeds. If internal Merge is due to interface requirements and requires Agree, Agree becomes principled as well.

On the other hand, I have also argued that enchantment with minimality and 'best design' considerations in the domain of language should not lead us to ignore or 'eliminate' structure without which human meaning would not be what it is: projections, in particular, or the idea that the semantic interface is built in stages or layers, the intentional one presupposing a purely conceptual or thematic one. As for the design of the derivational dynamics driven by Merge and Agree itself, the highly intriguing minimalist idea of a 'crash-proof' syntax that dispenses with the cancellation/crashing distinction should be kept in mind. If correct, it supports 'best design' considerations in a fairly astounding way, as does 'Strong Compositionality'—the claim that semantic interpretation of phrasal hierarchies is 'purely interpretive', either by tracking the hierarchies as existing at the final representation LF (Larson and Segal 1995), or as built up dynamically in a unified cyclic access to SEM (Epstein *et al.* 1998; Uriagereka 2002; Chomsky BEA).

The crucial insight here from a philosophical point of view, which I think has not been widely enough appreciated, is that *meaning* in its structural aspects might be viewed as an emergent byproduct of how structure is generated derivationally or dynamically, in a highly constrained fashion. The point is not only that matters of semantic interpretation, to cite Huang (1995: 155), can be 'to a large extent seen to pattern on a par with matters of form', an insight speaking in itself against the charge that generative grammar is a 'non-semantic' or 'syntactocentric' approach. The point is also not merely that syntactic and semantic form can be seen to *correlate* very tightly (correlation being a very weak relation that in particular neither means identity nor causation). The point is that if we wish to actually *explain* these correlations, or to know *why* a particular syntax is mapped to a particular semantics, it is not the semantic side of this dichotomy that we can appeal to. Contrary to a long philosophical tradition departing from Frege and the logical positivists, I have argued that it is much more plausible that the explanatory direction is the opposite one: that it is the syntax, the generative engine of language, that can be invoked to explain the form-meaning mapping, to the extent even that the distinction between 'syntactic' and 'semantic' structure may collapse. To the extent that semantic interpretation does pattern with linguistic form, semantics falls out from how the syntactic object is built, in several hierarchical layers.

We have thus been led to a strongly internalist conclusion as regards a possible science of human meaning. Our minds freely generate structures at two interfaces, which suit our purposes in conceptualization, on the one hand, and judgement, on the other: they take up such functional roles, but are not caused by them. Lawful in language, and subject to naturalistic inquiry, are the internal constraints imposed on the structures of our thoughts, not their external functions, a conclusion diametrically opposed to how analytic philosophy has sought to accomplish the naturalization of the linguistic mind.

Looking at some SEMs and concepts, we have regarded them as being intrinsically meaningful, but not as intrinsically 'representing' anything—in the same sense that the 'ideas' of the natural philosophers in the seventeenth and eighteenth centuries were not, on my view at least, 'representing anything'. This is to say that 'representation' does not enter as an explanatory notion, and that the internal mental representations postulated cannot be relationally defined. SEMs are plain structures that we assume are there in the mind, but they do not reach out to the world somehow. At least not directly: for by assumption, they are *used*, accessed by performance systems and employed to further purposes in language use and discourse. The 'intentionality' of a SEM perhaps reduces to that use-theoretic sense.

For naturalistic purposes this internalism is welcome, for an internalist attitude is precisely what would be adopted by a biologist studying the workings of some other organic system, like the immune system. It is also reassuring that we have reached a result on the meaning side of the grammar that is parallel to a commonly assumed one on the phonetic side, a parallel systematically suggested in Chomsky (2000): for PHONs do not 'represent' anything out there either. It would seem pointless to construct some external objects out of air molecules for internal PHONs to refer to or to be definable in terms of, for the sake of supplying them with 'phonetic values' in the way that SEMs are thought to be supplied with 'semantic values' or 'contents'.

Nothing in the stance on reference that I have been taking (which will be much further discussed in the accompanying volume Hinzen 2006a) has implications against *realism*. We should always interpret our theories realistically, pushing ontological and unification problems to one side. If we give up on the 'representational theory of ideas', as rationalism, in my understanding, does, then perhaps there is also a sense in which the realism controversy becomes no more formulable than Rorty's 'epistemological problematic'. On a representational theory of ideas, the mind may indeed not 'reach out' to the world, and the question of realism versus anti-realism poses itself. But on a more use-theoretic view our concepts cannot but mean the world, or have content. While we do distinguish between science and science fiction, we do so in terms of our criteria of understanding and experiment, not representation. Science aims for intelligibility, not reference.

There are limits of intelligibility, too, as when we realize that we have no grasp of what it is to apply an ordinary human concept, nor of where it gets its seeming determinacy of content from. We apply our concepts as they occur in our minds, but what it is that causes them, or how it is that we apply them, we do not know. We have ideas and make discoveries in a creative manner, particularly as children, when 'discovering' the abstract structure that underlies a language. But this apparently does not much involve processes of 'belief-formation', 'rationality', or 'justification of hypotheses'. More than an 'answer' to external constraints, it is the internally directed development of an organic system. We may try to apply our concepts 'rightly' or 'wrongly', but, on a deeper level, we just *act* when we do so, and expect, essentially without a reason, that others act the same way. This is what Wittgenstein suggested: justifications come to an end. Human nature, I add to this Wittgensteinian picture, is the bedrock where this happens (Hinzen 2004). It also appears to be an inherent part of human nature that the mind persistently generates what amounts to an illusion about its transparency for itself: we unavoidably think that we have 'reasons for our actions', that we 'know which rules we follow', but we do not. We do not in general control or direct our thoughts, we just think. Teachers may believe that they can cause a pupil to have ideas, but perhaps ideas are not caused; we certainly do not know what we mean when we say that behaviour is. We talk of persons, cities, houses, and chairs, and all of these things are distinct in highly specific ways, but ultimately we cannot explain, in a non-circular fashion, what causes them, and makes them distinct. 'Origin stories' for concepts in terms of 'experience', 'instruction', 'bootstrapping', 'theories', 'phase transitions', or 'causation' remain inconclusive both empirically and conceptually.

We try to find a rationale for why all this internal machinery is there, but what we seem to find is design which is beautiful and efficient, though purposeless, with external 'impurities' causing variation in an abstract underlying type. In the language case, it is the phonetic channel where we see best design considerations fail, and it is in relation to the communicative use of language that the design features of language seem opaque. So perhaps, it is more that we find ourselves having mental organs in our head, and use them as good we can, but they are what they are, and not bound to suit all uses to which we put them. There need be no resources in our mind to understand how we end up having the knowledge that these organs provide us with, how we apply it, and how it can be justified in terms of the world out there. Perhaps the only way to 'justify' mind design in terms of the world out there is by vindicating a form of 'perfect design', for design is then a reflection of more general design principles of nature, analogous to those we are accustomed to in physics.

If I am right, a novel philosophical landscape opens, a combination of internalism, rationalism, and methodological naturalism, largely as a consequence of the study of grammar in the biolinguistic tradition, which itself however is inspired by much older, though often forgotten, traditions in biological inquiry. Indeed it seems a novel approach to human *reason*, regarding it as a structure in nature, to be studied quite irrespective of notions like confirmation, representation, or the 'probabilty of truth'. Issues are now on the horizon that have to be dealt with, such as issues in the metaphysics of truth (for some thoughts, see Hinzen 2003a, 2005b, 2006b), or in the foundations of ethics, which I have not pursued here. But I have mentioned in passing Singer's (1999) attempt to constrain ethical theories by our knowledge of human nature (and see also Dennett's 'derivation of "ought" from "is"' in Dennett 1995, chapter 16). There is little, I have argued, to support the sweeping Neo-Darwinian picture of human nature that Singer, Dennett, or Dawkins defend and make the basis of their vision on ethics. It is a completely empirical question whether the apparent absence of functional design and external shaping we have found in language and concepts carries over to human morals.

There would be nothing incoherent in such a conclusion, as human morality depends on moral concepts, and these are part of an enormously intricate human conceptual system, which we have reasons to believe is highly constrained innately. Given what seem to be inherent methodological problems in the functionalist study of mind design (Chapter 3), there is no reason not to try an approach to the moral mind on a more abstract 'typological' level, in a non-functionalist vein. We should not *start*, that is, from the assumption that moral ideas are 'designed by natural selection to further the long-term interests of individuals and ultimately their genes' (Pinker 1997: 406; see Premack and Premack, 1994, for a more open-minded empirical study of human morality as a domain-specific cognitive faculty; and Katz (2000) for an overview over the state of the art). If the environment need not have had the power to create human morality (though it may have selected it), and the latter arises predominantly by way of internal constraints, this opens up a possibility: human nature may become a *positive* constraint on ethical thinking, not merely the negative one it is in Singer (1999). That is, it could be a *source* of human morality, not merely a deplorable *limitation* to it.

Ultimately, of course, what applies to concept application in general applies here: how we apply our concepts has no rationale in terms of referents out there, or what is true. As we turn to the ethical realm, we may be frightened to think this through to its logical conclusion. But this is no argument against internalism, much as the fear of Kuhnian relativism is no argument in favour of reference as a source of semantic stability. Maybe, though, we are just lucky, and our design is such that it simply does not come naturally to us that murder is good. As far as I can see, this is in fact quite likely, but the issue, as ever, is empirical.

References

Abler, W. (1989). 'On the particulate principle of self-diversifying systems', *Journal of Social and Biological Structures* 12: 1–13.
Abney, S. (1987). 'The English noun phrase in its sentential aspect', Ph.D. Dissertation, MIT.
Aboh, E. (2004). 'Topic and Focus within D', *Linguistics in the Netherlands*, 1–12.
Ahouse, J. C. and Berwick, R. (1998). 'Darwin on the mind', *The Boston Review* 23(2): 36–41.
Amundson, R. (1994). 'Two concepts of constraint', *Philosophy of Science* 61: 556–78.
—— (1998). 'Typology reconsidered', *Biology and Philosophy* 13: 153–77.
Anderson, S. R. and Lightfoot, D. (2002). *The Language Organ. Linguistics as Cognitive Physiology* (Cambridge: Cambridge University Press).
Antony, L. and Hornstein, N. (eds.) (2003). *Chomsky and his Critics* (Oxford: Blackwell).
Arthur, W. (2002). 'The emerging conceptual framework of evolutionary development biology', *Nature* 415, 14 Feb. 2002, 757–64.
Atran, S. (1990). *Cognitive Foundations of Natural History: Towards an Anthropology of Science* (Cambridge: Cambridge University Press).
Baker, M. (1997). 'Thematic Roles and Syntactic Structure', in L. Haegeman (ed.), *Elements of Grammar* (Dordrecht: Kluwer), 73–137.
—— (2001). *The Atoms of Language* (New York: Basic Books).
—— (2003). *Lexical Categories: Verbs, Nouns and Adjectives* (Cambridge: Cambridge University Press).
Baltin, M. and Collins, C. (eds.) (2001). *The Handbook of Contemporary Syntactic Theory* (Oxford: Blackwell).
Barber, A. (ed.) (2003). *Epistemology of Language* (Oxford: Oxford University Press).
Barkow, J. H., Cosmides, L., and Tooby, J. (eds.) (1992). *The Adapted Mind* (New York/Oxford: Oxford University Press).
Baron-Cohen, S. (1995). *Mindblindness: An Essay on Autism and Theory of Mind* (Cambridge, MA: MIT Press).
Barsky, R. (1998). *Noam Chomsky: A Life of Dissent* (Cambridge, MA: MIT Press).
Beatty, J. (ed.) (2001), *Thinking about Evolution: Essays in Honor of Richard C. Lewontin*, 2 vols. (Cambridge: Cambridge University Press).
Bell, C. (1833). *The Hand, Its Mechanism and Vital Endowments as Evincing Design*, Bridgewater Treatise, Treatise IV (London: William Pickering).
Belletti, A. (1990). *Generalized Verb Movement: Aspects of Verb Syntax* (Turin: Rosenberg and Sellier).
—— (ed.) (2004), *Structures and Beyond* (Oxford: Oxford University Press).
Bernstein, J. B. (2001). 'The DP Hypothesis: Identifying clausal properties in the nominal nomain', in Baltin and Collins (eds.), 536–61.
Berwick, R. C. (1997). 'Syntax facit saltum', *Journal of Neurolinguistics* 10(2/3): 231–49.
Bever, T., Fodor, J., and Garrett, M. (1974). *The Psychology of Language* (New York: McGraw-Hill).
Bickerton, D. (1981). *Roots of Language* (Ann Arbor: Karoma).

Bickerton, D. (1990). *Language and Species* (Chicago: University of Chicago Press).
Block, N. (1995). 'The mind as the software of the brain', in D. N. Osherson and E. E. Smith (eds.), *Thinking. An Invitation to Cognitive Science*, Vol. 3 (Cambridge, MA: MIT Press), 377–426.
Bloom, P. (2000). *How Children Learn the Meanings of Words* (Cambridge, MA: MIT Press).
Boeckx, C. (2004). *Bare Syntax*. MS, Harvard University.
—— and Hornstein, N. (2005). 'The varying aims of linguistic theory', in Julie Franck and Jean Briemont (eds.), *Cahier Chomsky* (Paris: L'Herne).
Borer, H. (2005), *Structuring Sense: An Exoskeletal Trilogy*, 2 vols. (Oxford: Oxford University Press).
Boysson-Bardies, B. (1999). *How Language Comes to Children* (Cambridge, MA: MIT Press).
Brandon, R. N. (1988). 'Levels of selection', repr. in Hull and Ruse (eds.), 176–97.
Brandt, R. (1988). 'John Locke', in J.-P. Schobinger (ed.), *Die Philosophie des 17. Jahrhunderts*, Vol. 3 (Basel: Schwabe & Co. AG), §29.
Brock, W. H. (1992). *The Fontana History of Chemistry* (London: Fontana).
Brody, M. (2003), *Towards an Elegant Syntax*, Routledge Leading Linguists (London: Routledge).
Brouwer, W. (1980). 'Einstein and Lorentz: The structure of a scientific revolution', *American Journal of Physics* 48(6): 425–31.
Caramazza, A. and Shapiro, K. (2004). 'Language categories in the brain: Evidence from aphasia', in Belletti (ed.), 15–38.
Carey, S. (1982). 'Semantic development: The state of the art', in L. Gleitman and E. Wanner (eds.), *Language Acquisition: The State of the Art* (Cambridge, New York: Cambridge University Press), 347–89.
—— (1998). 'Knowledge of number: Its evolution and ontogeny', *Science* 282: 641–2.
—— (2004). 'Bootstrapping and the origin of concepts', *Daedalus*, 59–68.
Carstairs-McCarthy, A. (1999). *The Origins of Complex Language: An Inquiry into the Evolutionary Beginnings of Sentences, Syllables, and Truth* (Oxford: Oxford University Press).
—— (forthcoming). 'The evolutionary origin of morphology', in Maggie Tallerman (ed.), *Language Origins: Perspectives on Evolution* (Oxford: Oxford University Press).
Chalmers, D. J. (1996). *The Conscious Mind* (Oxford: Oxford University Press).
Chametzky, R. A. (2000). *Phrase Structure: From GB to Minimalism* (Oxford: Blackwell).
—— (2003). 'Phrase structure', in Hendrick (ed.), 192–225.
Changeux, J. P. and Dehaene, S. (1996). 'Neuronal models of cognitive functions associated with the prefrontal cortex', in A. R. Damadio, H. Damasio, and Y. Christen (eds.), *Neurobiology of Decision-making* (Berlin/New York: Springer).
Cheney, D. L. and Seyfarth, R. M. (1990). *How Monkeys see the World: Inside the Mind of another Species* (Chicago: Chicago University Press).
—— —— (1997). 'Why animals don't have language', The Tanner Lectures on Human Values, Cambridge University, March 1997.
Cherniak, C. (1995). 'Neural component placement', *Trends Neurosciences* 18: 522–7.
—— (2005). 'Innateness and brain-wiring optimization: Non-genomic nativism', in A. Zilhao (ed.), *Cognition, Evolution, and Rationality* (London: Routledge).

Chomsky, N. (1959). A Review of B. F. Skinner's *Verbal Behavior*, *Language* 35(1): 26–58.
—— (1965). *Aspects of the Theory of Syntax* (Cambridge, MA: MIT Press).
—— (1966). *Cartesian Linguistics* (New York and London: Harper and Row).
—— (1970). 'Remarks on Nominalization', in R. A. Jacob and P. S. Rosenbaum (eds.), *Readings in English Transformational Grammar* (Waltham, MA: Ginn), 184–221.
—— (1972). *Studies on Semantics in Generative Grammar* (The Hague: Mouton).
—— (1986). *Barriers* (Cambridge, MA: MIT Press).
—— (1995). *The Minimalist Program* (Cambridge, MA: MIT Press).
—— (1998). 'Minimalist inquiries: The framework', *MIT Working Papers in Linguistics*; revised version in R. Martin *et al.* (eds.) (2000), *Step by Step* (Cambridge: Cambridge University Press), 89–156. Quoted as MI.
—— (2000). *New Horizons in the Study of Language and Mind* (Cambridge: Cambridge University Press).
—— (2001a). 'Derivation by Phase', in M. Kenstowicz (ed.), *Ken Hale: A Life in Language* (Cambridge, MA: MIT Press), 1–52. Quoted as DBP.
—— (2001b). 'Beyond Explanatory Adequacy', *MIT Occasional Papers in Linguistics* 20. Reprinted with revisions in Belletti (ed.), 104–31. Quoted as BEA.
—— (2002). *On Nature and Language*, eds. A. Belletti and L. Rizzi (Cambridge: Cambridge University Press).
—— (2003). 'Replies to critics', in Antony and Hornstein (eds.), 255–328.
—— (2005). 'Three factors in language design', in Linguistic Inquiry 36: 1, 1–22.
Churchland, P. S. (1981). 'Eliminative materialism and the propositional attitudes', *Journal of Philosophy* 78: 67–90.
—— (1996). 'Toward a neurobiology of the mind', in R. Llinás and P. S. Churchland (eds.), *The Mind-Brain Continuum* (Cambridge, MA: MIT Press).
Cinque, G. (1999). *Adverbs and Functional Heads* (Oxford: Oxford University Press).
Clarke, D. (1982). *Descartes' Philosophy of Science* (Manchester: Manchester University Press).
Clements, G. N. and Hume, E. V. (1995). 'The internal organization of speech sounds', in J. A. Goldsmith, (ed.), *The Handbook of Phonological Theory* (Oxford: Blackwell), 245–306.
Collins, C. (1997). *Local Economy* (Cambridge, MA: MIT Press).
—— (2002). 'Eliminating labels', in Epstein and Seely (eds.), 42–64.
Conway Morris, S. (2003). *Life's Solution: Inevitable Humans in a Lonely Universe* (Cambridge: Cambridge University Press).
Cosmides, L. and Tooby, J. (1992). 'The Psychological Foundations of Culture', in Barkow, Cosmides, and Tooby (eds.), 19–136.
—— —— (1997). 'Evolutionary Psychology: A Primer', <http://www.psych.ucsb.edu/research/cep/primer.html>.
Cottingham, J. (1976). *Descartes' Conversation with Burman* (Oxford: Clarendon).
Crain, S. and Pietroski, P. (2001). 'Nature, Nurture and Universal Grammar', *Linguistics and Philosophy* 24 (2): 139–86.
—— and Thornton, R. (1998). *Investigations in Universal Grammar: A Guide to Experiments in the Acquisition of Syntax and Semantics* (Cambridge, MA: MIT Press).
Crystal, D. (2000). *Language Death* (Cambridge: Cambridge University Press).

Culicover, P. (1997). *Principles and Parameters* (Oxford/New York: Oxford University Press).

Curtiss, S. (1977). *Genie: A Psycholinguistic Study of a Modern-day 'Wild Child'* (New York: Academic Press).

Damasio, A. (1999). *The Feeling of What Happens* (San Diego: Harvest Books).

Darnell, M., Moravcsik, E., Newmeyer, F., Noonan, M., and Wheatley, K. (eds.) (1999). *Functionalism and Formalism in Linguistics*, 2 vols. (Amsterdam/Philadelphia: Benjamins).

Darwin, C. (1859). *On the Origin of Species by Means of Natural Selection*, repr. 1968 (Harmondsworth: Penguin).

Davidson, D. (1986). 'A nice derangement of epitaphs', in E. Lepore (ed.), *Truth and Interpretation* (Oxford: Blackwell) 433–46.

—— (1990). 'The structure and content of Truth', *Journal of Philosophy* 87: 279–328.

Davies, P. and Gribbin, J. (1991). *The Matter Myth* (London: Viking).

Dawkins, R. (1976/1989). *The Selfish Gene*, 2nd edn. (Oxford: Oxford University Press).

—— (1986). *The Blind Watchmaker* (Norton: New York).

—— (1995). *River out of Eden* (Phoenix: Orion Books).

—— (1998). 'Universal Darwinism', in Hull and Ruse (eds.), 15–37.

Dennett, D. (1995). *Darwin's Dangerous Idea* (New York: Simon & Schuster).

Derrida, J. (1972). 'Fines hominis', in id., *Marges de la philosophie*, (Paris: Éditions de Minuit).

Descartes, R. (1637/1984). *Discours de la Méthode*, Introduction et notes par Et. Gilson (Paris: Vrin).

—— (1644/1983). *Principles of Philosophy*, trans. V. R. Miller and R. P. Miller (Dordrecht: Reidel).

Devitt, M. and Sterelny, K. (1987). *Language and Reality* (Oxford: Blackwell).

—— (2003). 'Linguistics is not Psychology', in Barber (ed.), 107–39.

Dirac, P. (1968). 'Methods in theoretical physics', in: A. Salam *et al.*, *From a Life of Physics; Evening lectures at the International Centre for Theoretical Physics, Trieste, Italy*. A special supplement of the International Atomic Energy Agency Bulletin, Austria.

Doolittle, W. F. (2000). 'Uprooting the Tree of Life', *Scientific American* 282 (2): 90–5.

Edelman, G. (1992). *Bright Air, Brilliant Fire* (New York: Basic Books).

Eimas, P. (1985). 'Sprachwahrnehmung beim Säugling', *Spektrum der Wissenschaft*, March 1985.

Eldredge, N. and Gould, S. J. (1972). 'Punctuated equilibria: An alternative to phyletic gradualism', in T. J. M. Schopf (ed.), *Models in Palaeobiology* (San Francisco: Freeman Cooper).

Elman, J. L., Bates, E., Johnson, M. H., Karmiloff-Smith, A., Parisi, D., and Plunkett, K. (1996). *Rethinking Innateness: A Connectionist Perspective on Development* (Cambridge, MA: MIT Press).

Emerton, N. E. (1984). *The Scientific Reinterpretation of Form* (Ithaca, NY: Cornell University Press).

Emmorey, K. (2001). *Language, Cognition, and the Brain: Insights from Sign Language Research* (Mahwah, NJ: Lawrence Erlbaum).

Epstein, S. (1999). 'Un-Principled syntax: The derivation of syntactic relations', in Epstein and Hornstein (eds.), 317–46.

Epstein, S. and Hornstein, N. (eds.) (1999). *Working Minimalism* (Cambridge, MA: MIT Press).

Epstein, S. and Seely, D. (2002). 'Rule applications as cycles in a level-free syntax', in Epstein and Seely (eds.), 65–89.

Epstein, S. and Seely, D. (eds.) (2002). *Derivation and Explanation in the Minimalist Program* (Oxford: Blackwell).

Ferry, L. and Renaut, A. (1985). *La pensée 68. Essai sur l'anti-humanisme contemporain* (Paris: Gallimard).

Fischer, K. (1994). 'Das Naturverständnis bei Galilei', in L. Schäfer and E. Ströker (eds.), *Naturauffassungen in Philosophie, Wissenschaft, Technik*, vol. 2 (Freiburg/Munich: K. Alber Verlag), 149–84.

Fodor, J. (1975). *The Language of Thought* (Cambridge, MA: MIT Press).

—— (1981). 'The present status of the innateness controversy', in id. (ed.), *Representations: Philosophical Essays on the Foundations of Cognitive Science* (Cambridge: Cambridge University Press).

—— (1983). *The Modularity of Mind* (Cambridge, MA: MIT Press).

—— (1990). *Reply to Dretske's 'Does Meaning Matter'*, in Enrique Villanueva (ed.), *Information, Semantics, and Epistemology* (Oxford: Blackwell), 28–35.

—— (1998). *Concepts. Where Cognitive Science Went Wrong* (Oxford: Clarendon).

—— (2000). *The Mind Doesn't Work that Way* (Cambridge, MA: MIT Press).

—— (2003). *Hume Variations* (Oxford: Clarendon).

—— (2004). 'Having concepts: a brief refutation of the twentieth century', *Mind and Language* 19(1): 29–47.

—— and Lepore, E. (2002). *The Compositionality Papers* (Oxford: Oxford University Press).

—— and Pylyshyn, Z. (1988). 'Connectionism and cognitive architecture: a critical analysis', *Cognition* 28, 3–71.

Fox, D. (2000), *Economy and Semantic Interpretation* (Cambridge, MA: MIT Press).

—— (2003), 'On Logical Form', in Hendrick (ed.), 82–123.

Frampton, J. and Gutmann, S. (1999). 'Cyclic computation: A computationally efficient minimalist syntax', *Syntax* 2(1): 1–27.

—— (2002). 'Crash-Proof syntax', in Epstein and Seely (ed.), 90–105.

Friedman, M. (1993). 'Remarks on the history of science and the history of philosophy', in P. Horwich (ed.), *World Changes: Thomas Kuhn and the Nature of Science* (Cambridge, MA: MIT Press), 37–54.

—— (2000). *A Parting of the Ways: Carnap, Cassirer, and Heidegger* (Chicago: Open Court).

Fromkin, V. A. (1997). 'Some thoughts about the brain/mind/language interface', *Lingua* 100: 3–27.

Fukui, N. (2001). 'Phrase structure', in Baltin and Collins (eds.), 374–406.

Galileo Galilei (1632). *Dialogo, Opere di Galileo Galilei*, 1890–1909, 2nd edn. 1929–39, ed. A. Favaro, edizione nazionale, vol. 7 (Florence: Giunti-Barbara).

Gallistel, C. R. (1990). *The Organization of Learning* (Cambridge, MA: MIT Press).

—— (1995). 'The replacement of general-purpose theories with adaptive specializations', in Gazzaniga (ed.), 1255–67.

Gallistel, C. R. (1998). 'Brains as symbol processors: The case of insect navigation', in S. Sternberg and D. Starborough (eds.), *Conceptual and Methodological Foundations*, vol. 4 of *An Invitation to Cognitive Science*, Series ed. by D. Osherson (Cambridge, MA: MIT Press).
—— and Gibbon, J. (2001). 'Computational versus associative models of simple conditioning', *Current Directions in Psychological Science* 10: 146–50.
Garber, D. (1992). 'Science and certainty in Descartes', in v. Chappell (ed.), *René Descartes*, Part I (New York: Garland), 284–322.
Gaukroger, S. (1993). 'Descartes: Methodology', in G. H. R. Parkinson (ed.), *The Renaissance and Seventeenth-Century Rationalism*, Routledge History of Philosophy, Vol. IV (London and New York: Routledge), 167–200.
Gazzaniga, M. (1992). *Nature's Mind* (New York: Basic Books).
Gazzaniga, M. (ed.) (1995). *The Cognitive Neurosciences* (Cambridge, MA: MIT Press).
—— (ed.) (1997). *Conversations in the Cognitive Neurosciences* (Cambridge, MA: MIT Press).
Gillett, C. and Loewer, B. (eds.) (2001). *Physicalism and its Discontents* (Cambridge: Cambridge University Press).
Gleitman, L., Cassidy, K., Nappa, R., Pappafragou, A., and Trueswell, J. C. (2005). 'Hard words', *Language Learning and Development* 1(1): 23–64.
Godfrey-Smith, P. (1996). *Complexity and the function of mind in nature* (Cambridge: Cambridge University Press).
Golinski, J. (1995). '"Matter" and "Mechanical Philosophy"', in J. Yolton *et al.* (eds.), *The Blackwell Companion to the Enlightenment* (Oxford: Blackwell).
Goldin-Meadow, S. and Mylander, C. (1990). 'Beyond the input given: The child's role in the acquisition of language', *Language* 66: 323–55.
Gooding, D. (1992). 'Putting agency back into experiment', in A Pickering (ed.), *Science as Practice and Culture* (Chicago: University of Chicago Press), 65–112.
Goodwin, B. (1994). *How the Leopard Changed its Spots* (London: Weidenfeld & Nicholoon).
Gopnik, M. (1990). '"A Rube Goldberg machine par excellence", Commentary on Pinker and Bloom (1990)', *Behavioral and Brain Sciences* 13(4): 734–5.
Gottlieb, G. (2002). 'Developmental-behavioral initiation of evolutionary change', *Psychological Review* 109: 211–18.
Gould, S. J. (1989). *Wonderful Life* (London: Penguin).
—— (2002). *The Structure of Evolutionary Theory* (Cambridge, MA: Belknap Press of Harvard University Press).
—— and E. S. Vrba (1982). 'Exaptation—A missing term in the science of form', repr. in Hull and Ruse (eds.) (1998), 52–71.
—— and Lewontin, R. (1978). 'The spandrels of San Marco and the Panglossian paradigm', *Proceedings of the Royal Society of London* B 205: 581–98.
Grimshaw, J. (1990). *Argument Structure* (Cambridge, MA: MIT Press).
Grodzinsky, J. (2004). 'Variation in Broca's region: Preliminary cross-linguistic comparisons', in L. Jenkins (ed.) (2004).
Grodzinsky, Y. and Amunts, K. (eds.) (2006). *Broca's Region* (New York: Oxford University Press).
Grohman, K. (2003). 'Successive cyclicity under (anti-)local considerations', *Syntax* 6 (3): 260–312.

Guasti, M. T. (2003). *Language Acquisition: The Growth of Grammar* (Cambridge, MA: MIT Press).
Hacking, I. (1982). 'Experimentation and scientific realism', *Philosophical Topics* 13: 71–87.
—— (1983). *Representing and Intervening* (Cambridge: Cambridge University Press).
—— (1992). 'The self-vindication of the laboratory sciences', in Pickering (ed.), 30–64.
Hadley, R. F. (2004). 'On the proper treatment of systematicity', *Mind and Machines* 14: 145–72.
Hale, K. and Keyser, S. J. (2002). *Prolegomenon to a Theory of Argument Structure* (Cambridge, MA: MIT Press).
Hallman, P. (2004). 'Symmetry in structure building', *Syntax* 7 (1): 79–100.
Harré, R. and Madden, E. H. (1975). *Causal Powers. A Theory of Natural Necessity* (Oxford: Blackwell).
Hammerstein, P. and Leimar, O. (2002). 'Ants on a Turing trail', *Nature* 418: 141–2.
Hauser, M. D. (1996). *The Evolution of Communication* (Cambridge, MA: MIT Press).
—— (2000). *Wild Minds: What Animals Really Think* (New York: Holt).
—— Chomsky, N., and Fitch, W. T. (2002). 'The faculty of language: What is it, who has it, and how did it evolve?', *Science* 298: 1569–79.
—— D. Weiss, and Marcus, G. (2002). 'Rule learning by cottom-top tamarins', *Cognition* 86: B15–B22.
—— E. S. Spelke (in press). 'Evolutionary and developmental foundations of human Knowledge; A case study of mathematics', in M. Gazzaniga (ed.), *The cognitive neurosciences*, vol. 3, Cambridge; MA: MIT Press.
Heim, I. and Kratzer, A. (1998). *Semantics in Generative Grammar* (Oxford: Blackwell).
Heidegger, M. (1952). *Über den Humanismus* (Frankfurt/Main: Klostermann 2000).
Hespos, S. J. and Spelke, E. S. (2004). 'Conceptual precursors to language', *Nature* 430: 453–6.
Hendrick, R. (ed.) (2003), *Minimalist Syntax* (Oxford: Blackwell).
Higginbotham, J. (1985). 'On semantics', in *Linguistic Inquiry* 16 (4): 547–93.
—— (1993). 'Grammatical form and logical form', in *Philosophical Perspectives* 7: 173–96.
—— (2002). 'Some consequences of compositionality', MS, University of Southern California.
Hinzen, W. (2003a). 'Truth's fabric', *Mind and Language* 18 (2): 194–219.
—— (2003b). 'Real dynamics', in J. Peregrin (ed.), *Meaning: The Dynamic Turn. Current Research in the Semantics/Pragmatics Interface*, 12 (Oxford: Elsevier), 91–118.
—— (2004). 'Synthese a priori bei Wittgenstein', *Zeitschrift fuer philosophische Forschung* 58: 1–28.
—— (2005a). 'Spencerism and the Causal Theory of Reference', *Biology & Philosophy*.
—— (2005b). 'Truth and the human clause', forthcoming in G. Siegwart and D. Greimann (eds.), *The Illocutionary Role of Truth* (Berlin: Walter de Gruyter).
—— (2006a). *An Essay on Names and Truth* (Oxford: Oxford University Press).
—— (2006b). 'Internalism about truth', *Mind and Society* (forthcoming).
Hinzen, W. and Rott, H. (eds.) (2002). *Belief and Meaning—Essays at the Interface*, Deutsche Bibliothek der Wissenschaften (Frankfurt: Haensel-Hoehenhausen).
Hirschfeld, L. and Gelman, S. (eds.) (1994). *Mapping the Mind* (Cambridge: Cambridge University Press).

Ho, M.-W. (1984). 'Environment and heredity in development and evolution', in M.-W. Ho and W. T. Saunders (eds.), *Beyond Neo-Darwinism. An Introduction into the new Evolutionary Paradigm* (San Diego: Academic Press), 267–89.

Hornstein, N. (1995). *Logical Form* (Oxford: Blackwell).

—— (2002). 'A grammatical argument for a neo-Davidsonian semantics', in G. Preyer and G. Peter (eds.), *Logical Form and Language* (Oxford: Clarendon Press), 345–64.

—— (2005). 'Empiricism and rationalism as research programs', in J. McGilvray (ed.), *The Cambridge Companion to Chomsky* (Cambridge: Cambridge University Press).

—— and P. Pietroski (2002). 'Does every sentence like this exhibit a scope ambiguity?', in Hinzen and Rott (eds.).

Huang, J. T. (1995). 'Logical form', in Webelhuth (ed.), 125–76.

Hull, D. (1978). 'A matter of individuality', *Philosophy of Science* 45, 335–60.

—— (1986). 'On human nature', in Hull and Ruse (eds.) (1998), 383–97.

Hull, D. and Ruse, M. (eds.) (1998). *The Philosophy of Biology* (Oxford: Oxford University Press).

Hume, D. (1739–40/1978). *A Treatise of Human Nature*, ed. L. A. Selby-Bigge, 2nd edn. (Oxford: Clarendon).

—— (1748/1975). *An Enquiry Concerning Human Understanding*, ed. L. A. Selby-Bigge, 3rd edn. rev. by P. H. Nidditch (Oxford: Clarendon Press).

Jackendoff, R. (1977). *X-bar Syntax* (Cambridge, MA: MIT Press).

—— (1994). *Patterns in the Mind: Language and Human Nature* (New York: Basic Books).

—— (2002). *Foundations of Language* (Oxford: Oxford University Press).

Jacob, F. (1982). *The Possible and the Actual* (Seattle: University of Washington Press).

James, W. (1880). 'Great men and their environment', lecture before the Harvard Natural History Society, published in the *Atlantic Monthly*, October 1880.

Jenkins, L. (2000). *Biolinguistics* (Cambridge: Cambridge University Press).

Jenkins, L. (ed.) (2004). *Variation and Universals in Biolinguistics*, (Oxford: Elsevier).

Johnson, K. (2000). 'How far will quantifiers go?', in Martin, Michaels, and Uriagerella (eds.), 187–210.

Jungius, J. (1630/1982). *Praelectiones Physicae*, ed. C. Meinel (Göttingen: Vandenhoeck and Ruprecht).

Jusczyk, P. W. (1999). 'How infants begin to extract words from speech', *Trends in Cognitive Sciences* 3 (9): 323–8.

Kamp, H. and Reyle, U. (1994). *From Discourse to Logic* (Dordrecht: Kluwer).

Karmiloff-Smith, A. (1992), *Beyond Modularity: A Developmental Perspective on Cognitive Science* (Cambridge, MA: MIT Press).

Katz, J. (1997). *Realistic Rationalism* (Cambridge, MA: MIT Press).

—— and Postal, P. (1991). 'Realism vs. conceptualism in linguistics', *Linguistics and Philosophy* 14, 515–54.

Katz, L. D. (ed.) (2000). *Evolutionary Origins of Morality* (Exeter: Imprint Academic).

Kauffman, S. (1993). *Origins of Order: Self-Organization and Selection in Evolution* (Oxford: Oxford University Press).

—— (1995a). *At Home in the Universe. The Search for Laws of Complexity* (London: Penguin).

—— (1995b). '"What is life?" Was Schrödinger right?', in M. P. Murphy and L. O'Neill, *What is Life? The Next Fifty Years* (Cambridge: Cambridge University Press).

Kayne, R. (1994). 'The Antisymmetry of Syntax' (Cambridge, MA: MIT Press).
Kenstowicz, M. (1994). *Phonology in Generative Grammar* (Oxford: Blackwell).
Kepler, J. (1611/1953). *Neujahrsgabe oder: Vom Sechseckigen Schnee*, trans. F. Rossmann (Berlin: Keiper).
Kim, J. (1996). *Philosophy of Mind* (Boulder, CO: Westview Press).
Kiss, E. K. (1991). 'Logical structure and syntactic structure: the case of Hungarian', in C. T. J. Huang and R. May (eds.), *Logical Structure and Syntactic Structure: Cross-linguistic Perspectives* (Dordrecht: Reidel), 111–48.
Kitcher, P. (1985). *Vaulting Ambition: Sociobiology and the Quest for Human Nature* (Cambridge, MA: MIT Press).
—— (1999). 'The Hegemony of Molecular Biology', *Biology and Philosophy* 14: 195–210.
Koyré, A. (1939/1966). *Études galiléennes* (Paris: Hermann).
Lakoff, G. (1971). 'On generative semantics', in D. Sternberg and L. Jakobovits (eds.), *Semantics: An Interdisciplinary Reader in Philosophy, Linguistics, and Psychology* (New York: Cambridge University Press), 232–96.
Landau, B. and Gleitman, L. (1985). *Language and Experience: Evidence from the Blind Child* (Cambridge, MA: Harvard University Press).
Langendoen, T. and Postal, P. M. (1984). *The Vastness of Natural Language* (Chicago: University of Chicago Press).
Langton, C. G. (1988). 'Artificial Life', in id. (ed.), *Artificial Life*, Santa Fe Institute Studies in the Sciences of Complexity, 6 (Reading, MA: Addison-Wesley), 1–47.
Larson, R. and Segal, G. (1995). *Knowledge of Meaning* (Cambridge, MA: MIT Press).
Lasnik, H. (1999). 'On the locality of movement', in Darnell *et al.* (eds.), 33–54.
—— (2000). *Syntactic Structures Revisited* (Cambridge, MA: MIT Press).
—— and Uriagereka, J. (2002). 'The poverty of the challenge', *The Linguistic Review* 19: 147–50.
Laurence, S. and Margolis, E. (2001). 'The poverty of the stimulus argument', *British Journal of the Philosophy of Science* 52: 217–76.
Legate, J. and Yang, C. (2002). 'Empirical re-assessment of stimulus poverty arguments', *The Linguistic Review* 19: 151–62.
Leiber, J. (1995). 'On Turing's Turing Test and Why the *Matter* Matters', *Synthese* 104: 59–69.
—— (2001). 'Turing and the fragility and insubstantiality of evolutionary explanations: a puzzle about the unity of Alan Turing's work with some larger implications', *Philosophical Psychology* 14 (1): 83–94.
Leibniz, G. W. (1686/1996). *Metaphysische Abhandlung* (Hamburg: Meiner).
—— (1704/1996). *Neue Abhandlungen über den menschlichen Verstand* (Hamburg: Meiner).
Lepore, E. and Ludwig, K. (2002). 'What is logical form?', in Preyer and Peter (eds.), 54–90.
Leslie, A. (1994). 'ToMM, ToBY, and Agency: Core architecture and domain specificity', in Hirschfeld and Gelman (eds.), 119–48.
—— (2000). 'How to acquire a 'representational theory of mind', in D. Sperber (ed.), *Metarepresentations* (Oxford: Oxford University Press), 197–224.
Lewis, D. (1983). 'Language and languages', in id., *Philosophical Papers*, vol. 1 (Oxford: Oxford University Press).
Lewontin, R. C. (1998). 'The evolution of cognition', in D. H. Osherson and E. E. Smith (eds.), *An Invitation to Cognitive Science*, vol. 3 (Cambridge, MA: MIT Press), 107–32.

—— (1993). *The Doctrine of DNA. Biology as Ideology* (London: Penguin).
Lickliter, R. and Honeycutt, H. (2003). 'Developmental dynamics: towards a biologically plausible evolutionary psychology', *Psychological Bulletin* 129 (6): 819–35.
Lindenmeyer, A. and Prusinkiewicz, P. (1990). *The Algorithmic Beauty of Plants* (New York: Springer).
Locke, J. (1690/1975). *An Essay Concerning Human Understanding*, ed. P. Nidditch (Oxford: Clarendon).
Loewer, B. (1999). 'A guide to naturalizing semantics', in B. Hale and C. Wright (eds.), *A Companion to the Philosophy of Language* (Oxford: Blackwell), 108–26.
Longobardi, G. (1994). 'Reference and proper names. A theory of N-Movement in syntax and logical form', *Linguistic Inquiry* 25 (4): 609–65.
Lowe, J. (2004). 'Dualism', MS, University of Durham, forthcoming in B. McLaughlin and A. Beckermann, *Oxford Handbook in the Philosophy of Mind*.
Lycan, W. (1994). 'Functionalism, I and II', in S. Guttenplan (ed.) (1994), *A Companion to the Philosophy of Mind* (Oxford: Blackwell), 317–32.
—— (2003). 'Chomsky on the mind-body problem', in Antony and Hornstein (eds.), 11–28.
Machamer, P. (1998). 'Galileo's machines, his mathematics, and his experiments', in id. (ed.), *The Cambridge Companion to Galileo* (Cambridge: Cambridge University Press).
Machover, M. (1996). *Set Theory, Logic and their Limitations* (Cambridge: Cambridge University Press).
Macnamara, J. (1982). *Names for Things* (Cambridge, MA: MIT Press).
Malachowski, A. R. (ed.) (1990). *Reading Rorty* (Oxford: Blackwell).
Marantz, A. (1984). *On the Nature of Grammatical Relations* (Cambridge, MA: MIT Press).
Marcus, G. (1998). 'Rethinking eliminative connectionism', *Cognitive Psychology* 37: 243–82.
—— (2001). *The Algebraic Mind: Integrating Connectionism and Cognitive Science* (Cambridge, MA: MIT Press).
Margulis, L., and Sagan, D. (2002). *Acquiring Genomes: A Theory of the Origin of Species* (New York: Basic Books).
Markman, E. M. (1989). *Categorization and Naming in Children—Problems of Induction* (Cambridge, MA: MIT Press).
Marler, P. (1991). 'The instinct to learn', in S. Carey and R. Gelman (eds.), *The Epigenesis of Mind: Essays on Biology and Cognition* (Hillsdale, NJ: Erlbaum), 37–66.
Martin, R. and Uriagereka, J. (2000). 'Some possible foundations for the minimalist program', in Martin, Michaels, and Uriagereka (eds.), 1–30.
Martin, R., Michaels, D., and Uriagereka, J. (eds.) (2000). *Step by Step: Essays on Minimalist Syntax in Honor of Howard Lasnik* (Cambridge: MA: MIT Press).
Martinez, D. E. *et al.* (1998). 'Cnidarian homeoboxes and the zootype', *Nature* 393: 748–9.
Martinich, A. P. (ed.) (1985). *The Philosophy of Language* (Oxford: Oxford University Press).
Mather, J. A. (1995). 'Cognition in cephalopods', *Advances in the Study of Behavior* 24: 317–53.
Matthews, G. H. (1961). *Hidatsa Syntax* (Cambridge, MA: MIT Press).
Mausfeld, R. and Heyer, D. (2004). *Colour Perception: Mind and the Physical World* (Oxford: Oxford University Press).
May, R. (1977). '*The* Grammar of Quantification', Ph.D. Dissertation, MIT.

Maynard Smith, J. and Szathmáry, E. (1995). *The Major Transitions in Evolution* (Oxford/New York: W.H. Freeman, Spektrum).

Mayr, E. (2000). 'Darwin's influence on modern thought', *Scientific American* July 2000.

—— (2002). 'Die Autonomie der Biologie', Zweite Walther Arndt Vorlesung, *Naturwissenschaftliche Rundschau* 55. Jahrgang, Heft 1, 23–9.

McClelland, J. L., Rumelhard, D. E., and the PDF Research Group (1986). *Parallel Distributed Processing. Explorations in the Microstructure of Cognition*, vol. 2 (Cambridge, MA: MIT Press).

McDowell, J. (1996). *Mind and World* (Cambridge, MA: Harvard University Press).

McGilvray, J. (1999). *Chomsky* (Cambridge: Polity Press).

McGinn, C. (1994). *Problems in Philosophy: The Limits of Inquiry* (Oxford: Blackwell).

McGonigle, B. O. and Chalmers, M. (2002). 'The growth of cognitive structures in monkeys and men', in S. B. Fountain, M. D. Bunserg, J. H. Danks, and M. K. McBeath (eds.), *Animal Cognition and Sequential Behaviour* (Boston: Uluwer Academic Publishers).

—— and Dickinson, A. (2003). 'Concurrent disjoint and reciprocal classification by *Cebus paella* in seriation tasks: evidence for hierarchical organization', *Animal Cognition* 6: 185–97.

Mehler, J. and Dupoux, E. (1994). *What Infants Know* (Oxford: Blackwell).

Meinhardt, H. (1995). 'Dynamics of stripe formation', *Nature* 376: 722–3.

Metzner, H. (2000). *Vom Chaos zum Bios. Gedanken zum Phänomen Leben* (Leipzig: Hirzel).

Millikan, R. (2003). 'In defense of public language', in Antony and Hornstein (eds.), 215–37.

Mijuskovic, B. J. (1974). *The Achilles of Rationalist Arguments* (The Hague: Martinus Nijhoff).

Mitchison, G. J. (1977). 'Phyllotaxis and the Fibonacci Series', *Science* 196: 270–5.

Molenaar, P. (1986). 'On the impossibility of acquiring more powerful structures: A neglected alternative', *Human Development* 291 245 51.

Moro, A. (2000). *Dynamic Antisymmetry* (Cambridge, MA: MIT Press).

—— Tettamanti, M., Perani, D., Donati, C., Cappa, S. F., and Fazio, F. (2001). 'Syntax and the brain: disentangting grammar by selective anomalies', *Neuro Image* 13: 110–18.

Mufwene, S. (2001). *The Ecology of Language Evolution*, Cambridge Approaches to Language Contact (Cambridge: Cambridge University Press).

—— (2002). 'What do pidgins and creoles tell us about the evolution of language?', Long abstract of a talk given at the conference 'Origin and Evolution of Languages', Collège de France, 27 September 2002.

Müller, G. B. (1990). 'Developmental mechanisms at the origin of morphological novelty: A side-effect hypothesis', in M. H. Niteck: (ed.), *Evolutionary Innovations* (Chicago: University of Chicago Press), 99–130.

Nagel, T. (1995). *Other Minds* (Oxford: Oxford University Press).

—— (1997). *The Last Word* (Oxford: Oxford University Press).

Neander, K. (1995). 'Explaining complex adaptations', *British Journal for the Philosophy of Science* 46, 583–7.

Newman, S. A. and Comper, W. D. (1990). '"Generic" physical mechanisms of morphogenesis and pattern formation', *Development* 110: 1–18.

Newman, S. A. and Müller, G. B. (1999). *Morphological evolution: Epigenetic mechanisms*, in *Embryonic Encyclopedia of Life Sciences* (London: Nature Publishing Group), <http://www.els.net>.

Newmeyer, F. J. (1996). *Generative Linguistics—A Historical Perspective* (London and New York: Routledge).

Nissenbaum, J. (2000). 'Investigations of covert phrasal movement', Ph.D. Dissertation, MIT.

Ospovat, D. (1981). *The Development of Darwin's Theory* (Cambridge: Cambridge University Press).

Orr, H. A. (1996). 'Dennett's Strange Idea', *The Boston Review*, summer 1996.

Osherson, D. N., Scarborough, D., and Sternberg, S. (eds.) (1998). *An Invitation to Cognitive Science, Vol. 4: Methods, Models, and Conceptual Issues*, 2nd edn. (Cambridge, MA: MIT Press).

Papineau, D. (2001). 'The rise of physicalism', in Gillett and Loewer (eds.), 3–36.

Parsons, T. (1990). *Events in the Semantics of English* (Cambridge, MA: MIT Press).

Peacocke, C. (2002). 'Three principles of rationalism', *European Journal of Philosophy* 10(3): 375–97.

Pennisi, E. (2002). 'Evo-Devo enthusiasts get down to details', *Science* 298 (5595), Nov. 2002: 953–5.

Penrose, R. (1994). *Shadows of the Mind* (Oxford: Oxford University Press).

Piattelli-Palmarini, M. (1989). 'Evolution, selection, and cognition: From "learning" to parameter setting in biology and in the study of language', *Cognition* 31(1): 1–44.

—— and Uriagereka, J. (2004). 'The immune syntax: The evolution of the language virus', in Jenkins (ed.), 342–78.

Pickering, A. (ed.) (1992). *Science as Practice and Culture* (Chicago/London: University of Chicago Press).

Pietroski, P. (2002). 'Function and concatenation', in Preyer and Peter (eds.), 91–117.

—— (2003). 'Small Verbs, Complex Events', in Antony and Hornstein (eds.), 179–214.

Pinker, S. (1994). *The Language Instinct* (London: Penguin).

—— (1997). *How the Mind Works* (New York: W. W. Norton).

—— (2002). *The Blank Slate: The Modern Denial of Human Nature* (London: Penguin).

—— and Bloom, P. (1990). 'Natural language and natural selection', *Behavioral and Brain Sciences* 13 (4): 707–84.

—— and Jackendoff, R. (2005). 'What's special about the human language faculty?', *Cognition* 95: 201–63.

—— and Ullman, M. T. (2004). 'The past and future of the past tense', *Trends in Cognitive Sciences* 6 (11): 456–63.

Plotkin, H. (1997). *Evolution in Mind* (London: Penguin).

Pollock, J.-Y. (1989). 'Verb movement, universal grammar and the structure of IP', *Linguistic Inquiry* 20: 365–424.

Popper, K. (1959). 'The problem of induction', repr. in M. Curd and J. A. Cover (eds.) (1998), *Philosophy of Science: The Central Issues* (New York: W. W. Norton), 426–32.

Postal, P. M. (1972). 'The best theory', in S. Peters (ed.), *Goals of Linguistic Theory* (Englewood Cliffs, NJ: Prentice-Hall).

—— (2004). *Skeptical Linguistic Essays* (Oxford: Oxford University Press).

Preyer, G. and Peter, G. (eds.) (2002), *Logical Form and Language* (Oxford: Oxford University Press).

Premack, D. and Premack, A. J. (1994). 'Moral belief: Form versus content', in Hirschfeld and Gelman (eds.), 149–68.

Pullum, G. and Scholz, B. (2002). 'Empirical assessment of stimulus poverty arguments', *The Linguistic Review* 19: 9–50.

Putnam, H. (1975). 'The meaning of "meaning"', in id., *Philosophical Papers*, Vol. 2, *Mind, Language and Reality* (Cambridge: Cambridge University Press), 215–71.

—— (1992). 'Replies', *Philosophical Topics* 20: 347–408.

Quine, W.V.O. (1960). *Word and Object* (Cambridge, MA: MIT Press).

—— (1969). 'Natural Kinds', in id., *Ontological Relativity and other Essays* (New York: Columbia University Press).

—— (1972). 'Methodological reflections on current linguistic theory', in D. Davidson and G. Harman (eds.), *Semantics of Natural Language* (Dordrecht: Reider), 442–54.

—— (1986). 'Reply to Gilbert Harman', in L. E. Hahn and P. A. Schilpp (eds.), *The Philosophy of W.V. Quine* (La Salle: Open Court), 181–8.

—— (1987). 'Indeterminacy of translation again', *Journal of Philosophy* 84: 5–10.

Raff, R. A. (1996). *The Shape of Life. Genes, Development, and the Evolution of Animal Form* (Chicago and London: University of Chicago Press).

Récanati, F. (1993). *Direct Reference. From Language to Thought* (Oxford: Blackwell).

Rey, G. (2003a). *Chomsky, Intentionality and a CRTT*, in Antony and Hornstein (eds.), 105–39.

Rey, G. (2003b). 'Representational content and a Chomskyan linguistics', in Barber (ed.), 140–86.

Rizzi, L. (1997). 'The fine-structure of the left periphery', in L. Haegemann (ed.), *Elements of Grammar* (Dordrecht: Kluwer), 281–337.

Rogers, G. A. J. (1996). 'Science and British philosophy: Boyle and Newton', in S. Brown (ed.), *Routledge History of Philosophy*, vol. 5 (London: Routledge), 43–68.

Rorty, R. (1980). *Philosophy and the Mirror of Nature* (Princeton, NJ: Princeton University Press).

—— (1986). 'Freud and moral reflection', in J. H. Smith and W. Kerrigan (eds.), *Pragmatism's Freud. The Moral Disposition of Psychoanalysis* (Baltimore/London: John Hopkins University Press), 1–27.

—— (1990). 'The priority of democracy over philosophy', in Malachowski (ed.), 279–302.

—— (1995). 'Philosophische Voraussetzungen der akademischen Freiheit?', in *Merkur* 550: 28–44.

—— (2001). 'Wider den Dogmatismus. Quine und die Philosophie des 20. Jahrhunderts', *Neue Zürcher Zeitung*, 17th–18th February 2001.

Russell, B. (1914/1993). *Our Knowledge of the External World* (New York: Routledge).

Schank, J. J. and Wimsatt, W. C. (2001). 'Evolvability: Adaptation and modularity', in Beatty (ed.), vol. 2, 322–35.

Schiffer, S. (1994a). 'A paradox of meaning', *Nous* 28(3): 279–324.

—— (1994b). 'Thought and language', in Guttenplan (ed.), 589–94.

Schlosser, G. and Wagner, G. P. (eds.) (2004). *Modularity in Development and Evolution* (Chicago: University of Chicago Press).

Schulthess, P. (1998). 'Die Philosophische Reflexion auf die Methode', in J.-P. Schobinger (ed.), *Die Philosophie des 17. Jahrhunderts*, vol. 1 (*Grundriss der Geschichte der Philosophie* begründet von F. Überweg) (Basel: Schwabe), 62–120.

Searle, J. (1992). *The Rediscovery of the Mind* (Cambridge, MA: MIT Press).

—— (2002). 'End of the revolution', *The New York Review of Books*, 25 April 2002.

Searls, D. B. (2002). 'The language of genes', in *Nature* 420 (6912): 211–7.

Singer, P. (1999). *A Darwinian Left* (New Haven, CT: Yale University Press).

Shea, W. (1998). 'Galileo Galilei', in *Grundriss der Geschichte der Philosophie begründet von F. Überweg,. Philosophie des 17. Jahrhunderts*, ed. J.-P. Schobinger, vol. 1, Part 2 (Basel: Schwabe), 777–815.

Slack, J. M. W., Holland, P. W. H., and Graham, C. F. (1993). 'The zootype and the phylotypic stage', *Nature* 361: 490–2.

Smith, N. (2002). *Language, Bananas and Bonobos* (Oxford: Blackwell).

—— and Tsimpli, I.-M. (1995). *The Mind of a Savant* (London: Blackwell).

Smolensky, P. (2000). 'Grammar-based connectionist approaches to language', *Cognitive Science* 23: 589–613.

Sober, E. (2001), 'The two faces of fitness', in Beatty (ed.), vol. 2, 309–21.

Spelke, E. S. (1994). 'Initial knowledge: Six suggestions', *Cognition* 50: 431–45.

—— (2000). 'Core knowledge', *American Psychologist* 55: 1233–43.

Stapp, H. C. (2004). *Mind, Matter, and Quantum Mechanics* (Berlin: Springer-Verlag).

Stewart, I. (1998). *Life's Other Secret. The New Mathematics of the Living World* (London: Penguin).

Stokhof, M. (1999). 'Could semantics be something else? Philosophical challenges for formal semantics', in J. Gerbrandy *et al.* (eds.), *JFAK50. Essays presented to Johan van Benthem on the Occasion of his Fiftieth Birthday* (Amsterdam: Amsterdam University Press).

—— (2002). 'Meaning, interpretation, and semantics', in D. Beaver *et al.* (eds.), *Words, Proofs, and Diagrams* (Stanford: CSLI Publications).

Stowe, L. A., Haverkort, M., and Zwarts, F. (2005). 'Rethinking the neurological basis of language', *Lingua* 115 (7): 997–1042.

Sulkowski, G. M. and Hauser, M. C. (2001). 'Can rhesus monkeys spontaneously subtract?', *Cognition* 79: 239–62.

Sutton-Spence, R. L. and Woll, B. (1999). *An Introduction to the Linguistics of BSL* (Cambridge: Cambridge University Press).

Svenonius, P. (2004). 'On the edge', in D. Adger, C. de Kat, and G. Tsoulas (eds.), *Peripheries: Syntactic Edges and their Effects* (Dordrecht: Kluwer), 259–87.

Szabolcsi, A. (1994). 'The Noun Phrase', in F. Kiefer and K. Kiss (eds.), *Syntax and Semantics 27: The Syntactic Structure of Hungarian* (San Diego: Academic Press), 179–274.

Tipton, I. (1996). 'Locke: Knowledge and its limits', in S. Brown (ed.), *Routledge History of Philosophy*, vol. 5 (London: Routledge), 69–95.

Thompson, D'Arcy Wentworth (1917/1966). *On Growth and Form* (Cambridge: Cambridge University Press).

Todd, L. (1990). *Pidgins and Creoles* (New York: Routledge).

Torretti, R. (1999). *The Philosophy of Physics* (Cambridge: Cambridge University Press).

Toulmin, S. and Goodfield, J. (1962). *The Architecture of Matter* (Chicago: University of Chicago Press).

Tomaselli, S. (1995). 'Human nature', in J. Yolton et al. (eds.), *The Blackwell Companion to the Enlightenment* (Oxford: Blackwell), 229–33.

Turing, A. (1950). 'Computing machinery and intelligence', *Mind* 49: 433–60.

—— (1952). 'The chemical basis of morphogenesis', *Philosophical Transactions of the Royal Society* B 237: 37–72.

Uriagereka, J. (1998). *Rhyme and Reason. An Introduction to Minimalist Syntax* (Cambridge: MA: MIT Press).

—— (2002). *Derivations. Exploring the Dynamics of Syntax* (London: Routledge).

—— (forthcoming). 'In defence of D-Structure', MS., University of Maryland. Quoted as DDS.

Voltolini, A. (2001). 'Why the computational account of rule-following cannot rule out the grammatical account', *European Journal of Philosophy* 9(1): 82–105.

Walsh, D. M., Lewens, T., and Ariew, A. (2002). 'The trials of life: Natural selection and random drift', *Philosophy of Science* 69: 452–73.

Webelhuth, G. (ed.) (1995). *Government and Binding Theory and the Minimalist Program* (Oxford: Blackwell).

Webster, G. and Goodwin, B. (1996). *Form and Transformation. Generative and Relational Principles in Biology* (Cambridge: Cambridge University Press).

Weinberg, S. (1976). 'The forces of nature', *Bulletin of the American Academy of Arts and Sciences* 29 (4): 13–29.

West, G., Brown, J., and Enquist, B. (1997). 'A general model for the allometric scaling laws in biology', *Science* 276: 122–6.

Wigner, E. P. (1960). 'The unreasonable effectiveness of mathematics in the natural sciences', *Communications of Pure and Applied Mathematics* 13: 001–14.

Williams, G. C. (1992). *Natural Selection: Domains, Levels, and Challenges* (Oxford: Oxford University Press).

Williams, E. (2003). *Representation Theory* (Cambridge, MA: MIT Press).

Wilson, E. O. (1975). *Sociobiology. The New Synthesis* (Cambridge, MA: Belknap Press).

—— (1978). *On Human Nature* (Cambridge, MA: Harvard University Press).

—— (1998). *Consilience* (New York: Knopf).

Wittgenstein, L. (1984). *Philosophische Untersuchungen*, Werkausgabe vol. I, 1. Aufl. (Frankfurt: Suhrkamp). Quoted as PU.

—— (1989). *Vortrag über Ethik*, in id., *Vortrag über Ethik und andere kleine Schriften*, ed. J. Schulte (Frankfurt: Suhrkamp).

—— (1991). *Das Blaue Buch*, ed. R. Rees, Werkausgabe vol. V (Frankfurt: Suhrkamp).

—— (1992). *Zettel*, ed. G. E. M. Anscombe and G. H. von Wright, Werkausgabe vol. 8 (Frankfurt: Suhrkamp).

Wynn, K. (1998). 'Psychological foundations of number: numerical competence in human infants', *Trends in Cognitive Sciences* 2: 296–303.

Yamada, J. E. (1990). *Laura: A case for modularity of language* (Cambridge, MA: MIT Press).

Yang, C. (2002). *Knowledge and learning in natural language* (Oxford: Oxford University Press).

—— (2004). 'Universal Grammar, statistics or both?', *Trends in Cognitive Sciences* 8:10.

Yolton, J. W. (1983). *Thinking Matter. Materialism in 18th-Century Britain* (Minneapolis: University of Minnesota Press).
—— (1984). *Perceptual Acquaintance from Descartes to Reid* (Oxford: Blackwell).
—— (1990). 'Mirrors and veils, thoughts and things: The epistemological problematic', in Malachowski (ed.), 58–73.
—— *et al.* (eds.) (1995). *The Blackwell Companion to the Enlightenment* (Oxford: Blackwell).

Index

abstraction 252
adjuncts 177, 182
AI 24
analyticity ix
association 262
adaptationism 170, 207
adequacy
  descriptive 161
  explanatory 162–164, 169
analytic philosophy 33–4, 40–41
artificial life 53
autonomy of syntax 220

Bauplan *see* type

categories 256–8
Carstairs-McCarthy 132–3, 136, 170, 244
cascades 248
chain 195
Chametzky, R. 174, 177, 180, 182–3, 186
chemistry 47, 76–8
Cherniak, C. 30
Chomsky, N. 6–7, 21, 42, 46–8, 62, 75, 86–7, 102, 109, 130–1, 133–4, 188–9, 211, 213–6, 239–45
C-I (conceptual-intentional) systems 120, 158
Collins, C. 185–6, 193
command unit 247–8
communication xii–xiii, 128–138, 183, 205, 207, 276
competence vs performance 20–22
compositionality 135, 242
Computational-Representational Theory of Mind (CRTM) 40, 107, 253
concepts 74, 258–267
conceptual
  vs. intentional information 178, 261, 274
  structure 179–80
  -intentional (C-I) systems 120

Condition on Theta-Assignment 241
conservativity 181, 183, 219, 242, 250–2, 273
constructions 197, 199–200, 207
conventions 233–4
crash-proof syntax 241
creativity 133–4
cyclicity 242–3, 246, 249, 273
  successive 198

Davidson, D. 80
Dawkins, R. xi, 30, 38–40, 103
Dennett, D. 95–6, 107
Descartes, R. 5–6, 56–8, 60–63, 67–70, 74, 78, 121, 134–5, 165
design 24–30
  bad xi, 24, 30, 249
  minimal 27
  optimal 239
  perfection xi, xiii, 26–8, 28–30, 165
Devitt and Sterelny 84–5
disembodiment 261
dualism
  metaphysical 60, 62, 96
  methodological 36, 45, 79–80, 83–5, 94, 103, 145, 254, 272
dynamic semantics 228

economy 168, 174, 205, 227
eliminative materialism 44–50
empiricism 251–2, 257, 262, 264, 269, 271–2
Enlightenment 10, 32
epistemology 253
Epstein and Seeley 243–6
existence 14–15, 226, 252, 259–60, 272
  conditions of 14–15
experiment 70–4
explanation 112–114, 161–2, 169, 224, 227–9, 231, 235, 272
  principled 169
expression 120, 232, 234

externalism 231, 244; see also internalism
'evo-devo' 92

fictions 42, 78
Fodor, J. 17, 24, 50, 265–6
form 14, 92, 105, 110–1, 257
formalism x–xi, 53–4, 105–6
foundationalism 68
Full Interpretation 227
functionalism 13–14, 22, 24, 31, 50–4, 99,
    101, 110, 213–16, 251–2, 254, 256, 264

Galilei, G. 4–5, 66–7, 70, 74, 252, 272
Gallistel, R. 19, 52
Goodwin, B. 112–13, 255
Gould, S.J. 11–12, 38, 109
Grass, G. 117

Heidegger, M. 15, 32–3, 59–60
Hornstein, N. 222
human nature 10–15, 35–40, 46, 89, 93, 96,
    110, 113, 165, 169–170, 254, 270, 272, 275
Hume, D. 3, 6, 8–9, 36, 261–2

Inclusiveness 183, 193
innateness 263–4
instruction 263
interfaces 250
internalism 12, 31, 54, 109, 138, 179, 214–16,
    224, 229, 232, 253–4, 271, 274–5
IS (initial state) 118, 161

Jackendoff, R. 136, 154–160, 222
James, W. 98
judgements 17, 41, 178, 260

Kant 15, 41, 59, 74, 78, 177, 256, 260
Kauffman, S. 37, 94
Kayne, R. 246
Kim, J. 64
Kitcher, P. 95, 110
knowledge 253–4
    limits of 23

labels 170, 184, 187–8
Larson 219, 229–231

Lasnik, H. 205
Leibniz, G.W. 268
Lewis, D. 140–1
LF 157, 160, 220–223–4, 232, 245–6, 248
Linear Correspondence Axiom 247
locality 198–9, 205, 207, 218, 229, 249
Locke, J. 4, 7, 55, 58, 61
logic 154, 255
Lycan, W. 51–2

Marcus, G. 48–50
Mayr, E. 38, 90, 106, 111–2
meaning 234, 248–50
    of words 221
mechanical philosophy 6, 8
mental causation 62–5
mentalism 251
Merge 188–190, 273
    internal 181, 216–18
method 67–71
methodological naturalism ix, 60
Minimalist Program xiii–xiv, 16, 71, 79,
    165–70
    philosophical essence of 250, 252
mirror 175
modularity 15–19
morality 276–7
Moro, A. 214–15
movement 194–219
    head 176
    A bar 177, 194–5
Müller, G. 93

names 159
natural philosophy 55
natural selection 97, 207
Neo-Darwinian Synthesis (NDS) 23,
    38–9, 91–2, 95
Newton, I. 6–7, 55, 60–1
normativity 40, 43, 139, 145, 146–7, 255,
    260
nouns 257
novelty 93, 98
'nullifying the argument from design'
    170
Numeration 120, 240–2

Penrose, R. 24, 53, 62
perfect design 165
performance 20
persons 261
phase transition 269
phases 199, 242–3
philosophy of language 40–44
philosophy of mind 44–54
PHON 120
phonology 122, 124
Pietroski, P. 178, 190–193, 222
Pinker, S. 38, 96, 99, 126
Plato 13, 21, 66, 114, 121, 165, 255, 268
Port-Royal 255
poverty of the stimulus 122–5
predication 176
Principle of Uniformity 164
projection 172
propositions 178, 180, 233, 242, 244
Prout, W. 59, 76–7
psychological reality 79, 83–4, 169
psychologism 251, 255
public language 139–144

quantification 200–5
questions 194–7, 204–5
Quine, W.v.O. 72, 81, 84, 86, 126, 270–1

rationalism xii, 9–10, 23, 34, 78–9
Recanati, F. 234
recursion 170
realism 78
reference 56, 75, 78, 258–62, 275
representation 18, 31, 40, 42, 65, 74–8, 84–5, 107, 231, 251, 253–4, 257–8, 264, 274;
  see also reference
  levels of 246; see also LF
  vs derivation 249–50
Rey, G. 48, 83–5, 164, 253–4
Rorty, R. 31, 34–6, 59–60, 256
Russell 41, 233, 260

Schiffer, S. 141–2
scope 194
Searle, J. 86–7
Segal, G. 228, 219, 229–231
SEM 120, 158, 220–238
semantics 235
  in layers 178, 193, 195, 209, 213, 215, 245, 274
sentence 175–6
'side-effect hypothesis' 93
S-M (sensorimotor) systems 120
Smolensky, P. 48
specifiers 180
Spell-Out 245–8
  Multiple 249
Spencer, H. 29, 98–99
subjacency 198
syntax 150–5
Szabolcsi, A. 175–6

thematic structure 175–7, 180, 182
thought 156–8, 178, 220–1
truth 253
truth-conditions 224
T-schema 225–6
Turing's Test 24–6, 51
type/typology 89–91, 106–8, 110, 114

UG 46, 89, 106–7, 110, 118–9, 121, 251
understanding 257
uninterpretable features 211–12
Uriagereka, J. 211, 218, 247–8, 250

virus model 218
Voltolini, A. 143–4

Williams, G. 11–12
Wittgenstein 56, 144–9, 234, 260, 270
words 248

X-bar scheme 172

Yolton, J. 56, 58, 61, 261

The manufacturer's authorised representative in the EU for product safety is
Oxford University Press España S.A. of el Parque Empresarial San Fernando de
Henares, Avenida de Castilla, 2 – 28830 Madrid (www.oup.es/en or product.
safety@oup.com). OUP España S.A. also acts as importer into Spain of products
made by the manufacturer.

www.ingramcontent.com/pod-product-compliance
Ingram Content Group UK Ltd.
Pitfield, Milton Keynes, MK11 3LW, UK
UKHW022152230426
12049UKWH00003BA/62